Praise for *Before* Brown

"Vivid, absorbing, and gracefully written, *Before* Brown explores the human cost of Heman Marion Sweatt's simple, but hard-earned, ambition: to get a good education. Gary Lavergne's gifts as a storyteller bring Sweatt's journey, and the context of his struggle, alive. With a novelist's eye for character and detail, Lavergne gives us an intimate portrait of Sweatt. His story reminds us that in the not-so-distant past—when a black man could be denied admittance to law school solely because of his race—'change' was slow-going. *Before* Brown is both a monumental work and a great read. Sweatt's story is one that every American should know."
—PAMELA COLLOFF, SENIOR EDITOR, *TEXAS MONTHLY*

"This is a story of human frailties and human fears and how individual courage and community resolve can overcome them. Lavergne's telling of the human drama around *Sweatt v. Painter* gives us a fuller and more accurate picture of that legal landmark in American history. He captures the physical and emotional price that was paid to bring Texas and America closer to their own ideals. The telling and the story are both inspirational."
—RICHARD W. LARIVIERE, PRESIDENT, UNIVERSITY OF OREGON

"This is a story that the nation should not forget, and it is told here with rich context and nuance. The battle for civil rights here is so much more than a successful Supreme Court case."
—TERESA SULLIVAN, PROVOST AND PROFESSOR OF SOCIOLOGY, UNIVERSITY OF MICHIGAN—ANN ARBOR

"Gary Lavergne has traced a significant chapter in the struggle to secure civil rights in this country—a struggle of collective triumph amid personal tragedy. *Before* Brown ably captures the complex, layered interplay of power, politics, and ideology that is the human drama in Heman Sweatt's story. Lavergne masterfully highlights key ethical, legal, and policy issues throughout the book. The careful reader sees that the intractable problems of justice and fairness that befuddled many in the past are still with us today, albeit in new forms. The moral of this story is there is unfinished work to be done by all of us."
—LODIS RHODES, PROFESSOR, LYNDON BAINES JOHNSON SCHOOL OF PUBLIC AFFAIRS, UNIVERSITY OF TEXAS AT AUSTIN

"*Before* Brown gives us much more than just a fascinating history of a courageous young Texan's refusal to settle for anything less than what a human being deserved. Gary Lavergne's masterful portrait of Thurgood Marshall (and the NAACP in the pre–MLK Jr. years) teaches us how he peacefully, and with dignity, challenged America to live up to the promises guaranteed in our Constitution."
—DANIEL J. SARACINO, ASSISTANT PROVOST FOR ENROLLMENT AND DIRECTOR OF ADMISSIONS, UNIVERSITY OF NOTRE DAME

"*Before* Brown is a meticulously researched and movingly written account of the African American community's efforts to integrate admissions at the University of Texas. Deftly interweaving political and legal history with personal biography, Gary Lavergne's account is a must for any who would wish to know the backstory of people and events in Texas that would lead four years later to the U.S. Supreme Court's landmark decision in *Brown v. Board of Education*."
—SAUL GEISER, RESEARCH ASSOCIATE, CENTER FOR STUDIES IN HIGHER EDUCATION, UNIVERSITY OF CALIFORNIA, BERKELEY

"It is clear that what started out as a straightforward biography of Heman Marion Sweatt ended up being a masterful overview of race, education, and social views of both African American and white Texans during the early to mid-part of the last century. Lavergne writes like a novelist, but his work is, in fact, a wonderful historical treatment of an important period in the history of the State of Texas. *Before* Brown is an emotional and very human look at the effects of public policy on a race of people. It is, in other words, not a history of facts, but a tragic and triumphant history of a people. *Before* Brown is a must-read for every Texan. I am so smitten by the book that I will suggest it be required reading for every freshman and first-year law student of Texas Southern University."
—DR. JAMES M. DOUGLAS, EXECUTIVE VICE PRESIDENT AND DISTINGUISHED PROFESSOR, TEXAS SOUTHERN UNIVERSITY

"What a great idea to bring to life the ordeal of Heman Sweatt, his fight for justice, and the landmark victory that paved the way to *Brown v. Board of Education*. And who better than Gary Lavergne, a talented writer and admissions officer at the center of other Texan breakthroughs in the quest for greater access to higher education, to write this compelling narrative?"
—PATRICK WEIL, DIRECTEUR DE RECHERCHE AU CNRS, CENTRE D'HISTOIRE SOCIALE DU XXE SIÈCLE, UNIVERSITÉ PARIS I PANTHÉON–SORBONNE

Before *Brown*

Jess and Betty Jo Hay Series

Before *Brown*

Heman Marion Sweatt, Thurgood Marshall,
and the Long Road to Justice

GARY M. LAVERGNE

University of Texas Press ⟁ Austin

Requests for permission to reproduce material from this work should be sent to:
Permissions
University of Texas Press
P.O. Box 7819
Austin, TX 78713-7819
www.utexas.edu/utpress/about/bpermission.html

⊗ The paper used in this book meets the minimum requirements of ANSI/NISO z39.48-1992 (R1997) (Permanence of Paper).

Library of Congress Cataloging-in-Publication Data
Lavergne, Gary M., 1955–
    Before Brown : Heman Marion Sweatt, Thurgood Marshall, and the long road to justice / Gary M. Lavergne. — 1st ed.
        p. cm.
    Includes bibliographical references and index.
    ISBN 978-0-292-72200-2 (cloth : alk. paper)
    1. Sweatt, Heman Marion, 1912–1982.   2. Segregation in higher education—Texas—History—20th century.   3. African American college students—Texas—Biography.   4. African Americans—Texas—Biography.   5. University of Texas at Austin—History—20th century.   6. Sweatt, Heman Marion, 1912–1982—Trials, litigation, etc.   7. Painter, Theophilus S. (Theophilus Shickel), 1889–1969—Trials, litigation, etc.   8. Marshall, Thurgood, 1908–1993.   9. African Americans—Legal status, laws, etc.—Texas—History—20th century.   10. Texas—Race relations—History—20th century.   I. Title.
    LC212.722.T4L38 2010
    344.764′0798—dc22
                                                          2009049278

For Bruce Walker

Contents

Acknowledgments

First, as always, is my wife and editor, Laura Gwen. This is the fourth book she has edited. On occasion our four grown children, Charles, Mark, Amy, and Anna (two social scientists and two journalists) gave me their advice and counsel.

This book is dedicated to Dr. Bruce Walker, the vice provost and director of admissions at the University of Texas at Austin. Since he hired me in September 2000, I have stood with him through emotional battles over affirmative action, automatic-admission-percentage plans, civil rights complaints and investigations, angry students, angry parents, angry donors, angry politicians of every persuasion, and a federal lawsuit. I have been an eyewitness to his courage and advocacy of access and justice. He is the kindest and most decent gentleman I have ever known, and he is the best friend I have ever had. During the writing of this book, I shamelessly exploited my friendship with Bruce and my colleagues on his staff, especially Michael Washington, who helped me locate historical locations in Austin. Elsewhere I received valuable advice and help from Lee S. Smith, the associate vice president for legal affairs, who should write his own book on the history of access to higher education in Texas. Kedra Ishop, registrar Shelby Stanfield, Andy Smith, Ted Pfeifer, Gwen Grigsby, Lodis Rhodes, Shannon Janes, Leo Barnes, Rudy Metayer, and Gerald Torres were great friends and advisors. On campus, the staffs of the Tarlton Law Library, the Perry-Castañeda Library, the Harry Ransom Humanities Research Center, and the Dolph Briscoe Center for American History were professional and invaluable. My good friend from *Texas Monthly*, Pamela Colloff, helped me stay on track during the early stages of writing.

In Houston, I am indebted to my very good friend Clarence Douglas, who spent days driving me through the Third Ward and the Paradise North

Cemetery. He introduced me to the Reverend William Lawson of Wheeler Avenue Baptist Church, who pulled me from despair to determination to finish this project. At the Houston Public Library, the staff of the Metropolitan Research Center made it possible for me to do an extraordinary amount of work in a short time. While in Houston, I was well fed and cared for by my dear cousins, Archie and Carrie Lavergne.

In Austin I had the privilege to meet Ada Anderson, a truly remarkable woman who is today a patron of the arts and a philanthropist. She was an indispensable source of information about Austin in the 1940s and 1950s. At the Austin Public Library, Karen Riles in the Austin History Center was very helpful in locating sources of information. At the Texas Capitol, the Texas Legislative Council was also instrumental in locating bills and reports relevant to this story.

Other colleagues in higher education I am indebted to include Jonathan Alger, vice president and general counsel of Rutgers University; Amilcar Shabazz, the chair of the W. E. B. Du Bois Department of Afro-American Studies at the University of Massachusetts at Amherst; James Douglas, a former president and the current executive vice president of Texas Southern University; Saul Geiser of the Center for Studies in Higher Education at the University of California at Berkeley; Teresa Sullivan, provost and executive vice president for academic affairs at the University of Michigan at Ann Arbor; and Richard Lariviere, the president of the University of Oregon.

Dr. Hemella "Mellie" Sweatt, of Ohio; Dr. James Leonard Sweatt III, of Dallas, Texas; and Anna Sweatt, of Arkansas, gave generously of their time and support. At Baker Botts, LLP, Joe Greenhill, a former chief justice of the Supreme Court of Texas, made time for an interview and provided some of his papers on the *Sweatt* case, including the notes he had with him during his argument before the Supreme Court.

I am fortunate to have a business relationship with James D. Hornfischer, my literary agent, who is also a licensed attorney. Jim continues to reconcile my esoteric intellectual interests with the real world of publishing (not an easy task). This is the fourth book we have worked on together.

I am also indebted to the staff of the University of Texas Press, especially William Bishel and Theresa May, and the faculty advisory committee for recognizing the value and relevance of this story and for allowing me to present it in narrative form. Other colleagues at UT Press, including Nancy Bryan, Allison Faust, David Hamrick, Sarah Hudgens, and Casey Kittrell, along with copy editor Kip Keller, are part of a remarkable publishing team.

No doubt there are others. For those whose names I have forgotten, be assured it was due to a fatigued mind, and not my heart.

Before *Brown*

Introduction

When I reported for football practice as a freshman on the campus of Church Point High School in Louisiana in the fall of 1969, the news on the insufferably hot and humid field was not about whether we were going to have a winning season but about how many "colored" students were going to report for school in a couple of weeks. Church Point High had enrolled a few African Americans as students the previous year, but my freshman class in 1969–1970 was going to be the first fully integrated one in the school's history—and one of the first in all of Louisiana.[1] Under a court order at the time, Church Point High School would first have an integrated freshman class, then a fully integrated high school the next year.

I remember that two African American freshmen, Walter Lewis, Jr., and "Big John" Bellard, reported to football practice that day two weeks before the opening of school. They were fourteen or fifteen years old, and they must have felt terribly alone. Two years before, three girls in my class, Desiree Guidry, Priscilla Meche, and Roslyn Duplechin, first broke the color barrier when they attended Church Point Elementary School as part of a "pre-integration" program to determine how the whites of Church Point would react to racial integration. Today, Duplechin believes that the program added to the smooth transition of the integration of Church Point schools, and I know her to be right. Until I wrote this book, I never thought of Walter, Big John, Desiree, Priscilla, and Roslyn as courageous. I see now that none of the rest of us, in my four years at Church Point High, ever had to summon the courage they had to walk through those doors.

Among the advantages enjoyed by white students at Church Point, our mothers, fathers, brothers, and sisters had gone there before us. We knew the principal and almost all of the teachers, aides, cafeteria workers, and janitors. The high school was in our neighborhood.

We were kids. I wish we had appreciated the history going on around us. The integration of Church Point High School went fairly smoothly compared to the battles that accompanied desegregation in most other places in Louisiana and the South, but I look back on that experience and wish we had all been kinder to one another. I wish I had had enough brains back then to recognize heroes. Perhaps not surprisingly, we tended to racially segregate ourselves while on campus, and thirty years later we did so again during our class reunion until a DJ played music and we all formed lines and danced.

The desegregation of schools like Church Point High came about because courageous black applicants to white colleges, like Heman Marion Sweatt, of Texas, went inside those institutions while they were still segregated, submitted applications to sometimes hostile administrators, and fought long court battles.

I want *Before* Brown to be more than a biography of a single plaintiff in a Supreme Court case. Having been an American history teacher for many years, I have learned that before attempting to teach anything, teachers should do what is called a task analysis. For example, before students can learn algebra, they must know mathematics, and before mathematics, they must know how to count.

This book tells a story and is intended for a general readership of students of all ages interested in the history of the American civil rights movement. As Hugh Kennedy stated in the foreword of one of his books, "I use the word 'story' deliberately. I have written a determinedly narrative history that concentrates on people and events."[2] The life of Heman Sweatt is an often-overlooked chapter in that remarkable history: the end of state-sanctioned racial segregation, usually associated with the *Brown v. Board of Education of Topeka* ruling in 1954, was a linear process that started much earlier. *Sweatt v. Painter* (1950) and its two companion cases are tragically neglected milestones in that process. The result of my task analysis of the Heman Sweatt story took me down a longer road than I imagined, but every mile was worth it. The road to victory in *Sweatt* and *Brown* was the result of more than just cogent legal reasoning and courtroom arguments. To the social-science purist, rigidly wedded to the architecture of a scholarly thesis, I make no apologies, but provide extensive citations for everything in this book.

The first chapters provide an overview of the Texas African American experience as seen through the eyes of a family of former slaves by the name of Sweatt. By definition, my task-analysis approach requires extensive backstory on topics like Texas's oppressive constitution and voting laws and practices like the white primary. In the middle chapters, I cover the impact of African American pastors, private black colleges, the National Association for the Advancement of Colored People, and African American newspapers as sources of hope for an oppressed people. Meanwhile, the Texas Permanent University Fund, the white primary, and the University of Texas represented examples of privilege for the white establishment. Each topic is a dot in the linear progression that was the long road to justice for Heman Marion Sweatt. I make the case that state-sanctioned segregation immediately after *Sweatt*, while not explicitly ruled unconstitutional, nonetheless became a legal and practical impossibility. The closing chapters are mainly about why Sweatt won his case.

Some of the material of this book is transcribed trial testimony. Direct and cross-examination of witnesses in a court of law can be as dramatic as any novel—it certainly is in this case—and I want readers to feel as if they are in the courtroom. But anyone with experience with transcripts and depositions (such as the Watergate transcripts) knows that reading words *exactly* as they were spoken can be maddening. Throughout this work, I alert the reader to the occasions I mildly edited spoken words purely for clarity.

Finally, writing about race is emotional and difficult. A story teaches nothing and serves no purpose unless it provokes emotion of some kind—satisfaction, laughter, sorrow, outrage, or fear. Effective storytelling is sometimes offensive. As W. E. B. Du Bois wrote in *The Souls of Black Folk*, our nation has not yet found peace from its sins; punishment for the sin of American slavery manifests itself in many ways, and one is persistent uncertainty about how to refer to African Americans.[3] My choice of words, especially decisions on when to use "black," "African American," and "Negro," and related decisions on when to capitalize certain words, reflect my sincere determination to be both sensitive and historically honest.[4]

CHAPTER 1

Prologue

*As a symbol, Heman Marion Sweatt marks the emergence of the Negro in Texas
as an adult and citizen.*

HOUSTON INFORMER, DECEMBER 1946

On February 26, 1946, Heman Marion Sweatt, a thirty-three-year-old, five-foot-five-inch, 130-pound mail carrier from Houston, entered the Main Building of the University of Texas at Austin (UT Austin). He carried with him a copy of his undergraduate transcript. His graduation from Wiley College in 1934 meant that he was qualified to enter the University of Texas Law School—except for one thing: he was an African American.

Sweatt was a member of a delegation from the Texas State Conference of the National Association for the Advancement of Colored People (NAACP). The group had been formed to meet with UT president Theophilus S. Painter. Painter assembled a small group of university administrators for the meeting.

At the time, the nine-year-old Main Building, capped by an imposing tower, was fast becoming the trademark of UT Austin, but for the visiting African American delegation, it was also a symbol of what they had been denied since the founding of the Republic of Texas—higher education.

The confrontation took place on the ground floor in Room 1. Then and today, it houses the Office of the Registrar. R. A. Hester, the president of the Progressive Voters League and leader of the NAACP delegation, began by reading a statement that included an assertion that Negro citizens of Texas were entitled to the same educational opportunities as whites. After much discussion, Hester signaled Heman Sweatt to speak up; Sweatt had said nothing up to that point.

Sweatt could not have been more courteous or deferential, which made his words all the more powerful. He asked for permission to speak, and then addressed the group in a soft, slow, measured tone. He wanted to be a lawyer, he said. Then he emphasized that he had a right to the same legal training as other Texas college graduates. At the time, Texas provided no professional schools for its black citizens, and if Texas really wanted to provide for the professional education of Negroes, it could. Then he presented Painter with a transcript from Wiley College and formally asked for admission to the University of Texas Law School.

The meeting was the opening round of what would become the lawsuit *Sweatt v. Painter* (1950).

Sweatt's application to the UT Law School set in motion events that appear surreal today. "Heman Sweatt will never darken the doors of the University of Texas," said Grover Sellers, the attorney general of Texas.

To keep this kind, gentle, mild-mannered, and introverted mailman from entering an all-white institution, the State of Texas spent millions of dollars in the 1940s to transform a glorified trade school, run by a "principal," into a university, complete with graduate programs. The Texas Legislature also created a parallel university, which had a law school before it had a mathematics department, where none had existed before. It was intended to be a "University of the First Class—for Negroes." While trying to prevent Sweatt from enrolling in UT Austin, a panicked Texas political establishment spent more money on what was called "Negro higher education" than it had during the entire previous history of the state.

The actions of Heman Marion Sweatt and his supporters seriously undermined the separate-but-equal doctrine and provided a precedent for racial segregation's legal demise in *Brown v. Board of Education*. From 1946 through 1950, Sweatt made it possible for the NAACP and its supporters to force America to deal with the true meaning of the Constitution, and as Sweatt said, it was a great example of the "progress of democracy."

In December 1946, the *Houston Informer,* one of the largest black newspapers in the country, chose Heman Sweatt as its "Man of the Year." The owner and editor, Carter Walker Wesley, himself a veteran of civil rights struggles, wrote: "As a symbol, Heman Marion Sweatt marks the emergence of the Negro in Texas as an adult and citizen. Older Negroes have gotten benefits for themselves and for their people by indirection—pleading, cajoling, making the appeal of the weak and mistreated Negro to some strong white person who would champion their cause. These older men always operated in twilight where deals and compromises and subterfuges could be made."[1]

By the time *Sweatt v. Painter* came before the U.S. Supreme Court,

Sweatt had become a lead player in a master plan by the NAACP to end American apartheid. The tale of Heman Sweatt is an overlooked but crucial chapter in a much larger drama that began long before his birth. Those who make history often travel a long and dangerous road; and they are never alone. From the 1920s through the 1960s, plaintiffs in civil rights cases literally put their names, and sometimes their lives, on the line. In the 1940s and 1950s in Texas, newspaper and magazine coverage made "Sweatt" a moniker for a monumental, and what some considered a "dangerous," social, educational, and legal change. The publicity made Heman Marion Sweatt a hero to some and a villain to others.

Finding an African American in Texas who was qualified to attend the University of Texas Law School, who could be relied upon to face microscopic scrutiny and a multiyear disruption of his personal life, who would follow through by walking alone through the doors of an all-white institution, who would be a man and do it with pride and dignity and not hate as others were hating him was not easy. The NAACP found such a person, a mailman, in a little house at 3402 Delano Street in the Third Ward in Houston.

CHAPTER 2

One of the Great Prophets

Where, after all, do universal human rights begin? In small places, close to home . . . They are the world of the individual person: The neighborhood he lives in; the school or college he attends; the factory, farm or office where he works. Such are the places where every man, woman and child seeks equal justice, equal opportunity, equal dignity without discrimination. Unless these rights have meaning there, they have little meaning anywhere. Without concerted citizen action to uphold them close to home, we shall look in vain for progress in the larger world.

ELEANOR ROOSEVELT, SPEECH TO THE UNITED NATIONS, MARCH 27, 1958

On June 19, 1865, General Gordon Granger, the newly appointed Union commander of the Department of Texas, stepped off his command ship in Galveston and announced that, henceforth, the Emancipation Proclamation was law in Texas. Approximately 250,000 Texas slaves were thereby freed.

But the news was not all good. The former slaves were warned not to assemble in towns, where they could not be protected, or to congregate near military outposts, or to follow in the footsteps of the army. Granger knew what to expect from the freedmen. They had nothing and nowhere to go. During the war, their large numbers had slowed the Union Army and strained its supplies and communications. So in Texas the former slaves were told to remain on the plantations that thrived on their backs and reach labor agreements with the landowners who had once enslaved them.[1]

Even before Granger reached Texas, slave owners from other states had migrated west, perhaps seeking refuge from the war itself, or desperately trying to avoid the inevitable loss of their "property."

Oral tradition and contemporaneous records have it that one slave family had been marched to the Waxahachie area, just south of Dallas.[2] That slave family would come to be known as "Sweatt." In 1870 there were many Sweatt families in the Waxahachie precinct of Ellis County; nearly all were from Tennessee, and about half of them were white. Richard Sweatt, a skilled freedman who worked in a blacksmith shop, would have been about seventeen years old at the end of the war. Sometime between then and the early months of 1870, he married a woman identified in the census as a mulatto named Silvia. In December 1870 they had a son whom they named James Leonard. The 1880 census indicates that neither Richard nor Silvia Sweatt could read or write, but ten-year-old "Lenard" is listed as being "at school."[3]

James Leonard Sweatt never grew taller than five feet six inches. As an adult, he was thin, balding, and bespectacled—all stereotypes of a meek and mild weakling. Yet he grew to be a "forceful man of great dignity."[4] Throughout his life, he was a "dramatic moral force for leadership," and a "Great Prophet for a whole community."[5]

During his late teens, James Leonard Sweatt entered Prairie View State Normal School and Industrial College, the only state-supported institution of higher education for African Americans in the state. In the mid-1880s, this alone made him one of the most educated African Americans in Texas, even though Prairie View was a grossly underfunded combination high school and trade school that taught such skills as broom making and mattress making.

Normal schools were set up to provide teacher training, and Prairie View's sole higher-education function was to produce teachers for "colored" public schools. Sweatt graduated with the class of 1890, which provided thirteen new black teachers for the entire Texas school-age African American population. Ten years later, two of the thirteen were deceased, eight were still teachers, one was a principal, and one was a professor of mathematics at the Lincoln Institute in Missouri. The remaining graduate, James Leonard Sweatt, had been a teacher and principal in Beaumont for a short time, but soon discovered that he could not reach financial security as a public school teacher in Texas. Around 1897, he moved about sixty miles west on the Old Spanish Trail to a city he thought held promise—Houston.[6] His decision was a good one. The gap between black and white teachers' salaries grew dramatically from 1900 to 1930, the period when he would have pursued his teaching career.[7]

By the time he graduated from Prairie View, James Leonard Sweatt had grown mightily unimpressed with the Jim Crow education he had received. Perhaps he didn't want to be part of a state-sponsored sham of educating the "colored" citizens of Texas. Many years later, one of Sweatt's sons would say, "My father was a graduate of Prairie View and he never had any respect for it."[8]

Life on Chenevert Street

As a result of its rapid growth, and unlike most cities of a similar age, Houston has no historic district and no clearly defined single black section. Throughout its history, blacks and working class whites settled mostly on the southern edges of the city, where vacant property was available. Each new expansion included its own section for nonwhites. To this day, black enclaves are spread throughout Houston, from the inner city's exclusive downtown area to its periphery, many miles away.[9]

James Leonard Sweatt's first known Houston address was in or near what is today the downtown business district. In the *Houston City Directory* for 1897–1898, he is listed as a postal clerk living at 202 Andrews Street. (He kept his postal clerk job for nearly fifty years.) After living on Andrews Street for about two years, he built a large white two-story wood-framed house at 2415 Chenevert Street in a racially mixed neighborhood on the city's edge with easy access to black residential clusters in the Third Ward.[10] In 1910, 7,662 (31 percent) of the 24,705 Houstonians living in the Third Ward were African Americans. At the time, only one in five black Houstonians was a homeowner.[11]

James Leonard Sweatt married Ella Rose Perry, an expert seamstress and a favorite of some of Houston's most prominent families. Her brother, Heman Perry, founded the Standard Life Insurance Company of Atlanta, one of the largest black-owned companies in the United States.

James and Ella Rose Sweatt had seven offspring, but two died as children: "Girlie Mae" at the age of nine and Ida Modena when she was only sixteen months old.[12] The Sweatts valued and insisted on scholastic excellence for their children. "At home our father always stressed the value of an education. He instilled in us the idea of integration from an early age," said one of his sons.[13] The Sweatts refused to allow their children to believe they could not compete with whites enrolled in exemplary public and exclusive private schools. The Sweatt children would be ready to enjoy the rights and privileges of full citizenship—should that day ever come. All the Sweatt offspring earned advanced degrees, an accomplishment that would be remarkable even today—for anyone; for an African American family with five children attending neglected and grossly underfunded Jim Crow high schools in the South at the turn of the century, it was phenomenal. Erma attended Columbia University and Wilberforce University, in Ohio, and later became a teacher; James, also called "Jack," attended the University of Michigan; John attended Iowa State, and Wendell, the University of Nevada.[14] Heman attended a black institution in Texas: Wiley College in Marshall.[15]

Heman Marion Sweatt, James and Ella's fourth child, was born on December 11, 1912. Those who called him "Heman" did not know him well. For all others, he was "Bill," although no one seems to remember how that came about. He looked like his father in every way and had great reverence for his dad: "My father was quite an historian and he taught me the subject at the table. We talked about black history, black problems . . . [He] was very sensitive and informed on the issues."[16]

There are conflicting accounts of what life was like on Chenevert Street in the early 1900s. In a 1946 newspaper interview, Sweatt said that while growing up, he played with white boys, who treated him well.[17] Two years later, in a letter to Walter White of the NAACP's national office, he proposed writing an autobiography in which he would detail his growing up in a southern city where there was a "real white picket fence behind which the children of one Negro family in a white neighborhood played, daring never to venture beyond it." He characterized his proposed book as the chronicle of a lifetime of struggles outside that white picket fence.

In the 1980s, based in part on an interview with Sweatt, historian Michael Gillette wrote that "[white] neighbors used the playground facilities at nearby Baldwin Park, [while] segregation compelled Heman to walk several miles to Emancipation Park, the only facility for Negroes."[18] The account of the segregation is certainly accurate, but the hardship created by the distance is not. Baldwin and Emancipation parks are both on Elgin Avenue and are only three-tenths of a mile from each other; it is not possible to walk several miles past one to get to the other.

A similar embellishment emerges from the description of Sweatt's walks to and from elementary school. Gillette writes: "On his two mile walks to Douglass Elementary School, Heman passed two all-white schools which he could not attend. One of them was Longfellow School and only blocks from his home."[19] The Longfellow School was very near the Sweatt home, three blocks away, but if Heman Sweatt went past it, his walk to Douglass Elementary was less than a mile.[20]

The meaning of the white picket fence and the distances he had to walk to the park and school are distractions anyway. Heman Sweatt would not become a heroic figure because he walked long distances to school or a playground. If a "colored" elementary school had been located next door to his home on Chenevert Street, it would still have been Jim Crow, and it would still have been appallingly unjust.

The irony is that residential racial segregation in the Third Ward, and especially in the Chenevert Street area, was minimal, especially for a southern city. In 1918, as Heman Sweatt approached his sixth birthday, five of the twenty-six households in a five-block area around his home were occupied by "colored" people.[21] Every day, black and white Houstonians lived mostly in harmony and in proximity to one another. Only racism can explain why social and educational integration was unthinkable.

Black-owned enterprises in the Third Ward centered on Dowling Street, a thoroughfare that included the eastern edge of Emancipation Park. By 1945, the area had about 25,000 African Americans. Their businesses were largely service establishments and "dispensers of food, drink, and entertainment."[22] A variety of other small businesses also thrived, including offices for twenty-two physicians, fourteen dentists, seven registered pharmacists, and four lawyers. If Third Ward African Americans chose to, they could exclusively patronize black-owned businesses, something that black newspapers of the day often encouraged their readers to do.

In 1945, the Negro death rate in Houston was almost twice that of the white population and, allegedly, second only to the death rate recorded for the Jefferson Davis Hospital. Such appalling health statistics are explained in part by what Lorenzo Greene observed in 1930: "The streets of Houston are terrible. This applies to the Negro section. They are mostly unpaved and many of them are as narrow as alleys."[23] Many of the ditches lining those streets were filled with stagnant sewage, easily spread by Houston's torrential rains and floods.

Tragically, outrageous racial stereotypes of the time contributed to such a sad condition. One news item reported that "the Negro is inherently afraid of a hospital" and "the Negro feels out of place going to a white hospital for treatment."[24] The irrational bigotry that produced the dangerous notion that anyone would actually prefer sickness and death to medical treatment also produced the belief that minimal school facilities sufficed for a Negro population uninterested in education.

Despite the difficulties they faced, and perhaps to some extent as a result of them, African Americans of the Third Ward built substantial support structures for their community.[25] The architects of these support structures were the professionals who worked to improve the lives of their neighbors. Pastors of black churches exerted more influence than any other group. From its inception, the congregation of Houston's first black church was involved politically in Houston affairs by hosting meetings of a biracial group called the Harris County Republican Club. "[The black man's] church was his school, his forum, his political arena, his social club, his art gallery, his conservatory of music."[26]

The "black man's church" was also where he found his soul, where he could be a man. If any place was beyond the white man's reach, it was the black church. If any person was truly independent of the white establishment, it was the black pastor. In 1936, the *Houston Post* reported that Houston had 440 churches; 204 (46 percent) of them were black, even though their parishioners made up only 21 percent of the population. Nearly 90 percent of the black churches were Baptist. (The Sweatt family attended the Wesley Chapel AME [African Methodist Episcopal] Church on Dowling Street.) Each church was "a peculiar sustaining force which gave [African Americans] the strength to endure when endurance gave no promise, and the courage to be creative in the face of [their] own dehumanization."[27] From those churches and others like them throughout the South emerged the leaders, and the soul, of the modern American civil rights movement.

Labor unions, an area in which James Leonard Sweatt was particularly active, also affected the quality of life of Houston's African American population. Sweatt saw organizing and collective bargaining as a way to combat the much larger issue of racism. He was convinced that such alliances opened the door to promotions for blacks and made their protests more effective. But during the first decades of the twentieth century, relations between black workers and labor unions were not good. By excluding blacks from membership, unions also prevented them from landing coveted skilled jobs and apprenticeships.

The genesis of James Sweatt's union-organizing activities was a decision by a white-owned insurance company, the Mutual Benefit Association, to enforce a "Caucasian clause" barring the issuance of insurance policies for southern black postal clerks. Sweatt and a number of others contacted similarly situated clerks, and by the summer of 1912, thirty-five of them formed a national organization. By October 1913, the National Alliance of Postal Employees was officially organized in Chattanooga, Tennessee. When in Houston, meetings were held in the Sweatt living room on Chenevert Street. Sweatt's good friend Henry L. Mims was the group's first president. As late as 1945, the National Urban League reported that "there is a branch of the National Alliance of Postal Employees in the Houston area. Negro postal employees, members of this union in the city, are credited with having given birth to this organization."[28]

The Klan in Houston

Despite the success of Houston's African American citizens in building supportive communities during Heman Sweatt's formative years, prevailing attitudes guaranteed his relegation to "second-class status."[29] Whites believed that there would be peace and racial harmony only if blacks stayed in their place. Some of the more delusional whites believed they lived in "Heavenly Houston" and based their conviction on comparisons of Houston with other, more troubled southern cities. For African Americans, segregation was not the only condition that invalidated the myth of "Heavenly Houston." Men and young boys like Sweatt and his brothers had to be careful and conscious of how they acted. The failure to stay in your place could include something as innocuous as looking white people directly in the eye. Intimidation was heightened after October 1920, when the Ku Klux Klan organized its first Houston chapter. Only one month later, 200 of the robed and hooded "Apostles of Hate" held their first cross burning in the city.[30]

Initially, the Klan's use of terror and violence was not based on race. The Klan's first victim in Houston was B. I. Hobbs, a white lawyer who had a reputation for filing large numbers of lawsuits on behalf of both white and black clients. On February 5, 1921, a gang abducted Hobbs and spirited him to an unknown location, where they cut off his hair and tarred and feathered him. After beating him severely, the Klansmen left him completely naked in the downtown business district in the middle of San Jacinto Street. The Klan then reinforced their presence by mailing hundreds of frightening letters to Houston residents.[31] In another incident directed against a white male, A. V. Hopkins, a white manager accused of insulting a group of high school girls in a public place, was kidnapped, beaten, and abandoned in March 1921. The next day, he fled Houston.[32] That April, William J. McGee, a white salesman, was accused of repeatedly bothering a group of girls. On the day after the Klan abducted him, he told reporters that he needed only six hours to leave Houston.[33]

"The Ku Klux Klan is here to perform a mission no other agency can reach," it warned the people of Houston. Despite the Klan's initial focus on white victims, Houston's African Americans knew not to be complacent, especially after the Klan's most horrifying attack.

On Sunday, May 1, 1921, Dr. J. Lafayette Cockrell, an African American dentist, was riding in a car with four or five others, including his wife and brother. On Conti Street, two large cars drove up and boxed in Cockrell's vehicle. Immediately, several men drew revolvers and surrounded the car. They ordered Cockrell to get out, and when he did, W. H. Cockrell, his brother, also got out. As the brother tried to read the license plate of an abductor's car, he was viciously assaulted. Mrs. Cockrell watched the mob drive away with her husband. For several hours no one knew where they had taken Dr. Cockrell or what they had done to him.[34]

Dr. Cockrell had come to the attention of the Klansmen a few weeks earlier when he pleaded guilty to a morals offense.[35]

Several hours after the Conti Street incident, the C. J. Wright Undertaking Company received an anonymous call requesting an ambulance and directing it to a shack south of Pearland, a small town about eighteen miles from the abduction site. Inside the shack, the attendants found the heavily anesthetized Dr. Cockrell. The ambulance took him to St. Joseph's Infirmary, where he was attended to by physicians on staff; Dr. Cockrell had been castrated.[36]

The horror infuriated the newly elected mayor of Houston, Oscar Holcombe, who called for an end to the violence and declared he was going to uphold law and order and not lose control of his city. The chief of police ordered every police officer to report to duty immediately to address the double challenge of hunting down the kidnappers and responding to reports of a looming general uprising by Houston's African Americans. (The rumors were unfounded.)

As soon as he was able to relate what had happened to him, Dr. Cockrell told Holcombe that after being taken to the shack, he was blindfolded. "I was seized and forcibly thrown to the floor and in spite of my struggles, overpowered. While I was struggling I was warned that if I continued to fight I would have my head knocked off. I was bound so that I could not move. Later, a can of ether was opened and I became unconscious. Then the ambulance came and I was taken to the infirmary." Mayor Holcombe asked the stricken dentist if he wanted police protection. Dr. Cockrell declined, saying, "I have nothing more to fear." The next day, the *Houston Post* reported that "Cockrell had been rendered completely sterile." According to the doctors who examined him, the castration had been performed by a "skilled surgeon."[37]

At the time, Heman Sweatt was nine years old. How James Leonard Sweatt explained all of this to his sons during conversations at the table "about black history [and] black problems" can only be imagined.

Sweatt at Wiley

In 1930, Heman Sweatt graduated from Jack Yates High School, where he had met Constance "Connie" Mitchell. Years later, the two were described as "high school sweethearts." But marriage would have to wait. Sweatt's parents wanted to provide a college education for all of their children.

The quest for a first-rate education for his children, however, was also a source of frustration for the elder Sweatt: "All of my children had to go out of this state to get their training when their white playmates got the same training at less cost and trouble right here in Texas," he said.[38] Higher education for African Americans eventually became a large issue during the last years of James Leonard Sweatt's life. But in 1930, both he and his sons had to face the realities of life for African Americans in Houston and everywhere else in Texas: unless a black man or woman wanted to become a teacher, there were no public higher-educational opportunities in Texas. Gifted and talented black high school graduates sometimes qualified to attend out-of-state universities, but few parents could afford the travel much less the tuition. Texas provided no assistance of any kind. Across the nation in 1931, one year after Heman Sweatt entered college, only 35,949 African American students were attending black higher education institutions. (A few others attended integrated colleges.) But even that small number is deceiving: one-third of that population was actually enrolled in elementary schools and high schools at institutions that were colleges in name only.[39]

Unlike his brothers and sister, Heman elected to stay in Texas and attend Wiley College in Marshall, in the far northeastern part of the state. Founded in 1873 by Bishop Isaac Wiley of the Methodist Episcopal Church and the Freedman's Aid Society, the school was the first black college established west of the Mississippi River; its mission was to prepare emancipated slaves for a promising future. Even today, Wiley markets itself as an institution "committed to providing students with a broad liberal arts and career-oriented education in a Christian environment." In its early years, Wiley aspired to become the Fisk University (the renowned African American institution in Nashville) of the West.

Sweatt entered with the freshman class of 1930. In 1933, Wiley became the first black college west of the Mississippi to be granted an A rating by the Southern Association of Colleges and Schools.[40] Years later when Sweatt became one of the most famous professional-school applicants in America, his lawyers worried about the timing of the A rating. Many graduate and professional schools did not admit applicants from unaccredited undergraduate colleges. Wiley was accredited for roughly two of Sweatt's four years there.

Sweatt majored in biology, and his teachers included James H. Morton, a chemistry teacher and civil rights activist who would later move to Austin, teach at Tillotson College, and become the president of the capital city's chapter of the NAACP during a crucial time in its history. James Leonard Farmer, a religion and philosophy teacher, is believed to have been the first African American in Texas to have a PhD.[41] Without question, however, the most influential of his teachers was Melvin Beaunorus Tolson.

Melvin Tolson was born in Moberly, Missouri, in 1900. By the time he was twelve, his first poem had been published in "Poets' Corner" in the

Oskloosa, Iowa, newspaper. An orator par excellence, he insisted that he had learned all he knew about public speaking from his white eighth-grade teacher, a demanding perfectionist who required him to repeat poems while she snapped her fingers to indicate when a word or syllable should be accented. Tolson arrived at Wiley in 1924 with a teaching appointment in English and speech, and over the next twenty-three years he became a legend. Beginning in 1937, he wrote a weekly column about African American life in America; entitled "Caviar and Cabbage," it ran in the *Washington Tribune.*

Melvin Tolson was a complicated man, as engaging as he was brash and as humble as he was pugnacious. His inner circle knew him to be a Marxist who could argue passionately for social reform based on the teachings of a caring and loving Jesus Christ. He cared deeply for people but had no patience for either "fence straddlers" or "extremists whose views he found simplistic."[42]

Tolson delighted in confronting and upsetting his students to the point of vigorous debate. His writings were provocative as well. "Historians are the biggest liars in the world," he wrote in "Caviar and Cabbage." In a column entitled "Is the White Man Worse than the Negro?" he began with "Now, since it soothes your vanity to think that another man is crazier than you."[43]

He also had no patience with simpletons. On July 31, 1943, in a "Caviar" column entitled "Who Said: This Is White Man's Country?" he wrote, "A Negro who thinks this country—the United States—is not his country is a damned fool. My native land! Where is it? It is where my mother gave me birth. My hometown is where I was born. Jesus was a Nazarene because He was born in Nazareth. I am just as American as President Roosevelt."[44]

Debate was central to Tolson's teaching method. Shortly after arriving at Wiley, he founded the Forensic Society. As relentless as his eighth-grade teacher, he grilled his debaters for a year before deciding whether they were good enough to represent Wiley. His students learned to identify, analyze, and respond to logical fallacies. Undoubtedly, his students also adopted his style: reasoning, satire, and, above all, eloquence. His team is believed to have participated in its first interracial debate in 1929, when it took on the team from Oklahoma City University.

In 1935, his team traveled west to take on the national champion debate team from the University of Southern California (USC). Upon arrival, Tolson sequestered his debaters and ordered them to prepare for the big event while he toured USC's speech department, which was as large as all of Wiley College. When he returned, the stir-crazy students asked whether they could venture out onto the USC campus. Tolson replied, "Oh, they're not so much. We'll visit them after we win the debate just to show them we're good sports."[45]

That evening, the Wiley team defeated USC in an auditorium filled with eleven hundred people.[46] (The incident was the inspiration for Denzel Washington's hit movie *The Great Debaters.*)

Although Heman Sweatt was not on that debate team, Tolson was one of his teachers. Many years later, when asked who had influenced him the most, Heman Sweatt identified his father, James Leonard Sweatt, and his teacher Melvin Tolson.[47]

Heman Sweatt graduated from Wiley College on August 8, 1934, with a bachelor of arts degree. From the 1940s to the present day, reports of Sweatt's academic acumen grew, mostly as a result of public-relations attempts to emphasize his qualifications for being admitted to the UT Law School. In 1946, the *Houston Informer* reported that "Sweatt was generally considered one of the most brilliant students ever produced by the local school system." Today, plaques and memorials emphasize his "outstanding [academic] credentials." In reality, Heman Marion Sweatt was a good and steady student who graduated from Wiley College in four years. A copy of his official Wiley transcript is in the *Sweatt v. Painter* files of the NAACP because association officials carefully reviewed it in January 1946. It shows a few As, but mostly Bs and Cs.[48]

Searching for a Role

After graduation, Sweatt worked at a number of jobs; in 1936, he became a teacher and substitute principal in Cleburne, Texas. The principalship had been vacated by his brother Jack when he left to attend the University of Michigan. While in Cleburne, Heman taught biology in what he described as "the most unsupervised school system for blacks that heaven ever conceived."[49] Like his father, he stayed in education for only a short time. After Jack's return in the spring of 1937, Sweatt attended the University of Michigan. His ambition was to become a physician, and during the 1937–1938 academic year, he enrolled in bacteriology, immunology, and preventive medicine classes. By the end of the spring semester, he had completed twelve graduate hours with a B+ average.[50]

While living on Glen Street in Ann Arbor, between the University of Michigan's main campus and University Hospital, Sweatt became acquainted with Lloyd Gaines, another out-of-state graduate student. Gaines was already a celebrity of sorts for being the plaintiff in a landmark suit against the University of Missouri. Sweatt later admitted that he was cool toward Gaines, largely because of the latter's inflated ego. He was, however, impressed with Gaines's knowledge of and commitment to civil rights.[51] Sweatt could not have known just how important this acquaintance would become—to him personally and to the cause of equal educational access.

At the end of his first year at Michigan, Sweatt returned to Houston for the summer of 1938. He did not like the brutal winters of the Great Lakes area, which reportedly took their toll on his health. He had already passed the postal service's civil service exam, and when he found temporary employment in the post office as a substitute carrier, he decided not to return to Ann Arbor. He lived with his parents for nearly two years before he married his high school sweetheart, Connie Mitchell.[52]

As a boy and young man, Heman Sweatt was molded by the activism of his father at home and the eloquence of Melvin Tolson at Wiley. These mentors responded to what they saw as the ignorance of racial prejudice with study and scholarship. When confronted by the utter un-Christianity of Jim Crow, they turned to Jesus Christ. They refused to respond to hatred with more hatred. And both of them refused to surrender their country to an establishment that oppressed them. As Tolson said, he was just as much an American as Franklin D. Roosevelt.

CHAPTER 3

The Cast of Characters

The world's a theatre, the earth a stage,
Which God and Nature do with actors fill.
THOMAS HEYWOOD, *APOLOGY FOR ACTORS*, 1612

Reconstruction was no more than a chapter in a history book for Heman Sweatt, who was born thirty-five years after federal troops left the South. He was a product, however, of the failure of Reconstruction to end injustice, a failure that made him keenly aware of his "place"—and the consequences of not staying in it. He was also molded by the men and women who challenged assumptions of Negro inferiority in Houston's Third Ward.

Included among these courageous citizens was Charles Norvell (C. N.) Love, a tall, slim albino whose eyesight was so poor that he had to hold written materials six inches from his face. In 1893, Love founded the *Texas Freeman,* the first African American newspaper in Texas and possibly the first west of the Mississippi. He ran stories documenting how white police officers mistreated black Houstonians.[1] In 1911, he put his activist words into action when he parked his horse in a restricted zone for eight hours in violation of an ordinance that prohibited "colored people" from hitching their horses on downtown streets for longer than thirty minutes. During the hearing that followed, he persuaded the city council to revoke the ordinance.

In his reporting and in a column he called "Man About Town," Love set a standard for Texas's African American journalists and defined their profession for the next seven decades. The readers of black-owned newspapers saw that progress toward full citizenship could be made—not as fast as they would like—but it could be made. In Texas, C. N. Love established the role of the black newspaper as a major institution in the struggle for equality.

Black-owned newspapers were more than sources of news and chronicles of events: they were a validation of the accomplishments of African American Texans, secular versions of the black church. They published stories about smart kids, accomplished artists, successful businessmen, educators, doctors, lawyers, scientists, heroes, and pretty girls who were also black.[2] While white Texas relegated black children to grossly underfunded elementary and secondary schools, and provided no meaningful higher-educational opportunities, black newspapers reminded readers that they should not accept racist notions.

Black newspapers also advocated policies and points of view, not just in columns and editorials, but in news items as well, without pretending otherwise. They promoted faith in the American system of law, and even though their readers lived in a nation that oppressed them and had enslaved their ancestors, black newspapers offered an extraordinarily patriotic view of America and its promise. At the same time, black newspapers defined manners and etiquette in a way acceptable to the African American middle to upper-middle class and, through exposure, disciplined and shamed those who were not a "credit to their race"[3]: "Nothing is more embarrassing to Negroes than to have drunken rowdies in public places, who not only embarrass the immediate circle, but embarrass the whole race by making whites think that Negroes are generally rowdy."[4]

Despite their general support for America's system of law, black newspapers did address injustices. C. N. Love was among the first to attack the tragically effective disenfranchisement of African Americans enforced by election statutes that excluded them from party primaries. In 1921, the same year in which the Houston KKK castrated a black dentist for getting too comfortable with white women, Love and other plaintiffs filed suit against G. W. Griffith, the chairman of the Harris County Democratic Executive Committee, in an effort to overturn Texas's election laws. *Love v. Griffith* (1924) eventually made it to the U.S. Supreme Court, which, incredulously, declared the case moot: "The rule promulgated by the Democratic Executive Committee was for a single election only that had taken place long before the decision of the Appellate Court. No constitutional rights of the plaintiffs in error were infringed by holding that the cause of action had ceased to exist. The bill was for an injunction that could not be granted at that time. There was no constitutional obligation to extend the remedy beyond what was prayed."[5] Love lost the first round, but the fight was not over. For the next twenty-three years, African Americans in Texas fought the oppressive white primary.

A contemporary of C. N. Love, Clifton Richardson, Sr., a graduate of

Bishop College, a black institution in Marshall, Texas, founded the *Houston Informer* in 1919. Under his leadership, the paper took militant stands on racial issues: uncompromising positions on antilynching laws, better educational opportunities for African American children, and equality in segregated public accommodations. When five African American males from Huntsville were nearly lynched after being accused of raping a fifteen-year-old white girl, Richardson reported the incident with his usual fearlessness. He exposed the truth about Huntsville officials who refused to press charges against the lynch mob. His brutal editorials on lynching and injustice caught the attention of the Ku Klux Klan; the group sacked the *Informer* office, burning many of its files and destroying its printing press.[6]

The *Informer* also weathered boycotts and other threats from angry racists. "N——, leave town. Don't let the sun go down on you," read a message posted on Richardson's door. But unlike white Klan victims, Richardson understood that he could not run and start a new life somewhere else. Not that he would have run anyway. Instead, he gathered trusted friends to defend his home and family. During the siege, Houston police chief Thomas Goodson paid him a visit and inquired, "Richardson, I understand you carry a pistol with you at all times." When Richardson confirmed the chief's suspicion, the latter responded, "I don't blame you."[7]

One of the friends Richardson called upon to help protect his house was a stout, five-foot-seven-inch businessman who was either crazy or utterly fearless. Julius White had a third-grade education, but by 1925, by any measure, he was a wealthy man. In her book *In Struggle against Jim Crow*, Merline Pitre describes White as the owner of a nightclub, a ranch, and several houses. He had "a great deal of liquid capital," that is, cash, enough cash to enjoy the company of both affluent blacks and whites.[8] He could have enjoyed his wealth and made life easier for himself by "staying in his place." But White did not amass his fortune by staying in his place, taking it easy, or being a nice guy. A brutal street fighter who had an overpowering personality and never backed away from anyone, White was regarded as one of the "meanest black men in town." In an interview with Darlene Clark Hine, James Nabrit, Jr., an acquaintance of White who later became president of Howard University, described White as "a hustler with no high school education, he ran women and had shot two policemen and was generally considered to be crazy."[9]

But Pitre appropriately points out that Julius White financed many of the early lawsuits against the white primary while at the same time sponsoring cultural events for Houston blacks, such as the art exhibits at the Colored

Carnegie Library.[10] He may have been a hustler, but Julius White was not just a hustler.

Carter Walker Wesley and the Battle for the *Informer*

Clif Richardson, Sr., continued to publish the *Informer* through the 1920s, and as the paper's reach expanded, it attracted investors who saw that it had potential for even greater growth. Chief among them was Carter Walker Wesley, an attorney who returned to his native Houston after a somewhat notorious tenure as a lawyer in Oklahoma. On April 6, 1927, Richardson entered into a business arrangement with Wesley and three other partners. The resulting corporation was the Webster-Richardson Publishing Company. The other investors were J. Alston Atkins (Wesley's law partner), S. B. Williams, and George H. Webster. Webster received 100 shares for the printing shop he owned; Richardson received 100 shares for the *Informer*; Wesley and Atkins paid $5,000 for 50 shares of common stock; and whatever shares remained (no one knows for sure) were sold to other investors. Richardson must have thought it was a sweet deal: he became the president of the enterprise and was retained as the editor of the *Informer*.[11]

Under Richardson's editorial leadership and with a $15,000 investment in state-of-the-art machinery, Webster-Richardson grew to be "the most efficient black publishing corporation in all of Texas."[12] The sweet deal, however, was short lived: there wasn't enough room for the monumental egos of both Richardson and Wesley.

Carter Walker Wesley was born in Houston in 1892. He attended Fisk University in Nashville, and shortly afterward was selected to attend a segregated army officers training camp in Des Moines, Iowa. After completing the program in October 1917, he was commissioned as an officer and shipped to Europe, where he served in some of the greatest battles of the war: Argonne, Verdun, and Oise-Aisne. By Armistice Day, he was a first lieutenant and the commanding officer of his unit.[13] After the war, he entered Northwestern University Law School in Evanston, Illinois, and graduated in 1922 before moving to Muskogee, Oklahoma, to join his friend J. Alston Atkins in a law practice. The legend is that he was "the first Negro on record to pass the Oklahoma Bar on his first try." In his first five years as a lawyer, he brought thirteen cases before the Oklahoma Supreme Court and won eleven of them.[14]

Wesley and Atkins's most famous case was that of Leonard Ingram, a

Creek freedman (that is, he was of mixed Indian and Negro ancestry). Ingram owned 160 acres of land that had been given to him as a payment to Indians when Oklahoma became a state. State officials did not know it at the time, but enormous oil pools lay below much of the Indian land. In opposition to the common practice of appointing white "guardians" of Indian property, Ingram wanted control of his land after oil was discovered there sometime before 1927. For this litigation, he retained the legal services of Wesley and Atkins.[15]

Ingram's lawsuit was successful. He regained control of his property, and Wesley and Atkins won another high-profile case. But the publicity destroyed their reputations in Oklahoma after it became known that they had collected approximately $40,000 in legal fees—an enormous sum at the time. Their law partner allegedly left them and formed his own firm to sue to recover some of Ingram's money. Wesley and Atkins left Oklahoma for the former's hometown of Houston. Whether, as has been claimed, "Wesley and Atkins were run out of Oklahoma" is debatable. What is certain is that they settled in Houston in 1927 with a lot of money to invest.[16]

As they relocated their law practice to Houston, Wesley and Atkins looked for investment opportunities. They formed a real estate and property management company called Safety Loan Brokerage with two other partners and a $25,000 investment. The investment proved lucrative until 1929 and the onset of the Great Depression.[17]

After 1929, Atkins concentrated on the law practice, and Wesley turned his attention to the Webster-Richardson Publishing Company. He wanted control of the *Houston Informer.* In his way stood Clif Richardson, a formidable obstacle who *was* the *Informer;* he had founded it and been its editor since 1919. Richardson was a hero to many literate African Americans who religiously followed his attacks against racial discrimination. He repeatedly put his life at risk for what he believed and, specifically, for Houston's black population. Only someone as audacious as Carter Wesley would even attempt to unseat such an icon—but he did.

Wesley and Richardson's relationship deteriorated through the spring and summer of 1930. Wesley was a hard-nosed businessman who demanded that strict business procedures be followed, while Richardson was more lax. As the auditor of the corporation, Wesley pushed for a more sophisticated bookkeeping system and closer scrutiny of the money flow. They could not get along, and of the two, Wesley was clearly more competitive—and ruthless. The final split reportedly occurred when Richardson delayed the publication of the *Informer's* August 16, 1930, issue, which allegedly contained offensive, tabloid-like information. The feud grew even bitterer when the corporation (Wesley) sued Richardson.[18] By the end of that year, Richard-son gave up and announced the formation of a new black newspaper called the *Houston Defender*. By January 3, 1931, Wesley possessed undisputed con-trol of the *Informer*. The split became official on January 14 when a majority of its stockholders voted to change the name of the Webster-Richardson Publishing Company to Webster Publishing.

Wesley dealt Richardson's hope of competing against his former part-ners a near-fatal blow when he convinced an even greater journalistic icon, C. N. Love, to merge his *Texas Freeman* with the *Informer*. The result was the *Houston Informer and Texas Freeman*.[19] By 1932, Wesley was the treasurer of the corporation and general manager and editor of the newspaper. Only one year later, he clashed with yet another of his partners, George Webster, resulting in the latter's withdrawal from the corporation.

Under Carter Wesley's leadership, the *Informer* became the most suc-cessful black newspaper in Texas history. From 1931 to 1946, its circulation increased elevenfold—from 4,765 to 44,024. While almost all other black newspapers depended on white-owned machinery, the *Informer* was printed at its own Houston plant, which became one of the largest employers of black workers in Houston. By the start of World War II, the *Informer* had grown from an eight-page to a twenty-page newspaper. From the 1930s through the end of the 1950s, the *Informer* reached beyond Houston to sev-eral other cities, each with its own edition.[20]

Wesley used the *Informer* to become one of the most powerful and influ-ential African Americans in Texas. He knew it, and for the rest of his life, he refused to be ignored. Whether engaged in a trivial argument, pursuing a business goal, reaching a personal objective, or presenting a case before the U.S. Supreme Court, Carter Wesley never suffered pangs of self-doubt. In business and politics, he was ruthless.

Through his column, "Ram's Horn," Wesley skewered whomever he wanted. He could be just as critical of blacks for moral weakness as of whites for bigotry: "I recently bought a car through a Negro salesman. His name was John Austin. He promised everything under the sun and ended up by not doing anything, not even promising the service guaranteed with the purchase. If John Austin were giving cars away at half price, I wouldn't buy another one from him. In my book he's the biggest liar since the days of Iago."[21]

Two months later Wesley was beaten by two white Texas state troopers in a rural area in Montgomery County, north of Houston. According to the officers, the incident began when a white man named George Borning complained to the police that Wesley had waved at him. Incredibly, the police pursued Wesley as if he had committed a crime. According to Wesley, an officer named H. R. Owens said, "We have the complaint that you were disturbing the peace and waving at white people on the highway. What are you doing waving at white people, n——?"

It is inconceivable that Wesley let that pass without a retort of some sort. He was knocked into a ditch and kicked repeatedly. Within a few days, the *Informer* reported details of the incident, and according to Wesley, it "swept Negroes into a frenzy."

"Frenzy" might have been melodramatic, but in Austin, where the *Informer* was widely read, Dr. Everett Givens, a prominent black dentist, met with the governor's staff to register a complaint. On May 18, Wesley's trial took place in Montgomery County, and he acted as his own counsel. On the witness stand, he got George Borning to admit that the "waving" incident never happened. The judge dismissed the charges of resisting arrest and disturbing the peace, but Wesley was found guilty of speeding (95 miles per hour) and fined $50.[22]

Facing two armed state troopers in East Texas, who threw him in a ditch and kicked him, Carter Wesley refused to stay quiet and remain in his place. He would not be ignored, and even in East Texas, he got his way.

Richard Grovey

Carter Wesley was what his friend Richard Randolph Grovey described as a "New Negro": "The New Negro is the Negro who can see more Negroes than one . . . who has sense to realize that he is one of 15 million underprivileged people, and that he owes it to himself and his God to do everything possible to lift his people from the midst of economic death."[23]

Richard Grovey was a "New Negro" as well. Since 1917, he had owned and operated Grovey's Barber Shop in the center of the African American commercial section of the Third Ward. Since he depended on no white customers or sponsors, he could afford to be outspoken and militant, and he had the temperament and education to be both. Born in rural Brazoria County, south of Houston, near a hamlet called Sweeny, Grovey graduated from Waco Colored High School in 1910. After earning a degree at Austin's Tillotson College in 1914, he was a principal of a "colored" school until he clashed with the white superintendent. The latter had instructed Grovey to hire a "woman of questionable virtue."[24]

Grovey's reputation as an enthusiastic advocate for the African American community took him to all parts of Texas to speak out on two issues he took quite personally: the white primary and the need for African Americans to support one another by patronizing black businesses. In a speech at a banquet honoring him as "Man of the Year, 1939," Grovey said, "For the Negro the best milk is the milk sold by the company that employs Negroes."[25] On this occasion and many others, Grovey was recognized as a literate and articulate, albeit militant, advocate for political and economic rights.

The vehicle for Grovey's activities was the Third Ward Civic Club, which counted Julius White among its members. The organization sought to bring all blacks, from highly educated professionals to uneducated common laborers, together for a common good. For many blacks, Grovey was a symbol of hope.[26]

The Sweatts knew all of Houston's black civic and religious leaders of the time, largely through their membership in civic organizations. Grovey's Third Ward Civic Club, Julius White's Harris County Negro Democratic Club, and the Bi-Racial Harris County Republican Club were but three of several, probably dozens, of clubs in Houston formed for a variety of reasons from the 1920s to the 1950s; they experienced various levels of success and lasted for various lengths of time. Nearly every African American enclave in Texas had such groups.[27] While the clubs' raison d'être was to bring about the inclusion of African Americans into the political, educational, and cultural life of mainstream America, they virtually ignored half of the population they ostensibly sought to serve—women.

Lulu Belle Madison White

Even the most militant of male black leaders, like Grovey, defined freedom in masculine terms: "I've lived as long as I want without a right to be a citizen. I intend to fight to my dying day—in order that the Negro's right to be a man not be curtailed."[28]

The prevailing attitudes of the times might absolve leaders like Grovey, White, and Wesley for excluding women from their civic deliberations, and the mentality was not exclusively Texan. In 1906, when describing the goals of the Niagara Movement, W. E. B. Du Bois said, "We shall not be satisfied with less than our full manhood rights." In an era when the wealthy excluded the poor, whites excluded nonwhites, and native-borns excluded immigrants, powerful men excluded women in politics and business.

And yet, it would be a mistake to believe that civil rights advocacy was a male-only activity. In Houston, women had their own clubs, like the Grand Court of Calanthe and the Eastern Star, and a multitude of other service organizations. Many of the men's groups also had women's auxiliary branches. These and other women's organizations worked hard to raise money for political and charitable causes that improved the quality of life in their communities.

One prominent female black activist was Lulu Belle Madison. She was born in 1900 in Elmo, Texas, a hamlet built along the Texas and Pacific Railway tracks in Kaufman County, east of Dallas. After attending Butler College in Tyler for a short time, she moved to Houston, where she met and married a man twelve years her senior—the volatile nightclub owner Julius White.

Lulu (also known as "Lula") White aspired not only to be among the influential but to be influential herself. She and Julius were a prominent power couple in Houston's African American circles. She was a member of several women's clubs and service organizations and was well known for the Sunday-afternoon teas she hosted in her spacious home in the Third Ward at 2620 Tuam Street. After a short teaching career, she devoted all of her time to the cause of full citizenship for all African Americans.[29]

Standing five feet and six inches and weighing more than 250 pounds, Lulu White had a commanding appearance. She was every bit as fearless as her husband, Julius, and she could be, as Merline Pitre wrote, bold, brave, and loud on some occasions, and amiable and dignified on others. She tried to become a member of Houston's influential Bi-Racial Committee, but when her application was denied—because she was a woman—she looked elsewhere. There were plenty of organizations for men, and her husband was active in nearly all of them, but only one included women: the NAACP.[30]

The second half of the 1930s was a turbulent time for the Houston NAACP chapter. During what became a de facto reorganization of the chapter, Lulu White caught the eye of the national organization and she emerged as a major player. By 1943, the Houston chapter was the largest in the South, and by then she had become the first paid employee in the history of the NAACP in Texas. Julius White contributed much to her success. According to Michael Gillette, the Whites' large home was frequently used for meetings, and Julius provided the chapter with two rooms of office space in the Pilgrim Building in downtown Houston. Her office was on the second floor of the four-story building, but she didn't spend a lot of time there. Julius also provided a car, which she used after being appointed the director of the Houston NAACP Youth Council.[31]

Washington and Du Bois

During the time Heman Sweatt was in Houston, from the 1920s through the 1950s, successful and accomplished African American leaders included a brutish underworld figure (Julius White), his equally determined wife (Lulu Belle Madison White), a barber (Richard Grovey), and a lawyer-turned-newspaperman (Carter Wesley). Nearly all black families also turned to their pastors for inspiration, both spiritually and in civic matters. Clashes and disagreements among such strong and spirited people were inevitable, and no issue was more volatile than deciding where to begin the fight for equality. There were difficult choices to make about what steps should be taken first and about the best strategy to pursue. For example, there was little debate about the need to educate African Americans, but educate them in what? Where should their education take place: in white-controlled integrated schools or in equally funded but segregated black-run schools? Of course, the debate was not limited to Houston; it was part of the national African American experience. But the long road to justice for Heman Marion Sweatt was directly affected by the debate among African American teachers, and his story should be read in that context.

Booker T. Washington, the best-known and most influential African American educator at the dawn of the twentieth century, thought that immediate large-scale industrial education was the best and most realistic means of lifting the Negro race. He grounded this decision in the conditions of the real world, where racial segregation was, at least temporarily, a fait accompli. In his autobiography *Up from Slavery*, Washington concluded that the economic future of African Americans in the South was tied to the extent to which blacks could be educated in the industrial arts. He saw no realistic role for Greek and Latin in the life of a black family living in a shack with a dirt floor. He advocated self-reliance, hard work, study—much of which later came to be known derisively as "accommodation."

In one of the most famous speeches in American history, the "Atlanta Compromise Speech," delivered September 18, 1895, at the Cotton States and International Exposition in Atlanta, Washington incurred the permanent and unforgiving wrath of black activists and intellectuals.

> The wisest among my race understand that the agitation of questions of
> social equality is the extremest folly, and that progress in the enjoyment
> of all the privileges that will come to us must be the result of severe and
> constant struggle rather than of artificial forcing. No race that has anything
> to contribute to the markets of the world is long in any degree ostracized
> . . . The opportunity to earn a dollar in a factory just now is worth infinitely
> more than the opportunity to spend a dollar in an opera-house.[32]

Washington saw protest as a distraction from the necessary day-to-day toil of people desperately needing to elevate themselves. But what truly angered his detractors was a sentence, earlier in the speech, that has defined and haunted Washington's legacy to this day: "In all things that are purely social we can be as separate as the fingers, yet one as the hand in all things essential to mutual progress."[33]

Washington believed that craftsmanship, trades, industrial skills, and agricultural science, complemented by a virtuous personal life, would eventually make blacks indispensable to the American economy. He reasoned that in a profit-driven capitalist economy, management and workers could be counted on to do one thing—pursue their own best interest. Under such conditions, whites would find it profitable to accept African Americans as citizens and integrate them into American society.[34]

On the other hand, W. E. B. Du Bois, the first black man to earn a PhD from Harvard, saw a classical, liberal education as the only safeguard against white oppression. African Americans were not bodies or machines for merely producing wealth. "In the history of nearly all other races and peoples the doctrine preached at such crises has been that manly self-respect is worth more than lands and houses, and that a people who voluntarily surrender such respect, or cease striving for it, are not worth civilizing." He saw activism, confrontational political action, and an unrelenting drive for civil rights as steps on the road to citizenship and the realization of what he called "full manhood rights." His vision for educational access, however, was not as inclusive as Washington's; he favored the development of a Jeffersonian-type intellectual elite he called the "Talented Tenth."[35]

> Again, we may decry the color-prejudice of the South, yet it remains a heavy fact. Such curious kinks of the human mind exist and must be reckoned with soberly. They cannot be laughed away, nor always successfully stormed at, nor easily abolished by act of legislature. And yet they must not be encouraged by being let alone. They must be recognized as facts, but unpleasant facts; things that stand in the way of civilization and religion and common decency. They can be met in but one way,—by the breadth and broadening of human reason, by catholicity of taste and culture.[36]

Du Bois argued that Washington's industrial-education approach denied Negroes the "breadth and broadening of human reason" and left it exclusively for whites: "And above all, we daily hear that an education that encourages aspiration, that sets the loftiest of ideals and seeks as an end culture and character rather than bread-winning, is the privilege of white men and the danger and delusion of black."[37]

Frontline, a PBS series, featured the Washington–Du Bois debate in a segment called *The Two Nations of Black America.* Indeed, the notion of a monolithic conspiratorial mindset for black America has always been a racist myth. Throughout the twentieth century, the debate within the black community over industrial versus liberal education expanded to include other issues: protest versus self-reliance, litigation versus sit-ins, and, especially, an Afrocentric education provided by predominantly black institutions versus integration. There were often painful debates over state and local issues as well, so that by the late 1940s, Heman Sweatt's aspirations would become the center of this intraracial divide in the black community in Texas, and especially in Houston.

In 1905, Du Bois, then a professor at Atlanta University, called a meeting of black intellectuals who opposed Booker T. Washington's moderate approach. Twenty-nine like-minded black intellectuals met from July 11 through July 14 on the Canadian side of Niagara Falls in Fort Erie and formed the Niagara Movement, a confrontational organization with specific goals.[38] Membership in the movement, however, was always small, and its finances were always strained. Perhaps it floundered because it excluded the energy of women and the resources of liberal whites. Ultimately, the Niagara Movement became historic not because of what it was but because of what it would eventually become.

The Birth of the NAACP

The catalyst for that transformation was one of the most notorious race riots in American history. The incident began with the arrest of an African American male on August 14, 1908, only blocks from Abraham Lincoln's historic home in Springfield, Illinois. The man had been accused of sexually assaulting a white woman and was housed in the city jail, located on the town square. The jail also housed another black prisoner, a suspect in the murder of a white man.

As the white mob in the town square grew larger, Springfield officials, fearing that the jail would be stormed and the prisoners lynched, surreptitiously evacuated the two men through a back door and into the waiting car of a local restaurant owner, safely relocating them to the county jail. Instead of going home when they learned that the prisoners had been moved, the mob went on a rampage. They burned the restaurant and car of the white man who had cooperated with the police. The hysteria did not stop until the Illinois governor called in the National Guard. News reports shocked and angered the nation, especially the old Union states, which had been presented with the undeniable reality of rioting whites and lynch mobs outside of the old Confederacy.

One of the reporters covering the tragedy was William English Walling, a University of Chicago– and Harvard-educated socialist who had just returned to America from czarist Russia. He and his Russian wife, Anna, were in Chicago when the Springfield riot broke out. Apparently they arrived in time to witness some of the mob violence, and were amazed and horrified by what they saw: murder, violence, entire sections of a city in ashes, and hundreds of frightened African Americans with no place to go. His article on the riot was entitled "Race War in the North," and he characterized African American oppression as the "permanent warfare" of whites against blacks.[39]

Walling's vivid and disturbing descriptions so shocked a *New York Post* writer named Mary White Ovington that she wrote to him and suggested that concerned social reformers should start a movement to stop the abuse of African Americans and, by extension, fight the dramatic increase of state-level segregation laws. In early 1909, Walling, Ovington, and Dr. Henry Moskowitz, a Jewish civil rights advocate, met in a small New York apartment and envisioned a new association, one that included whites and blacks, men and women.[40]

Its first activity was to hold a national conference on the centennial of Abraham Lincoln's birthday (February 12, 1909). Oswald Garrison Villard, the grandson of the abolitionist William Lloyd Garrison, sent out the invitations. Fifty-three people attended. The group convened again in May 1910, and shortly afterward the organization gained strength when W. E. B. Du Bois's Niagara Movement joined what was, at the time, largely an all-white group called the National Negro Committee. In short order, five founders, Du Bois, Villard, Ovington, Walter E. Sachs, and John Haynes Holmes, incorporated the organization under the laws of New York and took the name National Association for the Advancement of Colored People—the NAACP.[41]

During the NAACP's formative years, Du Bois was the only black among its first officers. A towering intellectual, he was hardly representative of oppressed blacks. Warren St. James, in his study of the NAACP as a pressure group, maintains that the association's greatest problem during its first forty years was an inability to reach masses of African Americans, especially in rural areas—places like East Texas and the cotton fields of the Deep South, where it was needed most (the population Booker T. Washington wrote of in *Up from Slavery*). Its headquarters were in New York City, far removed from the bulk of oppressed black Americans. The NAACP attracted moderately and highly educated middle-class African Americans, most of whom were politically active and in positions to see the opportunities denied them.[42]

In 1912, a young white woman who was studying the life and conditions of southern Negroes visited Houston as part of her research. She interviewed Negro leaders about ways to improve blacks' quality of life, and in the course of a conversation, she informed them of a new advocacy group, the NAACP. Immediately, a group of black leaders formed a membership committee and looked into establishing a Houston chapter. James Leonard Sweatt was one of the eleven charter members. As his son Heman grew to adulthood, he, too, became active in the NAACP.[43]

From the beginning, the relationship between the NAACP's national office and individual Texas chapters was a rocky one. But both sides understood that they needed each other. In Texas, the Houston chapter was the key, not just because of its size, but because of its money and its access to extraordinarily talented men and women. And, alas, that included Carter Wesley; he knew it, and he would not allow himself to be ignored.

The Houston NAACP chapter was organized in the small back room of a grocery store owned by R. T. Andrews. He became its first member, and from the back of that store emerged the Texas pioneers of an organization that took on the twin weapons of the oppression of African Americans: racial segregation and the white primary.

The battle against the white primary came first.

CHAPTER 4

Iron Shoes

A lawyer is either a social engineer or he is a parasite on society.
CHARLES HAMILTON HOUSTON, HOWARD UNIVERSITY LAW SCHOOL

In 1926, Justice Louis Brandeis, a liberal and the originator of applying social science to litigation, quietly confided to the president of Howard University that the Supreme Court was sympathetic to Negro civil rights but that repeatedly cases were lost because of substandard briefs, shabby preparation, and facile arguing.[1]

A logical extension of Brandeis's point was that a new generation of first-rate attorneys needed to be graduated from law schools serving African Americans. The most obvious source of those lawyers was Howard University, in Washington, D.C. Decades later, Thurgood Marshall recalled that in the 1920s and 1930s, the unaccredited Howard University Law School was derisively referred to as the "dummy's retreat." Howard Law had few or no academic standards, and most instruction took place via a night school that catered to students burdened by full-time day jobs. Judge Robert L. Carter later wrote in his autobiography that the unaccredited school produced graduates who were not able to pass the bar exam, and as a result, they remained waiters, postal workers, and porters, as if they had never attended a law school.[2] But when Brandeis made his embarrassing, albeit accurate and honest, comment, the architect of a remarkable transformation of Howard Law was already on the faculty.

Charles Hamilton Houston was the son of William Le Pre Houston, a Washington lawyer, and Mary Hamilton Houston, a popular hairdresser whose customers included many of Washington's ruling elite. Charles Houston's academic talent became apparent while he attended the M Street

High School, the first classical Negro high school established in the United States, and became the only black student to enroll in Amherst University's entering class of 1911. He graduated in 1915 and returned to Washington to teach literature at Howard University. During World War I, he entered the army as a lieutenant, one of more than 2,000,000 African Americans who registered for the military; 367,000 served overseas. His military service was a life-altering experience plagued by naked racism, abuse, and harassment. While still in uniform, Houston turned to reading the law, so that by the time he returned to America in February 1919, he had decided that his "battleground was in America, not in France." He decided to become a lawyer and dedicate his life to the realization of racial justice.[3]

Much of the historiography of World War I focuses on how the Allied armies redrew the map of Europe and brought about the downfall of a number of centuries-old monarchies and empires. Few historians connect the war to the end of legal segregation in America, but service overseas exposed thousands of patriotic African American soldiers and sailors to racially tolerant European countries. The disparity between European liberality and the shameful treatment American black soldiers received at home left a legacy of resentment among black veterans like Charles Houston and Carter Wesley. Upon their return, these men refused to be fools. "I felt damn glad I had not lost my life fighting for this country," Houston remembered bitterly. The war's effect went beyond veterans. In 1917, membership in the NAACP was about 10,000; shortly after the end of the war, in 1919, it had exploded to nearly 80,000.[4]

After leaving the military in 1919, Houston entered Harvard Law School. He edited the law review and earned his law degree. By 1924, he had returned to Washington to teach at Howard Law School, which was in a house at 420 Fifth Street, NW. While there, he used his Harvard contacts to establish a close but informal relationship between the two universities. He wanted Howard to become a "Harvard" for American blacks. In 1930, he joined the administration as a dean, and his accomplishments in educational reform can be described only as phenomenal. In less than two years, the school of law was accredited by the American Bar Association and granted membership in the Association of American Law Schools.[5]

But the emergence of Howard Law School as the "West Point of Negro Leadership" was not without pain. Since its inception, Howard Law had been the source of about 75 percent of America's black attorneys, and that alone prompted some historians to characterize its night school as "admirable." Houston's father was a product of Howard's night school. But Charles

Houston saw mediocrity and incompetence.[6] Going from quantity to quality took courage. Houston envisioned Howard Law as the source of a cadre of talented black lawyers who would spread throughout the nation, but especially the South, to change the life of the African American. Ironically, his vision of quality and high standards exposed him to accusations of elitism.

Houston was an insufferable perfectionist who attacked Howard Law's status quo by abolishing the night school, restructuring the curriculum, hiring highly skilled and trained teachers, and implementing America's first law program specializing in civil rights. Undoubtedly, he discovered that turning a formerly open-admissions institution into a more selective one meant the need to deny places to formerly "qualified" applicants—some of whom became angry. But Houston also understood that no one was well served by enrolling students who were tragically unprepared to graduate or pass the bar afterward. The days of raising hopes and producing graduates who would ultimately be humiliated by failing the bar and returning to jobs traditionally taken by less-educated blacks had come to an end at Howard Law School.

Houston thought that "the social justification for the Negro lawyer as such in the United States today is the service he can render the race as an interpreter and proponent of its rights and aspiration." And as academic excellence and rigor took firm root at Howard Law, Houston's students heard certain sacred postulates more and more often: "Men, you've got to be social engineers"; "A lawyer is either a social engineer or he is a parasite on society"; "The only justification for Howard Law School . . . is necessary work for the social good."[7]

Houston saw that in a court of law, with its majesty, rigid rules and procedures, sworn testimony, and judicially assured relevance, there was hope. There was hope for a process in which an African American lawyer could face a white official, or anyone else who could be subpoenaed, and ask questions in the light of public scrutiny: "We used the courts as dissecting laboratories to extract from hostile officials the true machinations of their prejudices; and . . . the resulting exposures were often enough in themselves to produce reforms. Likewise we use the courts as a medium of public discussion, since it is the one place where we can force America to listen."[8] He could have added that although litigation for racial justice almost always began with defeat in the hopelessly racist atmospheres of southern district courts, victory became a little more probable with each appeal as hearings moved up the judicial hierarchy—farther away from Jim Crow county seats and judges elected in white primaries.

Nathan Margold and the Strategy for Desegregation

As Charles Houston continued to oversee the development of talented black lawyers, he enhanced an already close relationship with the national office of the NAACP and constructed a comprehensive legal approach to end school segregation. In 1930, the NAACP retained one of Houston's Harvard friends, Nathan Margold, to produce a legal strategy for attacking segregation. Margold delivered an impressive 218-page analysis of how best to attack school segregation, pointing out, for example, that the litigation should take place in border states, where passions were cooler than in the Deep South.

Margold also recommended that the NAACP direct its efforts to challenging grossly underfunded schools for African Americans as an unconstitutional violation of the equal protection clause of the Fourteenth Amendment. His recommendation, however, was not a direct attack on segregation. Margold argued that rulings on the unconstitutionality of unequal segregation would force state officials either to achieve true racial separation and equality or to integrate schools. The former would necessarily require states to duplicate all services: two sets of everything, including schools. And because no state could afford such a dual set of services, institutions, and bureaucracies, ultimately blacks and whites would have to attend the same schools.[9]

The Margold Report also noted that many southern states (including Texas) already had equality provisions in their constitutions. So in some circumstances the proper legal remedy might be a writ of mandamus, which is a motion to order a public official to immediately obey or enforce an existing law. Margold argued that there was no difference between separation and discrimination by statute, on the one hand, and separation and discrimination by administrative rules, on the other. For the latter, the threat alone of legal action could result in more educational opportunities for African Americans.[10]

Nathan Margold could not have been more prophetic had he used a crystal ball to predict what Heman Sweatt was to achieve twenty years later in Texas. The downside of the Margold Report, however, was that it entertained the possibility that separate could be equal, or what Antonio Maceo Smith later sarcastically referred to as "good segregation."

Meanwhile, Walter White, the chief secretary of the NAACP, had determined that the association needed a full-time staff lawyer to direct its legal activities. In 1934, the NAACP board of directors voted to offer Charles

Houston the job. He was ready to leave Howard, perhaps because he was already very active in the association and his students were circulating petitions protesting his absenteeism. On July 1, 1935, he went from being part-time NAACP counsel to a full-time staff attorney. With a budget of less than $5,000, Houston became a social engineer. He formed a legal advisory committee to develop a plan of action based on the Margold Report. Its foundation was Margold's theory that the white establishment was not willing to pay for truly equal separation.[11]

Houston's connections in the legal establishment, the law schools, and the courts were impressive. But ultimately his greatest and most enduring contribution to the goals of the NAACP was his mentoring of a young, long, and lanky lawyer from Baltimore named Thurgood Marshall.

Thurgood Marshall and *Pearson v. Murray* (1936)

"I started work with the NAACP when I was in my second year of law school," Marshall once said.[12] He was one of Charles Houston's best students—"I don't know anything I did in the practice of law that wasn't the result of what Charlie Houston banged into my head"—and he had a passion for justice and for becoming the social engineer Houston so often spoke about. Marshall also adopted Houston's work ethic. As a student, he called his teacher "Iron Shoes," and often complained about the workload Houston imposed, but as a lawyer, he worked every bit as hard as his academic progenitor. Marshall commuted from Baltimore to Washington every day and worked so hard on his studies that he is reputed to have lost fifty-five pounds in one year. Marshall had energy that was both inspiring and annoying, and he had a singular gift that improved with experience and time: he was engaging and charming—even to redneck sheriffs, lawyers, and judges who kept him out of their restrooms and didn't let him use their water fountains. In most cases, they couldn't help but like him.[13]

Marshall was a complex man. Perhaps his civility and charm were sincere, or perhaps he understood that hatred, even when it is returned, is a parasite on the intellect. He graduated magna cum laude from Howard Law in 1933, and for a short time struggled to establish a private practice in Baltimore. In less than two years, his relationship with the NAACP evolved from doing volunteer work to becoming a member of Charles Houston's staff—a position that paid $2,400.

But even before his move to New York, Marshall had become involved in the case of Donald Murray. Murray, who graduated from Amherst College in 1934, was from Baltimore, like Marshall. He wanted to attend the University of Maryland School of Law, but was denied admission because of his race. Under Maryland's constitution and laws, Murray could attend all-black institutions like Morgan College or the Princess Anne Academy, or he could accept an out-of-state "scholarship" that Maryland provided for young African Americans to attend Howard Law School. Marshall had no problem showing that Morgan and Princess Anne were not options, since neither had a law school; Princess Anne was, in fact, a junior college until the state made it a branch of the University of Maryland. Maryland's equality argument rested solely on the notion that its policy of paying black students to leave its borders meant that they would thereby receive an education comparable to that provided by Maryland Law. Marshall argued that Murray's exclusion from the state's only law school was at variance with both Maryland's laws requiring equality and the equal protection clause of the Fourteenth Amendment.[14]

Maryland argued that "the law school is not a governmental agency, required by the [Fourteenth Amendment] to give equal rights to students of both races." Because it derived most of its income from tuition and fees, the law school was a private organization. And just in case the court held that Maryland Law was a public institution, the state added that "the admission of Negro students is not required because the amendment permits segregation of the races for education, and it is the declared policy and the practice of the state to segregate them in schools, and that although the law school of the university is maintained for white students only, and there is no separate law school maintained for colored students, equal treatment has at the same time been accorded the Negroes by statutory provisions for scholarships or aids to enable them to attend law schools outside the state." Finally, Maryland argued that even if the court held that Maryland Law was a public institution, and that the out-of-state scholarships failed to provide equality, the remedy for Murray was not admission to Maryland Law, but the establishment of an "equal" law school for Negroes.[15]

In fact, Maryland had enacted laws to provide professional-school programs for African American students at Morgan College and the Princess Anne Academy, but it had yet to take any action to make such programs possible. Murray was an adult and a citizen of Maryland, and he wanted to attend a law school in his home state. Neither in-state black institution offered to him had a law school, just the promise that one day there would be one.

In January 1936, Maryland's supreme court handed Thurgood Marshall, who had been at the bar for only two years, and his master teacher, Charles

Hamilton Houston, a comprehensive victory for their client. The court shot down every argument for segregation Maryland had put forward:

> The one corporation [University of Maryland] could not be both a public and a private one . . . a distinction between agencies which do and those which do not collect fees from individual users of their facilities would not support a distinction between private and public character . . . There is no escape from the conclusion that the school is now a branch or agency of the state government. The state now provides education in the law for its citizens. And in doing so it comes under the constitutional mandates applicable to the actions of the states.[16]

To the argument that out-of-state scholarships met the equal-protection requirement, the court ruled that offering African Americans the option of attending law school outside the state at increased expense fell far short of providing facilities equal to those for white students. They added that the number of "colored students" who might be affected was irrelevant.

The only issue left unanswered was whether out-of-state scholarships per se satisfied the equal-protection guarantees of the U.S. Constitution; the Maryland court ruled that since the U.S. Supreme Court had not ruled on the issue, that they "need not discuss it now."[17]

The effect *Murray* had on the morale of the NAACP and its supporters cannot be understated. On its face, it was limited to the boundaries of one rather small border state. For Charles Hamilton Houston, it must have been a validation of his unrelenting demands for quality and hard work. The case opened the doors of the University of Maryland Law School to all citizens of Maryland, and that was an enormous victory for equal rights.

Missouri ex rel. Gaines v. Canada (1938)

Two months before earning a bachelor of arts degree from Lincoln University, Missouri's all-black institution, Lloyd Gaines sent a request to the registrar of the all-white University of Missouri for a law school catalogue. All the registrar's staff knew was that the request came from 1000 Moreau Drive in Jefferson City; it was a routine request, and the office sent the catalogue.

In August 1935, Gaines applied for admission to the University of Missouri Law School. Registrar Sy Woodson Canada didn't realize that Gaines was African American until he received transcripts from Lincoln University. The University of Missouri was segregated, and Canada referred Gaines to the president of Lincoln University. Lincoln's president communicated the obvious to Gaines: there was no law school at Lincoln or anywhere else in Missouri for African Americans. The president referred Gaines to the superintendent of Missouri schools to secure an application for an out-of-state scholarship as provided for African Americans under Missouri law.

In court, Missouri argued that it intended to meet the separate-but-equal test by elevating the quality of education at Lincoln University to the level of the state's flagship university, but doing so would take time; in the meantime, Gaines should accept the scholarship to become a lawyer. The state also admitted that in accordance with its constitution, state court rulings, and laws, Gaines was rejected solely because he was black.

During July 1935, Charles Hamilton Houston had contacted a black Harvard-educated St. Louis attorney named Sidney R. Redmond for help in preparing a legal challenge to Missouri's segregation of its higher-educational institutions and professional schools.[18] Decades after the events in question, and despite later denials by Gaines and the NAACP of any connection to their simultaneous and complementary activities, Redmond described how he had given Gaines the postcard to request the law-school catalogue when the two met in Redmond's office. What was indisputably true, however, was that neither Houston, who developed the legal strategy, nor Redmond, who did most of the litigating, knew much about their new client.[19]

During the *Gaines* litigation, Houston and the NAACP discovered that the selection of a plaintiff for a long, difficult, and stressful case mattered a great deal.[20] Gaines proved to be a high-maintenance plaintiff. As Juan Williams wrote, "Gaines wanted the NAACP to treat him like a star." He craved attention from the press and everyone who knew him, and then maintained that the attention he asked for was putting him under a great deal of pressure. To keep Gaines busy, the NAACP paid for him to work on a master's degree from the University of Michigan.[21] During his time there, he came to know Heman Sweatt; Sweatt thought Gaines was rather arrogant.

Keeping Gaines busy and quiet in Michigan was worth it to the NAACP. Houston saw the Missouri suit as the key to the NAACP's effort to desegregate schools nationwide; he intended to take the case all the way to the Supreme Court. Houston argued that if no separate schools existed for black students, integration was the only remedy. The timing was also right; since 1935, Franklin Roosevelt had appointed two liberal justices to the bench.[22]

After losing in Missouri district court and the Missouri Supreme Court, *Gaines* reached the U.S. Supreme Court during the 1938–1939 term.[23] The

Court stopped short of striking down the separate-but-equal doctrine, but it did make constitutional compliance in the absence of integration much more difficult for a state to achieve. First, the Court said that Gaines's right to an education was a personal and individual one. Even though the state had argued that the small demand for a black law school did not justify the state's investment, the Court said that it did not matter how many other African Americans applied: Missouri had to provide the school.

Second, the Court unambiguously struck down the practice of using out of state scholarships to satisfy the state's duty to provide a separate but equal education for African Americans: "Manifestly, the obligation of the State to give the protection of equal laws can be performed only where its laws operate, that is, *within its own jurisdiction*. It is there that the equality of legal right must be maintained" (emphasis added).[24] The Maryland Supreme Court had said much the same thing in *Murray*. With *Gaines*, the idea of using out-of-state scholarships to meet the test of separate but equal legally ended forever and everywhere in the United States.

Finally, the Court made clear that the promise of future equality, that is, the planned establishment of a separate law school for black Missourians, did not make temporary discrimination constitutional. The Supreme Court sent *Gaines* back to Missouri with instructions to admit Lloyd Gaines to the University of Missouri Law School or provide a law school for him within its borders: "We are of the opinion that . . . petitioner was entitled to be admitted to the law school of the State University in the absence of other and proper provision for his legal training within the State."[25]

Now, all Jim Crow states could either open their universities and professional schools to all citizens or establish duplicates of every program of every school to accommodate a relatively small number of African American students. From the beginning, Charles Houston reasoned that since no state could afford such duplication, Jim Crow states would be forced to integrate.

But it didn't work out that way. In early 1939, the Missouri legislature ordered that a separate law school for African Americans be opened by September 1, 1939. Additionally, it authorized the board of curators of Lincoln University to open new schools and programs for blacks "as the need arose." Gaines rejected the separate law school for blacks at Lincoln University, claiming it was not equal to the white school at the flagship University of Missouri. The Missouri Supreme Court remanded the case to district court in St. Louis, and the case appeared headed for the U.S. Supreme Court a second time.

Complicating the NAACP's plan was the fact that Lloyd Gaines was a troubled young man. He left Michigan and returned to St. Louis on December 31, 1938. Shortly afterward, he left for Kansas City to look for a job; after an unsuccessful search he moved to Chicago. At five in the evening on March 4, 1939, he mailed his mother an eight-page letter from the Stock Yards Postal Station in Chicago.

> As for publicity relative to the university case, I have found that my race still likes to applaud, shake hands, pat me on the back and say how great and noble is the idea, how historical and socially significant the case but—and there it ends. Off and out of the confines of publicity columns, I am just a man—not one who has fought and sacrificed to make the case possible, one who still is fighting and sacrificing—almost the "supreme sacrifice" to see that it is a complete and lasting success for thirteen million Negroes—no!—just another man. Sometimes I wish I were a plain, ordinary man whose name no one recognized.[26]

He roomed at a Chicago YMCA until March 7, 1939, when he ran out of money. His fraternity brothers at the Alpha Phi Alpha house in that city took up a collection and allowed him to stay there. About a week later, Gaines told his landlord that he was going out to buy postage stamps. He was never seen nor heard from again.[27]

In the meantime Charles Houston was preparing for another round of litigation to attack Missouri's new Jim Crow law school. When he returned to Missouri in October 1939 for the new district trial, he was shocked to learn that Gaines had not been heard from for seven months. Gaines was not required to attend the retrial, but under the rules of the court, he was required to make himself available for the state to depose. On October 11, 1939, Houston informed the district court judge that his client was missing. The NAACP orchestrated a frantic nationwide search, but to no avail. In January 1940 there was still no clue to his whereabouts, so the judge dismissed the case.

Years later, Sidney Redmond admitted that his client may have felt as though the NAACP were taking advantage of him. "There was a feeling—not commonly discussed, of course—that Gaines seemed to feel that he wasn't getting enough out of being used as a guinea pig, and wanted more in a personal sort of way."[28] Redmond also described the Gaines family as being reluctant to help the NAACP. That Lloyd Gaines might have been abducted and "eliminated" was never taken seriously by NAACP leaders, who surely would not have feared making public accusations or calling for an investigation. It is difficult, indeed impossible, to believe that Sidney Redmond, Charles Houston, and Thurgood Marshall would have stayed silent in the face of the abduction of their client. According to Marshall, when the NAACP needed Gaines most, he disappeared.

The *Gaines* case consumed much of Charles Houston's time and energy for more than three years and cost the NAACP more than $25,000.[29] In a letter to his wife, Houston confessed, "Rest is what I need, but there is too much to do in such a short time."[30]

CHAPTER 5

The Shadow of Failure

To know defeat is to know sin; it is the ultimate blasphemy against the American theology.
JAMES JACKSON KILPATRICK, *THE SOUTHERN CASE FOR SCHOOL SEGREGATION,* 1962

For almost all their lives, James Leonard and Ella Rose Sweatt watched other people enjoy full democracy without enjoying it themselves. But they were not passive observers. During Heman Sweatt's formative years, he saw his father organize workers and participate in church activities and civic organizations in Houston. The organizations they built and what they learned during those years established the machinery that the younger Sweatt used to fight for higher education for black Americans.

The organizational machinery first emerged as a civic force combatting the effects of a masterpiece of disenfranchisement—the Terrell Election Law of Texas. Its provisions effectively removed the umbrella of equal protection for African Americans guaranteed by the Fourteenth Amendment and voting rights under the Fifteenth Amendment. Texas election laws neutralized whatever hopes African Americans harbored as a result of the Civil War and Reconstruction. And that was exactly the way Terrell wanted it.

Alexander Watkins Terrell was born in Virginia in November 1827, grew up in Booneville, Missouri, graduated from the University of Missouri, and studied law in the office of a local judge.[1] He was admitted to the Missouri bar in 1849 and practiced law in St. Joseph until he moved to Austin in 1852. He developed a close friendship with Texas icon Sam Houston and set up a successful law practice. Within five years, he was elected a state district judge in Travis County, where Austin is located.

At first, Terrell was not vocal about whether he was for or against secession. However, in 1863, Terrell ended whatever speculation there may have been about his true loyalty. He enlisted in the Confederate Army and joined the First Texas Cavalry, where he was quickly promoted to brigadier general. Before his promotion could become official, however, Confederate military leaders from Texas were either handing over their swords in surrender or fleeing to Mexico.

Terrell fled to Mexico. He served in Maximilian's army until it became clear that President Andrew Johnson's vision of Reconstruction and reconciliation included the liberal dispensing of presidential pardons to former Confederate officers.

Upon his return to Texas in 1866, Terrell practiced law in Houston for a year before isolating himself from Reconstruction on a plantation in a rural area about 100 miles north and east of Austin. For four years he led the quiet life of a gentleman farmer before returning to a law office in Austin. Soon he was back in politics; by 1876, he was a state senator. With only two brief interruptions, for the next thirty years he represented the Austin area in either the Texas House of Representatives or the Texas Senate.[2]

During his time in the Texas Legislature, he fit the profile of a former-Confederate politician, conveniently forgetting that in many countries he would have been charged with treason and hung for taking part in a rebellion. He felt humiliated, bitter, and livid over Reconstruction politics, which he took personally. From the late 1870s through the first decade of the 1900s, Terrell introduced or sponsored numerous disenfranchisement bills, including ones to levy poll taxes and require literacy tests for jury service. His racism was deep and harsh, and he was only slightly more tolerant of immigrants and poor, uneducated, and impoverished whites.[3]

Terrell was an angry man, perhaps because much of what he stood for was haunted by the shadow of failure. In 1962, James Jackson Kilpatrick, editor of the *Richmond News Leader,* authored a controversial and somewhat offensive book entitled *The Southern Case for School Segregation.* Kilpatrick argued that the South (and, by association, Terrell and other Confederates) could not be understood without recognizing that "alone among all the regions of the Union, the South has known defeat. To know defeat is to know sin; it is the ultimate blasphemy against the American theology . . . Failure—permanent, total, unqualified failure—is unknown. It is intolerable. It shatters the grand American illusion . . . But the South has known failure. It has known what it is to do one's best, to fight to exhaustion, and to lose."[4] Terrell and thousands like him refused to face the reality and consequence of Confederate failure. He was haunted by his past and surrounded by freedmen, the reminders of failure—permanent, total, unqualified failure.

The first Terrell election laws, enacted in 1903, presumed that the Civil War amendments to the U.S. Constitution applied only to general elections for federal office (that is, only for congressional seats and the Electoral College). Terrell's bills established direct primaries as the method of selecting party candidates, who then represented their parties in a general election open to all. After the end of Reconstruction in 1876, when Texas became a one-party state, the law meant that the Democratic primary selected the only viable candidate for the general election. In fact, one-party Democratic politics took root in all southern states, and for the next hundred years, the old Confederacy was the "Solid South" for the Democratic Party.

In January 1905, Terrell expanded disenfranchisement through additional bills. One made it a crime to pay a poll tax for an African American; another empowered the executive committee of a political party to define its membership, thus allowing them to exclude whomever they wanted from the party's activities.[5] The exclusion of blacks from a primary made it a "white primary."

Even under the oppressive Terrell Election Law, however, African Americans were able to vote in some areas of the state if the local Democratic officials who controlled party eligibility allowed them to do so.

But the situation became even worse in 1921 when the U.S. Supreme Court ruled in *Newberry v. U.S.* that primaries were not elections within the meaning of the Constitution but were *"merely methods by which party adherents agree upon candidates whom they intend to offer and support for ultimate choice by all qualified electors."* The Court added that laws governing elections do not necessarily apply to primaries: *"the two things are radically different"* (emphasis added).[6]

This hands-off attitude toward political-party activities set the Texas Democratic establishment in motion. During the Texas regular legislative session of 1923, Senator R. S. Bowers, of Caldwell, introduced Senate Bill 44, which stated, "In no event shall a Negro be eligible to participate in a Democratic Party election." What followed was even more breathtaking: "And should the Negro vote in a Democratic primary election such a ballot shall be void." Election officials were also directed to be proactive in the destruction of ballots cast by black voters. SB 44 passed both houses, and was presented to Governor Pat Morris Neff, an 1897 graduate of the University of Texas and a future president of Baylor University, who let the bill become law without his signature.[7]

In *Black Victory,* historian Darlene Hine wrote: "The emergence of a literate and economically viable black professional and business class meant that an increasing number of blacks could pay the poll tax." Additionally, black newspapers like Carter Wesley's *Informer* and Clif Richardson's *Defender* spearheaded extensive campaigns to get black voters to pay those taxes. In 1928, William King's *Dallas Express* promoted a poll-tax drive by quoting respected black leaders like Bishop John McKinney: "You should not be less than a citizen. Pay your poll tax." In editorials, King argued, "You are a man if you have the poll tax in your pocket."[8]

Nixon v. Herndon (1927) and Nixon v. Condon (1932)

The Texas that Heman Sweatt grew up in was a hotbed of suffrage struggles, which began with the efforts of Dr. Lawrence A. Nixon, a forty-one-year-old African American physician from El Paso who had helped establish one of the first NAACP chapters in Texas. Nixon was loyal, reliable, mature, educated, and economically independent of the white population—an ideal NAACP plaintiff. El Paso, being situated on an international border, was far less racially volatile than the formerly Confederate East Texas and the states of the Deep South.[9]

On July 26, 1924, Nixon, a member of the Democratic Party, stood before two election judges, C. C. Herndon and Charles Porras. It was not as frightening as it could have been: Herndon and Porras were his friends. As Nixon recalled, "They inquired after my health." Then Nixon presented a receipt for payment of Texas's poll tax. "Dr. Nixon, you know we can't let you vote," one of the judges said. "I know you can't let me vote, but I've got to try," Nixon replied.[10] Nixon then presented the two election officials with a statement, prepared by the NAACP, confirming that he had been denied the right to vote in a primary election because he was a Negro. It was the truth; Herndon and Porras readily signed it.[11]

Nixon sued Herndon and others, arguing that the Texas white-primary laws violated the Fourteenth and Fifteenth Amendments of the U.S. Constitution. When the case reached the Supreme Court, the defendants (Texas election officials) made no argument, but the State of Texas submitted a brief.[12]

When the Court ruled on March 7, 1927, Justice Holmes's reasoning could not have sounded a more optimistic note for the NAACP:

> We find it unnecessary to consider the Fifteenth Amendment, because it seems to us hard to imagine a more direct and obvious infringement of the Fourteenth . . . "What is this [the Fourteenth Amendment] but declaring that the law in the States shall be the same for the black as for the white;

that all persons, whether colored or white, shall stand equal before the laws of the States, and, in regard to the colored race, for whose protection the amendment was primarily designed, that no discrimination shall be made against them by law because of their color."[13]

Then, after chastising Texas for such a clear constitutional violation, he "instructed" the state on how to make its disenfranchisement law constitutional: "States may do a good deal of classifying that is difficult to believe rational, but there are limits, and it is too clear for extended argument that color cannot be made the basis of a *statutory classification* affecting the right set up in this case" (emphasis added).[14]

In other words, it was clear that Texas had violated the basic civil rights of African American Texans—because it had done so through statute. If the political party sought to do the same thing, however, it could do so as a private entity not governed by state law.

In response, members of the Texas Democratic Party in the legislature replaced what had been struck down in *Herndon* with "every political party in this State through its State Executive Committee shall have the power to prescribe the qualifications of its own members and shall in its own way determine who shall be qualified to vote or otherwise participate in such political party." Shortly afterward, the Executive Committee of the Texas Democratic Party produced a regulation that eliminated African Americans from membership in the Democratic Party.[15]

On July 28, 1928, Dr. Nixon presented himself to election judges James Condon and C. H. Kolle in El Paso's ninth precinct. Condon and Kolle declined to furnish a ballot for Nixon and told him that in order to vote, he would have to get an order from the chairman of the Democratic Executive Committee of El Paso. After an unsuccessful search for the chairman, Nixon returned to the polling place and was denied again. This time Condon signed a statement affirming that Nixon was not allowed to vote solely because of his race.

Nixon v. Condon was decided on May 2, 1932. Again, the Court acknowledged the obvious: "The legislative purpose was . . . to prevent Nixon and other Negroes from participating in . . . [primaries that are] equivalent to an election."[16] Incredibly, the Court struck down the executive committee's regulation not because it denied equal rights to African American voters, but because the regulation, again, came from the wrong source. The Court ruled that the executive committee had become an organ of the state when it acted independently of the Democratic Party: "They are then the governmental instruments whereby parties are organized and regulated to the end that government itself may be established or continued." Just as Justice Holmes had done in *Herndon,* Justice Benjamin Cardozo gave Jim Crow states "instructions" on how to lawfully exclude blacks: "Whatever inherent power a state political party has to determine the content of its membership resides in the *state convention*" (emphasis added).[17]

Less than three weeks later, the Texas Democratic Party met and adopted a resolution that stated: "Be it resolved that all white citizens of the State of Texas who are qualified to vote under the Constitution and laws of the State shall be eligible to membership in the Democratic Party and, as such, entitled to participate in its deliberations."[18] Carter Wesley and James Nabrit, Jr., attempted to appear before the Resolutions Committee but were never recognized. The resolution was not universally supported by all white Texas Democrats: some had been elected, in part, with black support; others were uneasy about the possibility that a select few whites might use their new power to disenfranchise their white political opponents also.[19] But despite a lack of universal support, the white primary remained so completely effective that it was in fact the only method of disenfranchisement used in Texas and much of the rest of the South.[20]

Grovey v. Townsend (1935)

Although the NAACP was involved in the *Nixon* cases, the association actually favored a more deliberate strategy than random and individual state-by-state cases against the white primary. Many in the NAACP, including the white attorneys who had done almost all of the legal work, also believed that the Supreme Court was still too conservative for a successful challenge.[21]

Houston's African American leadership, on the other hand, saw no need to follow the lead of a national organization. Carter Wesley, his law partner, J. Alston Atkins, and James Nabrit Jr., the Houston trio, joined forces with Richard Randolph Grovey to challenge the Texas white primary on their own.

After *Condon,* a case Houstonians considered meaningless, all four men believed that it was important for black attorneys to direct the legal struggle and argue Texas cases against the white primary. They wanted to solidify the African American community around a common cause. The resentment they felt against the NAACP had festered since the litigation of *Condon,* a case Wesley and Nabrit wanted to present before the Court themselves but that was instead presented by three white New York NAACP attorneys.

Others in the Houston community joined in the fight. Julius White once again put his money where his mouth was. He too was impatient with the "wait and see" attitude of the NAACP.

Houstonians were electrified by talk of a bold move, but elsewhere, black leaders were gravely concerned. Richard D. Evans, a Yale-educated African American attorney from Waco who had represented Charles N. Love in his white-primary case, passionately begged the Houstonians to drop their plans for an independent court challenge. Dr. Lawrence Nixon and the national office of the NAACP also asked the Houston trio to wait for more favorable conditions—like the appointment of more liberals to the Court.

But the Texas group was not intimidated by the NAACP, which they considered aloof and ineffective. Third Ward African American civic clubs like Julius White's Harris County Negro Democratic Club and Richard Grovey's Third Ward Civic Club, as well as numerous women's clubs, black pastors, and their congregations, rallied around Grovey, who announced on July 1, 1934, in a letter to the editor of the white-owned *Houston Post* that Blacks would present themselves as Democrats and demand to vote in primary elections.[22] "We plan to use reason, the public press and the Courts to let the world see Texas Democracy as it really is . . . The voters know that this howl about the purity of the white man's party primaries is a cloak behind which many office holders can deal Negroes the most wicked hands."[23] White leadership in Houston and all of Texas, however, may have been distracted by the *Post*'s front page headline that day: "Fear of Civil War Grips Germany after Revolt: Hitler in Undisputed Control with Nation Armed for Rebellion."

As promised, Richard Grovey presented himself on July 28, 1934, to election officials and demanded an absentee ballot for the Texas Democratic primary. Citing Texas Democratic Party rules, county clerk Albert Townsend refused. The Houston trio, Wesley, Atkins, and Nabrit, fully expecting the rejection, sued Townsend in a justice of the peace court in Harris County.[24]

Grovey v. Townsend was first heard in a justice of the peace court, where the Houston trio knew they were going to lose. Grovey asked for ten dollars in damages. Under Texas law, a case could not be appealed in state courts if it sought less than twenty dollars in damages, so *Grovey* could not be heard by a Texas court of appeals or the state supreme court. Once the justice of the peace in Houston ruled, the case went directly to the U.S. Supreme Court.[25]

Carter Wesley wrote in the *Informer* that "never before since Negroes were disenfranchised by the Terrell Election Law has there been such widespread interest on the part of Negroes all over the state in a common point of view and a common objective."[26]

The U.S. Supreme Court heard the case on March 11, 1935. The Houstonians presented a direct attack on the white primary's constitutionality: any attempt by Texas or a political party to interfere with the right to vote was unconstitutional because the primary was an election under the meaning of the Constitution; the state is unavoidably involved in elections when it passes laws describing who is eligible to vote in primary and general elections—party conventions are merely arms of the state; and the Texas Democratic Party is merely an arm of the national Democratic Party, which had never adopted racial restrictions in its primaries.[27]

On April 1, 1935, the Supreme Court decided *Grovey.*

> The primary is a party primary. . . .
>
> . . . We are not prepared to hold that in Texas the state convention of a party has become a mere instrumentality or agency for expressing the voice or will of the state.
>
> . . . The argument is that as a negro may not be denied a ballot at a general election on account of his race or color, if exclusion from the primary renders his vote at the general election insignificant and useless, the result is to deny him the suffrage altogether. [To say so] is to confuse the privilege of membership in a party with the right to vote for one who is to hold a public office.[28]

The defeat could not have been more crushing. Richard D. Evans, of Waco, who had "begged" the Houstonians not to proceed with *Grovey,* fumed: "Their fido pack went bear hunting and treed a skunk." Dr. Lawrence Nixon, who had endured two Supreme Court cases as a plaintiff and had heeded the advice of the NAACP to wait awhile before trying again, bitterly wrote that the Houstonians had succeeded in "tearing down everything that had been built for them."[29] To Nixon, proceeding with a white-primary case without the expertise and resources of the NAACP was incompetent and stupid.

The NAACP did its best to distance itself from the debacle. But as Walter White, the organization's secretary, lamented, "Years of hard work and heavy expense appeared to have gone for naught."[30] James Marshall, an attorney associated with the NAACP, carefully reviewed *Grovey v. Townsend* and concluded that the Houston trio had badly handled the case.[31]

After such universal criticism, most lawyers would not want to bring any further attention to themselves—but not so with Wesley, Atkins, and Nabrit. Indeed, their criticism of the NAACP intensified. Incredibly, Wesley argued passionately that the *Grovey* failure was really an NAACP failure to develop a white-primary case using black attorneys, both at the Supreme Court and in local trials.

Trouble in Houston

Once the finger-pointing subsided, the national office of the NAACP and African American Houstonians quietly admitted that they needed each other. Richard Grovey assured the black population that his case was not the end of the fight to vote—"unless the Negroes of Texas stayed on their knees and made it so."[32]

Wesley and company knew they had to step back and allow the NAACP to take control of cases headed to the Supreme Court. Failure in *Grovey* also had a profound effect on African American leaders in Texas. As one historian put it, "In order to prevent further disaster, it was decided to organize the Texas Conference of [NAACP] Branches and make it the legal spearhead."[33]

Carter Wesley, Alston Atkins, and James Nabrit, Jr., continued to be active, albeit divisive, leaders of Houston's African American population. Even after their complete and humiliating defeat in *Grovey*, the Houston trio—who by themselves made up 10 percent of all of Texas's black attorneys—could not be dismissed by anyone in Texas or in the national office of the NAACP because they brought money and energy to the fight. Wesley was on his way to making the *Informer* the most influential black newspaper in Texas, and he had ambitions to expand to New Orleans and other large southern cities.[34]

The NAACP also took seriously Wesley's insistence on hiring black attorneys. The *Grovey* fight coincided with Walter White's push for the NAACP's board to appoint Charles Hamilton Houston as a special counsel. Talk of his appointment had been going on for some time, and so it may not have been the direct result of Texan demands. Still, it gratified Wesley and Atkins and allowed them to save face. The arrival of Charles Houston changed the NAACP's approaches to litigation for voting and educational rights.[35]

The NAACP in Houston seemed hopelessly divided. C. F. Richardson, Sr., Wesley's bitter former business partner and chief competitor in the newspaper business, was a popular president of the Houston branch. But he too had his problems. In the late 1930s, Richardson faced rather serious charges of misusing NAACP funds. During the presidential election of 1940, he compounded his problems by publicly endorsing fellow Texan John Nance Garner over FDR, in violation of the NAACP's rule against political endorsements.

Houston NAACP members were divided into two political factions: those who supported Richardson (the Garnerites) and those who supported Wesley. During the summer of 1939, Wesley used the *Informer* to unmercifully attack Richardson and the Garnerites. The national NAACP office looked at the unfortunate, at times childish divisiveness in Houston with dismay. Walter White dispatched an NAACP field organizer and former newspaper reporter, Daisy Lampkin, to Houston to investigate the conflict. Lampkin's review included phrases like "the worst I've ever seen," "unbelievable," and "one grand mess" and described shady financial dealings, petty bickering, and even threats of murder.[36] At one point, she considered calling for the revocation of the Houston chapter's charter. After reading the report, Walter White fumed at the potential damage those "grafters and crooks" could do to the association in Texas.[37]

Over time, the Houston NAACP chapter did regain its functionality. Atkins and Nabrit moved out of Houston to pursue academic careers. Although Wesley remained in the city, he concentrated his energies on the newspaper business. In September 1939, the epicenter of the bitter factionalism, Clif Richardson, Sr., died of Bright's disease.[38] Lulu White (Julius's wife) became the acting president of the chapter and worked to restore order.

In November 1939, the pastor of the Good Hope Baptist Church, the charismatic Albert A. Lucas, was elected to a full term as president.[39] Nearly four decades after he first met the Reverend Lucas, Thurgood Marshall remembered him as "one of the finest gentlemen you'd ever run across. In the glove compartment of his car he had two items—a Bible and a .45 [caliber pistol]. And his answer was very simple, 'I'll try the Bible first.'"[40]

Lucas's preaching was so effective that he was accused of starting a riot in Detroit after a ten-minute speech. The *Houston Informer* once reported: "He not only says almost anything he wants in his pulpit but is human enough to talk the language of all men in the street."[41] He had a talent for using rousing orations, not as a call to arms, but as a call for calm and reason: "I am saying to you that we will win some of the things that we should have and that we are entitled to if we are willing to fight hard enough for them . . . Our fights are all within the democratic framework and, therefore, are not to be fought with the sword, nor without outside help."[42]

The Reverend Lucas's tenure as president of the Houston NAACP was not an easy one. In March 1940, an open meeting at the Olivet Baptist Church turned into a brawl. The most complete account of the embarrassing incident is by one of the participants—Carter Wesley. The chapter had assembled to discuss whether another suit should be initiated to challenge the Democratic white primary. The Garnerites proposed a resolution to postpone the suit so as not to embarrass the Garner presidential campaign. They added that if another suit were filed, it would eliminate any chance that the upcoming Texas Democratic Convention would vote to allow blacks to vote in the primaries. In speaking against the Garnerite-sponsored postponement, Richard Grovey and Carter Wesley countered that Democrats could have voted to allow blacks the ballot long ago and had never done so. While Grovey had the floor, he undiplomatically denounced the Garnerites as "a sinister force which would take from us constitutional rights." A Garnerite named Alphonse Mills, seated several rows in front of Wesley, became so enraged that he leaped over rows of chairs and pews onto Wesley, and "the two engaged in a dog-fight."

Apparently, the fight spread throughout the church before Lucas and others with clearer heads restored order. Afterward, Mills said that he "beat the devil out of Carter Wesley." In the *Informer*, Wesley wrote, "Alphonse Mills went home with a bloody head and a swollen face." But in a rare moment of contrition, Wesley added, "It was unfortunate that the fight took place in a church."[43]

Lucas's attempts to bring order to the Houston NAACP enhanced his reputation enough that he was elected president of the Texas State Conference of Branches of the NAACP during its May 10–12 meeting at the First Congregational Church in Corpus Christi. But the highlight of the conference was the appearance of Thurgood Marshall from the National Office. The Texas State Conference of Branches took control of Texas's legal attack on the white primary and handed the responsibility over to the National Legal Committee of the NAACP, which was controlled by Marshall. To ensure local input, William J. Durham, a black attorney from Sherman, was retained as Texas's resident counsel, and in what was a conciliatory gesture, Carter Wesley and another attorney were appointed his assistants.[44]

William J. Durham was born in 1896 in Sulphur Springs and served in World War I before studying law in the office of a white lawyer from Sherman. After several attempts, Durham passed the bar and set up a practice in Sherman in 1926.

He witnessed racial terrorism first hand during the trial of a black man accused of raping a white woman in May 1930. A mob killed the defendant by burning the Grayson County courthouse; the judge and other county officials had to be rescued from the second floor by the fire department. Not even the legendary Texas Ranger Frank Hamer, the man who would track down and kill Bonnie and Clyde four years later, could control the horde. The Texas Ranger creed of "one riot, one Ranger" didn't work in Sherman in 1930. Mob mentality so completely possessed the vigilantes that they fished the charred remains of the defendant out of the ashes of the courthouse and hung them from a tree on Mulberry Street in the black business section. Stores were looted to build yet another fire beneath the hanging corpse of the murdered and mutilated defendant. The lunacy continued with the burning of the black business district, including William Durham's law office.[45]

Sherman's black business section never fully recovered from the abomination of May 1930, but Durham stayed in Sherman for the next thirteen years. He could afford to take civil rights cases because he had a lucrative practice as counsel for an insurance company. His civil rights cases included equal-pay lawsuits for black teachers, and he developed a reputation as a first-rate lawyer. In 1954, legendary Dallas County district attorney Henry Wade (who would become famous for prosecuting Jack Ruby for the murder of Lee Harvey Oswald) said of Durham that "he is as good, or better, than any other lawyer I have worked against in this office."[46]

Antonio Maceo Smith

Juan Williams described Antonio Maceo Smith as a "commanding man who smoked big, pungent cigars." In the *Handbook of Texas,* he is referred to as "Mr. Civil Rights of Texas." Today, thirty years after his death, students at A. Maceo Smith High School in Dallas still refer to him simply as "the Man."[47]

Maceo Smith, who was born in Texarkana on April 16, 1903, graduated from Fisk University before moving to New York and working his way through New York University's MBA program. After graduate school, he founded the Harlem Advertising Agency and lived in New York until 1931, when he returned to Texarkana. Then he moved to Dallas, where he organized a life insurance company.[48]

Maceo Smith was a natural organizer. Amilcar Shabazz described him as someone who could bring about a "rising mood of optimism."[49] He energized the Negro Business League and reorganized the Dallas Negro Chamber of Commerce, serving as its executive secretary. In 1936, he was elected secretary of the Dallas NAACP. In addition to his civic and business responsibilities, he was the assistant general manager of Negro participation in the Texas centennial celebration of 1936, securing an astounding $100,000 grant from the federal government for black participation.[50]

Maceo Smith became the organizational force behind the NAACP's Texas State Conference of Branches, which became even more effective when he left the private sector in 1938 to become a race-relations officer for the federal government's housing authority. Rather than being isolated in an office with white colleagues (who didn't want him there) in Fort Worth, Smith was assigned a secretary and space in a housing project in Dallas. Using funds provided by the federal government, and ignored by white colleagues uninterested in what he was doing, Smith traveled to housing projects throughout Texas, promoting good race relations by frequently meeting with African American leaders (of NAACP branches) on the local level.[51]

The emergence of Maceo Smith as a statewide figure and the establishment of the Texas State Conference of Branches meant that the association was no longer as vulnerable to the internal squabbles of individual chapters. The state conference could establish additional chapters in midsize cities, finance court actions, obtain plaintiffs, and, most importantly, coordinate litigation and civil action with the national office. The Texas conference also gave chapters access to larger pools of talent and the opportunity to discipline one another to follow roadmaps developed by the national association.[52] In short, there would be no more overdependence on the Houston chapter's money and lawyers and no more renegade cases like *Grovey*. People like William J. Durham would check persons like Carter Wesley, and vice versa. Most significantly, henceforth, Thurgood Marshall would call the shots during litigation, whether Carter Wesley liked it or not.

CHAPTER 6

The Second Emancipation

The Texas Primary case was the greatest . . . That, to me, was the greatest one . . . It changed the whole complexion in the South.
THURGOOD MARSHALL, 1978

Sometime in the spring of 1940, Thurgood Marshall enjoyed a pleasant evening in Dallas with his friends Maceo and Fannie Smith. Over dinner and drinks, Marshall convinced Maceo Smith that the time had come for black Texans to put the defeat of *Grovey,* five years earlier, behind them and challenge the Texas white primary again. As the executive secretary of the NAACP's Texas State Conference of Branches, Smith responded to Marshall's suggestion by calling for the conference's Legal Redress Committee to meet in Dallas on May 5, 1940.

Six weeks earlier on March 20, the NAACP Legal Defense and Educational Fund (also called the LDF) had been incorporated and made largely independent of the national association. Marshall was its first director-counsel, and he took control of it. During the meeting of the Legal Redress Committee on May 5, Marshall had little trouble getting Texans to agree that the white primary should be challenged, that it should be done in Texas, that a fund drive needed to be started, that the case would be handled by the state conference and the LDF, and that, if necessary, the case should go all the way to the Supreme Court.[1]

From the Dallas meeting, most of the participants drove south to Corpus Christi for the annual meeting of the state conference. Marshall electrified the delegates with his own brand of preaching and a solemn promise to maintain control over the upcoming white-primary lawsuits. Maceo Smith called the meeting the "greatest in the history of our state conference." In a letter to Walter White, Marshall noted, "Now this Texas group will really go to town."[2]

The Dallas and Corpus Christi meetings set up the organizational and funding mechanisms needed to battle both the white primary and Sweatt's subsequent assault on segregation.

The first step in the new challenge to the white primary was the selection of a plaintiff. Marshall did not want all their hard work aborted by the disappearance of a plaintiff, as his mentor Charles Houston had experienced in the *Gaines* case. Marshall, Maceo Smith, the Reverend Albert Lucas, William Durham, and Carter Wesley became the major players in the careful screening and selection of a dependable plaintiff.

Maceo Smith recommended Clifton Richardson, Jr., the thirty-year-old heir to his father's newspaper, the *Houston Defender,* and an activist like his father. Predictably, Carter Wesley made serious objections: as the publisher and editor of the most powerful black newspaper in Texas, he would be placed in the unenviable position of covering the heroic efforts of a rival newspaper editor and the son of a bitter personal and business rival. "[The] use of Mr. Richardson as plaintiff," Wesley wrote, "seems a stubborn intent to impose upon my paper without any corresponding gain to the case or to the NAACP . . . My protest is that young Mr. Richardson does not merit the right to be plaintiff and will automatically secure from me a great deal of publicity which I am not willing to give a competitor unless he merits it."[3] Richardson (like his father) accused Wesley of pettiness and treachery. The cause needed Carter Wesley, so before the fight could become another bitter and divisive Houston rivalry, the Reverend Lucas recommended two of his parishioners, Dr. Lonnie Smith, a dentist, and Sidney Hasgett, variously identified as a hod carrier, a mail carrier, and (by the *Houston Directory*) as the secretary-treasurer of a local labor union, to serve as plaintiffs instead.[4]

Both Hasgett and Smith presented themselves to election judges during the Democratic primary elections in the summer of 1940. On July 27, Smith attempted to vote in the first round, and was denied a ballot by an election judge named S. E. Allwright. During the runoff on August 24, both Smith and Hasgett tried. Smith was again turned away. Hasgett was accompanied by Carter Wesley, Richard Grovey, and Julius White. The election judge tersely asked, "You haven't been coming up here for the past nine or ten years. Now speak out, who sent you here?" Wesley shot back that the black citizens of Houston had. Richard Grovey argued that Hasgett was merely asking for the same voting privileges Mexican Americans enjoyed in Democratic primary elections. The election judges, Theodore Werner and John Blackburn, called the local Democratic headquarters for directions about what to do; they were told to ask Hasgett, Wesley, and Grovey to leave.[5]

In January 1941, Thurgood Marshall and William Durham filed suit against Werner and Blackburn for denying Hasgett the right to vote. It was the fourth NAACP voting-rights suit in fifteen years. Hasgett sued for $5,000 in damages in federal court. Marshall was not interested in the kind of shortcut the Houston trio had taken in *Grovey;* he wanted to build a case with a complete appellate record to present to the Supreme Court. The process would take longer and be more expensive; the Houston crowd would have to develop patience.

During the district court hearing on April 25, 1941, Marshall and Durham argued that the Democratic primary was an election authorized by the state and that to deny Hasgett the ballot was a violation of the Fifteenth Amendment. As Carter Wesley wrote in the *Informer,* a general election in Texas was a "perfunctory gesture." Marshall presented a large body of statistics showing that every winner of a general election in Texas since 1859 had been a Democrat—except two. Not surprisingly, on May 5, 1941, the judge ruled that the election judges had acted legally by preventing Sidney Hasgett from voting in the August 1940 Democratic primary runoff.[6] No one in the Houston crowd was surprised at the *Hasgett* ruling. Marshall kept assuring everyone that it was worth the time and expense to build a record through the complete appeals process. *Hasgett* was on its way to the court of appeals.[7]

Exactly three weeks later, Marshall completely reversed himself and strongly argued that *Hasgett* should be dropped. He had good reason. On May 26, 1941, the U.S. Supreme Court rendered a decision in *U.S. v. Classic* that changed everything. What was remarkable was that *Classic* was a Louisiana case that had nothing to do with the white primary.

On September 10, 1935, Senator Huey Long of Louisiana was gunned down in Louisiana's capitol, in Baton Rouge. From the time of his election to the governorship in 1928 to his assassination, Long had completely dominated Louisiana politics with dictatorial fervor. Like Texas, Louisiana was a one-party state, and the only election that mattered was the Democratic Party primary. Candidates were either "Long" or "anti-Long," but they were all Democrats. During a primary election held on the fifth anniversary of Long's death, five anti-Long voting commissioners in New Orleans's Tenth Ward altered eighty-three votes for one candidate, cast fourteen votes for another candidate, and counted all of them as votes for a third candidate. The Justice Department charged Patrick Classic, a voting commissioner, and four others with fraud.

In *Classic,* the federal government argued that the fraud committed by the commissioners during the primary election deprived New Orleans voters of their rights under the Constitution. The justices had before them a clear-cut case of an attempt to steal a seat in Congress—during a primary rather than during a general election. If the Court followed the logic of *Grovey* and the *Nixon* cases, it would have to rule that the fraud committed in the New Orleans primary was a private matter for the Democratic Party to resolve. In other words, the Court had to decide whether stealing votes, during the only election that mattered in places like Louisiana and Texas, was a crime.[8]

The justices could not allow such an abomination, and although the majority opinion did not mention *Grovey,* they knew their ruling in *Classic* overruled it.[9] The Court could not have provided Marshall with a clearer precedent.

> The practical operation of the primary in Louisiana is, and has been since the primary election was established in 1900, to *secure the election* of the Democratic primary nominee for the Second Congressional District of Louisiana.
>
> . . . The primary in Louisiana is an integral part of the procedure for the popular choice of Congressman. The right of qualified voters to vote at the Congressional primary in Louisiana and to have their ballots counted is thus the right to participate in that choice.[10] (emphasis added)

Thurgood Marshall called the decision "striking and far-reaching." And although Durham and Marshall's argument in *Hasgett* was similar, Hasgett had not been denied the right to vote for a member of Congress. Deciding to drop the *Hasgett* case would prove to be easier than breaking the news to African American Texans.

In *Black Victory,* Darlene Clark Hine described in a masterly way the efforts, drives, collections, and solicitations conducted to finance the white-primary lawsuits. African American Texans were united as never before. Concerted newspaper fundraising campaigns headlined Carter Wesley's *Houston Informer,* Clif Richardson, Jr.'s *Houston Defender,* and L. I. Brockenbury's *Dallas Express.* Thousands of volunteers, like Heman Sweatt, walked door-to-door and asked for anything a household could give—some could give only pennies and nickels. African American churches across the state took up extra collections, and over a period of years, there were more cake and cookie sales than could be counted. *Hasgett* was the fourth try, and some black Texans were getting tired and discouraged. Now, Thurgood Marshall was telling them to start all over again.

Some in Texas believed that the NAACP had botched the case. In 1978, Marshall recalled that Texans had told him, "We want you to know, this is the last go-round; we've contributed four times before, if you lose this one, forget about it."[11] In *Grovey*, Houston's impatient trio, despite ultimately losing, had gotten them from a justice of the peace court in Houston to the U.S. Supreme Court in one step. From the very beginning, Julius White had been in the forefront of the battle against the white primary, having been a plaintiff and the financial backer of a number of suits and motions for injunctions. He watched Commissioner Werner turn Sidney Hasgett away. It mattered when Julius was not happy, and he wasn't. He let Thurgood Marshall know that he "had better win the next case or not return to Texas."[12]

Marshall was probably pleasantly surprised to learn he had the support of the Texan who mattered most, Carter Wesley. Wesley knew where the Supreme Court was headed. The Court had provided the road map in *Classic,* but *Hasgett* wasn't the case that would force it to strike down the white primary.

Smith v. Allwright (1944)

After a careful review, Marshall, Wesley, and a few others determined that it was not necessary to locate a new plaintiff. During the summer Democratic primaries of 1940, Dr. Lonnie Smith had tried to vote at every opportunity: at the 48th precinct of Harris County in the Fifth Ward on July 15; in the first round of the primary on July 27; and again during the runoff on August 24. Each time he was turned away. The July 27 primary included the nomination of candidates for the U.S. Senate and House of Representatives. S. E. Allwright, the election judge, had refused to give Smith a ballot.[13]

On April 20, 1942, Thurgood Marshall and William J. Durham argued in federal district court that the Democratic Party had no characteristics of a private organization; it had no constitution, rules, or bylaws; its source of authority was the election laws of Texas. Following the *Classic* road map, they argued that *Smith v. Allwright* should be governed by *Classic,* in part because Democratic primaries in Texas, as in Louisiana, were the only elections that mattered. Three weeks later, on May 11, the judge ruled that *Classic* was not applicable but *Grovey* was. As in *Grovey*, the judge ruled that the Democratic Party was a private organization and that a primary was not an election in the eyes of the U.S. Constitution.[14]

At the Fifth Circuit Court of Appeals, both sides made the same arguments, and the result was the same. The Fifth Circuit affirmed the application of *Grovey* rather than *Classic.* Chief Judge Joseph C. Hutcheson, Jr., was particularly hard on Thurgood Marshall, whom he grilled with questions for three hours—only to rule against him. On his way out of court, Marshall told Hutcheson, "Well, I'm going to the Supreme Court."

"Of course," replied the judge.

According to Marshall, a few weeks later he ran into Hutcheson, who asked, "Have you filed your petition for certiorari, yet?"

"No, sir," replied Marshall.

"Well, why don't you hurry up? You know you're going to win."[15]

In November 1943, Marshall and Durham appeared before the Supreme Court, along with William Hastie, a well-known and respected civil rights attorney, for oral arguments. Marshall began with a history and the nature of Democratic primaries in Texas and their similarities to the Louisiana primaries ruled on in *Classic*. Hastie followed with a direct attack on *Grovey*. Although Durham stood ready to address Texas-specific questions, he never addressed the Court because those questions never came up. Carter Wesley was in the courtroom. He noted that the justices asked almost no questions. Some opponents of the white primary were concerned about the uncharacteristic silence of the justices during arguments and about the failure of Texas Democrats to show up to argue their case. But shortly afterward the Texas attorney general, Gerald Mann, requested to address the Court on behalf of the State of Texas. The court scheduled a rehearing on January 12, 1944. As the Court later observed, the attorney general "urged substantially the same grounds as those advanced by the respondents."[16]

On Monday, April 3, 1944, the Supreme Court finally put to rest the question of the constitutionality of the white primary and, more specifically, whether it violated the Fifteenth Amendment.

The *Smith v. Allwright* ruling began with an uncommon admission by the Supreme Court that it (the Court) had been the cause of confusion: "The District Court denied the relief sought and the Circuit Court of Appeals quite properly affirmed its action on the authority of *Grovey v. Townsend* . . . We granted the petition for certiorari to resolve a claimed inconsistency between the decision in the *Grovey* case and that of *United States v. Classic*."[17] The justices admitted that *Grovey* and *Classic*, both relatively recent decisions, could not coexist. The mea culpa continued with an admission of questionable rulings in the *Nixon* cases.

The Supreme Court then made up for decades of inaction and obfuscation with one of the most unambiguous decisions in its history:

> It may now be taken as a postulate that the right to vote in such a
> primary for the nomination of candidates without discrimination by the

State, like the right to vote in a general election, is a right secured by the Constitution. . . .

. . . Here we are applying, contrary to the recent decision in *Grovey v. Townsend,* the well established principle of the Fifteenth Amendment, forbidding the abridgement by a state of a citizen's right to vote. *Grovey v. Townsend* is overruled.[18]

It was as comprehensive a victory as Thurgood Marshall could have hoped for. *Smith v. Allwright* had a majority of 8–1. The only dissenter was Justice Roberts, the author of *Grovey.* He accurately pointed out that *Classic* never mentioned *Grovey* and thus could not have overruled it. It didn't matter; *Smith* overruled it. The white primary died on April 3, 1944. Undoubtedly, Thurgood Marshall would have argued that one reason for victory was that a more thoughtful and forceful record had been developed in *Smith* than in *Grovey.* Perhaps, but sitting on the Supreme Court that Thurgood Marshall faced in *Smith* were eight justices appointed or reappointed by Franklin Roosevelt; all voted for the NAACP position. When *Grovey* was argued, seven of the justices had been appointed by conservative presidents Hoover, Taft, and Coolidge.

African American voters, especially in Texas, were overjoyed by the *Smith* ruling. Lulu White called it the "Second Emancipation of the Negro," and Daisy Lampkin shouted, "We are free at last."[19] Thirty-four years later, Thurgood Marshall, reflecting on his remarkable career, wrote, "The Texas Primary case was the greatest . . . That, to me, was the greatest one . . . it changed the whole complexion in the South."[20]

The results of *Smith* were swift and dramatic: in Texas, the percentage of eligible African American voters who were registered had been only 9.24 percent in 1940; it had doubled to 18.5 percent by 1947; and by 1952 it had reached 31.31 percent.[21]

The judicial victory also demonstrated how important it was for local NAACP chapters, the state conference, and the national association to work together. Brilliant legal strategy and tactics by the NAACP had replaced the crushing defeat of the renegade-sponsored *Grovey* with a "Second Emancipation," but only after the NAACP realized that, in some ways, Carter Wesley and Alston Atkins had been right: success was inextricably linked to close coordination with black attorneys and black state and local leaders. It was not happenstance that Thurgood Marshall "dictated the last rough draft of the *Smith v. Allwright* brief in the *Informer* office . . . to [Carter] Wesley's secretary," and that Wesley is listed as one of eight authors of the brief.[22]

After winning the Supreme Court case, Dr. Smith was threatened and harassed for a time; his friends took turns guarding his home in the Fifth Ward. Eventually, he was able to take great satisfaction during the first set of Democratic primaries that followed, when African American Texans went to the polls and voted without any major incidents.[23]

As Amilcar Shabazz wrote, "The voting rights victories won the NAACP a great deal of credibility in Texas."[24] On the local level, Lulu White's membership drives more than doubled the Houston chapter's enrollment from 5,679 in 1943 (the year before *Smith*) to 12,000 in 1945 (the year after *Smith*). Lulu White made a difference at the state level as well. She and Juanita Craft, another NAACP field operative, traversed Texas to organize new branches and reawaken many others. According to Michael Gillette, the number of branches increased from 36 to 104.[25]

The next great challenge was the desegregation of public elementary and secondary schools and higher education. Filled with a sense of hope and empowered with the right to vote, African American Texans set their sights on opening the doors of Texas's constitutionally designated "University of the First Class." It was time to find another plaintiff and go back to court.

A Brief Constitutional History of Public Education for Black Texans

The history of public higher education in Texas is inextricably linked with the transformation of enormous tracts of public land from near-worthless wilderness and desert to some of the most valuable property on earth. A subplot of that history is whether African American Texans would ever have access to that public wealth.

In 1839, only three years after the Battle of the Alamo, Republic of Texas president Mirabeau Lamar set aside 220,000 acres to establish an endowment for a public university.[26] The decision required no political courage—land was the one thing Texas had plenty of. At that time, Texas was struggling to survive, and thus the establishment of a public university for its white citizens wavered with each threat to the young republic's existence. There were no provisions for what was called "Negro education" of any kind in the Constitution of 1836. After Texas joined the Union the first time, a few churches in some cities provided whatever education blacks received.[27]

The Texas Constitution of 1866 mentioned a system of education for "Africans and their children," but the financing of these schools was to come from taxes on blacks themselves—an extraordinarily weak economic base.

The sum of constitutional support for black education was a phrase: "It shall be the duty of the Legislature to encourage schools among these people." Elsewhere, the constitution provided for the existing perpetual school fund to be used exclusively for the education of whites. In Washington, the Radical Republican Congress found that unacceptable because it did not meet the conditions set forth for Texas's readmission to the Union, one of which was the ratification of the Fourteenth Amendment and its equal protection clause. Texas responded with the Constitution of 1869, which provided for the education of all inhabitants age six to eighteen. It made no provision for higher education for either whites or blacks per se, but the prior and continued existence of the land endowment for higher education should have meant that African Americans would not be excluded from the benefits of such a promising state asset—the assurance of equal educational opportunity had been a condition for readmission to the family of states.[28]

Texas was readmitted to the Union in 1870, but when Reconstruction ended, in 1876, so did any inclination Texas might have had to honor the equal-protection conditions of its readmission. The Texas constitutions from the days of the Republic to the times of Heman Sweatt were the products of a southern-leaning white political class. As in the rest of the South, the policy of separate and unequal in Texas was based, as Melvin Banks wrote, on "the time worn argument that whites paid a disproportionate per capita amount of taxes."[29]

The constitutional convention of 1876 occasioned the first serious discussion of a free public-education system and a state-supported system of higher education in Texas's history. During the debates, serious opposition was raised to any form of tax-supported schools. Reactionary whites thought of several counties in East Texas where blacks were a majority, or nearly a majority, of the population. They considered the educating of everyone in those counties to be little more than a dangerous experiment. At the time, the state had six private colleges for whites and two for blacks; this seemed sufficient for those content to limit literacy to an economic and political oligarchy. Pro-education delegates, however, successfully implanted into the constitution the higher-education provisions that would dominate much of the debate over Heman Sweatt's attempts to go to law school sixty years later. One such provision was article VII, section 10:

> The Legislature shall, as soon as practicable, establish, organize and provide for the maintenance, support and direction of a *university of the first class*, to be located by a vote of the people of this State, and styled "The University of Texas." . . . (emphasis added)

Just as significant was the following section:

> It is hereby declared that all lands and other property heretofore set apart
> and appropriated for the establishment and maintenance of "The University
> of Texas," together with all the proceeds of sales of the same, heretofore
> made or hereafter so to be made, and all grants, donations and appropria-
> tions that may hereafter be made by the State of Texas or from any other
> source, shall constitute and become a *permanent university fund.*[30] (emphasis
> added)

For African Americans, there was article VII, section 14:

> The Legislature shall also when deemed practicable, establish and pro-
> vide for the maintenance of a College or *Branch University* for the in-
> struction of the colored youths of the State, . . . and no money [shall be]
> appropriated out of the general revenue, either for this purpose or for the
> establishment and erection of the buildings of the University of Texas.
> (emphasis added)

Years later, bitter debates took place over the meaning of section 14. African
Americans interpreted it to mean that a "colored" university, a branch of
the University of Texas, was authorized by the constitution and that with
such authorization came access to the Permanent University Fund (which
became the official name of the endowment) for the construction and maintenance of that branch.

Once the proposed constitution was ratified in February 1876, it became
the duty of the legislature to pass enabling legislation to meet the mandated
higher-education provisions. Five years later, the legislature passed an act
creating a "university of the first class" for its white citizens. The state held
an election to determine its location, and Austin was chosen to host the undergraduate and professional schools; Galveston was chosen for the medical
school.[31]

On May 5, 1882, the legislature approved a call for an election to determine the location of the "Section 14 colored university." A number of
locations were nominated, and the election was held on November 7, 1882.
Austin won with 18,329 votes, followed by Prairie View and Houston.[32]

By November 1882, all the state had left to do to fulfill its constitutional
mandate to establish a university for its African American citizens was to
pass laws to actually create and fund the school. But there was a hitch: the

creation of such a university was left exclusively to the legislature, to be accomplished "when deemed practicable."

It never deemed the project practicable.

Prairie View

On August 14, 1876, only a few months after the ratification of a new state constitution, the Texas Legislature did make a gratuitous attempt to establish an agricultural and mechanical college for African American students. On a dilapidated plantation owned by the widow of a former Confederate colonel, the state instructed the President of Texas A&M to oversee what was called the Alta Vista Agricultural College. The chief campus administrator was not a "president," as at most colleges, but a "principal." At the time, "principal" was not a diminished title, because it signified that the holder was the chief administrator of a branch. (The president of Texas A&M was also the principal of the white branch.)[33] Eight black males enrolled on March 11, 1878, becoming the first black students to ever enroll in a Texas state college; their tuition was $130 for nine months. Within three years, Alta Vista closed from a lack of students. In 1879, Governor Oran Roberts proposed that the institution become a normal school (that is, a training school for teachers). Alta Vista was reestablished as Prairie View Normal School, and it was from that school that James Leonard Sweatt became a certified Texas teacher.[34]

Significant progress in "Negro education" came only with Congress's passage of the Morrill Act of 1890, also called the Second Morrill Act. It provided a dedicated and reliable source of funding for black higher education and called for an end to racial discrimination: "No money shall be paid for the support of a college where a distinction of race or color is made in the admission of students." This overdue call for simple fairness, however, ended when southern congressmen inserted a clause that forced a federal sanctioning of segregation: "The establishment and maintenance of such colleges separately for white and colored students shall be held in compliance with the provisions of this act."[35]

By 1891, the Texas Legislature, for all practical purposes, had to be forced to pass enabling legislation to comply with the provisions of the Second Morrill Act when the U.S. treasurer refused to release federal funds allotted to Texas. On March 14, 1891, Prairie View began receiving 25 percent of the federal funds designated for agricultural and mechanical colleges in Texas.[36]

From 1876 through 1901, Prairie View was an agricultural school and then a normal school. In 1896, the Colored Teachers State Association of Texas (CTSAT) pushed for a curricular expansion into classical and scientific studies. The CTSAT also advocated that Prairie View be the designated "colored branch university" promised to African American Texans in the Constitution of 1876. Prairie View would then have been entitled to allocations of money from the Permanent University Fund. By 1901, the legislature had set aside $2,500 to make Prairie View a "classical" college but had taken no action on making it the branch university.[37]

From its declaration of independence from Mexico, to its annexation as a state, through the Civil War and Reconstruction, and until 1946, Texas made only one attempt to provide higher education for its African American citizens: when it took advantage of the Morrill acts and their mandates, which allowed Texas to spend grants from the federal government. And the state accepted these funds mainly because it had to spend money on blacks in order to receive significantly more funds to spend on whites. Indeed, the history of higher education in Texas for African Americans is tragic. By the 1890s, the white political establishment in Texas had managed to achieve what Congress had intended to be an impossible result. Adherence to the Fourteenth Amendment of the U.S. Constitution and the "impartial provision" of section 7 of the Texas Constitution should have ensured that if a white state university "of the first class" was established, one for blacks would be also—the operation of the law was supposed to make it impossible for one to be practicable without the other. It did not work out that way.

So from 1876 to 1947, Prairie View was all that black Texans had in the way of publicly supported higher education, and what public support it received was meager. On July 24, 1915, for example, voters were presented with a statewide referendum that would have allocated 600,800 acres of state land for agricultural and mechanical colleges. Prairie View would have gotten 150,000 of those acres, but the proposal was voted down by a substantial margin. A similar proposal was defeated again in 1919.[38]

In some parts of Texas, African American participation in that election was limited, or even nonexistent, because of the Terrell Election Laws.

Heman Sweatt and the Poor State of Higher Education for Blacks

When Heman Marion Sweatt returned to Texas from the University of Michigan, he lived for a short time with his parents. By April 1940, he had married Connie Mitchell, his high school sweetheart, and had purchased a small, two-bedroom home at 3402 Delano Street. When World War II broke out, he tried to enlist in the military on two occasions and was rejected both times. Heman was not as healthy as a young man his age should have been. In his later years, he recalled that he had returned from the University of Michigan, not because of any academic problem (he had a B+ average), but because his thin and frail body, conditioned to the heat and humidity of the Texas Gulf Coast, could not tolerate the extremely cold Great Lakes winters.

In the 1940s, small homes crowded the middle-class Delano Street neighborhood, populated with some of Houston's more-educated African Americans. Heman was a Wiley College alumnus, and Connie had studied home economics for two years at Austin's Samuel Huston College. While living on Delano Street, she taught at a neighborhood school a few blocks away. Her favorite pastime was sewing, and she undoubtedly supplemented what she already knew with what her mother-in-law, Ella Rose Sweatt, was able to share.[39]

Sweatt's work for the post office started as a part-time position. For African Americans, postal work was a good and steady job, one subject to federal civil-service regulations. By the late 1940s, senior mail carriers were making approximately $3,750 a year—much better than what was usually available to most young black men, even those with an undergraduate college education. In 1945 the Houston post office employed 335 blacks, 225 of whom were carriers, like Sweatt. More importantly, in the shadow of the Great Depression, postal work was as "recession proof" a job as a worker, black or white, could hope for.

During the second half of the 1940s, Heman Sweatt lived a routine life. Early every morning he boarded a city bus to the post office, where he sorted and loaded mailbags for house-to-house delivery. His route rarely changed during his decade-long tenure as a mail carrier. It was a rectangular zone measuring four by seven city blocks, located due east of downtown Houston and north of what is today the University of Houston. The area was largely residential, but also included small retail shops serving the neighborhood.[40] Mail delivery during Houston's steamy summers was hard and taxing work, especially for someone who had never been particularly robust. Getting a promotion to an indoor position, such as a clerk, was coveted by most of the carriers, especially ambitious and educated ones like Sweatt. According to Sweatt, federal civil-service regulations prohibited racial discrimination in the awarding of such positions. But postmasters had the option of choosing one of three top candidates, and they always appointed whites. As a result, blacks never could be supervisors, because a minimum requirement for su-

*

pervisory positions was experience as a postal clerk. Frustrated by this lack of simple fairness, Sweatt became heavily involved in the activities of the National Alliance of Postal Employees (NAPE). In March 1944, with the help of an attorney, Sweatt carefully prepared a written grievance against the postal service. In it, he documented workers' concerns with citations from civil service and post office policies and regulations. He liked that kind of work, and it brought about an interest in the law, specifically in the use of the law to fight discrimination.[41]

But the reality was that Sweatt couldn't do much to pursue his ambition to become a lawyer. Only five public institutions in the South offered graduate work in the arts and sciences to African Americans; there were six in education and four in agriculture. None of those institutions offered PhD programs or professional schools.[42]

Public elementary and secondary education in the South was similarly neglected. During the school year 1937–1938, nineteen states (and the District of Columbia) maintained school systems segregated by law; 78.6 percent of all African Americans lived in those states, where they made up 23.1 percent of the population. But "colored" schools received only 4 percent of the funding spent on public education. In a school year in which the national average per-pupil expenditure for education was $99, white funding in the South was less than half that amount ($44.31), and funding for African American pupils was less than one-eighth ($12.57).[43]

A measure of the struggle black colleges faced in Texas can be seen in the tenure and pay of faculty. In a 1944 survey of eight black senior colleges in Texas, 55 percent of faculty members had only five years of experience or less; 2 percent had more than twenty years. About 75 percent of faculty members surveyed made less that $1,560 a year—about 42 percent of a senior mail carrier's salary. The story of young James Leonard Sweatt, who in the 1890s left the teaching profession after only one year, and young Heman Sweatt, who in the 1930s did the same thing, described a pattern.[44]

In 1932, while Sweatt was an undergraduate student at Wiley College and in a period when sound teaching in higher education required a library with a minimum of 50,000 volumes, only five black institutions in America had libraries with 20,000 or more volumes; 72 percent had fewer than 10,000 books; almost 10 percent had no library at all. Sadly, even those abysmal library statistics were exaggerated. One college president was reputed to have counted the hymnals in the campus chapel as part of the institution's library collection. Another boasted a library of 16,000 volumes, but a subsequent audit by a reporter and a librarian located only 500 usable books. Indeed, books were such a valuable commodity that one institution kept its library hidden in an attic and another kept its books in a wooden cage to protect them from possible use by students.[45]

So if Heman Sweatt, an adult and citizen of Texas, had the ambition and the means to become a lawyer, where was he to go?

Emboldened by the decision in *Gaines,* and with a financial and political infrastructure fashioned by *Smith v. Allwright* in place, and with a faith in the Constitution more mature than that of their opponents, Thurgood Marshall, A. Maceo Smith, Carter Wesley, Lulu and Julius White, William Durham, and dozens of others were ready to enter the fray and mobilize to break down the racial barriers of Texas's "university of the first class."

During World War II, as America battled fascist racial supremacy overseas, Ralph Bunche, Howard University's chair of political science, emerged as a sage. While many African Americans, including members of the Sweatt family, considered turning to communism as a road to becoming treated as adults and citizens, Bunche counseled African Americans to keep faith in the American ideal:

> It is the Constitution and the ideals of the American Revolution which gave the Negro the persistent belief that he was entitled to equality of rights . . .
>
> . . . The fight will be lost the moment the United States finds itself marooned in a totalitarian world . . .
>
> . . . There are those also who say that it is of little consequence to the Negro whether this country maintains its present pseudo-democratic institutions or becomes nationalistic or totalitarian. This is dangerous advice for the Negro; it is an insidious type of defeatism . . .
>
> . . . The Negro citizen has long since learned that "special" treatment for him implies differentiation on a racial basis and inevitably connotes inferior status.[46]

Indeed, it would have been foolhardy to fight the battle of the right to vote in a democracy only to abandon democracy itself. It would also be a mistake to believe Bunche to be an accommodationist: his advice to southern whites was equally astute: "The Southern white man is at a disadvantage—he can either be a reactionary Democrat or forgo his rights in the political process . . . No section of the country produces such virile and vituperative demagoguery; none is so unprogressive and politically bigoted. The South pays a high price for its white supremacy."[47]

CHAPTER 7

A University of the First Class

In Latin America whoever is not black is white: in Teutonic America whoever is not white is black.

JAMES BRYCE, 1ST VISCOUNT BRYCE,

THE AMERICAN COMMONWEALTH, 1910

Shortly after Dr. Lonnie Smith and Sidney Hasgett were refused the ballot during the 1940 summer Democratic primaries, black civil rights groups in Texas, although firmly united by the *Hasgett* and *Smith* cases, found themselves appealing to the same constituencies and duplicating one another's efforts. The NAACP's Texas State Conference had been formed to coordinate and improve communication and fund-raising among the association's chapters, but that crucial reform did not extend to other African American civic and political organizations. On May 8, 1941, Maceo Smith issued an appeal to African American groups throughout Texas for fund-raising to support the NAACP's litigation of the *Hasgett* case. On January 10, 1942, a number of African American groups met and formed an umbrella association called the Texas Council of Negro Organizations (TCNO).[1]

Already known for his organizational genius, Maceo Smith was appointed chairman, and Joseph Rhoads, a remarkable educator and the president of Bishop College, was elected president. The TCNO focused its fund-raising and energy on the white-primary cases, but it also considered education. Its priorities for education, however, were not always consistent with the position taken by the national office of the NAACP. At first, the TCNO platform focused on the equalization of educational opportunities and facilities more than on the NAACP-preferred goal of integration.[2]

The struggle for educational rights during Sweatt's time took place amid tensions between two black factions. Their differences were often bitter and irreconcilable. The equalization crowd favored an infusion of funds to significantly improve black institutions. They demanded the establishment of a constitutional "university of the first class for Negroes" and the (considerable) upgrading of Prairie View to a genuine university. The integration crowd, on the other hand, demanded that the doors of the University of Texas and other whites-only institutions be opened to everyone.

The schism was neither new nor indigenous to Texas: Given adequate resources, where should African American students be educated? In predominately black schools run by black administrators who understood the plight of being black in America, or in integrated schools with historically white identities and largely controlled by whites? In an integrated world, what would become of African American culture and traditions? What would become of the most gifted and talented black students, inadequately educated in historically neglected and poorly funded schools, if they were suddenly enrolled in schools with the white progeny of generations of wealth and privilege?

Thurgood Marshall believed in integration; Carter Wesley believed in equalization as providing an option for blacks who did not choose integration. Marshall saw "separate" as inherently unequal, and his teacher, Charles Houston, believed that justice was not possible in a segregated society.[3] Others, like W. E. B. Du Bois, saw separateness and "voluntary segregation" as a matter of black pride: "[The black man] would not Africanize America, for America has too much to teach the world and Africa. He would not bleach his Negro soul in a flood of white Americanism, for he knows that Negro blood has a message for the world. He simply wishes to make it possible for a man to be both a Negro and an American, without being cursed and spit upon by his fellows, without having the doors of opportunity closed roughly in his face."[4]

Plessy v. Ferguson (1896) and *Gong Lum v. Rice* (1927)

During the life and times of Heman Sweatt the legal justification for closing the doors of opportunity to African Americans came from the Supreme Court case *Plessy v. Ferguson*, a case about segregation in railcars. On June 7, 1892, Homer Adolph Plessy used a ticket he purchased to board a first-class passenger railcar on the East Louisiana Railway. He purposefully sat in a coach restricted to white passengers. Almost immediately, the conductor ordered him to get out of first class and move to that part of the train reserved for colored people. When Plessy refused, the conductor notified a policeman, and the two men hoisted Plessy out of his seat and threw him off the train. Homer Plessy was taken to the Orleans Parish jail and arraigned for willfully and criminally violating Louisiana segregation laws that had been enacted almost exactly two years earlier.[5]

Homer Plessy was a sociological problem: biologically and mathematically (as far as his racial heritage) nearly white, but socially and politically completely black. Plessy could very well have been "whiter" than many others seated in the same railcar. His attorney represented him as being seven-eighths Caucasian, but in late nineteenth-century Louisiana, Plessy was a Negro because one of his eight great-grandparents, a great-grandmother, was black.[6]

If Homer Plessy had been in Cleveland, he would have been white because under Ohio law, the preponderance (greater weight) of his blood was Caucasian. But in North Carolina, he might or might not have been black, because the law there was that "any visible admixture of black blood stamps the person as belonging to the colored race." Was he visibly black enough to be a black? In Detroit, he would have been white because in Michigan the predominance of Caucasian blood had to "only be three-fourths" for someone to be considered white.[7]

In May 1896, the Supreme Court issued a ruling in *Plessy v. Ferguson* that was second only to the *Dred Scott* decision in its dehumanization of African Americans.[8]

> The object of the [Fourteenth] amendment was undoubtedly to enforce the absolute equality of the two races before the law, but, in the nature of things, it could not have been intended to abolish distinctions based upon color, or to enforce social, as distinguished from political, equality, or a commingling of the two races upon terms unsatisfactory to either.[9]

The Court followed that the lack of absolute equality did not necessarily imply the inferiority of one group.

> We consider the underlying fallacy of the plaintiff's argument to consist in the assumption that the enforced separation of the two races stamps the colored race with a badge of inferiority. If this be so, it is not by reason of anything found in the act, but solely because the colored race chooses to put that construction upon it.[10]

Plessy meant that it was within the police power of a state to determine who was white and who was black and that the segregation of accommodations for each could meet the equal-protection mandate of the Fourteenth Amendment if those accommodations were equal.

In transportation or education or any other human endeavor, absolute and precise equality, of course, is not possible. No two schools will ever have the same number of books and pencils. Nor can they ever have exactly the same quality of faculty teaching in separate buildings made with exactly the same number of bricks. Under *Plessy*, the tests were those of reasonableness, good faith, and the public good.[11]

From 1896 through the 1950s, *Plessy* was applied to cases upholding segregation in public education. It became the judicial foundation of the "separate but equal" doctrine, and its meaningless test of reasonableness led to the goal of "substantial equality" rather than equality itself. So by the time Heman Sweatt aspired to attend law school, "separate but equal" had been watered down to "separate but substantially equal." Other corrupt interpretations further perverted any hope for true equality, such as the notion that equality meant that taxes paid by white citizens should go to white schools and taxes paid by black citizens should go to "colored schools," which were controlled by white school boards. But as Justice Harlan wrote in his dissent in *Plessy*, "The thin disguise of 'equal' accommodations . . . will not mislead anyone, nor atone for the wrong this day done."[12] And as Patricia Lefforge Davis wrote, *Plessy* "preserved the South from judicial Reconstruction."[13]

During Heman Sweatt's time, the ambiguities of codified racial classifications remained. Even outside of the old Confederacy, at least eighteen states, some with no Jim Crow laws, had statutes forbidding whites from marrying blacks or mulattos.[14] The irony was, of course, that miscegenation laws also restricted the freedom of whites; the question in those states was "Who is white?"

But what was a state to do with a citizen who had neither black nor white blood? In the 1920s, Mississippi's Rosedale consolidated high school district faced that conundrum when Gong Lum, a Mississippi citizen, business owner, and taxpayer, attempted to register his daughter, Martha, in the school attended by white students. Lum was of Chinese descent. Nine-year-old Martha was required by Mississippi's compulsory-attendance laws to attend school. At the opening of school, the elder Lum successfully registered Martha at Rosedale consolidated high, but at noon recess, the superintendent notified her that she would not be allowed to return because the district's board of trustees had decided that Rosedale was to be all white. Martha, they said, belonged in the "colored" high school.[15]

Gong Lum refused to accept the school district's decision. His argument was not that segregation was wrong, but that Martha was not a member of a colored race, nor was she of mixed blood—she was pure Chinese. Lum took his complaint to a Mississippi district court and won when the judge issued a writ of mandamus ordering school officials to admit Martha. The Rosedale trustees won a reversal in Mississippi's Supreme Court.[16]

In 1927, former president and Chief Justice William Howard Taft delivered the *Gong Lum* opinion for the U.S. Supreme Court. "The right and power of the state to regulate the method of providing for the education of its youth at public expense is clear," he wrote.[17]

So, on the first day of school nine-year-old Martha Lum was not colored—until about noon, when the superintendent told her she was colored. Shortly afterward, a Mississippi district court told her she was not colored, and then the Supreme Court of Mississippi made her colored again. And with that, Martha Lum remained colored—in Mississippi.

Undoubtedly, Gong Lum, her father, could have moved his family somewhere else and become not colored again.

Cumming v. Richmond County Board of Education (1899) and *Berea College v. Kentucky* (1908)

The first fifty years of the separate-but-equal doctrine inspired by *Plessy* was truly an era of judicial delusion. The federal government, especially its courts, functioned under the belief that it was powerless to interfere with state control of public education. One of the first tests of the separate-but-equal doctrine came from the city of Augusta, Georgia. On July 10, 1897, the Richmond County school board levied $45,000 in taxes on its citizens for the support of a school system. At the time, all pupils paid tuition to attend public schools. African Americans living in that jurisdiction never challenged the right or the wisdom of the school board to collect the taxes until the same board voted to fund the white high school and close the black high school. The reason for closing the colored high school, it explained, was that if money were provided for sixty black students in a high school, there would not be enough to educate the more than three hundred black students in the elementary grades. The board would have to "turn away three hundred little negroes who are asking to be taught their alphabet and to read and write."[18]

In *Cumming v. Richmond County Board of Education* (1899) the U.S. Supreme Court focused almost solely on whether the federal government had jurisdiction in a matter considered a state duty—education. The ruling was that the Richmond County school board was not choosing to educate white students only, but instead was accommodating as many African American students as it could afford to. The Court believed the policy was in the best interest of the greatest number of black children, especially since a private high school for African Americans was available for the same tuition that they would have paid to attend a public school.[19]

The next Supreme Court case involving race and education came from Kentucky and involved a private college in Berea, a small town in Madison County. Berea College quietly operated a coeducational and desegregated school until March 1904, when the Kentucky legislature passed the "Day Law," which made it illegal for any school to accept both blacks and whites as pupils.[20]

The trial court found Berea College in violation of the law, and the Kentucky Court of Appeals upheld the lower court's ruling. The case made its way to the U.S. Supreme Court. In November 1908, in a 2,400-word decision, the Supreme Court destroyed Berea's progressive heritage when it decided to limit its review only to the question of whether a state had the power to regulate its own "corporate creatures": "We are of the opinion . . . that it does come within that power, and, on this ground, the judgment of the Court of Appeals of Kentucky is affirmed."[21]

In *Cumming, Berea,* and *Gong Lum,* the Court held that the discretion of the states to regulate their own public and private schools did not conflict with the Fourteenth Amendment of the U.S. Constitution.[22]

The Bi-Racial Conference on Negro Education in Texas

Missouri ex rel. Gaines v. Canada, the 1938 ruling whereby the Court told Missouri it had to provide equal educational opportunities to all citizens within its borders, represented a remarkable change insofar as it forced segregated states to provide for the education of African Americans in one of two ways: they could integrate their whites-only institutions, or they could provide substantially equal schools (*Gaines* is discussed at length in Chapter 4). The power of the state to enforce segregation was unchanged: *Gaines* did not overrule *Plessy* or *Cumming.*[23] The challenge to the states was to provide "better segregation."

The implications of *Gaines* for Texas were immense. At the time of the *Gaines* ruling, Texas had no public graduate or professional schools for African Americans; it did not even have the sort of out-of-state scholarships that the Supreme Court ruled insufficient. It was against that background that Texas's flagship university presidents, Homer Rainey of the University of Texas and Thomas O. Walton of Texas A&M, along with L. A. Woods, the superintendent of public instruction, called for an education summit in Austin in the summer of 1942. Approximately seventy educational and political leaders attended, forming what became known as the Bi-Racial Conference on Negro Education in Texas (commonly called BCNET).[24] With the blessing of Governor Coke Stevenson, the conference created a steering committee that coordinated several subcommittees.

African Americans on the steering committee represented intraracial divisions about what direction improvements in "Negro education" should take. In *Advancing Democracy,* Amilcar Shabazz described it as a clash of philosophies embodied by W. R. Banks, the principal of Prairie View A&M, who had dedicated much of his life and career to the college and wanted to see it become a substantial, predominantly black university, and Joseph Rhoads, the president of Bishop College, who initially advocated that Texas supply a new "university of the first class" for blacks, as promised in the Texas Constitution. (Later he was to join the integrationists.)[25]

Almost two years later, BCNET issued a report summarizing its findings. It documented what everyone knew: "It is quite apparent that if the Negro race is to have an educated leadership within its own ranks, higher education, including graduate and professional education, is absolutely essential."[26] More informative was the description of the state of higher education for African American Texans, because the report delved into the status of private institutions like Joseph Rhoads's Bishop College and Heman Sweatt's alma mater, Wiley College. The six private black colleges in Texas were all founded separately by different religious and charitable organizations. Their locations made no strategic sense. Only two had a building set aside for a library. The only black public institution, Prairie View, had no building for its meager book collection. Having no library was identified as the single greatest challenge the institution faced.[27]

For W. R. Banks, BCNET was more than just a commission. For the first time in his long and frustrating career, Texas's white educational (and political) leadership was looking seriously at his school and actually considering making improvements. It didn't matter to him that whites' motivation for such a review had nothing whatsoever to do with a genuine or altruistic concern for African American Texans. His instinct was to do what he had been doing for decades: seize any opportunity, make any pitch, and do anything for his struggling and neglected institution. For the first time, Banks saw an opportunity to get a library for his students. Perhaps it is not surprising that he and his faculty and staff dismissed the idea of integration and opposed the creation of a new black university in Austin or anywhere else in Texas. The possibilities presented by BCNET, additions and improvements considered unimaginable only a few years earlier, took hold of Banks and his pragmatic followers. They envisioned, at last, a chance for blacks to educate their sons and daughters in a way that had been denied them since Stephen F. Austin became an empresario west of the Sabine River in the 1820s.

President Rhoads rejected such investments in Prairie View A&M. Perhaps he saw Prairie View as the embodiment of everything that was unjust. Maybe he saw it as James Leonard Sweatt had: a place where an education could be secured, but not one worthy of respect—and no amount of money could erase that legacy. Rhoads was fully aware of what Missouri was doing with Lincoln University, and he understood what *Gaines* now required of Texas. He did not want to let Texas "off the hook" and allow Prairie View to be used in the same way. Until his conversion to the integration viewpoint, Rhoads had an uncompromising vision of Texas's constitutional guarantee of a first-class university for Negroes: he wanted a new university in Austin.[28]

The BCNET report also addressed two options that clearly could not be reconciled with the *Gaines* decision. The first was the expansion of a newly created out-of-state tuition program of the type that the Supreme Court had expressly ruled unconstitutional. The second was an outgrowth of the Southern Governors Conference, which considered creating a consortium that would administer a single set of exemplary graduate and professional schools for all southern African Americans, institutions equal in every way to any single southern flagship university. While it would have been amusing to see southern governors like Earl Long, Theodore Bilbo, Herman Talmadge, and Orval Faubus fight one another over the educational patronage of professional schools none of them really wanted, the idea was not taken seriously long enough to determine where such schools would be located or how they would be funded and administered. As the BCNET report stated, "Securing the cooperation of the states to the extent of insuring the stability of financial support and educational policy is practically impossible."[29]

So BCNET ultimately became just another white-supremacist meeting that produced a racist report: "Admission of Negroes to existing state universities for whites is not acceptable as a solution of the problem of providing opportunity for graduate and professional study for Negroes, on two counts: 1) public opinion would not permit such institutions to be open to Negroes at the present time; 2) even if Negroes were admitted they would not be happy in the conditions in which they would find themselves."[30] W. R. Banks, Joseph Rhoads, and the rest of Texas's African American leaders had heard it all before. Again, at the time of the report, Banks and Rhoads looked to the

Texas Constitution for the delivery of the long-promised "colored branch" of the University of Texas. What they disagreed on was which institution was to fill that mandate: Banks wanted to make Prairie View the "first-class university for Negroes"; Rhoads wanted the new institution in Austin that the people of Texas had voted for in the 1880s. Either way, any university for African Americans was required by state and federal law to be "substantially equal" to the best one offered to whites. In Texas, that standard was the University of Texas at Austin.

Dissension at the University of Texas

The University of Texas at Austin has always been controlled by a board of regents. Each regent is appointed by the governor and confirmed by the state Senate. In political circles, the appointments are among the most prestigious patronage prizes available to a governor. And so for most of its existence, the governance of the University of Texas System has largely reflected the political philosophy of governors who, like Coke Stevenson and "Pappy" O'Daniel, were often frugal and reactionary southern-leaning Democrats.[31]

Faculty and students, however, have often delighted in an "enlightened" or youthful rebelliousness against the Texas white establishment. In 1947, adult Texans favored segregated universities by a ratio of 25:1, and 85 percent opposed the admission of blacks to UT in particular. At UT, the majority of students favored the admission of black students and supported efforts to break the color barrier.[32] Non-Texan visitors were (and still are) often surprised at how liberal the UT family could be. In 1946, NAACP lawyers Thurgood Marshall and Robert Carter were said to be impressed with the attitude of UT students.[33]

The best-known ideological rift between the UT family and the Texas establishment (in the form of the board of regents and elected officials) took place in 1944. In what law school dean W. Page Keeton called the "big fight," university president Homer Rainey threw down the gauntlet when he called a special meeting of the faculty on October 12, 1944, and publicly leveled sixteen charges against the regents. He alleged violations of academic freedom, especially attempts to fire economics instructors who supported Franklin Roosevelt's New Deal, and interference with the effective administration of the university. The regents responded with two days of hearings, and at nine on the evening of November 1, 1944, they fired President Rainey.[34]

During the 1940s, Texas politicians were gravely concerned about "radicalism" in Texas education. Governor W. Lee "Pappy" O'Daniel stated publicly that it was time for the people of Texas to regain control of the University of Texas. O'Daniel's successor, Coke Stevenson, complained to Rainey: "It is one thing to have full freedom to teach the truth as each of us understands the truth to be, and . . . another thing to take advantage of one's position in a public school to teach atheism, communism, and other isms that tear down and destroy all that you and I have been taught to believe in."[35] (Ironically, Homer Rainey was a very devout Christian; he had been an ordained Baptist minister since the age of nineteen.) It was Pappy O'Daniel's and Coke Stevenson's regents who ousted Rainey.[36]

Charges of communist infiltration at UT continued well into the 1950s, in the 1960s during the Vietnam War, and, arguably, until the fall of the Soviet Union. Rainey and other UT presidents received many letters and complaints like that from M. L. Fleming, of Amarillo: "There is no definite line of demarcation between an avowed communist and a great many dissenters known as New Dealers, or otherwise." E. M. Biggers, of Houston, wrote to the regents directly: "Why spend billions to combat communism in distant parts of the world, while we spend millions teaching it at home?" In 1948, L. D. Fretwell, enraged by campus radicalism, wrote to the university president: "I am so mad I could bust."[37]

J. Frank Dobie, a giant in the world of southwestern folklore and literature and a UT faculty member, wanted to "bust" as well—but for very different reasons. His tremendous reputation in academic circles notwithstanding, he represented the radicalism that Governors O'Daniel and Stevenson detested. Dobie thought segregation was "a loyalty to fallacies and prejudices, not loyalty to constitutional and Christian principles of justice."[38] Pressure to remove liberal professors from the UT faculty angered Dobie so much that his comments drew the attention and ire of Governor Stevenson, who issued a statement: "If I were a member of the Board of Regents, I would remove Dobie without batting an eye . . . The removal of Dobie from the faculty would be just a question of eliminating a disturbing influence."[39]

The regents responded by passing a resolution stating that all faculty on leave (which happened to include Dobie) had to return to their teaching duties. Dobie had spent the previous year on personal leave and wanted to extend that leave through the fall of 1947. He applied for that extension on April 22, 1947; he wanted to teach half sessions in the spring. The application was endorsed by the English Department chairman and approved by the dean of the College of Liberal Arts. When it reached the desk of Rainey's successor, President Theophilus Painter, he rejected the request.[40]

Dobie refused to resign. When he did not report to work for the fall semester in 1947, Painter terminated him. A file in the President's Office Records of UT accurately illustrates the paradox that is the relationship between UT and alumni, elected leaders, and the citizens of Texas. While the staff, and especially the faculty and students, mourned the loss of the most distinguished of UT's teachers, other Texans rejoiced. M. L. Massingill represented the prevalent reaction of the regents and the politicians: "The fewer Dobies and Raineys we have at the University of Texas, the better it will be."[41]

Paying for College

Shortly after the disappearance of Lloyd Gaines, a number of suits were instituted to force states to live up to their responsibilities for providing an equal educational environment for their African American students. As Thurgood Marshall was to write many years later, "At the time the best strategy seemed to be an attack against the segregation system by law suits seeking absolute and complete equalization of curricula, faculty, and physical equipment on the theory that the extreme cost of maintaining two 'equal' school systems would eventually destroy segregation."[42] In theory, such a legal strategy was a good one: no state could afford to duplicate its educational systems to satisfy the separate-but-equal doctrine. In 1946, Missouri spent $500,000 to graduate one student from a black law school and ten students from a black journalism school at Lincoln University. State legislators and administrators offered deluded definitions of what was equal, and popularly elected state district judges went along with them.

It soon became evident that the "equalization" approach could be circumvented, as state officials in states like Missouri and Kentucky created Jim Crow schools at existing black colleges. As more of America's black leaders abandoned hope of ever being taken seriously by southern and border state courts and legislatures, the movement to engage in a direct attack on segregation gained momentum, especially in the NAACP.

Texas had more at stake than integration versus equalization. Creating a higher-educational system for African American citizens also raised the question of how to pay for it. Early in its history, Texas set aside vast tracts of land—the only thing that it had in abundance—for the sole purpose of funding a university of the first class; according to the Constitution of 1876, the money generated from the lands would be called the Permanent University Fund (PUF). Almost fifty years after land was first set aside to fund a state university, the University of Texas formally opened in Austin on September 15, 1883, although classes had been held before that date in the temporary capitol a few blocks south on Congress Avenue.

In April 1883, the legislature had passed a bill adding 1,000,000 acres of unappropriated public-domain land to the PUF territory. The act stipulated that the land was set aside as a permanent endowment for the University of Texas and its branches. One of those branches was to be a separate "Negro college." Eventually, the PUF came to include more than two million acres of desolate, nearly uninhabitable land, mostly in West Texas, that no one believed had significant commercial value. The UT regents held on to the land in the hope that the vast tracts might be worth something some day—then it could be sold.

From 1876 to the first quarter of the twentieth century, the area generated a little revenue from sheep-grazing leases. Disposable income for UT was further depressed by a Texas law putting the principal of the PUF off-limits. Only money earned by the money in the PUF could be spent; this spendable money came to be known as the Available University Fund.[43]

On May 27, 1923, at an oil rig called the Santa Rita No. 1 in Reagan County, a driller named Carl Cromwell looked down into the hole he had been working on for 646 days and noticed bubbles rising from the casing head. After averaging only 4.7 feet of drilling a day since beginning work at that location, Cromwell hit the "Big Lime" dolomitic sands about 3,000 feet below the surface. Rather than continue work at the rig, he and a coworker rushed to lease available acreage surrounding Santa Rita No. 1.

Santa Rita (the patron saint of the impossible) wouldn't wait. Even without further drilling, on the very next day, May 28, the rig gushed oil with such a fury that it covered a 250-square-yard area with thick black liquid.[44]

No other incident has ever had such a profound effect on Texas higher education as the Santa Rita gusher. The University of Texas became one of the most heavily endowed universities in the United States. By 1925, the PUF was growing by $2,000 a day and no end seemed in sight. Since the PUF had been set aside exclusively for UT in the state constitution, the state legislature voted in 1931 to split the proceeds from the windfall with Texas A&M by making the latter a branch of UT. (The split was two-thirds for UT and one-third for Texas A&M.)

By 1944, Texas rigs accounted for 45 percent of all U.S. oil production. African American leaders, especially from Austin, correctly pointed out that the Texas Constitution of 1876 called for a "university of the first class for Negroes." It was to be a branch of the University of Texas, and therefore would have access to the Available University Fund. Construction of this new, constitutional university could begin with proceeds from the fund.

From 1931 through 1946, UT received $15.7 million from the Available University Fund, and nearly all of it went to permanent improvements. If the state constructed a black university that had access to the fund, there would necessarily be less money for UT and Texas A&M. In an effort to preserve their hold on the PUF, the regents of the two flagship universities met in Fort Worth and set up a special committee to study their institutions' responsibilities "in the matter of Negro education." They also recommended that the governor appoint yet another biracial committee to investigate the matter.[45]

The recommendation was just another promise. What appeared to be more substantive, however, were the actions of the state legislature in 1945. The legislature understood that the defeat of the white primary meant that similar litigation in the area of education before an increasingly sympathetic U.S. Supreme Court was inevitable. In January 1945, the Texas A&M regents announced that they intended to make Prairie View a first-class university. Four months later, the legislature responded with SB 228, which authorized Prairie View to teach any graduate- or professional-level course offered to whites at UT. It also changed the school's official name from Prairie View Normal and Industrial College to Prairie View University. The bill passed the Senate with a unanimous vote and the House with only five nays. Governor Coke Stevenson quickly signed the bill into law.[46]

SB 228 was just another promise. What is remarkable is that Texas's political leaders seemed to believe they were being generous. Inserting "university" in Prairie View's name did not change its functions or course offerings. The legislature did substantially increase Prairie View's budget, but the additional money was not specifically earmarked for the establishment of graduate or professional schools; the action was more like an attempted payoff than a genuine attempt to provide education for the state's African American citizens. In theory, courses available to whites on campuses like UT but otherwise unavailable to blacks anywhere in Texas were to be offered at Prairie View as the demand justified the need, that is, not until a black student asked for it.[47]

African American leaders in Texas were never fooled by the legislature's disingenuous attempts at mollification. At the time the Texas Legislature passed SB 228, Maceo Smith wrote to Thurgood Marshall: "I have said to my colleagues here that you cannot make a university by the Legislature voting to change the name of Prairie View College to Prairie View University. *It's going to take legal action to accomplish the desired results*" (emphasis added).[48]

CHAPTER 8

"A Brash Moment"

*Statesmanship could save much money, much pain and much anguish; ignorance
and reactionism will cost the people dearly.*
CARTER WESLEY, *HOUSTON INFORMER*, OCTOBER 27, 1945

In June 1945, the *Dallas Morning News* estimated that it would take
$25,000,000 to build a "Negro university" remotely equal to UT and that to
do so Texas would have to dip into the Permanent University Fund (PUF).[1]
Despite the politicians' rhetoric, no one seriously believed the Texas Legislature would set up an "equal" Negro university. Few believed Texas would
even honor its commitment to its shamefully inadequate out-of-state tuition
assistance, which had already been ruled unconstitutional in *Gaines*. In an
article in the academic journal *Phylon*, W. E. B. Du Bois quoted an editorial
in the *Dallas Morning News* that admitted the tuition scheme was "a rather
ridiculous side-stepping of an obligation."[2]

Some white leaders clearly thought serial promises would mollify blacks.[3]
Even when improvements to black education were attempted, the results
were hardly adequate. Prairie View became a university in name only, offering new programs and curricula it had no money to implement, no faculty
to teach, and no library to support. Texas had not provided for a new building of any type on the Prairie View campus since 1925, and there were no
appropriations for any in the future.[4]

Immediately after the successful challenge he helped wage against the
white primary in *Smith v. Allwright*, Thurgood Marshall exploited the stat-
ure he had earned to direct the education efforts of all African American
leaders in Texas. Marshall and his allies understood that such a moment
might never again present itself. In early 1945, only six months after *Smith*,

the NAACP's Texas State Conference called for the integration of the University of Texas because African Americans had no other professional schools to attend. Their legal strategy, however, was not yet an unambiguous, direct attack on segregation. The conference retained William J. Durham and charged him with developing a legal brief. Maceo Smith, the executive secretary of the conference, forwarded the brief to Marshall on April 9, 1945. Smith's message included an invitation for Marshall to come to Texas for further discussions.[5]

During a meeting in Dallas on June 2, 1945, the conference finalized a blueprint for litigation against UT. The NAACP made no attempt to keep its plans secret. Indeed, it positioned itself for maximum publicity: Maceo Smith publicly announced that Texas's flagship was now a legal target for securing higher-educational opportunities for African American Texans.[6] Within days, in a letter to the president of the Texas conference, Marshall gave the go-ahead to raise $10,000 for prosecuting Texas equalization cases. The conference was responsible for raising the money, while the national NAACP was to handle the litigation.[7]

Less than two weeks later, Marshall wrote a letter to Kenneth R. Lampkin, an Austin attorney, asking for information on applying to the UT Law School.[8] At the time, Lampkin was Austin's only black attorney. He was also very active in the NAACP. His office was located in a building shared by one of Austin's four black dentists—a Howard Dental School graduate named Everett H. Givens. Lampkin had represented Givens in a lawsuit forcing regental action to establish the long-awaited branch university for African Americans promised in the Texas Constitution of 1876.[9]

Givens v. Woodward (1946) was a petition for a writ of mandamus to force Texas to create a segregated black university. Such an action would normally have incurred the wrath of the NAACP's preference for integration, but Marshall was not concerned. Unlike Carter Wesley's equalization efforts, *Givens* exclusively invoked article VII, section 14 of the Texas Constitution of 1876. Marshall and Wesley slowly became competitors over the meaning of the equal protection clause of the U.S. Constitution. For Marshall, the mere establishment of a "Negro branch" of the University of Texas did not necessarily make it equal in the eyes of the federal Constitution—he could always argue that whatever Texas set up would have to be integrated.

Since *Givens* involved only Texas state courts, its uneventful adjudication moved rather swiftly. The district court overruled Givens's motion on September 25, 1946, saying that it lacked jurisdiction. The appeals courts ruled that the Texas Constitution enabled the legislature to create a university for people of color, but it did not mandate it. The legislature had sole authority to decide when the establishment of a "colored branch of UT" was "practicable."[10]

Taking the Fight to Texas

In an article for the *Journal of Negro Education* in 1955, William H. Jones argued that Texas was a good place to battle segregation because it had cosmopolitan intellectual centers in places like Austin. He used the example of the UT student newspaper, the *Daily Texan:* "They exhibited a surprising liberalism—a liberalism over and beyond anything that the commercial newspapers were free to disclose, because they owed no obligation to any particular political or economic interest." Jones also pointed to the state's large military installations and its highly diversified transient population. Alwyn Barr of Texas Tech argued that since Texas was more urbanized than other southern states, it was beginning to "shed its Confederate heritage." And as Melvin Banks pointed out, "Negroes in the larger towns and cities fared much better in the enjoyment of educational opportunities" than their brothers and sisters in remote rural areas. Literacy in urban enclaves like the Third Ward in Houston, where Heman Sweatt lived, made possible what reactionary whites feared: a successful black professional class with ambition and money. By the mid-1940s, Texas had also grown well beyond the borders of Confederate-dominated East Texas counties.[11]

Many African Americans worked on the campus of the University of Texas, but as Carolyn Jones wrote, "[They] journeyed from their homes in east Austin across East Avenue to the cafeterias, dormitories, and classrooms of the University where they held jobs cooking and cleaning." For those employees and other black Austinites, the University of Texas was merely a job and a symbol of discrimination.[12]

And yet it was because of the university and the state's growing bureaucracy (which included representation from those parts of the state without a Confederate legacy) that Austin was considered rather enlightened, at least by Texas standards. In a 1984 oral history interview conducted by the Austin History Center, W. Astor Kirk, a legendary African American activist from Austin, was asked whether black men and women were treated better in Austin than the rest of Texas. Kirk replied: "Basically, yes in the sense that the white intelligentsia here . . . were more open than what I found in Houston and Dallas and to some extent San Antonio. There were a number of whites in this town at that time who basically were not prejudiced, but they did recognize what the system was, and they probably did not have the courage to behave in ways that were consistent with their own beliefs."[13]

Outspoken liberal whites like Homer Rainey and J. Frank Dobie were not alone in Austin. In east Austin, the faculties of the predominantly black Tillotson College and Samuel Huston College, public school teachers, and sixty-six preachers formed an intellectual circle neatly matching the demographic of an African American bourgeoisie attracted to the goals and activities of the NAACP.

The NAACP also had a strategic reason for selecting Texas as a battleground: with the breathtaking state-owned resources Texas had at its disposal, if it could not afford to pay for separate equality for its African American population, no other segregated state could either.[14]

The NAACP also believed that graduate and professional schools were ideal targets. In most southern and border states, the question was not whether there were separate-but-equal facilities, but whether there were facilities for African Americans at all. Texas, for example, had no black law school. In such an atmosphere, Thurgood Marshall argued, meeting the separate-but-equal standard required the wholesale duplication of a state's entire graduate- and professional-school system. Such an investment for "so few Negroes" was a financial impossibility. Segregated states would have no choice but to integrate existing institutions.[15]

Law schools were a particularly attractive target. Every judge and almost every lawyer the NAACP was to come into contact with had graduated from a law school. It was common knowledge that law schools varied in quality; lawyers knew which ones were exemplary. If a state was to create a law school for African Americans, the separate-but-equal doctrine required that it be equal to the best one offered to whites. Law schools were also ideal targets because the students were older and more mature, which made it unlikely that emotional parents would become involved. Many law students were married and almost all were men, which eased the concern over interracial fraternization between the sexes.

In 1933, William Hastie, a Harvard Law graduate, wrote that an ideal African American plaintiff would be a person of "outstanding scholarship . . . neat, personable, and unmistakably Negro . . . [who] shows the whites in the community that these are Negroes . . . who measure up in every respect to collegiate standards."[16]

Looks mattered, but so did courage, stamina, and dependability. The plaintiff in the Texas law school case would become the "face" of the struggle, so he would have to possess unassailable admission credentials: an impressive transcript and a degree earned from an accredited institution. He would also have to be a person who understood and accepted the probability that his family would be scrutinized and possibly harassed during the time it would take to secure a decision from the U.S. Supreme Court—about four years.

Paradoxically for the plaintiff, in some ways victory might be more frightening than defeat. It would mean that after a successful decision, as newspapers covered every move and recorded every word, this person would have to walk (probably alone) through the doors of a previously all-white school, enroll, and perform. Every test, every grade, and every classroom recitation might be scrutinized.[17]

Finding such a plaintiff would not be easy, and it turned out to be even more difficult than anticipated. By August, William Durham, in a letter to the NAACP, lamented: "The plaintiff is our biggest worry, but I hope to see Carter [Wesley] soon and see if we can find a plaintiff."[18] Months earlier, the Texas conference had selected one member from each of its three major branches to serve on a committee to choose the right plaintiff. They were Maceo Smith (Dallas), Carter Wesley (Houston), and Kenneth Lampkin (Austin). They worked for months during the summer and into the fall of 1945. In the meantime, the "soldiers" of the Texas NAACP, like Lulu White, worked to raise money for litigation. Carter Wesley's newspapers were especially valuable: he kept the story in the news even when there was little to report. Throughout Texas and much of the south, African Americans saw running tallies of the amount collected for the education lawsuit. Not since the final battle over the white primary had African American Texans been so focused and united.

By August 1945, after reviewing five men as possible plaintiffs, the committee determined that three could be denied by UT Law School for reasons other than their race. One of the other two, Grover Washington, who was president of the Texas Youth Council, was qualified and seemed to be willing to enter the fray until his family objected. Afterward, Maceo Smith suggested William Durham's assistant, Crawford B. Bunkley, Jr., but Bunkley already had a law degree from the University of Michigan Law School. The committee considered asking Bunkley to apply for a master's of law degree instead, but both Bunkley and Thurgood Marshall were unenthusiastic about that idea. Marshall pointed out that universities traditionally had more leeway when it came to accepting or denying graduate-school applicants. Bunkley was willing to be a "last resort," but even then he admitted to Thurgood Marshall, "Frankly, I am not too interested in doing so."[19]

Heman Sweatt Steps Up

By the end of September, Marshall had nearly given up on finding a plaintiff for a law-school suit and was beginning to think that Texas should consider an elementary or high school suit instead. Again Marshall turned to Carter Wesley for advice, but just as the selection committee was giving up on the idea of a law-school suit, Lulu White came through with startling news. On October 10, 1945, she wrote Marshall to announce, "I think I have a plaintiff for the Education Case."[20] Lulu White's energy was without limits. She was consumed with the goal of equal citizenship rights. She also understood and exploited what Merline Pitre called the "transcendent leadership" of black preachers.[21] And so perhaps it is not surprising that she found a plaintiff in a church.

In African American churches, membership in the NAACP and raising funds for its causes became connected to an unquestioned and largely unchallenged moral authority. The Reverends T. J. Goodall and Earl Boone of Antioch Baptist Church and Albert Lucas of Good Hope Baptist Church were but three of hundreds of preachers throughout Texas who opened their sanctuaries and meeting halls to NAACP organizers. In Houston, when meetings were not held in a church hall they were often held at Emancipation Park in the Third Ward—a public facility that had been purchased by a coalition of black churches and donated to the city for the use of the African American population. In the spring of 1978, Thurgood Marshall recalled: "Eighty percent of the branches of the NAACP when I went there were run by ministers, in churches. Ninety-eight percent of the meetings were held in Negro churches."[22]

In early October 1945, during an evening meeting at the Wesley Chapel AME Church on Dowling Street in Houston's Third Ward, Lulu White presented an overview of the search for a plaintiff for the University of Texas Law School case. Her presentation included a plea for a volunteer to serve as plaintiff. In *Advancing Democracy*, Amilcar Shabazz described a "hush" falling over the meeting: "The brothers and sisters present looked strangely at White and then searched the faces of their peers." It was during this dramatic pause that Heman Marion Sweatt, a thirty-two-year-old mail carrier, stood up and with a "soft but certain voice . . . said he would do it."[23]

Years later, Sweatt described the episode as a "brash moment."[24] It probably was. He was aware of the exasperating nine-month search for a plaintiff by Texas's NAACP leadership. During that time, he betrayed no indication that he was considering becoming the plaintiff. Only a week before the "brash moment," during a regional training conference in Fort Worth, NAACP leaders voiced frustration over their seeming inability to find a suitable plaintiff. No mention was made of Heman Sweatt during that conference, and he is not mentioned in any of the surviving communications among the Texans or with Thurgood Marshall. On that fateful night in the Wesley Chapel AME meeting room, even though he was in a church he attended regularly and where everyone knew him, he seems to have caught everyone by surprise.[25]

Undoubtedly, many wondered why he would volunteer for such a grueling civic service. Sweatt had a nice home and a well-paying job at the post office. It was a federal position, one sufficiently removed from local and state control to allow for political and civic activism. His wife was a teacher in the local school. He was also just a few weeks shy of his thirty-third birthday and had not been a college student for about a decade.

On the other hand, in interviews years later, Sweatt seemed to contradict his own "brash moment" characterization when he revealed that his interest in the law started more than a year earlier, in March 1944, when he and an attorney named Francis Scott Whitaker prepared racial-discrimination grievances for a meeting with the postmaster. Sweatt indicated that about this time he decided to leave his job to go to law school, possibly at the University of Michigan. (Why he considered returning to the harsh climate that had adversely affected his health years earlier is not clear.)

Whether his decision to become a plaintiff was thoughtful or brash, Heman Sweatt was not prepared to proceed without the support of his family. They gathered at the Chenevert Street home of the aging patriarch and sage, James Leonard Sweatt, and during a large Sunday dinner, the family discussed Heman's decision to place himself before the public as the face of the assault on the exclusion of African Americans from Texas colleges and universities. The reaction of the educated and activist Sweatt family was predictable: all were supportive. His brothers, John and Jack, did voice reservations about their brother's age and whether the family could afford the endeavor. (They evidently did not understand that the NAACP would bankroll the litigation.)

Sweatt's brother John is reported to have asserted that only "Joe Stalin" could force American whites to accept justice for African Americans.[26] Such a radical outlook was not uncommon among young black men of the time. In his memoirs, Robert Carter, who was Thurgood Marshall's associate at the NAACP Legal Defense Fund, noted: "Socialism and Communism were very attractive concepts for a poor Black intent on securing the benefits available to a similarly situated white man. Communism professed dedication to equal rights and benefits for all without racial barriers."[27]

But if Thurgood Marshall had been a part of the discussion around the Sweatt family's table, he would have been disturbed by brother John's connection of communism with the struggle for racial justice. Marshall understood that if the public ever associated the NAACP with communism, no elected official anywhere in the United States would stand with the NAACP—for anything. Indeed, as the Sweatt family gathered, the NAACP was actively purging itself of communists. According to Marshall: "Around World War II, we decided to get rid of [the communists in the NAACP]. We wouldn't even allow them to come to a meeting. We ran them out."[28]

Connie Sweatt was not as thrilled about the idea of her husband becoming a plaintiff as the rest of his family. Indeed, there was much to fear. Sweatt was not the only person who would have to live with his decision. His home, income, future, and reputation were hers as well. Undoubtedly, his new visibility and, in some circles, celebrity or notoriety would take him away from their home more often than she was used to. Was she to be alone while he was away? If someone were to attack her home, what would she do? How was she to handle harassment? The Third Ward might not have been the most dangerous place for civil rights advocates to live (Lulu White and Richard Grovey lived unmolested only blocks away), but it wasn't "Heavenly Houston" either.

Both Heman and Connie Sweatt also weighed the consequences of the decision for their long-term financial security. At the time of his decision, Sweatt was a full-time mail carrier and a part-time employee of Carter Wesley's *Informer* newspaper. Accounts differ, but after an initial meeting at Sweatt's home with William Durham and Lulu White, Sweatt apparently felt better about becoming a plaintiff: "When I saw the kind of support that was going to be given me, well, it solidified my assurance for me making the move."[29]

The young couple's concern for their financial future was serious enough that they traveled to Dallas for a second meeting with Durham and Maceo Smith to discuss specifics of the financial arrangements between them and the Texas Association of NAACP Chapters. Under the terms of the agreement they reached, the association would underwrite court costs and legal fees as well as Sweatt's travel and subsistence expenses related to the adjudication of the case. Beyond that, Maceo Smith is reputed to have assured Sweatt that if the litigation succeeded, assistance would become available for educational and living expenses while Sweatt attended UT Law School.[30]

There is another possible explanation for Sweatt's caution and concern over personal finances. According to W. Astor Kirk, who was Sweatt's contemporary, a civil rights activist, and a plaintiff in a desegregation case against UT, Sweatt never really aspired to be an attorney. If true, then Sweatt was giving up a very good and secure job to become trained in a profession in which he had little or no interest. The Austin History Center's African American collections include a vertical file on Kirk, which contains a transcript of an oral-history interview conducted on August 29, 1984. While talking about his own attempts to enroll in UT's graduate school, Kirk indicated that even though he was denied admission, "there was not the kind of animosity that there was in the Sweatt case." The reason, Kirk said, was that he "was able to convince people that I really wanted to get an advanced degree and that to some extent this made a difference."[31] Kirk then elaborated:

> Well, he [Sweatt] was active with the NAACP, and they needed a plaintiff and nobody else as far as I could tell, nobody else was willing to be a plaintiff. So . . . he probably didn't want a legal education, but he was willing to be a plaintiff. We all knew in those days, he knew, that it was going to be rather dangerous work for anybody to be a plaintiff . . . I can be immodest at this point. Nobody believed that Sweatt really wanted to go to law school.[32]

What is certain is that Heman Sweatt received assurance that he would not be responsible for the legal expenses associated with his pending lawsuit. It also seems clear that Maceo Smith promised that his educational and living expenses were to be covered once he entered UT Law and that he would be guaranteed a level of comfort equal to that of his earning power as a mail carrier.

Sweatt indicated to Durham and Smith that the last step in his decision-making process was to ask for guidance from his employer. He was not referring to the postal service, where he worked full-time, but to Carter Wesley at the *Informer*, where he worked part-time as a circulation manager. Neither Sweatt nor Wesley ever spoke or wrote of the details of their discussion, but in a letter to Thurgood Marshall almost a year later, Wesley claims to have been the one who convinced Sweatt to become a plaintiff.[33]

By early November, the *Dallas Express* reported that William Durham was ready to proceed with a lawsuit against the University of Texas. All that was needed, he said, was authorization from the NAACP executive committee. The reality was not that simple. The NAACP had to be sure that there was no question about Sweatt's academic qualifications for admission and that the sole reason for his certain denial was that he was an African American.

At the time, admission requirements to UT Law School were surprisingly simple: the applicant had to be at least nineteen years old, furnish satisfactory evidence of good moral character, and hold a bachelor's degree from UT or some other acceptable institution. In a letter to Thurgood Marshall dated January 28, 1946, William Durham announced that "Mr. Sweatt has agreed to file suit against the Regents of the University of Texas."[34] While that letter was making its way to New York, Marshall sent a letter to Durham in Dallas. He was concerned that Sweatt's alma mater, Wiley College, had not been accredited until 1933, the year before Sweatt's graduation. (This meant that about two-thirds of Sweatt's undergraduate coursework had been completed at an unaccredited school.) Wiley therefore might not be "acceptable" to the UT administration, and its formerly unaccredited status might be used as a basis to deny Sweatt admission. Marshall instructed Durham to have Sweatt apply anyway. With "luck," Sweatt would be denied for no other reason than his race. Ideally, Marshall hoped for a letter from the UT president similar to the letter provided by the president of the University of Oklahoma in the case of Ada Lois Sipuel. He acknowledged that she was in every way qualified to be admitted—except for her race.[35]

On February 16, 1946, Carter Wesley's *Houston Informer* came uncomfortably close to leaking the NAACP's plans when it reported that, according to a reliable source, someone had been found who would be willing to be a plaintiff in a lawsuit against the state. Anyone keeping up with current events knew that the suit would be aimed at UT. When the paper added that it was likely to take place within the next thirty days, astute observers could easily determine that the next registration period on the Austin campus was to begin on February 26. With about $7,200 already collected and a well-known plaintiff who was widely recognized as a "marvelous person, a quiet man committed to justice," all that remained was the delivery of an application to the University of Texas Law School.

It is quite possible that in the history of the University of Texas, no other application had ever been so painstakingly developed and scrutinized—for the express purpose of being rejected.[36]

CHAPTER 9

The Great Day

Ye shall know the truth and the truth shall make you free.
JOHN 8:32, INSCRIBED ABOVE THE SOUTH ENTRANCE OF THE
UNIVERSITY OF TEXAS MAIN BUILDING AND TOWER

Shortly after the UT regents fired President Homer Rainey in 1944, they appointed Theophilus Shickel Painter acting president. A Virginian by birth, Painter had moved to Texas to become an adjunct professor of zoology in 1916. By 1921, he was a tenured associate professor, and he became a distinguished professor in 1939. His zoological specialty was in the field of genetics, and in those circles he was known for brilliant research on the cytology (the study of cells) of spiders and his investigations into the chromosomes in the salivary glands of fruit flies. The Yale-educated Painter had little or no administrative experience; he was the quintessential "faculty type." In 1946, the regents ignored faculty opposition and formally appointed him president.[1]

Painter's presidency should be considered in the following context: he was in a very difficult position at a tumultuous time. The university was reeling from the most wrenching ideological schism in its history. The regents wanted a nonconfrontational chief executive, and Painter proved to be an ideal choice. He was far more malleable than Rainey, and, in general, he cooperated with rather than opposing political and regental attempts to intimidate UT's more outspoken and militant professors. Painter's opportunistic termination of J. Frank Dobie was revelatory: most college presidents would have fought hard to keep such an accomplished and prolific writer.

Of more immediate concern to the board of regents at the time, however, was the future of UT's hold on the Permanent University Fund. Painter and the regents were clearly frightened by the possibility of being forced to create a constitutional university of the first class for Negroes, one that would have access to the PUF.

During the 1946–1947 fiscal year, the PUF held approximately $65,000,000 in assets and produced $1,472,000 for the Available University Fund, the part of the PUF that can be spent. In 1946–1947, the University of Texas received $988,000 from that source.[2]

Texas politicians had four options for providing "equal" higher educational opportunities for its African American citizens: create a constitutional university—a branch of the University of Texas—for African Americans (and thus further divide the Available University Fund); create a segregated state university through legislative mandate; dramatically increase funding for Prairie View A&M; or desegregate the University of Texas at Austin.

The boards of both UT and Texas A&M knew that the NAACP, which was active in many other southern states, was planning to litigate for the desegregation of existing higher-educational institutions. The Texas State Conference of Branches had made no secret of its money-raising activities. As discussed in Chapter 7, the UT and Texas A&M boards held a joint meeting in Fort Worth in January 1946 to consider how to provide higher education for African Americans. Their call for yet another meaningless biracial commission turned out to be not nearly enough.[3]

The Meeting

With a Wiley College transcript in hand, Heman Marion Sweatt joined a distinguished group of African Americans at Samuel Huston College in Austin on February 26, 1946: "The great day arrived."[4]

Sweatt and the other members of the delegation representing the NAACP's Texas State Conference of Branches had gathered for a meeting with UT president Painter.[5] R. A. Hester, president of the Progressive Voters League, a Dallas-based organization Maceo Smith helped to create in the mid-1930s, led the group. The Reverend C. D. Knight and Dr. B. E. Howell were also there from Dallas. Artemisia Bowden, the president of St. Philip's College, arrived with two other San Antonio members, Euretta Fairchild and the Reverend E. J. Wilson. James Jemison, the fiery Lulu White, and Clif Richardson, Jr., the thirty-five-year-old editor of the *Houston Defender,* accompanied Sweatt.

From the Samuel Huston campus, the delegation headed west across

East Avenue toward the University of Texas's landmark Main Building and Tower. The trip was only a few blocks, but the racial and educational gulf between the east and west side of East Avenue was much wider.

In 1946, the UT Main Building and Tower, a Works Progress Administration (WPA) project, had been occupied for only nine years. The Available University Fund contributed about $2,800,000 to help cover construction costs. The edifice sits atop College Hill, and on the west, east, and south, landscaped "malls" lead to where the university's Main Building has always stood. It was an area everyone knew as the original "Forty Acres."

The Main Building is a four-story structure housing administrative offices, reading rooms, and libraries. "Main" wraps itself around the Tower on three sides, making a contiguous structure of the two. The twenty-seven-story Tower, which was intended to house library collections and a number of centers for advanced study, rises from the north side of the Main Building. The whole complex was grossly overbuilt to support the enormous weight of the hundreds of thousands of volumes and manuscripts required to serve Texas's university of the first class.

The Main Building and Tower quickly became the trademark of the University and a symbol of Austin, but for the Sweatt delegation, it was also a symbol of what African Americans were being denied: a vast world of knowledge in an elegant and scholarly setting. Below the windows of the northeast and northwest wings are carved the names of fourteen giants of Western letters.[6] The east, north, and west faces display gold-leaf letters of the five alphabets from which English is derived: Egyptian, Phoenician, Hebrew, Greek, and Roman. Inside are majestic stained-glass windows and large oil portraits of past educators and benefactors. The entrance to the main library was the Hall of Six Coats of Arms, named for the six countries that had claimed Texas during its history. Sixteen ceiling beams in the east reading room, also called the Hall of Noble Words, were elaborately decorated with quotations and supported by brackets exhibiting famous printers' marks. The west reading room, called the Hall of Texas, was similarly constructed, but with a Texas history theme, including, on the brackets, hand-painted seals of nations that have contributed to Texas's population.[7]

In the Main Building and Tower alone, the University of Texas housed Asian, Middle Eastern, Indian, Sanskrit, Chinese, Japanese, Arabic, and Persian collections as well as numerous research centers. The one-room Stark Library on the fourth floor, by itself, contained more than 12,000 volumes associated with nineteenth-century English poets and novelists. That single room had more books than approximately 70 percent of all predominantly black colleges in the United States.[8] Walnut woodworking, wrought-iron metalwork, and wood carvings over the doorway adorned the nearby Wrenn Library, which was modeled after the library of Sir Walter Scott.

No African American had ever been able to use those facilities, and Heman Sweatt's delegation had no illusions about whether Texas's political leadership would ever build something separate and remotely equal for African Americans on the other side of East Avenue.

The meeting between the Sweatt delegation and President Painter took place in Room 1 on the ground floor of the Main Building. The ground floor was more like the Tower than the elegant upper floors of the Main Building; it was proletarian in look and functionality. Its shiny, smooth floor tiles made for easy cleaning and buffing but were treacherously slippery on rainy days. The midsize ceramic tiles on the walls were fashionable and functional for the time, able to withstand smudges from the hands of the thousands of people who would eventually walk the main hallway connecting the east and west entrances. Main 1 was (and still is) located on the southeast corner of the main hallway.

Sweatt and his entourage probably parked along 24th Street in an area traditionally reserved for visitors. As the delegation walked toward the Tower, some of the students smiled and said hello.[9]

President Painter greeted the group at Main 1. Painter's selection of supporting staff was revealing: Vice President James C. Dolley, Registrar Edward J. Matthews, and Scott Gaines, a land attorney for the board of regents. The Sweatt delegation presented itself to Painter as "representing the interests of the Negro citizens of Texas in procuring immediate public higher education facilities and instruction for Negroes in the professional courses in the state, such as medicine, law, pharmacy, dentistry, journalism, and others."

R. A. Hester, the first of the delegation to speak, read a statement declaring that Negro citizens of Texas were entitled to the same educational opportunities as whites. Hester used the *Gaines* case from Missouri as authority for claiming that Texas was not living up to its legal responsibility.[10] Hester's statement ended with a direct question to Painter: "We want to know just what has been done in regard to Point 12, Section C of the 12-point program that you outlined to the press January 20, 1946?"

Point 12 called for the appointment of a committee to study how to provide higher education for African American Texans. Hester and the delegation knew perfectly well that neither Painter nor anyone at Texas A&M had done anything. No one present noted whether Painter was embarrassed or annoyed, but to his credit he gave an honest answer: he had done practically nothing.

Painter then tried to steer the dialogue to something more positive by asking the group for suggestions about how to define the educational needs of African American Texans and the "most practical and realistic means to achieve them." Hester did not fall for the attempt at diversion: "We are not here to discuss or try to solve the race problem. The Negro citizens of Texas are seriously interested and concerned about provisions for them in graduate and professional schools. We want to know what the committee has done. *What is available now?* Not tomorrow, next week, or next month. We need training for our returning GIs and our children who must compete with others in their own state for jobs with inferior education" (emphasis added).

Hester's concern for returning GIs was a valid one. Only eight months later, in a report to Painter, E. J. Matthews wrote: "The chief difference between 1940–1941 students and those of 1945–1946 is *veterans*. In the former year 32 percent of the semester hours registered for were in freshman courses and 61 percent were in lower division courses, while in 1945–1946 the corresponding figures were 42 percent and 74 percent" (emphasis in the original).[11]

To Painter's answer that all that was immediately available was out-of-state scholarships, Hester shot back: "The present state aid is not only inadequate but unsatisfactory. Not only is the student penalized because it costs them more to live in other sections, but most of those who go away to study at the State of Texas' expense in more liberal sections decide to stay there and Texas Negroes do not get the advantage of their training." Hester also summarily dismissed state plans in Senate Bill 228 to upgrade Prairie View A&M: "We know of the change in the name of Prairie View from a college to a university. But all of that is a long range program, which at the present rate of progress will take years to be completed. We want to know what the state can offer the Negro now in the various phases of higher graduate and professional study."

Painter claimed to be sympathetic to the demands of the delegation: "I think that the Constitution does provide for the establishment of a university for Texas Negroes. I personally believe something can be worked out. I have talked to several legislators and found them willing and in agreement with me in a program of enlarged facilities. In this connection I believe that Prairie View's appropriation is larger for the next two years than it has ever been." He then asked the delegation for their names and asked for suggestions to forward to what was to become Governor Stevenson's new biracial committee.

Hester explained that what African Americans wanted was the "divorce" of Prairie View University from the control of the Texas A&M board and the establishment of a graduate and professional school in a large urban area. "The law is plain and it is up to the legislature to provide the funds. We do not object to separate schools if they are equal, but we do not want them separate if they are separate in order to be unequal," Hester emphasized. Hester knew Texas would never build an institution equal to the one hosting him at that very moment. All he had to do was look around and see what would have to be duplicated.

The only testy exchange occurred when President Painter mused that the graduate and professional schools the delegation wanted could start on a small scale and gradually grow as course demands warranted. He even suggested that the first courses could be offered as early as the fall of 1946. Hester and the others in his group got visibly agitated, frowned, and argued that no student should be denied training in a field because of a small demand, especially when white Texans were afforded the same training at the same time.

When Painter spoke of limited state budgets for programs, Lulu White could no longer restrain herself. She reminded the UT administrators that UT and Texas A&M were appropriated more than $10,000,000 of additional state money during the 1945 regular session of the Texas Legislature. This money, she asserted, could be diverted to the establishment of graduate and professional schools for African Americans.

"What would you have us do, close down the white schools for a year?" Registrar E. J. Mathews sarcastically asked. "That would not be a bad idea. It would give us an opportunity to catch up with you in training," White shot back.

Perhaps Hester saw that the meeting was going in the wrong direction, or maybe he thought that there had been enough talk. Texan African Americans had heard it all before—more promises from biracial committees and requests for patience. For whatever reason, Hester signaled Sweatt, who had sat quietly throughout the entire meeting, to speak up.

Heman Sweatt could not have been more courteous or deferential, which made his words all the more powerful. After asking for permission to speak, he addressed the group in a soft, slow, and measured tone. He wanted to be a lawyer, he said, and he had a right to the same legal training as other Texas college graduates. Furthermore, if Texas really wanted to provide for professional schools, it could find the money to do so. He made it clear that as an adult and a citizen of Texas, an out-of-state tuition package was unacceptable to him, even if only while a law school for African Americans was under construction. "I cannot go out of state to school, and I cannot wait indefinitely until some provision is made."[12] Then he presented Painter with a transcript from Wiley College and formally asked for admission to the University of Texas Law School.

For fans of poetic justice, it would be satisfying to make Sweatt's application even more heroic and his confrontation more dramatic by claiming that President Painter and his staff were tactically surprised or strategically outmaneuvered in some way. But Painter calmly accepted the transcript because he knew it would be forthcoming. He did not know it would be coming from Sweatt per se, but he undoubtedly had been waiting for this moment. For months, newspaper reports had described NAACP meetings and strategy sessions preparatory to a legal assault on segregation at the University of Texas. A few weeks earlier, Carter Wesley's *Informer* had reported that the "NAACP Education Fund Reache[d] the Half-Way Mark" when the account had $5,560.55 of deposits toward a goal of $10,000.[13]

On the day Sweatt handed over his transcript, Painter wrote a letter to the attorney general: "It was apparent, however, that this is to be the test case on the question of the admission of Negro students in the higher educational institutions of the State."[14] Moreover, Painter knew the meeting would involve an admissions issue of some sort; there was no other reason for him to involve the registrar or to hold the meeting in the area that served as the Admissions Office. (In 1946, the UT registrar also functioned as the dean of admissions.) Painter's office was a floor above, in Main 101, in a suite of offices that had much more comfortable meeting rooms.

As Heman Sweatt handed his transcript to Painter, Matthews interjected that Sweatt's application was not necessary. He spoke of his certainty that funds would be available for his law-school education somewhere other than the University of Texas. The university officials then engaged in a conversation that can be described only as condescending and offensive, even for the time.

Matthews, apparently reveling in his own enlightenment, assured the NAACP delegation that he "did not have any more than the normal amount of prejudice against Negroes." Part of his unsolicited yet "down to earth" advice to Sweatt was a warning of "grave dangers." Matthews added that African American Texans were on the verge of having unimagined educational facilities built for them, but a lawsuit could change everything. (No mention had been made by the delegation of a lawsuit, which indicates that Painter and the other university officials already knew of the real reason for the delegation's visit.) Sweatt did not comment on Matthews's thinly veiled warning. In all likelihood, he simply stared back and wondered how the registrar of a constitutionally designated flagship university did not understand that he was warning African Americans of the loss of something they, in fact, had never had.

Vice President Dolley, in what was perhaps an equally condescending tone, encouraged Sweatt to "think twice and choose the course that offers the most promise of success." President Painter then spoke fondly of a black man he knew, admired, and worked with. They grew up together, he said, "but he never let me eat with him and I wondered why until I was older."

The meeting ended when Painter informed the delegation that Matthews was not officially accepting the application, but that he [Painter] would request an attorney general's opinion on how the university should respond.

Painter wrote, "The members of the committee stated that the applicant was acting for himself, and that they simply permitted him to accompany them for their conference in regard to the general subject of furnishing higher educational advantages to the negro race in this state."[15] Shortly after the meeting, during an interview with the Associated Press, Sweatt expanded upon that deception by emphasizing that he was not a member or "guinea pig" of any "crusading Negro group."[16]

Later on the day of the meeting, Sweatt forwarded his University of Michigan transcript to Vice President Dolley and in an attached letter added: "I send [the Michigan transcript] as additional evidence of my qualifications for study in the University of Texas School of Law, and in supplement of my Wiley College (Marshall, Texas) credits which I gave you today during the conference with a group of citizens interested in Negro education. *A conference in which I was a mere visitor*" (emphasis added).[17]

R. A. Hester and Lulu White's obfuscations were even more blatant. "[Sweatt's application was] just as much a surprise to us," Hester said. Lulu White, the person who convinced Sweatt to become a plaintiff, said publicly that the NAACP was "not contemplating a lawsuit." Years later, Sweatt dismissed the harmless concerted deception merely as "playing the game."[18]

The NAACP delegation's deception did not really matter much because no one believed it anyway. Less than a week later, the *Daily Texan* reminded its readers that "this move has been expected since the summer of 1945 when the state president of the [NAACP's Texas State Conference of Branches] indicated that such action was being contemplated by the association."[19]

The NAACP litigation machinery had set its sights on Texas. The day after the Sweatt-Painter confrontation, William Durham sent Thurgood Marshall a telegram: "His application has been presented at school. Authorities are waiting on the opinion from Attorney General."[20] Three weeks later, Maceo Smith sent a letter to Carter Wesley: "According to plan, the proposed legal action will be backed squarely by the NAACP."[21]

Of all the contemporaneous commentary and news coverage of the February 26, 1946, confrontation between Heman Sweatt and Theophilus Painter, Clifton Richardson, Jr., best appreciated and most accurately described the historic change in Texas race relations. Of course, he had the advantage of having been an eyewitness, but his observation was no less prophetic: "The whites of Texas are faced with a dilemma which will no longer allow them room to procrastinate. They can no longer seek to dissuade us by the worn-out approach that 'I love Negroes since I had a black mammy and grew up with black boys.'"[22]

The Immediate Aftermath of the Meeting

After his encounter with Heman Sweatt, President Painter returned to his office in Main 101 and crafted a letter to Grover Sellers, the attorney general of Texas. Painter was surely aware of the legal assistance he was giving Sweatt as he dictated the opening paragraph:

> Your official opinion is respectfully requested upon the following inquiry:
>
> Application was made today by Heman Marion Sweatt, of 3402 Delano Street, Houston, Texas, for admission as a student in the Law School of the University of Texas. *This applicant is a citizen of Texas and duly qualified for admission into the Law School at the University of Texas, save and except for the fact that he is a negro.*[23] (emphasis added)

The stipulation did not escape the attention of Carter Wesley. In his *Houston Informer* column three days later, he wrote, "Dr. Painter, acting president, is to be commended for not attempting to dodge the issue by pretending that there was any other reason for barring the Negro."[24]

Indeed, in a single sentence, Painter reduced the issue to one of naked racial discrimination. He denied any notion Sellers might have had to challenge Sweatt's credentials or qualifications for admittance. It is also significant that Painter requested the opinion as quickly (the same day) as he did; he did not instruct the registrar to verify the authenticity of Sweatt's transcript or investigate Wiley College's accreditation—actions that are not uncommon in the admissions process, especially for applications to graduate and professional schools.

Given the political climate in Texas, Thurgood Marshall could not have asked for a more accommodating request for an attorney general's opinion. As Carter Wesley observed, "Dr. Painter put the politicians on the spot."[25]

Painter continued: "The applicant accompanied a group or committee which stated that it represented the interests of the negro citizens of this State in procuring immediate public higher educational facilities and instruction for negroes in professional courses within the State, such as medicine, law, pharmacy, dentistry, journalism and other similar professional subjects."[26] His letter reached the attorney general's office the next day. For Heman Sweatt, life would never be the same. In the immediate aftermath of the news bulletins, Sweatt continued to claim that he was not representing anyone but himself and that he had accompanied the NAACP delegation after having asked two members whether he could attend the meeting.[27]

The response on campus to Sweatt's application was, as one newspaper put it, "surprisingly favorable." An informal poll of a number of law students showed that the majority could not see anything wrong with having an African American as a classmate. The level of campus support for Sweatt was significant enough for Carter Wesley's *Houston Informer* to headline a story "U.T. Students for Sweatt."[28]

Sweatt was the talk of the campus, and passions became even more intense with the appearance of Sweatt's former teacher at Wiley College, Melvin B. Tolson. In a "standing room only" setting, Tolson delivered one of the most dramatic and memorable speeches in the university's history. Memories of the ousted president Homer Rainey and current events leading to what would soon be the unceremonious departure of J. Frank Dobie painfully divided the university family. For two hours, before a stunned and mesmerized audience, Tolson, the master poet, used epigrams and eloquence in a fearless presentation to disgrace myths of racial and socioeconomic superiority. His speech included public support for Dobie: "During great crises and struggles for human rights, many intellectuals get cold feet, and to warm them they climb into an ivory tower . . . They talk about 'spiritual' values. That's a form of hypocrisy that keeps them from fighting dirty battles, these bloody struggles, for racial justice and democracy."[29]

Other states offered a preview of what Sweatt could expect. Missouri, the first state faced with a Supreme Court order to provide a separate-but-equal opportunity for a black student (Lloyd Gaines), developed the blueprint for segregated states. Rather than admit Gaines to the University of Missouri Law School, politicians sought to forestall his entrance by creating makeshift graduate and professional schools at Lincoln University, the state's black university. Missouri bought $10,000 worth of books and spent about $75,000 to start a law school it claimed to be the equal of its flagship. In its first year, Lincoln University Law School enrolled thirty-four black students; that number fell as World War II progressed, and by 1944 the school had closed; it reopened in 1945 as black veterans returned from Europe. At the time of Sweatt's 1946 application, nineteen law-school students were enrolled at Lincoln.[30]

Indeed, after *Gaines,* Missouri changed Lincoln University from a small liberal arts college to a vehicle charged with meeting court rulings. Graduate programs appeared after the Missouri Legislature appropriated $200,000 for new departments.[31] Missouri's hurried establishment of a makeshift school and Gaines's mysterious disappearance delayed the NAACP's return to the Supreme Court for a judicial showdown over whether Missouri's response satisfied the mandate in *Gaines.*

In Oklahoma, only a month before Sweatt's meeting with Painter, a young black woman named Ada Lois Sipuel and her attorney, Amos T. Hall, had a similar meeting with the University of Oklahoma's president. Sipuel, an honor graduate of Langston College, applied for admission to the University of Oklahoma Law School. In her autobiography, Sipuel recalled that while rejecting her application, the president of the university, Dr. George Lynn Cross, "smiled as if to say, 'I'll give you anything you need to get into court.'"[32] Then he dictated an extraordinarily accommodating letter, citing the laws the NAACP would have to challenge and conceding that Sipuel was qualified in every way and was being denied admission solely because of her color.

In Oklahoma state district court in Cleveland County, Hall filed a writ of mandamus to compel university officials to admit her; it was denied. Thurgood Marshall joined Hall for arguments before the Oklahoma Supreme Court, but it affirmed the lower-court ruling. Eventually, the U.S. Supreme Court would rule in Sipuel's favor and remand the case to district court with instructions that Sipuel was entitled to an equal education within the state's borders (citing *Gaines*) and adding that it must be offered at the same time. What was instructive for Texas was that it was no secret that Oklahoma would respond to *Sipuel* as Missouri had responded to *Gaines:* in five days, Oklahoma created a makeshift law school at Langston College that was supposed to be "equal" to the fifty-year-old University of Oklahoma Law School.[33]

Little mystery existed about what was going to happen next in Oklahoma and Texas: Missouri's patently absurd attempt to set up in a few days Jim Crow professional schools equal to those of flagship universities, in order to serve a dozen or so Negro students, was spreading to other border and southern states, largely because Lloyd Gaines's disappearance had delayed a second appearance before the U.S. Supreme Court.

Texas and Oklahoma politicians were ready to exploit the issue for political gain. Sipuel later admitted, "From the very beginning I realized that resistance was coming primarily from certain elected officials, the legislature, and constitutions and laws of the state of Oklahoma."[34]

The Attorney General's Opinion

In September 2005, ninety-one-year-old former Texas Supreme Court chief justice Joe Greenhill, when asked what he remembered about Texas attorney general Grover Sellers, tilted his head, took a breath, and said, "Not real smart, but loveable."[35]

Sellers had become attorney general in 1944. He was a Democrat with ambitions to become governor. On February 27, 1946, when he received Painter's request for an opinion on Heman Sweatt's application, Sellers was winding down his two-year term as attorney general and gearing up for the Texas gubernatorial campaign of 1946.

On the home front in Texas, the end of World War II saw heated and bitter politics that crystallized divisions within the Democratic Party. It was a time of economic and social transfiguration: Texas was irretrievably moving from a rural to an urban state. During the governor's race of 1946, former UT president Homer Rainey emerged as the candidate of progressive Democrats. Attorney General Sellers's political base consisted entirely of anti–New Deal conservatives, sometimes called Texas Regulars.[36]

On March 16, 1946, Sellers released opinion O-7126, "Re: Whether a person of negro ancestry, otherwise qualified for admission into the University of Texas, may be legally admitted to that institution."[37] Its contents pleased his political base.

Sellers began with a summary of the facts: Heman Marion Sweatt was a citizen of Texas who was qualified for admission to the University of Texas Law School. Although he was a Negro, and although the Texas Constitution and statutes mandated segregation, Sweatt, citing *Missouri ex rel. Gaines v. Canada* (1938), argued that the education he sought was guaranteed to him and, further, that the education he sought was available nowhere else in Texas. In view of the apparent conflict between *Gaines* and Texas law, Painter wanted guidance on how to proceed with Sweatt's application. On page 2, Sellers inserted what would become infamous commentary: "The wise and long-continued policy of segregation of races in educational institutions of this State has prevailed since the abolition of slavery, and such policy is found incorporated not only in the Constitution of the State of Texas but also in numerous statutes. The constitutionality of such a policy and of laws in accord therewith has been repeatedly sustained" (parenthetical citations removed). He then cited *Gaines* as the "controlling case as to whether the policy of segregating races in Texas operates to 'abridge equal privileges and immunities of citizens of the United States.'"

Gaines, Sellers explained, unquestionably held that it was "the duty of a State to provide equal educational advantages within the State and that if such was not done it would constitute a discrimination in violation of the Constitution of the United States."

In the next paragraph he was more direct: "There is no doubt that if equal educational advantages are not provided for the applicant within the State, he must be admitted to the law school of the University of Texas." Sellers did not attempt to circumvent the mandatory duty of the state to provide equal educational opportunities for Texan African Americans. The state could do so in one of two ways: it could admit Sweatt to the University of Texas Law School, or it could provide for equal educational opportunity in a segregated setting. Sellers chose to focus on what Texas was not required to do: "It is not required, however, that the State maintain[,] in a condition of idleness and non-use[,] facilities to afford the applicant these advantages . . . The applicant is not deprived of any constitutional right until application has first been made to the proper authorities and the applicant's rights have been unlawfully refused" (parenthetical citations removed). In other words, the mandate of the state to provide separate-but-equal facilities, if it decided not to integrate its institutions, was not a duty until there was a demand for it. Sellers acknowledged that Sweatt provided the demand for a law school for African Americans in Texas, but he added: "The state is entitled to a reasonable notice that the facilities providing equal educational advantages are desired before its established policy of segregation is abrogated."

Sellers's "reasonable notice" logic meant that Sweatt's law-school education would have to wait until the state could establish the school for him. On its face, "reasonable notice" was a promise akin to the "when deemed practicable" condition for the establishment of a "colored" university (article VII, section 14 of the Texas Constitution of 1876). The difference, however, was that article VII was permissive, that is, the legislature did not have to do anything, whereas Heman Sweatt's application created a mandatory duty for Texas to act upon his request. To meet this mandatory duty, Sellers cited Senate Bill 228 of the Forty-ninth Legislature (1945), which, as Texas's good faith reaction to *Gaines*, changed Prairie View's name to "Prairie View University" and authorized it to teach any graduate- or professional-level course offered to whites at UT.

> *Whenever there is any demand for same*, the Board of Directors of [Texas A&M University], in addition to the courses of study now authorized for

said institution, is authorized to *provide for the establishment of courses in law, medicine, engineering, pharmacy, journalism, or any other generally recognized college course* taught at the University of Texas, in said Prairie View University, which courses shall be *substantially equivalent to those offered at the University of Texas.* (emphasis in the original)

Sellers added that although SB 228 had permissive language, "a direction contained in a statute, though couched in merely permissive language, will not be construed as leaving compliance optional." He continued:

All of the foregoing considered, it is concluded that the segregation of races in educational institutions in Texas may not be abrogated unless and until the applicant in good faith makes a demand for legal training at Prairie View University, gives the authorities reasonable notice, and is unlawfully refused.

Three weeks later, Sellers announced he was running for governor.[38]

Battle Lines Are Drawn

Immediately upon receipt of the attorney general's opinion, Theophilus Painter dictated a letter to Heman Sweatt and enclosed the transcripts Sweatt had submitted as his credentials for admission. Painter also enclosed a copy of the AG's opinion, adding, "This opinion is self-explanatory, and you will note that in accordance therewith it becomes necessary at this time to finally refuse your application to the Law School of the University of Texas." Painter had been made aware that William Durham was Sweatt's attorney, and he sent a copy of the letter to Durham's Dallas office.[39]

On March 17, 1946, the *Houston Post* reported that Sweatt was "bewildered" by Sellers's opinion. Reportedly, Sweatt had already "bought new shoes and a hat" and had packed to leave for Austin.[40] In fact, Sweatt and his supporters could hardly have been surprised at Sellers's action, since it was exactly what they had been planning for. Sellers's negative opinion was necessary for litigation to proceed. The opinion still elicited angry reactions from African American leaders in Texas. Sellers further enraged blacks when he announced that a "suitable law course could be set up [for Sweatt] in forty-eight hours."[41]

Two days after Sellers released his opinion, Sweatt penned a letter to Maceo Smith in which he described his reaction as "vomitous contempt." In a letter to William Durham, Carter Wesley added that "Sellers' opinion is as big a fraud as a competent lawyer could dare to make even in a state that has been given over to legal fiction and fraud through the years." In the next day's edition of the *Houston Informer,* Wesley blasted Sellers and described the opinion as "devious and contradictory."[42]

On February 26, 1946, Heman Sweatt's application to the University of Texas Law School jump-started competing legal machines. Governor Coke Stevenson's administration scrambled to create some semblance of the graduate- and professional-school opportunities that generations of African Americans had been pleading for and had been promised in the Texas Constitution. But the reactionary governor proceeded from a ridiculous and fatal flaw: he believed that African Americans would "settle" or even be grateful for his paltry offers. One Texas official is reputed to have said, "If a niggra wanted to study the law, all that was needed was one room, one professor, and one book."[43]

The pistons of the NAACP's legal machine fired as well. When he received his copy of Painter's rejection of Sweatt's application, William Durham contacted Maceo Smith and told him that now nothing stood in the way of filing a suit against the University of Texas. Grover Sellers commenced his defense of the State of Texas (and his campaign for governor) by assuring white supremacists that "Heman Sweatt will never darken the door of the University of Texas [so long as I am in office].[44]

Richard Sweatt. Heman Sweatt's grandfather was a former slave who had been moved during the Civil War from Tennessee to Ellis County, Texas. He was a blacksmith. Courtesy of Dr. James Leonard Sweatt III.

James Leonard Sweatt, Sr. Heman Sweatt's father was considered by friends and family to be a strong but fair man who demanded excellence from all of his children. Courtesy of Dr. James Leonard Sweatt III.

Heman Marion Sweatt with an unidentified little girl, c. 1917. Courtesy of Hemella L. Sweatt, MD.

Santa Rita No. 1, which was drilled on University of Texas lands in Reagan County, came in on May 28, 1923. The well proved that the area was rich in oil; revenue from it earned unimagined wealth for the Permanent University Fund. Prints and Photographs Collection, Santa Rita, Dolph Briscoe Center for American History, University of Texas at Austin (di-02265).

Heman Marion Sweatt as a young man, c. 1924. Courtesy of Hemella L. Sweatt, MD.

Heman Marion Sweatt as a graduate of Jack Yates High School, 1930. Courtesy of Hemella L. Sweatt, MD.

Clifton Richardson, Sr., the founder and editor of the *Houston Informer* and the *Houston Defender,* c. 1930. African American editors like Richardson, C. N. Love, and Carter Wesley supported the cause of equal citizenship rights in both their columns and news stories. Courtesy of the Defender Media Group.

Clifton Richardson, Jr., c. 1940. An eyewitness to Heman Marion Sweatt's initial confrontation with UT president Theophilus Painter, he later provided the most complete account of the historic meeting. Courtesy of the Defender Media Group.

Heman Marion Sweatt at about the time of his application to the UT Law School, 1946. Courtesy of Hemella L. Sweatt, MD.

Heman Marion Sweatt and his wife Connie Mitchell Sweatt at the time of his application to the UT Law School, 1946. Juanita Jewel Shanks Craft Collection, 1939–1948, Dolph Briscoe Center for American History, University of Texas at Austin (di-05059).

Left to right: Connie Sweatt, James Leonard Sweatt, Sr., Heman Marion Sweatt, and Ella Rose Sweatt at the time of Heman's application to the UT Law School, 1946. Prints and Photographs Collection, Heman Sweatt, Dolph Briscoe Center for American History, University of Texas at Austin (di-01642).

Newspaper publisher Carter Walker Wesley, *far right,* one of the most influential African Americans in Texas during the struggle for voting and educational rights, c. 1946. His heated arguments with Thurgood Marshall and other NAACP leaders were often personal and bitter, but he never wavered in his support for Heman Marion Sweatt's efforts to desegregate the UT Law School. Juanita Jewel Shanks Craft Collection, 1939–1948, Dolph Briscoe Center for American History, University of Texas at Austin (di-05058).

T. S. Painter, *left,* the acting president, and Dudley K. Woodward, the chairman of the University of Texas board of regents. Woodward directed the university's efforts to keep Sweatt out of the UT Law School. Prints and Photographs Collection, Theophilus S. Painter, Dolph Briscoe Center for American History, University of Texas at Austin (di-05061).

Heman Marion Sweatt testified that William Durham, *right,* was his attorney, but many lawyers worked on the *Sweatt* case, including Thurgood Marshall, *center,* of the NAACP. Photo by R. C. Hickman. R. C. Hickman Photographic Archive, Dolph Briscoe Center for American History, University of Texas at Austin (e_rch-0078).

Lawyers, including Thurgood Marshall, *far left,* C. B. Bunkley, *second from left,* William Durham, *third from left,* and Attorney General Price Daniel, *back to camera,* in a conference with Judge Roy Archer, *fourth from left,* during the trial of *Sweatt v. Painter* in the 126th District Court of Travis County, Texas, 1947. Juanita Jewel Shanks Craft Collection, 1939–1948, Dolph Briscoe Center for American History, University of Texas at Austin (di-05060).

Heman Marion Sweatt speaking at a rally, c. 1947. After applying to the University of Texas Law School, Sweatt became a popular speaker at gatherings in support of full citizenship rights for African Americans. Juanita Jewel Shanks Craft Collection, 1939–1948, Dolph Briscoe Center for American History, University of Texas at Austin (di-04794).

The 13th Street law school, derisively called the "basement school" by Thurgood Marshall. This picture shows that the entrance to the school was about four steps below street level. *Sweatt v. Painter* (1950), Relator's Exhibit 2.

Heman Marion Sweatt in line to register for the fall semester of 1950. He was not the only African American to enroll, but he received all the attention because the U.S. Supreme Court had ordered his admission. Prints and Photographs Collection, Heman Sweatt, Dolph Briscoe Center for American History, University of Texas at Austin (di-01127).

Thurgood Marshall arriving at Love Field in Dallas, c. 1950, for one of his many court appearances to litigate for voting rights and access to public schools for African Americans in Texas. Photo by R. C. Hickman. R. C. Hickman Photographic Archive, Dolph Briscoe Center for American History, University of Texas at Austin (e_rch-0167).

A. Maceo Smith, the organizational genius behind a number of African American civic and civil rights organizations, c. 1955. Photo by R. C. Hickman. R. C. Hickman Photographic Archive, Dolph Briscoe Center for American History, University of Texas at Austin (e_rch-0348).

Heman Marion Sweatt with his family at their home in Atlanta, Georgia, c. 1970. Courtesy of Hemella L. Sweatt, MD.

Heman Marion Sweatt as a guest of the University of Texas Law School, October 1974. He made several appearances, including an informal session with more than a hundred students. Prints and Photographs Collection, Heman Sweatt, Dolph Briscoe Center for American History, University of Texas at Austin (di-01641).

CHAPTER 10

"Time Is of the Essence"

Let's not be stampeded by social reformers from the North and East. The Sweatt case is nothing but a guinea pig case sponsored by those who wish to break down our southern laws.

STATE REPRESENTATIVE EUGENE MILLER (D-WEATHERFORD), ON THE FLOOR OF THE TEXAS HOUSE OF REPRESENTATIVES, FEBRUARY 1947

In June 1945, eight months before Heman Sweatt's application, Marshall sent a memo to Maceo Smith making it clear that the NAACP was to lead all efforts to integrate the University of Texas. Carter Wesley found such exclusivity patronizing and demeaning. Efforts to avoid open warfare between the two hardheaded men vanished on September 3, 1946, when Carter Wesley's Southern Negro Conference for Equal Educational Opportunities (SNCEEO) released an open letter addressed to "Friend" and sent it to what was apparently an NAACP-generated list.

The letter unveiled a new fight for the equalization of educational facilities and opportunities and was signed by Wesley as president of the SNCEEO and Maceo Smith as president of the Texas Council of Negro Organizations. The letter specifically stated that the SNCEEO would involve itself in cases the "NAACP is not likely to want to work in."[1] The announcement was consistent with Wesley's passionate belief that the struggle for black citizenship rights should include equalization and integration and should be fought simultaneously "on every front." When Lulu White received the letter, she exploded in anger and sent the flier and a handwritten note to Walter White at the NAACP's New York headquarters.

Walter:
Read this d—— thing. We do not need any other kind of organization in Texas. I need help down here. The Texas Council of Negro Organiza-

tions is enough. If the NAACP is spearheading this case why have any other organization to compromise over? Maceo is bound to have an organization to accept the segregated college for Negroes. The same people are members and working with the NAACP. Then Maceo and Carter call them to form some kind of an organization to make plans for a separate university. I may be wrong Walter, but this is nothing but a sellout set back to us. . . . I know full well it is Maceo's idea."[2]

The philosophical feud between the equalization and integration factions might not have been so heated if it had been limited to angry letters over long distances between Marshall and Wesley. Instead, it involved the always-volatile Lulu White and Wesley's *Houston Informer*.

In October 1946, Marshall tried to impress upon Wesley how serious he was about the threat the SNCEEO posed to the NAACP: "This letter is not only marked 'Personal', but is considered 'Personal' and for once, I am serious." He argued that if the SNCEEO went against the advice of the NAACP, then it would be considered a competing organization. "The problem of temporary segregation or a little segregation is much like a woman being a little pregnant . . . The Negroes in Texas will most certainly end up in two divided camps, and I do not believe it is possible to be in both camps at the same time." Marshall concluded with a sentence that became his mantra: "It is one thing to 'take' segregation that is forced upon you and it is another thing to ask for segregation."[3]

The low point came in a December 23, 1946, letter to Marshall in which Wesley characterized Marshall's insistence that the NAACP maintain complete control over Texas segregation cases as a "stupid idea." He called Marshall a "stupid man" and said that the NAACP could "go to hell," adding in a postscript: "You damned ingrate, who the hell do you think it was that insisted that the NAACP lawyers be called in before the petition was filed in the Smith Case?" Wesley also indicated that he could have said more, but he "refrained from expressing [himself] on the dumbness of Lulu White."[4]

Carter Wesley refused to concede control of African American activism in Texas to the hegemony of the NAACP. The Wesley-Marshall feud was a battle for the hearts and minds of the African American community in Texas, specifically its intelligentsia and professional class.

Thurgood Marshall and Walter White were justifiably concerned about making an enemy of Wesley, who distributed more newspapers than any other black man in Texas. Almost immediately, Walter White wrote Wesley: "To say that I am surprised [by your letter's] tone and content is about as mild a statement as I can make without running afoul of the postal laws . . .

We expect such attacks from Bilbo [Theodore Bilbo, a racist and reactionary U.S. senator from Mississippi], not from one of our own."[5]

On the same day Walter White sent his letter to Wesley, Marshall sent a letter that easily matched Wesley's for anger and venom. Marshall said that Wesley's letter had "narrowness that is unbelievable." Then he hit Wesley where it hurt: "If you want to know what I think about it, I think *Grovey v. Townshend* was not only one of the biggest mistakes made in the fight for Negroes' rights, but it set the fight against primary elections back at least fifteen years."[6]

As the *Sweatt* case worked its way through Texas courts and Marshall and Wesley exchanged postal barbs, Wesley also attacked Lulu White and the NAACP in the *Houston Informer,* accusing them, among other things, of having communist sympathies. On December 29, 1946, Lulu White called Walter White to complain. Walter White described his conversation with her in a memo to Marshall the next day: "Lulu White telephoned me (collect) from Houston yesterday morning saying Julius insists that she resign because Carter Wesley and Maceo Smith are making the fight a personal one."[7] In a letter to John Jay Jones, the president of the Texas State Conference of NAACP Branches, Wesley indicated that he knew that Lulu White's anxiety came as much from her husband, Julius, as from her public feuding. Lulu White would not run away from a fight, Wesley confided; it was Julius—"he can't handle criticism of his wife."[8]

At the end of 1946, Lulu White submitted a letter of resignation from her position and membership in the Houston branch of the NAACP. Rather than accept her resignation, the branch's board set up a meeting, during which Lulu White cited letters to Marshall and articles by Wesley as the reasons for her resignation. According to Wesley, "Attorney Herman Wright (a liberal, white activist lawyer from Houston) got up immediately after the reading of her letter and made an impassioned attack on me, and went so far as to say that he thought that I should apologize to Mrs. White. I spoke immediately after him . . . and he scrambled over himself to change positions . . . I will whip Thurgood's ears off, the same as I whipped Wright's ears off Tuesday night."[9] Wesley added that Lulu and that "long-headed Thurgood" wanted exclusiveness that he would never accept: "I am afraid the matter has gone too far now for any attempt at compromise."[10]

Marshall claimed that the integrationists he represented were better at getting equal facilities in a shorter period of time than the equalization crowd.[11] Indeed, as the two men exchanged letters, southern states were scrambling to build new schools for blacks and to increase funding for existing "Negro colleges"—not because of an altruistic awakening to the virtue of equalization, but because those states did not want to integrate white institutions.

Throughout the rest of January 1947, the Marshall-Wesley quarrel continued, and more and more people learned of the verbal warfare. Wesley seemed obsessed with upsetting Marshall. "You are a plain coward, and you show yourself to be a man of little ability and of little mentality," he wrote on January 18, 1947, the day after he had submitted a letter of resignation from the local, state, and national NAACP. His farewell included an explanation of his position on separate equality and a long description of a meeting in which he and Lulu White had descended into a bitter argument. He complained that he had been slandered and that communists had infiltrated the Houston NAACP branch.[12]

On January 28, Wesley attacked Marshall again: "I acknowledge receipt of your letter of January 22. It completes the picture of your mental shallowness, and your bankruptcy in integrity." Later in the same letter, Wesley may have inadvertently revealed his real problem with Marshall: the apparent snubbing of William J. Durham in the litigation ending the white primary. When Marshall, William Hastie, and Durham appeared together to argue the case before the U.S. Supreme Court, Durham stood ready to address issues of Texas law, but never spoke. "I still have not forgiven you for what you did to Durham in the *Smith* case."[13]

Of course, Wesley's resignation from the NAACP did not mean he was going away. By the end of January, James Nabrit, Jr., a lawyer and friend of both Marshall and Wesley, tried to mediate a truce by suggesting that they "sit down and battle it out among themselves." In May, Maceo Smith wrote to Marshall that he [Smith] had "had a talk with Carter Wesley a few days ago and he is 'almost' convinced that he was off on a tangent."[14] That was about as far as Wesley would go toward admitting a mistake or showing remorse for anything.

The Carter Wesley–Lulu White–Thurgood Marshall feud was more than just a sometimes-entertaining argument between intelligent, albeit egotistical and stubborn, people. The bitter division destroys the notion that the civil rights movement was fomented by "outsiders" who manipulated the African American population in the South. Many white southern reactionaries wanted badly to believe that the "Negro problem" came from a new generation of carpetbaggers determined to end the peaceful coexistence of the races in the South: agitators who caused trouble by stirring up susceptible southern blacks, who would otherwise have been content to leave well enough alone. Far from controlling the African American population in Texas, the national association, especially Marshall, had to fight hard to maintain the support of Texas NAACP branches—the most troublesome of which, by far, was the Houston branch.

Apparently at the direction of Walter White, Gloster Current, the new director of Branch and Field Services at the NAACP's national office, looked into the infighting in Texas. In his report, Current described three factions: Carter Wesley's adherents, who wanted full citizenship and access by equalizing schools that blacks would control; Lulu White's followers, including Heman Sweatt, who wanted to immediately desegregate white institutions, beginning with the University of Texas; and Maceo Smith, who seemed to straddle "both sides of the fence."[15] Current could have added that outside the NAACP were conservative black school officials and other state and county employees who held positions controlled by white school boards and county commissioners. This group limited their activism to lobbying for improvements to the newly renamed Prairie View University.[16]

For the rest of 1947, Carter Wesley used letters, meetings, and the *Houston Informer* to pound Lulu White and Thurgood Marshall. In justifying his position on the need for equalization before integration, Wesley wrote: "Mrs. White and the NAACP are in a separate Negro Building. They are separated in the buses. Their children or their relatives go to separate schools. They attend separate churches. They play in separate parks. Even on the streets they walk separately and stay separated. Despite these facts Mrs. White stubbornly refuses to recognize that we live in a separated world in Houston and in Texas. If she were not so stubbornly dense, she would realize that inasmuch as we are separated, we should demand our right to equality."[17] Marshall and Wesley exchanged malevolent letters through all of 1947. For Walter White, it was tiresome: "Don't Texans ever write short letters?"[18]

By October, Marshall was accusing Wesley of being an "unmitigated liar." At the end of the year, Marshall gave up and invoked a merciful end to his and Wesley's bickering: "I note that you are right back where you started," Marshall wrote, "and I can see no need on my part to continue this correspondence."[19] But in one form or another, the fighting would continue until Lulu White's death in 1957.[20]

Opening Salvos

In the late 1940s, the only issue that seemed to consistently unite the Texas NAACP was the cause of Heman Marion Sweatt. By the end of 1946, the *Sweatt* case had evolved from an attempt to establish separate graduate- and professional-education programs for African American Texans, as R. A. Hester had demanded during the February 1946 meeting with UT president Painter, into a direct attack on segregation. All sides believed the case would bring benefits. Marshall thought Texas would find it impossible to provide a law school for blacks that would be taken seriously; Texas would eventually buckle under the expense of duplicating everything and be forced to integrate. Wesley saw Texas's answer to *Sweatt*, the establishment of a new university for African Americans, as an exciting opportunity to build stronger black-controlled institutions—integration could come later. Even accommodationists like W. R. Banks saw immediate improvements taking place at Prairie View.

When it seemed evident that Texas would follow in the footsteps of Missouri and Oklahoma and create a makeshift Jim Crow law school, Marshall called a meeting of high-powered civil rights lawyers in Atlanta on April 27 and 28, 1946, for an evaluation of legal strategy. The group, which apparently did not include any attorneys from Texas, decided that forcing integration by making equalization too expensive was not working—at least not fast enough. Using equalization to achieve integration had resulted only in delays as states created makeshift Jim Crow schools. Every makeshift school in every state would have to be sued for being unequal, and popularly elected state district judges could be counted on to rule that the makeshifts met constitutional requirements.

In his memoirs, Robert Carter, Marshall's young associate at the NAACP, recalled that during the Atlanta conference, the group agreed that cases for law-school admission in Oklahoma and Tennessee should be "vigorously pursued," and litigation in Louisiana and South Carolina would be filed immediately. Litigation in Texas was a "possibility."[21]

Three weeks later, on May 16, 1946, about three months after his visit to UT, Heman Marion Sweatt filed suit against Theophilus S. Painter in the 126th District Court in Austin, Travis County, Texas.

Responses to *Gaines*

The University of Texas had considered the creation of a law school for African Americans as early as 1941, when Charles T. McCormick, the dean of UT Law, asked one of his faculty members, George Wilfred Stumberg, to look into how Texas should respond to the *Gaines* ruling of 1938.[22]

Stumberg wrote to flagship law schools in each of the southern and border states and found that the responses to *Gaines* varied. Arkansas and Kentucky received applications from African Americans, but their college credits were found to be deficient. In South Carolina, the law school referred the matter of a black applicant to its board of trustees, which appointed a special committee to study the question. The committee asked the law-school faculty to draft a bill authorizing and requiring the Normal College of South Carolina, a black institution, to establish a law school. The bill passed the state's House of Representatives but was amended to death in the Senate. Without enabling legislation for a black law school, the dean turned to persons he considered "colored leaders," who in turn "persuaded" the applicant to withdraw.[23] By 1947, however, South Carolina was back in federal court. The court ruled that South Carolina could do one of three things: admit the applicant, John H. Wrighten, to the white law school; set up a new law school for African Americans; or close the white law school.[24]

In Louisiana, two black students inquired about law-school admission. Acting dean Ira Flory reported that he handled the matter by "persuading the applicants that entry was impossible at this time." But he added that such persuasion would not work forever. He betrayed frustration by indicating to Stumberg that no one at Louisiana State University was willing to address the problem until it "becomes absolutely necessary."[25]

Applicants for admission to the University of Florida Law School who had not done their undergraduate work at the University of Florida (a segregated institution) had to demonstrate their readiness for law-school work by passing scholastic and legal aptitude tests. In Tennessee, black applicants went to court to require the University of Tennessee to enroll them as students in the graduate and law schools. The Tennessee Legislature responded with an act creating a branch of the University of Tennessee Law School for African Americans. The suit was then dismissed by the Tennessee courts as being moot.[26]

Stumberg identified North Carolina as the state that had done the most to address the *Gaines* ruling. A school of law had been set up at the North Carolina College for Negroes at Durham. The dean of the University of North Carolina School of Law served as the dean for the new Negro law school, and the teaching staff was made up of men who were part of the faculty of the University of North Carolina. By the end of the year, North Carolina had spent $10,600 on five students, two of whom could not return because of academic problems.[27] To keep the Jim Crow school running, North Carolina faced the prospect of spending even more money on three second-year law students and another entering class of five to ten students.

Two states did not exercise the option of creating separate Jim Crow schools. Arkansas and West Virginia could not afford to create the "Negro schools," and so admitted African Americans to whites-only graduate and law schools in 1948 and 1940, respectively.[28]

Five years before Heman Sweatt submitted his application, George W. Stumberg foresaw a day of reckoning for Texas: "In the long run southern schools will have to provide equal separate facilities for higher education or, of course, in the alternative have to admit negroes to schools furnishing instruction to whites."[29] In retrospect, it seems remarkable that Texas could ignore a decision like *Gaines* for as long as it did. From 1938 to 1946, Texas fiddled with biracial commissions, regental resolutions, university name changes, statements by university presidents, and a lot of other talk.

Then Heman Marion Sweatt changed everything.

Sweatt Files Suit and Sellers Replies

On the day Sweatt filed suit in the 126th District Court in Travis County, Texas, William Durham sent a telegram to Thurgood Marshall: "Sweatt case filed District Court Travis County Austin, Texas today. Will notify tomorrow of date of hearing."[30]

Two days later, on May 18, the 126th District Court served Painter with a citation informing him that Sweatt had filed suit against him, Charles T. McCormick, E. J. Matthews, and each member of the University of Texas board of regents. Painter, Matthews, and McCormick consulted the regents, and all decided to retain the attorney general to answer Sweatt's application for a writ of mandamus. Painter's formal request went to Grover Sellers on May 20, 1946.[31]

Reaction to Sweatt's petition by top Texas political officials was swift and pointed: if Sweatt wanted a law school, Texas would set one up for him. Sellers announced that a "suitable law curriculum" could be set up at Prairie View in two days. Governor Coke Stevenson was even more delusional: all that Sweatt's training required, the governor said, was one good lawyer, one set of encyclopedias, and one set of *Texas Statutes*.[32] Neither the press nor anyone in the legislature asked Stevenson why, if that was all Sweatt needed, there was a premier law school at the University of Texas with a library stocked with thousands of books and dozens of first-rate faculty members.

President Painter, Dean McCormick, and Registrar Matthews made no public comment.

Public reaction to Sweatt's application varied from complete support— "For three years I was on active duty with the United States Navy . . . in an effort to rid the world of bigotry and racial intolerance"—to complete hatred: "If that [n——] is allowed to enter the University of Texas just consider me no longer an ex-student of the University of Texas."[33]

In his petition for a writ of mandamus to compel his admission, Sweatt swore that he "was arbitrarily and illegally rejected pursuant to a policy, custom or usage denying qualified Negro applicants equal protection of the laws, solely on the ground of his race and color."[34]

A May 18, 1946, *Dallas Morning News* article entitled "Prairie View Negro's Place" repeated Governor Stevenson's promise to make funds available to Prairie View through a deficiency appropriation if Heman Sweatt were to request instruction "in good faith" there.[35] Stevenson made no attempt to estimate how much money it would take to fund the law school he had in mind for Sweatt, but if he truly believed that a law school curriculum need consist only of a copy of *Texas Statutes*, a set of encyclopedias, and a "good lawyer," it could not have been much. Clearly, it was Stevenson who was not acting in good faith. Two weeks earlier, the *Dallas Morning News* had run an editorial entitled "He Wants to Be a Lawyer," which stated: "But when Heman Marion Sweatt is an old man, he may have learned that a litigant can win a suit and lose a cause."[36]

The reality was that Sweatt was already winning. Soon after he applied to law school, the January 20, 1946, plan that had been announced by the boards of UT and Texas A&M—the blueprint for which Painter admitted "practically nothing" had been done—was put into high gear. Before the end of the next summer, Henry Allen Bullock reported in the *Journal of Negro Education* that "in a few short months a legal suit secured for Negroes and their education an amount equal to one-half of all the money appropriated for Negro education over a third of a century."[37]

The rush to create and fund Negro education where none had existed before confirmed Sweatt's revolutionary beliefs. In a letter to Lulu White, the introverted mailman the *Daily Texan* described as a "devout young Christian" wrote: "We have come as far as we have only because we have chosen the RADICAL method—RADICAL."[38]

Dudley Kezer Woodward, Jr., chairman of the UT board of regents when Sweatt filed his lawsuit, was a UT alumnus who had been president of the senior class and editor of the *Cactus* yearbook at the time of his graduation. From UT, he went to the University of Chicago Law School, graduating in 1908. In November 1944, he had been appointed to the regents at the height of the "big fight" with President Homer Rainey.[39]

Woodward was a dignified-looking man with a shock of white hair and wire-rimmed spectacles. He had been an attorney in powerful law firms for about fifty years, and he knew what elements made for a good law school. As the first district-court hearing of *Sweatt v. Painter* drew near, Woodward denied reports that he and President Painter had discussed plans to establish a "special school for Negroes" in Austin. A few days earlier, on June 6, 1946, he and Painter had been spotted in Houston, reportedly scouting locations for the establishment of a Negro university, including a law school for Heman Sweatt. When confronted with the reports, Woodward replied that the stories were "exaggerated." He added that he, Painter, and other state and university officials were addressing matters "on which there would be no statement at this time."[40] Rumors circulated that Houston was the logical choice for the new law school for Negroes since it had a large African American population with many lawyers and was accessible to both state and federal courts.[41]

African American leaders in Texas also suggested, publicly and privately, that the establishment of a new, properly funded and staffed segregated black university could be an acceptable alternative to integrating the University of Texas. On June 14, Heman Sweatt gave and signed a deposition in Houston in which he indicated that he would attend a separate law school if it were the equivalent to UT Law.[42] In a letter to the editor of the *Austin American,* Bishop College president Joseph Rhoads wrote:

> Negro leaders in Texas are virtually unanimous in the conviction that Prairie View should be retained as an A&M College of the highest possible rank and that such an achievement will necessitate, among other things, the divorcement of its administration and control from the institution for whites at College Station. Too, they are equally convinced that a separate accredited state university should be established as speedily as is consistent with sound educational procedure, in an urban community that will make easily accessible the co-operation and resources required for graduate and professional study, observation, practice, and research.[43]

To white political and educational leaders like Sellers and Woodward, Rhoads seemed to be suggesting that acceptable segregation was possible and that the state should be granted a reasonable amount of time to thoughtfully establish new black institutions. In less than a year, that is, after the NAACP made a firm commitment to abandon equalization and begin a frontal attack on segregation, Rhoads would completely change his position.[44]

Indeed, Sweatt's application brought about a number of remarkable comments and position changes. On May 24, 1946, the *Dallas Morning News* editorialized that "Texas owes its Negro population an opportunity for the same type of higher education offered other races. That is simple justice and plain duty, not merely a constitutional matter. That opportunity is not now provided." But like Rhoads, within a year the newspaper changed position.[45]

By June 15, 1946, Attorney General Sellers had filed an answer to Sweatt's petition for a writ of mandamus. The state argued that the petition was "improperly and prematurely" filed and that it should have been directed against the Texas A&M board of regents. Under Texas law, it was Texas A&M's responsibility, as the "guardian" of Prairie View A&M, to provide the legal training Sweatt had requested—not the University of Texas and its officials. Sellers also answered that the State of Texas had provided for separation of the white and Negro races in educational institutions, including institutions of higher learning, since 1845. Such provisions for segregation were still both statutory and contained in the Texas Constitution of 1876.[46]

The First Day in Court

The first hearing of *Sweatt v. Painter* took place in the Travis County Courthouse on Guadalupe Street, between 10th and 11th Streets, just west of the Texas Capitol. The 126th District Court was located on the fourth floor.[47]

On Monday morning, June 17, 1946, Judge Roy C. Archer called the court to order. Archer was later described by a former Texas chief justice as "reasonably smart, but totally political."[48] Judge Archer knew he was going to rule against Sweatt, and so did everyone else. Dudley Woodward and T. S. Painter were present for part of the proceedings, but when it became apparent that much of the day would be spent haggling over legal points and stipulations, the men left and did not return—not even for Archer's ruling.

During the afternoon session, the attorneys built a record with extensive stipulations of fact. Most significant was that Heman Sweatt, as a graduate of Wiley College and a postgraduate student at the University of Michigan, was fully qualified scholastically to be a first-year law student—as President Painter had acknowledged in his request for an attorney general's opinion on February 26. The state also conceded that Sweatt was denied admission "solely on account of his race and color" and that there has never been a state-supported law school for African Americans. Sweatt was denied access to the University of Texas Law School because state law required the segregation of the white and colored races in schools. Sweatt's lawyers conceded that Senate Bill 228 of the most recent Texas Legislature authorized the board of directors of Texas A&M to establish a law school for Negroes and that there was $125,000 available for that purpose. By the end of the day, African Americans made up about two-thirds of the courtroom crowd. Judge Archer was ready to announce his decision, which came almost immediately after the arguments concluded.[49]

Archer acknowledged Sweatt's qualifications to attend the law school and found that his civil rights had been violated because the state had denied him the opportunity to gain a legal education while granting it to others (whites). This state action deprived Sweatt of the equal protection of the laws guaranteed by the Fourteenth Amendment. Archer also cited Senate Bill 228, noting that it

> places a mandatory duty . . . to provide university courses in law for [Sweatt] substantially equivalent to those provided at the University of Texas; *and that the constitutional rights of the relator* [Sweatt] *will be amply preserved if such a course in law is established within the State of Texas and made available to relator within a reasonable time from the date hereof.* (citations omitted; emphasis added)

The ruling went on:

> It is therefore ordered that no writ of mandamus issue at this time and that if within six months from the date hereof a course for legal instruction substantially equivalent to that offered at the University of Texas is established and made available to [Sweatt] within the State of Texas in an educational institution supported by said State, the writ of mandamus sought herein will be denied, but if such a course of legal instruction is not so established and made available, the writ of mandamus will issue; and it is further ordered that this court retains jurisdiction of this cause; and that this cause be continued upon the docket of this court from term to term; and that at the expiration of said six months period, to wit, on the 17th day of December, 1946, at 10 o'clock a.m. a hearing will be held to determine the then existing facts and whether said Law School has or has not been established; whereupon the Court will enter its final order herein.[50]

After adjournment, most of the African Americans in the gallery crowded to the rail to congratulate and shake William Durham's hand. Durham publicly thanked Judge Archer and stated that the decision was "extremely fair and impartial."[51] Durham could afford to be magnanimous; he knew that the hearing was merely an exercise in building a record for an eventual appearance before the only court that mattered—the U.S. Supreme Court.

Heman Sweatt continued to make fictitious public comments that the hearing and whatever was to come were the result of his independent desire to enter a law school.[52]

Even Coke Stevenson understood that between June 17 and December 17, 1946, he was going to have to come up with much more than just a book of *Texas Statutes*, a set of encyclopedias, and a good lawyer.

CHAPTER 11

"The Tenderest Feeling"

It is a loyalty to fallacies and prejudices, not loyalty to constitutional and Christian principles of justice.

J. FRANK DOBIE, IN A SPEECH ON RACIAL SEGREGATION, DECEMBER 16, 1946

In August 1876, the State of Texas established an agricultural and mechanical college for its African American students. But from that date until the day Heman Sweatt applied to the University of Texas Law School, progress toward higher education for African Americans was no more than a story of an occasional group, committee, or biracial commission appointed to study educational injustices and empowered to do nothing. Generations and decades passed without any significant funding for higher education for Texas blacks.

But after February 26, 1946, the Special Joint Committee on Higher Education for Negroes in Texas, the latest version of the commissions that had done "practically nothing," came alive. By July 5, 1946, the group had issued a recommendation that Prairie View become a full-fledged agricultural and mechanical college and that for all other instruction, the state establish a "first-class university for Negroes." The report suggested that the new university be located in Houston and supervised by the UT regents.[1]

The report also resulted in a resolution appearing as an agenda item entitled "Higher Education for Negroes in Texas" at the joint meeting of the UT and Texas A&M governing boards in Corpus Christi on July 13, 1946. Not surprisingly, the boards of the two universities with access to the Permanent University Fund recommended in the resolution that the new black university not be designated a constitutional university, which would exclude it from sharing in the proceeds of the Available University Fund. The boards also petitioned Governor Coke Stevenson to appoint a biracial committee to detail plans for the construction of the schools.[2]

It took Governor Stevenson less than five days to appoint seven men to the biracial committee. Mark McGee, of Fort Worth, served as chair. The black members were W. R. Banks, the longtime principal of Prairie View, and Dr. M. L. Edwards, a physician from the small East Texas town of Hawkins.[3] The group met on July 25, only one week after their appointment, and voted to hold public hearings on August 8 at the Texas Capitol. On July 26, Maceo Smith of the Texas Council of Negro Organizations contacted the "Negro Leaders in Texas" to prepare for the hearings. Eighty-three members of the council met on August 3 and developed a presentation for the biracial committee. In a letter to Robert Carter at the NAACP, Smith stated that the August 3 meeting was not an NAACP event and that the group had selected Joseph Rhoads of Bishop College and Carter Wesley to present the position of the council at the August 8 hearing.[4]

President Painter's planned testimony parroted a plan developed by D. K. Woodward, the chairman of the board of regents, which would establish a Negro university through legislative statute and pay for it through state appropriation, rather than through the $60 million PUF. As if to claim an endorsement, Painter recalled that when he asked the Sweatt delegation whether there was any agreement among African American Texans about what educational facilities they wanted, he was told that Prairie View should become the "Negro A&M" and that "a real Negro university [should] be established in some urban center."[5]

Shortly before the first meeting of the biracial committee, Dr. Edwards argued that African Americans were "most concerned with whether the new institution will have high standards." Perhaps he envisioned another Howard or Fisk, or another Meharry Medical College (like Fisk, a premier black institution in Nashville). Such an institution could have a major impact on the supply of medical professionals serving African Americans, not only in Texas but throughout the South.

The much-anticipated public hearing opened on Thursday, August 8, 1946, at ten in the House Chamber of the Texas Capitol. About 350 African Americans filled the galleries to hear Governor Stevenson open the meeting with a prepared statement. To the surprise of many, Stevenson stayed for the two-hour hearing and listened intently while UT president Painter presented his views. The commission heard testimony that establishing a first-class university for Texas Negroes would cost approximately $6,500,000 and that if the money came from the Available University Fund, only $3,200,000 would be left for UT and Texas A&M to share.

Joseph Rhoads and Carter Wesley stunned the audience when they rejected the offer of a statutory university and demanded a constitutional branch of the University of Texas. Rhoads invoked article VII of the Texas Constitution of 1876, which enabled the establishment of a "branch university for the colored" of the state. "In the scope and quality of its offerings, facilities, faculties, and other essential services," Rhoads said, "a Branch University . . . must be the equivalent of all other units of the university system; otherwise, as a device for racial segregation, it will fall short of its purpose in its inception."[6]

Maceo Smith called the meeting a "spectacle, long to be remembered," and marveled at the unity the Texas African American leadership exhibited in the preparation and delivery of the position taken by the Texas Council of Negro Organizations.[7]

The thrill of such a successful presentation, planned and developed in Texas by Texans, resulted in a new spirit of confidence and independence from the NAACP's national office. Two weeks later, Maceo Smith sent a telegram to Robert Carter in New York, warning him that the Houston NAACP was on the verge of filing its own equalization suit. Carter immediately sent a pointed telegram to the president of the Houston Chapter, the Reverend A. A. Lucas, telling him that if the Houston NAACP filed its own suit, it could endanger the association's national campaign. (Thurgood Marshall had been on medical leave, and Carter undoubtedly saw the ghost of *Grovey v. Townshend*.) He more or less ordered Lucas not to proceed with any suit unless it had been reviewed by the national office.[8]

There was no surprise about what the biracial committee would ultimately recommend to the governor and legislature: the plan Dudley Woodward and others were developing to upgrade Prairie View and create a new Negro university in Houston was fairly well known, and had been reported in newspapers as early as June 20. Texas A&M president Gibb Gilchrist was already publicly explaining that Houston was the best location for the new university because it had Negro hospitals, trained medical personnel, and other Negro professionals. He also added that one-ninth of all African Americans in Texas lived in or near that metro area and that there were many job opportunities for ambitious students hoping to work their way through college.[9]

Houston also seemed ideal for another reason: the Houston College for Negroes (HCN). The origin of HCN dated back to 1925, when a Wiley College professor named J. T. Fox offered extension courses at what was called the "Old Colored High School." One year later, Jack Yates High School opened its doors, and in 1927 the success of the extension courses led to the use of Yates's new campus as the home of what was called the Houston Colored Junior College. By 1934, the Houston Independent School District decided that the institution could sufficiently support itself to pay rent, and the name was changed to the Houston College for Negroes.[10]

In 1944, HCN's administrators presented a plan for expansion that included a move to a newly purchased fifty-three-acre site on Cleburne Avenue. In 1946, HCN moved into Fairchild Hall, the only completed permanent structure on the campus. The site also housed a number of temporary buildings, including a vocational building and an industrial-arts shop to educate and produce artisans and skilled workers. Its vocational mission was very much what Booker T. Washington had advocated decades earlier.[11]

Juanita Craft and the Austin NAACP Branch

Austin, Texas, should have been an ideal location for an active branch of the NAACP. It was the home of two private black colleges, Tillotson College and Samuel Huston College, which meant that there was a supply of energetic, passionate, and educated young-adult African American students. Austin was also a city large enough to have an African American professional class, which served about 21,000 blacks living mostly in east Austin. Four black dentists and four doctors practiced medicine. There was only one lawyer, Kenneth Lampkin, but in all of Texas there were only twenty-three black attorneys. East Austin also had a healthy supply of black churches: sixty-six preachers served in thirty-six Christian churches, about half of which were Baptist. One of the largest was the Ebenezer Baptist Church, located high atop an area of the city called Robertson Hill. The congregation had been founded in 1875, and by the late 1940s and early 1950s, Pastor Robert L. Lowe and his flock were on the verge of constructing a new sanctuary costing an estimated $250,000.[12] (The building still towers over the city.)

Austin was also the home of the University of Texas and the state capital, which was populated by Texans from all parts of the state, not just the eastern counties of the former Confederacy. At the time, UT had an enrollment of more than 17,000 students, plus faculty and staff, from all over the world.[13] As the Heman Sweatt saga played out, it became evident that the Austin chapter of the NAACP was not as active as it should have been and that valuable human capital was not being used.

Despite its inactive NAACP chapter, Thurgood Marshall and Robert Carter were said to be surprised at the attitude and openness of Austin in 1946. In December, after meeting a group of UT students, Marshall was moved to write that he "believed that the best weapon we have to destroy segregation is the fairmindedness of the average young person in this country."[14] Two years later, UT polls indicated that nearly six in ten students approved of the desegregation of their campus, especially the graduate and professional schools.[15]

Shortly after Heman Sweatt's court appearance in June 1946, it became evident that the NAACP needed an active and powerful Austin chapter. Marshall had never expected Judge Archer to order Sweatt's enrollment in UT Law, so he knew that he and his entourage would be back in Austin for at least one more hearing in the 126th District Court. The NAACP branch in Austin needed to be functional because the 126th District Court, the State Court of Civil Appeals for the Third Supreme Judicial District, and the Texas Supreme Court were all located there.

The challenge of reviving the Austin NAACP Chapter fell to an activist from Dallas named Juanita Craft, who had first attracted the attention of the NAACP during the white-primary fight. She knew Austin. She was born in 1902 only a few miles north in a small town along the Chisholm Trail called Round Rock. In 1935, she joined the Dallas branch of the NAACP, and in 1944 she became the first black woman to cast a ballot in Dallas County. Two years later, she became a field organizer of the NAACP's Texas State Conference of Branches, a new job that, in April 1946, presented her with her first big challenge—reviving the Austin branch.[16]

Craft's success in Austin was due in large part to the emergence of James H. Morton as an NAACP leader. Morton, affectionately known as "Little Doc," was a chemistry professor at Samuel Huston College and had been a colleague of Melvin Tolson at Wiley College. While at Wiley, he had taught Heman Sweatt. From Wiley, Morton went to the University of Chicago, where he earned a master of science degree.[17]

James Morton was elected president of the Austin NAACP branch on November 15, 1946. Only three days later, he and Kenneth Lampkin attended a meeting of UT student organizations. University officials, apparently after being alerted that fund-raising was planned, warned the organizers that such activities were barred from campus; the meeting was moved across Guadalupe Street to the YMCA building. Sixty students from seventeen campus organizations attended a two-and-a-half-hour meeting presided over by a student named John Stanford, Jr.[18] The *Dallas Morning News* reported that it was the "first time in history that a group of students at the university, in a public meeting, had endorsed the principle of admitting Negroes to the school."[19]

Morton explained in a "slow and distinct" voice what the general objectives of the NAACP were and how the Austin branch intended to become involved in Heman Sweatt's case. He emphasized that the overall goal was to secure the constitutional rights of African Americans in the United States. The NAACP intended to do that in three ways: equalizing the salaries of black teachers to those of whites, repealing Jim Crow laws in the South, and launching a program for African Americans to acquire higher education.[20]

In an "easy and affable" manner, Kenneth Lampkin reviewed the facts of *Sweatt* and pointed out that it was not a "one of a kind" suit. He related the facts of *Gaines* and similar cases pending in Louisiana and Oklahoma.[21]

The Reverend Edward Brown, a Baptist minister and an associate secretary of the University YMCA, delivered a stirring talk titled "Segregation from the Christian Point of View." He said that "as Christians, we must do away with racial segregation, for before God we are all the same." He added that segregation was destructive of whites as well as blacks: it created a "superiority complex of the white race." When not preaching, Brown also stated that segregation was not a practical approach for solving the "problem of Negro education." Separate and equal required too much duplication. Brown estimated that nine new black colleges would be required to equalize black higher education in Texas with its white counterparts: it would take five teachers colleges like Prairie View; plus technological, agricultural, and arts and industries institutions like Texas A&M; and another comprehensive university like UT.[22]

The meeting was not without dissention, however. Jack Lewis, the director of youth work at the University Presbyterian Church, raised questions about the wisdom of unqualified and unconditional support for the cause of Heman Marion Sweatt and called for more flexibility. But after a discussion, the group voted down that position and passed a resolution written by the Reverend Brown: "We, the undersigned, hereby endorse and intend to support the National Association for the Advancement of Colored People's efforts for equal educational opportunities, as evidenced in the case of Heman Marion Sweatt, seeking admission to the University of Texas Law School."[23]

Texas reactionaries were appalled. The November 21, 1946, issue of the *Dallas Morning News* included an editorial entitled "Sixty Present."

This gets us back to the net fact that sixty students want Negroes in the law school. It is reasonably certain that the total number of students who are of that mind is larger than sixty. But it is not certain how many. It is time that noses are counted. The taxpayers of Texas will be interested to know how far this trend has gone, and just who is who and why. Very probably the bulk of Texas churchmen will also be interested. A complete poll of the entire 17,000 students would be interesting. From the standpoint of studying "infiltration liberalism," it might prove important as well. Let's have the poll.[24]

At UT, registered student organizations have to be composed exclusively of students, which meant that everyone in the university's new NAACP branch was white. The association celebrated the idea of an all-white chapter on the UT campus, but within the next few months, the Austin NAACP branch would discover what generations of UT administrators already knew: controlling activist UT students was no easy undertaking. For the next year, fighting and bickering between the Austin and university branches of the NAACP sapped valuable time and resources that should have been spent supporting the Sweatt cause.

For months, James Morton had to deal with the unruly students and heated arguments among campus radicals, who sometimes interfered in the affairs of the Austin branch. Maceo Smith called it an "ugly situation." It didn't seem possible: racial tension between two branches of the NAACP. According to Smith, a member of the university branch named Marion Ladwig used the NAACP for the "propagation of political idealism." Not content to rid the university branch of its communists, Ladwig went so far as to campaign for the integration of Austin churches. Morton felt that the adults in the older and established Austin branch should be able to exert some control over the upstart students. But the national association valued student participation in the NAACP, and the UT branch was its first white branch at a segregated university. It showed that if black students were to enroll, they had a good chance of being accepted by other students—a point Thurgood Marshall would have to make during the *Sweatt* trial.

The national association showed no inclination to exert authority over the young white renegades of the UT branch. "Please don't do anything to threaten the UT NAACP Chapter while the Texas case is going on," Roy Wilkins wrote to Morton. The university chapters of the NAACP, Wilkins insisted, were units of the national association and not subject to the authority of local branches. Shortly afterward, a disgusted Morton resigned his presidency.[25]

Of greater concern to the association was whether Texas NAACP branches would remain united behind Heman Sweatt. Walter White, Thurgood Marshall, Gloster Current, and Robert Carter must have wondered what was going on in Texas. Only a few weeks after the first *Sweatt* hearing, Heman Sweatt had to assure Lulu White that "I CAN BE POSITIVELY

DEPENDED UPON TO ATTEND THE UNIVERSITY OF TEXAS
IF WE ARE FORTUNATE ENOUGH TO GAIN ENTRANCE" (all
caps in original).[26]

During the summer and fall of 1946 in Texas, nearly simultaneously, warfare broke out between Lulu White and Carter Wesley over local control of the Houston branch, between Thurgood Marshall and Carter Wesley over whether to fight for integration or integration and equalization, between socialists and communists at UT over who would control the university branch, and between the university and Austin branches over everything from Heman Sweatt to lynching to segregated churches.

The Worrisome Sweatt?

In his report to Governor Stevenson, Chairman Mark McGee of the biracial commission recommended that a "Negro University" be established by an act of the legislature, which would make it a statutory university not entitled to the proceeds of the PUF.[27]

The report also said that the "university of the first class for Negroes" should be located on a central main campus in a major urban center: Houston, Dallas, Fort Worth, or Waco, in that order of preference. It should be a fully accredited institution comparable to UT in the arts and sciences; Prairie View was to be upgraded to an institution comparable to Texas A&M in its role as an agricultural and mechanical college. The legislature needed to provide for the funding as soon as possible, no later than the 1947 regular session, which was scheduled to convene in a few weeks. The governing board for the new institution should be composed of not less than nine citizens of Texas and should have both black and white voting members.[28]

The promise of a new university and a dramatically enhanced Prairie View would not satisfy Judge Archer's ruling. In June, Archer had ruled that the state had six months (until ten in the morning on December 17, 1946) to have an alternative law-school education ready for Heman Sweatt, or he was to be enrolled at UT Law. To meet that requirement before the deadline, the Texas A&M board of directors met on November 27, 1946, and passed a resolution acknowledging Senate Bill 228, which enabled them to provide for a law school (and other schools) at Prairie View. The board resolved that if Heman Sweatt or any other applicants offered themselves to the registrar at Prairie View—bringing with them an acceptable official transcript and other credentials, including a certificate from the dean of the University of Texas Law School that they were scholastically prepared for a course of law equivalent to that given at UT—they would be admitted to Prairie View Law School for the semester beginning in February 1947. The resolution further stated that the law-school courses would be offered in Houston and taught by "qualified Negro attorneys." Immediate funding for the new school would come from a deficiency appropriation already promised by Governor Stevenson, who had estimated the start-up cost to be about $50,000. No longer arrogantly claiming that all Heman Sweatt needed was a copy of *Texas Statutes*, a set of encyclopedias, and a good lawyer, Stevenson announced that the bulk of the money was to be spent on a new law library.[29]

As the date for the *Sweatt* rehearing drew near, Heman Sweatt became more of a "celebrity." He became the symbol of the fight for African American access to all that Texas offered its white citizens. But in New York, both Thurgood Marshall and Walter White had concerns about Sweatt and whether he was a good choice for plaintiff in such an important case. White was disturbed by a letter he had recently received from Sweatt. "It is occasionally necessary for me to glance up at the 'Jim Crow' signs above me to be assured that I am in Houston rather than Stalingrad," Sweatt wrote in his usual elegant penmanship. But it was another sentence that really concerned White: "Very frankly, I have agreed with the opinions of so many persons accused of being communistic that I loathe to deny that I am one."[30]

The NAACP was purging itself of communists during that same period. If Sweatt ever said such a thing in public, it could be disastrous—not just for the Texas case, but for everything the NAACP was trying to accomplish. Almost immediately, White contacted Thurgood Marshall, but there was not much either man could do.[31] The second *Sweatt* hearing was only a month away.

On the other hand, if William Hastie's 1933 description of an ideal plaintiff was valid (outstanding scholarship, neat, personable, and "unmistakably Negro"), then Sweatt was an ideal plaintiff. Throughout the entire *Sweatt v. Painter* saga, Heman Sweatt conducted himself in a way that allowed no one to argue that he should be excluded from UT for any reason other than that he was African American. Sweatt, personally, never became enough of an issue to divert attention from the real issue of state-enforced racial discrimination.

Student leaders like John Stanford, Jr., made it a point to alert President Painter that students were forming organizations to support Sweatt.[32] In November 1946, the Campus Guild, the largest cooperative house of UT students and an important moderate group, passed a resolution, by a vote of 41 to 6, offering membership to Sweatt as soon as he was admitted to the university. The Campus Guild's support was significant because in November 1946 approximately 95 percent of its members were veterans returning from war.[33]

Heman Marion Sweatt had class, a fact that should not be underestimated or dismissed simply because it cannot be measured. Pivotal constituencies like white moderates and liberals found that quality appealing in him and, thus, warmed to his cause. The longer and more often he was in the news, the more apparent it became that irrational hatred was the only reason he was being excluded from anything he was otherwise qualified to join.

But not all veterans were smitten by Sweatt, of course. Price Daniel, of Liberty, Texas, returned from the Pacific theater after being discharged from the United States Army in May 1946, just six weeks before Heman Sweatt's first hearing in Austin. Daniel was different from the other veterans in that he was already a political giant. He was married to a great-great-granddaughter of the single greatest Texan of all, General Sam Houston. Before the war, Daniel had been unanimously elected Speaker of the Texas House of Representatives. After one term, he enlisted in the army as a private, and by the end of the war he had reached the rank of captain. Upon his return to Texas, he immediately began a successful campaign to become the youngest state attorney general in the United States. On the night of June 17, 1946, as news of Judge Archer's *Sweatt* decision reached all parts of Texas, Daniel let it be known during his campaign that Texas needed a "militant, hard fighting attorney [general]."[34]

After winning the attorney generalship in 1946, Daniel aimed to be that hard-fighting attorney general, but his timing was slightly off. The *Sweatt* rehearing was set for December 17, 1946; Daniel would not take office until January 1947. Grover Sellers was to make one last appearance in court to represent Texas in the case of *Sweatt v. Painter.*

The Rehearing

Heman Sweatt's second courtroom appearance was one of the most anticipated events in the history of Austin. Only one month earlier, the Austin NAACP branch had launched a fund-raising and public relations campaign, which culminated in a mass meeting on December 16 in east Austin's new Dorie Miller Auditorium. UT students had distributed more than 5,000 leaflets for the event. The meeting, cosponsored by the Austin NAACP and UT students, was intended to demonstrate the support Sweatt had on the UT campus. Sweatt was among those scheduled to speak.[35]

James Morton introduced Lulu White, who presided over the program. The theme of the evening was Christian values. The Houston NAACP branch president, the Reverend Albert Lucas, delivered a stirring sermon: "The issue is not far distant when we shall study together, work together, go to heaven together—and those who go elsewhere—let *them* go together."[36]

J. Frank Dobie, who by then had become a virulent critic of the UT administration and board of regents, called upon those who would deny Sweatt his place in a classroom to think about what they were supporting: "It is a loyalty to fallacies and prejudices, not loyalty to constitutional and Christian principles of justice . . . It is a terrible thing to condemn a human being to the blackness of ignorance . . . No man who walks with another hanging around his neck or riding his back, walks free."[37] Jim Smith, the president of the UT student body, invoked the Almighty as well when he called for "Christianity, democracy, equality, and justice now!"[38]

When Sweatt took the stage, he directed some of his remarks at those opponents of his cause who were still clinging to the peculiar chivalry of protecting white women. He introduced his wife, Connie, and confessed: "I want to get a legal education at the university, not a wife."[39] He might not have been the most eloquent speaker that night, but after the conclusion of the rally, hundreds of people crowded the stage to meet him.[40]

The Dorie Miller Auditorium rally was a smashing success. Estimates of attendance ranged from 700 to 2,000. Given the description of the crowd by the press and some of the participants, as well as the size of the auditorium, it is likely that about 1,500 people attended.

Thurgood Marshall was ecstatic. After Judge Archer delivered his ruling the next day, Marshall was still talking about the rally. In a telephone conversation with Walter White, he could not get over the size of the crowd and the apparent support Sweatt had in Austin. Spectators had "jammed every available space" during a mass meeting conducted in a "public meeting place."[41]

The proceedings of the 126th District Court of Travis County the next morning were not to start until ten, but by nine all 300 seats were taken, the aisles were full, and people were standing against the wall. The entrance to the court was jammed with others struggling to see and still others in the hallway doing their best to hear. UT law students were among the first to arrive; they claimed the choice seats in the jury box. Ironically, the de facto seating pattern reflected living patterns in Austin itself: African Americans were on the east side and whites were on the west. The first two rows on the east side were taken by NAACP officials.[42]

When Heman Sweatt arrived, he went to the front of the courtroom and found that the plaintiff's table had six chairs, all taken by his lawyers and those from the NAACP. He sat on the floor near the wooden railing and made himself as comfortable as he could.[43]

Grover Sellers began with an overview of the November 27, 1946, resolution passed by the board of directors of Texas A&M in response to Senate Bill 228.[44] Sellers argued that it showed good faith from the state and that Sweatt was going to get his law-school education. The resolution, Sellers pointed out, called specifically for the law school to be substantially equal to the one at UT Austin. Funding for the new school, Sellers continued, had already been guaranteed by the governor through a deficiency appropriation. All Sweatt had to do was present himself to the registrar at Prairie View's new law school, located in Houston, and his training could begin in February 1947.

Marshall answered that a resolution is insufficient evidence. Judge Archer had not ruled six months earlier that the state present a resolution; the state had been ordered to produce a law school. The "scrap of paper" did not ensure Sweatt's right to enter an adequate university.

"A Negro student is not required to wait one minute longer than a white student," Marshall thundered, as he argued that Heman Sweatt had already had to wait six months. And the burden did not stop there: Sweatt and other Negro applicants had to obtain a certificate from the law-school dean, stating that they were qualified. "His efforts are more," Marshall added.

Marshall, looking directly at Judge Archer, boomed: "Your order, sir, was given six months ago. Five months later, the A&M directors got around to passing a resolution. It took them five months to pass a resolution to get started. I don't see how at that rate they expect to have the school in operation in February."

Grover Sellers rose to argue: "Whether you and I agree with the doctrines of our forefathers, it is our duty to uphold the law as they made it."

Sellers knew that in Archer's 126th District Court he was going to win his case; he should have stopped talking and waited for the ruling. Instead, he continued: "I want to see the Texas Negro have educational opportunities equal to those offered the whites, but in the constitutional way, which demands that the schools be segregated." During the previous summer, Sellers's unsuccessful gubernatorial campaign had exploited the prejudices and fears many people had about *Sweatt v. Painter,* so his assurance that "I have nothing but the tenderest feeling for this applicant" drew derisive laughter from African Americans in the courtroom. "I would not be in this court to oppose him today if Prairie View failed to give him the law training he seeks," insisted the lame-duck attorney general.

By the end of the day, the courtroom crowd had thinned out considerably and the spectator section largely consisted of NAACP representatives and a few diehard UT students. Marshall and Durham already knew what the ruling was going to be, so they asked Judge Archer for an immediate final judgment rather than another hearing in February 1947. Assenting, Judge Archer began, "Of course this is a matter that should have been disposed of many, many years ago. We are interested in Sweatt, the individual, but far more in all the colored people of the South." In his written judgment, Archer said that he was

> of the opinion that the said order of June 26, 1946, has been complied with in that a law school or legal training substantially equivalent to that offered at the University of Texas has now been made available to the Relator [Sweatt] and that the Relator may now obtain legal training within the State of Texas at the Prairie View University . . . And, further, the Court is of the opinion that provision for legal training for the Relator at said Prairie View University does not constitute any abridgment or denial of his constitutional rights.[45]

Judge Roy Archer denied Sweatt's petition for a writ of mandamus. Marshall requested that Archer's judgment include a stipulation that the only evidence presented by the state was the Texas A&M resolution. Archer denied the motion.[46]

Immediately after Judge Archer adjourned the hearing, Durham, Marshall, and Sweatt's other attorneys stood for photographs. Other Sweatt supporters wanted to have their pictures taken with Marshall, who towered over almost everyone in the courtroom. At first, Sweatt wasn't included in the photos; he sat quietly and alone in the jury box, reading Archer's judgment as his lawyers took center stage. Eventually, someone called him to pose.[47]

Marshall took the time to tell reporters that the *Sweatt* case was but one of several similar cases the NAACP was involved in. Suits had already been filed in Oklahoma and Louisiana, and a fourth was to be filed in South Carolina. Durham left no doubt that the *Sweatt* case was not over: "We intend to take Sweatt's case to the Supreme Court if that action is necessary, and for that reason we did not leave jurisdiction of the case in Judge Archer's court, but asked for a final judgment in order to service notice of appeal." The Third Court of Civil Appeals, located in Austin, was to receive the appeal.[48]

Sweatt had been offered a law-school education in Houston provided by

Prairie View University. Everyone knew he was not going to enroll and that his case would move forward. Speaking to reporters, he indicated that at that moment he planned to go back to being a mail carrier: "After all, I've got a home to keep up. I am using the money now that I have saved to go to school. Well, anyway, it looks like I'll get out of law school in 1956 doesn't it?"[49]

Marshall returned to the home of his host, a fifty-two-year-old dentist named Lewis Mitchell. Mitchell lived in east Austin on San Bernard Street, only a few houses from the home of Austin NAACP branch president James Morton. Mitchell's wife, Carolyn, a New York University graduate and faculty member of both Samuel Huston and Tillotson colleges, saw to it that Marshall was made as comfortable as possible.

Immediately after Archer's ruling, the Mitchells hosted an informal cocktail party that Sweatt attended. A *Daily Texan* reporter named Bill Hughes noted that Sweatt wore a gray suit with a polka-dotted silk tie "tied in an unbelievably small knot" and shined "ox-blood" shoes. Hughes quoted Sweatt as saying that he and his siblings were inspired to pursue an education by his father, a former schoolteacher who was now a retired railway mail clerk. His dad had graduated from Prairie View College, Sweatt explained, but he did not want his children to go there. His father wanted his children to attend institutions with much higher academic standards. Sweatt also claimed he first became interested in the law after witnessing racial discrimination in the postal service. "I decided that I wanted to be a lawyer," Sweatt said, "and I didn't want to go a thousand miles away from my home and people to do it, so I applied for admission to the University of Texas." Sweatt should have left it at that, but he again promoted the fiction that he was not a tool of the NAACP:

> No one except my wife, not even my father, knew of my plans. One day I picked up a copy of the *Houston Post,* and read that a committee was to come to the University to discuss advanced education for Negroes in Texas. I got permission to sit in on that conference, at which Dr. Painter was present. Contrary to rumor, only two of the fifteen people who attended the conference knew that I had my credentials with me. Only after the filing of my petition did the National Association enter the controversy. Even my original petition was filed through my friendship with Mr. Durham.[50]

Hughes reported that Sweatt believed in the Constitution, and so he believed he had a chance to ultimately win: "We will carry the case to the Supreme Court of the United States, if necessary." [51]

Sweatt left the Mitchells' party early to attend a dinner in his honor at the Campus Guild, the group that had offered him membership should he ever be admitted to UT. After dinner, he spoke to some of the students and thanked them for their support.[52]

The day after the court hearing and before leaving Austin, both Thurgood Marshall and Heman Sweatt went to the boardroom of Samuel Huston College to attend a meeting of the executive committee of the Texas NAACP. Both Marshall and Sweatt attended because of item 2 on the agenda: Equalization of Educational Opportunity.[53]

Item 2 was to deal squarely with the SNCEEO-TCEEO efforts to equalize educational facilities, which Marshall believed competed with the NAACP's desegregation efforts. Everyone who needed to be there to iron out differences and bury hatchets had been invited: Thurgood Marshall, Carter Wesley, Lulu White, and Maceo Smith. All of them had attended the trial the day before; there must have been great anticipation of the meeting by the invitees. The executive committee meeting began at noon, but the clash of the titans was not meant to be: Carter Wesley did not show up.[54]

Three days later, on December 21, 1946, Carter Wesley appeared conciliatory when he wrote in his column that "any impartial spectator would admit that the lawyers [Marshall and Durham] for Sweatt were the best lawyers in the court." Two days later, in a letter to Marshall, Wesley wrote, "You are a stupid man" and a "damned ingrate."[55]

Carter Wesley was a complicated man.

CHAPTER 12

The Basement School

After years of agitation it suddenly became "imperative" that the Negroes have a university and have it now. Why and what started it all? The firing on Fort Sumter?

AUSTIN AMERICAN, FEBRUARY 28, 1947

A poll taken a couple of weeks after the *Sweatt* trial decision in December 1947 found that, by a ratio of eight to five, African American Texans favored the creation of a university for Negroes rather than the integration of the University of Texas.[1]

Despite the poll, Thurgood Marshall still believed that the black community was solidly behind his attempts at integration. After all, the NAACP had raised $34,000 to litigate the *Sweatt* case, and such a result could have happened only with widespread grassroots support. His assessment of support was undoubtedly true, but even though he consistently and vehemently opposed equalization, his efforts were producing real results in Texas for the equalization faction. As he explained, "When the state thought the *Sweatt* case was an equalization case they changed the name of Prairie View and provided no money. When they saw it was a direct attack on segregation they appropriated $2,600,000 to construct a new university."[2] The integrationists who recruited Sweatt, raised the funds, and litigated the case were, perhaps paradoxically, bringing about the greatest equalization effort in American history.

Sweatt v. Painter kept African American leaders in Texas together because both the integrationist and the equalization factions were reaping benefits. Carter Wesley more accurately defined what most African American Texans wanted, but it was Thurgood Marshall and Heman Sweatt who were delivering it. The only issue that Carter Wesley, Maceo Smith, Thurgood Marshall, and Lulu White could agree on from 1946 to 1950 was that even after the establishment of a law school for African American Texans, if Heman Sweatt wanted to go to the University of Texas Law School, he should be able to do so, and so his case should be fought to the finish.

Price Daniel was aware of the integration-equalization division within the African American community, but he did not always understand it. His judgment was clouded by his insistence that African American activism resulted from meddling northern agitators like Thurgood Marshall. On March 21, 1947, only five days before he was to appear before the Texas Third Court of Appeals, Daniel announced that "a recent Belden Poll shows the majority of Texas Negroes favor separate schools." Then he continued rather condescendingly:

> What the majority of Texas Negroes need above all else today is sincere leadership within their own ranks dedicated to obtaining equal educational opportunities in the best separate schools that can be built . . . If they put education first and ditch the New York advisers whose primary aim is destruction of our segregation laws, Texas will soon have the best Negro university in the land. This is evident from the present attitude of the Legislature and the Governor in recently providing over $3,000,000 for the new Negro University in Houston.[3]

Daniel's statement also included a warning:

> The cold reaction of the NAACP minority leadership will prove a serious political blunder for the whole race if local leaders do not organize soon and cooperate fully with efforts now being made by public officials of Texas to provide the schools to which such citizens are fully entitled under the laws of our state.[4]

Daniel was asking African American Texans to trust him, the new governor, Beauford Jester, and the legislature. The vast majority of Texas blacks had never seen Thurgood Marshall in person, after all, so how could an outsider be trusted? What Daniel did not understand was what many black Texans did see: their local NAACP chapters were led by the few (and thus extraordinarily valuable) doctors and dentists who cared for them, the lawyers who defended them, the neglected and underpaid teachers who educated them, and the preachers who led them in prayer and provided the moral compasses of their neighborhoods. Daniel was asking African American Texans to turn their backs not on New Yorkers, but on Texans like Lulu

White, Dr. Lonnie Smith, Dr. Lewis Mitchell, William J. Durham, Kenneth R. Lampkin, James H. Morton, W. Astor Kirk, and the Reverend Albert Lucas.

The new governor whom Daniel wanted African Americans to trust was Beauford Jester, a UT alumnus who had been accepted to Harvard Law School but who earned his Juris Doctor degree at UT Law. After returning from the battlefields of World War I, Jester practiced law in his hometown of Corsicana.[5] He would eventually serve as both a UT regent and a railroad commissioner.[6]

As Daniel encouraged African Americans to accept what they were being "given," Prairie View's W. R. Banks was assigned the responsibility of organizing and opening the new school that had been authorized by the Texas A&M directors. He began by meeting with a black attorney in Houston named William C. Dickinson. Dickinson had earned a bachelor's degree at Pomona College in California, a bachelor of laws degree from Harvard, and a master of laws degree from Boston University in 1907. He was to be paid $5,000 a year for full-time work, if necessary.[7]

According to Carter Wesley, Dickinson had a good reputation for being meticulously careful in the types of cases he brought before the court. He headed a general practice of law, but his cases were largely probate, divorce, and small property matters. Curiously, at first Dickinson denied any knowledge of his role in the creation of the makeshift law school, but he soon admitted that he had been contacted by Banks.[8]

Carter Wesley attacked Dickinson in a number of ways, including his age and lack of relevant experience, and with the venom he usually reserved for Lulu White:

> So far as is known he has not returned to school or taken any refresher courses since 1907 . . . So it is this man, who finished in 1907, and who has a very small library in his office, who is to be pitted against the professors of law at the University of Texas . . . It is this man, who has not taught law, who is expected to walk into the classroom and master automatically the art of teaching, to such an extent that he can equal the experienced teachers of the University of Texas . . . It is this man, who must be well past 70, who is expected to do the arduous study necessary to master the subjects that are to be taught, and to teach enough students by himself to qualify Sweatt to be equal with the students of the University of Texas.[9]

Dickinson's partner, Henry Stuart Davis, Jr., was available if an additional teacher should become necessary. He was a graduate of Morehouse

College and Northwestern University Law School. Even though North-western Law was Carter Wesley's alma mater, that did not spare Davis from a scathing attack in the *Houston Informer.*

> As to Henry Stuart Davis, dispose of him by saying that the least said the better . . . he went to California and had a bad experience with the Bar Association and returned to Texas to practice. His bad experience was al-legedly in the attempt to pass the California bar. Davis admits freely that he is not claiming to be qualified to teach law. These are the men whom Dr. Banks led his committee to see, and these are the men referred to be-fore the court Tuesday, when Assistant Attorney General Littleton told the court that he expected to establish a school at Houston, under Prairie View, and have two competent, Negro instructors.[10]

But it was W. R. Banks who took the brunt of Wesley's outrage for participating in the grand deception of creating the makeshift law school and calling it equal to the University of Texas Law School. "Now that the issues are clear and the Negroes and whites are divided, Dr. Banks' dou-ble role of talking big to the Negroes, and then going up talking sweet to the whites, with neither side ever knowing what he said to the other, is ended."[11]

E. L. Angell, the assistant to the president of Texas A&M and secretary of its board of regents, described the Prairie View Law School as a suite in an office building at 409½ Milam Street in Houston. The "suite" consisted of two, possibly three, rooms. Angell emphasized that the rooms had been completely renovated and furnished with new furniture and office equip-ment. The dean of UT Law had furnished approximately 400 basic law ref-erence books chosen from a list required for the education of first-year law students. The estimated cost of the forthcoming library was to be $25,000–$30,000—at least half of the $50,000 that Governor Coke Stevenson had approved as a deficiency appropriation.[12] To Carter Wesley it was "nothing but a foolish and cheap insult to Negroes."[13]

Price Daniel fully expected eager and grateful black students to file ap-plications as soon as the school opened on February 1, 1947. He believed that the state would then be able to present the school, its faculty, and its contented students as evidence of having fulfilled Judge Archer's mandate. And it perhaps was reasonable to believe that at least a few qualified African Americans would apply. What was being offered, after all, was not available anywhere else in the South; at the time, blacks were attending white public colleges in only two southern states.[14]

For two weeks, from February 1 to February 14, the Prairie View Law School awaited the arrival of applications—none came. Not one.

Daniel announced that the law school's failure to attract even one student was due not to its inequality but to the fact that the NAACP had organized a boycott. He was right about the boycott but wrong about the reason why no one applied.[15]

Daniel's immediate challenge was that the Negro law school he envisioned as being populated by students when the *Sweatt* case came before the Third Court of Appeals was a monumental flop. Near the end of the registration period, on February 10, 1947, William Durham and Thurgood Marshall filed an appeal brief representing a change in the NAACP's legal strategy for *Sweatt;* it directly attacked segregation: "The terms 'separate' and 'equal' cannot be used conjunctively in a situation of this kind; there can be no separate equality."[16]

Senate Bill 140

As the registration period of the Prairie View Law School came to an end on February 14, 1947, the Fiftieth Legislature of Texas worked feverishly on a bill to create a university of the first class for Negroes. The Stewart-Moffett Bill, also known as Senate Bill 140, was based on recommendations in the report of Governor Coke Stevenson's Bi-Racial Commission. The true intent of SB 140 was evident in the first section:

> The Legislature of Texas deems it impracticable to establish and maintain a college or branch of the University of Texas for the instruction of colored youths of this state without the levy of taxes and the use of the general revenue for the establishment, maintenance and erection of buildings as would be required by Section 14 of Article VII of the Constitution of Texas, if such institution were established as a college or branch of the University of Texas.[17]

Section 1 of SB 140 made it clear that the new Negro university was not to be a branch of the University of Texas and, therefore, not a constitutional institution having access to the Permanent University Fund.

> Therefore, it is the purpose of this Act to establish an entirely separate and equivalent university of the first class for negroes with full rights to the use of tax money and general revenue fund for establishment, maintenance,

erection of buildings and operation of such institution as provided in Section 48, Article III of the Constitution of the State of Texas.

Section 2 established that the Texas State University for Negroes (TSUN) was to be located in Houston and was authorized to teach the arts, sciences, literature, medicine, pharmacy, dentistry, journalism, and education. Prairie View was to remain an agricultural and mechanical college offering courses in agriculture, mechanics, engineering, and natural sciences and was to remain under the control of the Texas A&M board of directors. Both institutions were authorized to add courses upon the demand of an applicant.

Section 3 authorized Governor Jester to appoint a board of directors "to be composed of nine persons and to consist of both white and negro citizens of this state." Section 5 empowered the board to select a site, and Section 6 empowered the directors "to proceed with the construction of all necessary buildings and other permanent improvements thereon."[18]

Sections 9 and 10 provided for what African American Texans had been waiting for since the Constitution of 1876: money—not just the promise of money, but real money: $2,000,000 for the acquisition of land; $500,000 (that is, $1,000,000 for the biennium) for support and operation; $100,000 for Prairie View to offer courses upon demand until August 31, 1947; $150,000 for TSUN to offer courses upon demand beginning September 1, 1947. The total appropriation for the new university equaled $3,250,000.[19]

Senator Lacy Stewart, the sponsor of SB 140, knowing of plans to convert the Houston College for Negroes campus into a "comprehensive" university, announced that he had traveled to the site and that "if we have any building at the University of Texas superior in construction I don't know what it is." He described the fifty-three-acre site in Houston as being about halfway between the Rice Institute and the University of Houston.[20]

During Senate hearings on the measure, Dudley Woodward, Jr., warned: "If this university is not established you may expect rulings which will open any state institution to Negro youth not afforded equal opportunities in education." In the *Houston Informer,* Carter Wesley complained that the hearing had been conducted without notifying any black leaders "working on the university question."[21]

Debate over SB 140 was not contentious: the legislature was nearly unanimous in the opinion that if it did nothing, "the United States Supreme Court will rule that your child and my child will have to attend school with Negroes."[22] Black leaders made no serious attempt to halt the spending of such large amounts of money on "Negro education." Even though the steps were attempts to sustain segregation, this was real money, and the NAACP had decided to argue that separate was inherently unequal. So as Carter Wesley would have said gleefully, let the whites build the school.

Most of the debate over SB 140 concerned details. J. F. Ward, of Rosenberg, argued against Houston as a location because it was a "hotbed of Negro reformers." Ward feared exposing the "country Negro" to "all the evils, joints, and dives in Houston." A few other legislators insisted that the state had already met its burden to satisfy judicial mandates. Tom Martin, of Fredericksburg, had "no objection" to the principle of an equal university for blacks, but he didn't want the state to spend "enormous" amounts of money when the state already had Prairie View.[23]

Henry E. Dodd, an African American representing the Travis County Conference on Equal Educational Opportunities for Negroes, argued during hearings on the bill for a constitutional amendment, rather than a bill, to create the Negro university; doing so would give the institution some insulation from possible future anti-Negro political spasms. Then he assured the white legislators that "we just want a first-class university. We don't want social equality." But not all of Dodd's testimony was conciliatory. After one legislator insisted that, in fact, there were very few blacks eligible for the academic rigor of the University of Texas, Dodd shot back: "Certainly we don't have many Negroes wanting higher education. We've had trouble getting lower education."[24]

The debate over SB 140 also included gratuitous blather about carpet-baggers and Yankee agitators. None of the rhetoric mattered: SB 140 was going to pass very quickly and by a wide margin. The *Dallas Morning News* called it "unbelievable speed."[25]

The real powers behind SB 140 were Dudley Woodward, Jr. (chairman of the UT board of regents) and Attorney General Price Daniel. Both men functioned as protectors of the University of Texas and watched carefully as the bill advanced toward final passage. The legislature did what Woodward and Daniel told them to do, and their instructions were based wholly on the defensive position in which Heman Sweatt had placed Texas.

As a result of the failure of the Prairie View Law School to attract any students, which meant that Texas had no law school for Negroes, Woodward announced that UT had been working on establishing a new law school in Austin in anticipation of legislative action. He added that the law school could be operating as soon as the governor signed the bill. The attorney general sent word to the House and Senate that if the bill was passed and signed the week before March 5, it would add materially to his defense against Sweatt's petition scheduled to be heard in the Third Court of Appeals on that same day. Daniel planned to argue that Sweatt's motion to be admitted to UT Law should be declared moot because a Negro law school had been established in Austin and a permanent school was being made ready in Houston for the fall semester of 1947.[26]

"It's a large order, a large price, but it's a price we will have to pay to keep the segregation clause in the Constitution," Dudley Woodward, Jr., warned the legislators.[27] SB 140 sailed through the Texas Legislature: it passed the Senate (25 yeas, 2 nays) on February 24; it was amended and passed by the House (122 yeas, 12 nays) on February 27; the Senate concurred with the House version (23 yeas, 3 nays) on March 3. The enrolled bill was sent to Governor Jester immediately, and he signed it at 1:50 p.m. Within minutes, registrar E. J. Matthews sent Heman Sweatt a letter offering him admission to a temporary law school to be set up in Austin. SB 140 was added to the *Texas Statutes* by the secretary of state less than twenty-four hours later.[28]

On March 5, 1947, the long-anticipated appeals-court hearing turned out to be anticlimactic. Price Daniel, Thurgood Marshall, and William Durham agreed to a motion for a three-week delay, which the court granted. On March 26, Justice J. M. McClendon announced from the bench that *Sweatt* would be remanded to Judge Archer's 126th District Court without prejudice to either party. Almost immediately, the retrial was set for April 28.[29]

What looked like a spirit of cooperation between Texas and the NAACP in their motions to remand for trial was specious. By returning to the district court, the NAACP saw an opportunity to retry *Sweatt* as a direct attack on segregation without having to file another suit or search for another plaintiff. All Heman Sweatt had to do was change his mind about what constituted an acceptable education in the law. He announced that he no longer had faith that Texas would ever produce a truly separate-but-equal law school capable of training him as thoroughly as it trained the white lawyers of his generation; the only acceptable solution was admittance to the UT Law School. The state saw a return to district court as an opportunity to continue to build upon SB 140 by presenting a new law school and a more compelling argument that the *Plessy* separate-but-equal test was being met in good faith by the state.[30]

A Makeshift Law School

Section 11 of SB 140 enabled the University of Texas regents to establish a temporary law school in Austin that was to function as the "School of Law of the Texas State University for Negroes." It made $100,000 immediately available for the establishment and operation of the school. To ensure that the makeshift school was immediately "comparable" to the University of Texas Law School, the legislature mandated that students have access to the State Law Library in the Capitol, which was used primarily by the Texas Supreme Court.[31]

The UT regents and administration moved furiously. On February 28, several days before Governor Jester signed SB 140, the regents authorized Chairman Woodward to organize the new law school in Austin. Its first semester was to run from March 10 through June 28. Woodward had already suggested to the regents and Attorney General Daniel that the dean of the UT Law School, Charles T. McCormick, also serve as the interim dean of the law school being set up for Heman Sweatt. Similarly, E. J. Matthews was to serve as the registrar.[32]

At three in the afternoon on February 28, the same day the UT regents authorized Woodward to organize the new law school, Dean McCormick met with the UT law faculty and presented a plan for the creation of the makeshift law school for African Americans. He indicated that he had worked out the plan with Price Daniel and Dudley Woodward. McCormick needed the backing, even if not the approval, of the faculty because much of the success of the plan depended upon some of the professors being willing to teach blacks in the makeshift school. The faculty approved the plan.[33]

At four, only a few minutes after the faculty meeting, McCormick met with the Budget Council to secure approval of additional pay for three law-school teachers who had agreed to teach classes in contracts, torts, and legal bibliography. The sum of the salaries was $2,000, or approximately a 50 percent supplement of their UT pay.[34]

The Budget Council's action and the legislative developments on SB 140 described above allowed Matthews to send Sweatt his long-awaited letter of admission to law school. The content of the letter had been dictated by Woodward six days earlier in a communication to Price Daniel. (Woodward disingenuously called his prose "merely suggestions.")[35]

Heman Sweatt's historic letter of admission to the "School of Law of the Texas State University for Negroes" was typed on plain white paper. Even the name of the school was typed, and the address was a post office box. Matthews explained that the Texas Legislature had authorized the establishment of a separate school of law equal in all respects to the University of Texas School of Law: "I am pleased to advise that your qualifications heretofore established and your application heretofore made will entitle you to attend the new school now being opened at 104 East 13th Street, Austin, Texas."[36]

Heman Sweatt had been accepted to a law school to which he had not applied; he had less than one week to report for classes 150 miles from his home. The contents of what was, for all other law-school applicants, a routine letter of admission were remarkable. Matthews summarized what would later become the state's defense against Sweatt's lawsuit. The 13th Street school was to be equal to the University of Texas Law School, Matthews emphasized, because the faculty was going to be the same, the State Library (an equal, perhaps better law collection than the UT Law Library) was to be available, and the school was shortly going to be certified by the American Bar Association and the American Association of Law Schools.[37]

Sweatt received his letter on March 4 and immediately forwarded it and other materials Matthews sent him to William Durham in Dallas, adding, "The same is self-explanatory and I await word from you regarding the type of reply (if any) in the best interest of the legal aspects of this case."[38] Sweatt later testified that he took the letter and traveled to Dallas to deliver it to Durham in person and remained there for almost a week. Durham instructed his client not to have anything to do with the Jim Crow law school on 13th Street.[39]

By then, the goal of the NAACP and the Texas Council of Negro Organizations was clear and uncompromising: in a resolution dated March 8, 1947, the TCNO declared "the Council can have no part in a legislative movement to establish makeshift segregated higher educational facilities for Texas Negroes." In a letter to Thurgood Marshall, Maceo Smith declared: "Plans are in the making to boycott the Austin Jim Crow law school and to set up plans for boycotting the proposed state university in Houston." The activism did not stop there. Smith also invited Marshall to speak at another mass meeting at Dorie Miller Auditorium planned for March 25, the night before the rescheduled appeals-court hearing.[40]

The "Austin Jim Crow Law School" Maceo Smith wrote about was the result of a request for bids the UT administration sent out on March 4 for the use of office space adjacent to or very near the Capitol. Proximity to the Capitol was the highest priority. As Woodward explained, "In this connection, it will be observed that library facilities are to be provided in the State Library, so that teaching quarters should be located as conveniently as possible to the Capitol."[41]

The space they secured was a three-story structure housing two businesses: the offices of Harold Young and Hubert McWhinney, the editors of the *Texas Spectator* newspaper, and the owner and primary occupant, an oilfield-services firm on the second floor called Odom and Ballanfonte Petroleum Engineering.[42]

The building was located at 104 East 13th Street, only twenty feet from a very narrow loop immediately outside the ornate railing surrounding the Capitol grounds. The entrance to the east and north sides of the Capitol was less than 100 yards away. It may have been the closest privately owned building to the Capitol. (The exact spot is now near the Texas Peace Officers Memorial, very close to the southern entrance of the Sam Houston State Office Building.)

UT leased four rooms, totaling 1,060 square feet, on the bottom floor for $125 a month. The budget for the school included an additional $3,000 reserve for the rental of additional rooms and floors as needed. From the 13th Street sidewalk, an entrance led to a hallway where a receptionist's desk was located. It also connected to a restroom. The other two rooms were intended to become classrooms and the beginnings of a law library. Plans were in place to move the school to the new Negro university in Houston as soon as possible.[43]

Like many other parts of the Heman Marion Sweatt story, the 13th Street law school has become clouded in folklore. For example, in an online collection of UT stories, Vivé Griffith writes: "In order to have a facility for law studies available before the trial, the state hastily set up a law school in Austin in the basement of a building on East 13th Street, in a low-income black neighborhood."[44] In fact, the area was neither black nor low income. Indeed, the building sat on some of the most valuable non-mineral-producing real estate in all of Texas.

Since 1947, an even more emotional debate about the makeshift law school has concerned whether the leased rooms were on the ground floor or in the basement. UT designated what was set up at 104 East 13th Street as the "School of Law of the Texas State University for Negroes," but it was hardly ever referred to by that official name; it was, and will forever remain, the "Basement School."

The negative context of "basement," as used by NAACP attorneys, especially James Nabrit, Jr., during the trial and in its media campaign was meant to imply that the rooms were dark, dingy, dungeon like, and underground. That is not an accurate description of the rooms leased by the state. On one side of the building, steps led to a second-floor gallery, giving it the function and appearance of a main entrance. Reaching the makeshift law school required descending two or three steps from the sidewalk on 13th Street to an area shaded by the gallery of the floor above. From there, two or three steps descended to a door, which was the entrance and exit to the rooms leased by Texas. Thus, the law school was on a floor below the main entrance, but only slightly lower than street level.

The End of the Basement School

Thurgood Marshall recognized the value of public relations. During the *Sweatt* litigation, Oliver Harrington of the NAACP national office assured Marshall that he was "working all [the] press."[45] The NAACP's efforts went beyond working the press. The association's members and the Texas Council of Negro Organizations continued to make it clear that they wanted nothing to do with the 13th Street school.

The *Course Announcement* for the spring 1947 semester consisted of three first-year classes: contracts, torts and legal bibliography, all three to be taught by UT Law teachers. On the day the 13th Street school opened, Dean McCormick wrote to President Painter that the salaries set aside for the teachers were "Holding—Pending Registrants."[46]

Registration for the spring semester of 1947 took place from March 10 to March 17. Governor Jester, Attorney General Daniel, and Dudley Woodward hoped that at least five and as many as ten black students would apply for admission.

Two days before the onset of the registration period, the Texas Council of Negro Organizations met and passed a resolution outlining its position on the 13th Street school. TCNO president Joseph Rhoads, claiming to represent thirty-one Negro organizations with a combined membership of about 500,000, publicly explained the position of African American leaders in Texas.[47] Regardless of promises and appropriations made by the legislature, the Texas State University for Negroes and Prairie View A&M had little chance of ever becoming "first-class" institutions, Rhoads said. "The University of Texas" described in the Constitution of 1876 belonged to all Texans. It approached first-class status because of a growing endowment, currently valued at approximately $65,000,000. No other state university, Rhoads thought, much less one grudgingly and hastily set up for a long-neglected racial minority, could ever enjoy resources equal to UT's share of the Available University Fund.

Rhoads emphasized that even other white state universities did not and could never measure up to UT's greatness as an educational institution because they were dependent solely upon money appropriated by the legislature. So it was foolish for African Americans to believe the legislature could be trusted to produce a public Negro university equal in every respect to the constitutional university in Austin, which had taken Texas from the time of the republic to the present to build. Rhoads mused that the Texas State University for Negroes might one day be a great school, but only if it was allocated a rightful share of the Permanent University Fund.[48]

Rhoads and the TCNO, along with Marshall and the NAACP, could not have been clearer: admission to the University of Texas was the only solution to the "problem of Negro education."

To discourage applications to the 13th Street school, black activists in Austin and Houston used a strategy Lulu White described in a July 1947 letter to Maceo Smith: "Let's see if we can develop a feeling of shame and embarrassment among the people who might enroll."[49] It had worked in Houston the previous month when W. R. Banks tried to set up a sham law school in the office of an elderly divorce lawyer. The Prairie View School of Law had not received a single application. It worked again in Austin in March. E. J. Matthews received three letters of inquiry on March 8 from prospects in Galveston, Fort Worth, and Marshall, but the communications did not include official transcripts and were not applications. A total of twelve inquiries—eleven letters and one visitation—arrived by the deadline. None formally applied. The most promising prospect, a grocer from Austin named Henry Doyle, publicly indicated that he was interested, but he declined to apply after the NAACP pressured him to desist.[50]

From March 10 to March 17, the *Daily Texan,* black newspapers, and Texas's big city dailies ran humiliating stories and pictures of UT administrators sitting alone in 104 East 13th Street, waiting for applicants that never arrived.

There is no record of who closed the 13th Street school at the end of the day on Monday, March 17, 1947, but the significance of the failure to attract a single student could not have escaped whoever locked those doors. Even before the closure, Governor Jester announced that he was "perplexed" why African American students wanting a career in the law did not take advantage of the new opportunity made available to them by the legislature and his administration.[51]

On Wednesday, March 19, Dean Charles McCormick wrote to President Painter: "I talked to Mr. Daniel, the Attorney General, this morning about the School of Law of the Texas State University for Negroes. Subject to your approval we have agreed upon the following procedure: After today the leased premises at 104 E. Thirteenth Street, Austin, Texas will be closed until further developments, and a notice will be placed on the door to the effect that inquiries may be made to Mr. Mathews [*sic*] as Registrar or to myself as Dean."[52] By the end of the day on March 19, McCormick addressed a letter to the postmaster of Austin, requesting that all mail addressed to the School of Law of the Texas State University for Negroes be forwarded to Dean E. J. Matthews, Registrar, Main Building 1, Austin, Texas.[53]

African American mail, if nothing else, was making it to UT's Forty Acres.

CHAPTER 13

A Line in the Dirt

A democracy that cannot deal fairly with its minorities cannot stand.
DALLAS MORNING NEWS, EDITORIAL, MAY 1, 1946

On Friday, March 21, 1947, Attorney General Price Daniel told an assembly of reporters that he was "disappointed" at the reaction of Negro leaders to the state's generosity: $3,350,000 appropriated to provide higher-education facilities for "colored" youth. African American Texans, the attorney general insisted, were being led astray by "some Negroes" whose "primary purpose . . . was to break down the segregation laws, not primarily to obtain an education."[1]

Much had changed since Judge Roy Archer's initial ruling: there was a Texas State University for Negroes in Houston and a temporary law school on East 13th Street in Austin. Daniel also presented a number of affidavits to the reporters, including one from E. J. Matthews, stating that Heman Sweatt had been officially informed that he had been accepted to the Texas State University Law School for Negroes, which was supposedly equal in every way to UT Law—an opportunity that Sweatt chose not to take advantage of. Other affidavits documented the establishment of the 13th Street facility and other efforts the state was making to provide the equality mandated by federal court rulings, especially *Gaines*.[2]

Sweatt's reaction to the state's efforts was predictable: an interim law school in Austin and a new university in Houston were not enough. "Assume I go to the interim law school for a year [and] then I transfer to the new university," Sweatt asserted, "how do I know what will be at Houston? The suit goes on."[3]

According to the NAACP's *Annual Report* for 1947, the historic brief filed by Sweatt's attorneys in response to Daniel's actions "opened an uncompromising legal assault upon segregation, *per se*."[4] The brief was the result of a collaboration between William Durham, Thurgood Marshall, and Marshall's colleague at the NAACP, Robert Carter, reflecting what Marshall and a group of lawyers had already concluded in their April 1946 meeting in Atlanta: equalization efforts had brought about what Maceo Smith called "bigger and better" segregation. From *Gaines* in 1938 to the remand of *Sweatt* in 1947, southern states had established six makeshift law schools and separate schools of journalism and library science.

Since both Marshall and Daniel agreed that a rehearing was desirable, the Third Court of Appeals set aside the trial court's judgment and ordered the cause "remanded generally to the trial court for further proceedings without prejudice to the rights of any party to this suit."[5]

The *Sweatt* case towered over other pending civil rights cases in the South. Marshall admitted that even though the NAACP was interested in cases in other southern states including Oklahoma, Louisiana, and South Carolina, "none of these present as thorough and complete an exposition of the fundamental points of law and interpretation at issue as the *Sweatt* case."[6]

Sweatt was the first case to make the claim that segregation per se violated the Fourteenth Amendment. Everyone knew *Sweatt* was headed for the Supreme Court, and when it got there, the NAACP would call for the outright reversal of *Plessy v. Ferguson*. It was a direct assault on a tradition that defined the South.[7]

Such a bold move, however, did not come without risks. As the *Daily Texan* noted: "Many reasonably liberal Texans who have strived honestly to overcome their natural and inherent prejudices will find completely unpalatable the new tack by the lawyers for Heman Sweatt . . . The die is cast in lawyer W. J. Durham's brief that emphasizes that 'there can be no separate equality.'"[8]

The Second Rehearing before Judge Archer

During a rally on the night of March 24 in Austin, Maceo Smith announced to delegations from nineteen different towns and cities that it would take an additional $20,000 to take *Sweatt* to the U.S. Supreme Court. More than $6,000 had already been spent. Hoping to pick up $1,000 that night, Smith motivated the crowd by declaring, "Every case we have taken to the United States Supreme Court we have won."

After Smith's pep talk came the highlight of the evening—Thurgood Marshall.[9] On the summit of Robertson Hill, in the meeting hall of Ebenezer Baptist, Austin's largest African American church, Marshall took center stage and regaled the audience with yet another assertion that the goal of the NAACP was the abolition of racial segregation. At one point he sarcastically answered Price Daniel's announcement that *Sweatt* was really about ending segregation: "I was deeply surprised that certain parties have just now found out that the NAACP is trying to abolish all segregation. Will you please tell them that the NAACP will only stop when segregation stops."[10]

Even if Daniel had only recently come to the conclusion that *Sweatt* was really about ending segregation, he did understand the gravity of the situation. He had announced that he would litigate *Sweatt v. Painter* personally, even though he was preoccupied with the hugely important tidelands controversy.[11] As a result, Daniel's bright and energetic thirty-three-year-old assistant attorney general Joe Greenhill handled much of the preparation of the state's defense of *Sweatt*.

Joe Greenhill was born in Houston and educated in the public schools there. At San Jacinto High School, he edited the yearbook while a student named Walter Cronkite, two years his junior, edited the school newspaper. Greenhill was a brilliant law student. He earned summa cum laude BA, BBA, and LLB degrees from the University of Texas and passed the Texas bar exam as a second-year law student. After graduating from UT Law, he returned to Houston to be an attorney. While in the U.S. Navy Reserve during World War II, he rose from the rank of ensign to lieutenant in the intelligence section, and then served as the executive officer on a fleet minesweeper called the USS *Control*, which patrolled in the Pacific.[12]

According to Greenhill, "Price Daniel said *Sweatt* was my case." Since 1947, Greenhill has insisted that his vigorous defense of Texas in the *Sweatt* case was not the result of racism, or personal or political ambition. "To me and the attorney general it was just a lawsuit." The law in Texas at the time was segregation, insisted Greenhill. "My client was Dr. Painter and the University of Texas. Either I could do my best or I could quit. I couldn't afford to quit."[13] He guided UT officials through the creation of the 13th Street school. For *Sweatt*, he was both the primary researcher and the author of briefs and motions.

Both sides had exemplary legal talent. Officially representing Heman Sweatt on the first day of that historic remanded trial were William J. Durham, Thurgood Marshall, C. B. Bunkley, Jr., and James M. Nabrit, Jr. Representing Texas were Attorney General Price Daniel and Assistant Attorneys General Jackson Littleton and Joe Greenhill.[14]

As always while preparing for trial, Thurgood Marshall sought the advice of many of his lawyer friends, particularly William Hastie. On April 3, he wrote to Hastie: "Judge Archer said that he understood the case was 'wide open' and that we should have a full hearing on the merits." Marshall abandoned the equalization strategy in favor of the direct attack. "So, whether we want it or not," Marshall continued, "we are now faced with the proposition of going into the question of segregation as such."[15] Hastie replied that for a direct attack against segregation to succeed, Marshall needed to give the court a basis for concluding that segregation at professional schools was unequal.[16] To use a Texas metaphor: "Marshall drew a line in the dirt in Texas" when it came to segregation.[17]

Judge Archer gaveled the court into session at ten on Monday, May 12th. The white press corps worked from a table usually reserved for the press, while black reporters were assigned the jury box. Marshall was concerned about press coverage. "I imagine that some of the publishers will rely on Carter Wesley for their coverage and it is for that reason that I am hoping that the *Afro* [a black newspaper] can arrange for independent coverage of the case in order that the anti-segregation point be fully covered," he wrote to Carl Murphy, an editor from Baltimore.[18] The NAACP requested coverage from at least fourteen African American newspapers as well as the major dailies and popular magazines. Marshall took the unusual step of asking Ollie Harrington of the NAACP's public relations department to come to the trial to "insure adequate coverage." (Afterward, Harrington sent thank-you letters to those that covered the trial.)[19]

Once again, the bailiff separated spectators according to race; blacks were moved to the east side. The hot and humid courtroom was made even more so by the close-packed spectators.

Almost immediately, William Durham asked for a two-hour recess to prepare a reply to a four-page document Price Daniel had presented to the court on why Heman Sweatt should not be permitted to attend the University of Texas. Archer granted a four-hour recess that took them through lunch.

After lunch, Price Daniel called D. A. Simmons as his first witness. Simmons was an alumnus of UT Law who had also been awarded honorary doctorates from the University of Montreal and Loyola University New Orleans. He had been active in the American Bar Association (ABA) on the local, state, and national level, and was testifying in this case as an expert on law-school standards. Daniel began his direct examination by establishing that the University of Texas Law School was ABA approved. More complicated were his efforts to demonstrate that the 13th Street school would become approved as well.

Simmons testified that during that morning's recess, Dean Charles Mc-

Cormick had taken him to the new law school for a tour. Simmons described the rooms and its contents, including shelves containing 150 to 200 books; the ABA requirement was a minimum of 7,500 books. Simmons knew that the Texas State Library and the Supreme Court Library had been made available to the students, so he walked over to the Capitol to check out those collections. He testified that "the books seemed to have been kept up to date, and [those libraries are] about a hundred or a hundred and fifty yards from this school." Daniel asked Simmons for the number of volumes in the Capitol's libraries, and Simmons indicated that he did not know but that he was willing to testify that "obviously there are a great deal more than 7,500 books and of a character that would afford an adequate legal education."[20]

Shortly into Simmons's testimony, Price Daniel posed a hypothetical question that neatly summed up the state's case:

> If the evidence in this case shows that in the building that you have already inspected, the University of Texas law faculty, the same faculty members, offered the same courses in law in that building, and with the library facilities of the Supreme Court Library that we have mentioned, and if the requirements for entrance are the same, the requirements for graduation are the same, as the Texas University Law School, if the evidence shows that the requirements for classroom study and all requirements contained in the catalogue of the University of Texas Law School must be met in the law school of the State University for Negroes, if the evidence shows what I have recited, in your opinion, will Texas University for Negroes Law School offer equal educational opportunities in law as that offered by the University of Texas?

Before Simmons could answer, Thurgood Marshall objected: Simmons was being asked to give a conclusion about what the law was—a duty limited to the judge. Archer overruled him and instructed Simmons to answer. He responded: "In my opinion, the facilities, the course of study, with the same professors, would afford an opportunity for a legal education equal or substantially equal to that given to the students at the University of Texas Law School."

Thurgood Marshall's cross-examination took more than an hour and focused on the value of accreditation to the law school and its students. He was particularly insistent on the issue of books:

> MARSHALL: If you had a university in Washington with no law library, but access to the Library of Congress, would you accredit that school?

SIMMONS: You are talking to me. I am only one of 185 delegates in the House of Delegates. I do not personally accredit anybody. If the law school you are talking about had trained professors, set up by Congress across the street, a hundred yards from that library, and the Act of Congress said this library shall be the library of that school, I would say, so far as I was concerned, I would say they had been furnished an adequate library [with] all of the books they could hope to read or study.

Similar exchanges between Marshall and Simmons took place over whether the law school under review should have a librarian, full-time professors, and a dean. Marshall placed Simmons in the unenviable position of having to argue that much of the enormous investment a state makes in its public law schools, including time, resources, libraries, teachers, and accreditation by the ABA and the Association of American Law Schools, did not make one school better than another.

Marshall persisted: "The important thing is that if this proposed school [could not] meet the requirements of the Association of American Law Schools, and the University of Texas does meet them; would you say that that is giving equal facilities?"

Simmons's reply was rather remarkable: "It wouldn't have the slightest effect on the student, whether he was a trained lawyer when he left the school or not."

The trial transcript clearly showed Simmons becoming more and more uncomfortable with Marshall's relentless cross-examination. "I am not arguing the law," an exasperated Simmons said. "I am not a lawyer in this case. I was just passing through the city. By reason of having been president of the [bar associations] from Houston to the United States. They asked me to talk about the standards. If you want me to argue about whether these facilities are worth as much as something else, you had better get somebody else."

Marshall was beginning to make the point that no matter how hard the state tried to pretend that the 13th Street school was equal to the UT Law School, it could never be. No lawyer in the courtroom could have missed the impact of Marshall's cross-examination. The argument that separate could not be equal and, therefore, that segregation could not be legal was beginning to take shape.

Price Daniel finished the first day by introducing the resolutions passed by the Texas A&M board of directors as evidence of Texas's efforts to provide educational equality for its African American population. He also reviewed a deposition by the Texas A&M official largely responsible for the creation of the Milam Street law school in Houston (the predecessor of the 13th Street school).

The African Americans in the courtroom reveled in what they were witnessing: talented black attorneys asking direct questions that required straight answers from the representatives of a system that had oppressed them and their ancestors for generations. The demolition of Simmons as witness, reported the *Houston Informer,* caused D. K. Woodward, Charles McCormick, and several others to remain in the courtroom after adjournment at the end of the first day: "Presumably, they were repairing their fences, which had been shaken considerably during the testimony."[21]

When the courtroom proceedings resumed on Tuesday, May 13, Attorney General Daniel reviewed SB 140, the legislation creating the Texas State University for Negroes in Houston. After the review, Daniel was ready for his first witness of the day: "I would like to call Mr. D. K. Woodward."

Woodward outlined the regents' creation of the 13th Street school. Daniel's questions emphasized the location, specifically, how close 104 East 13th Street was to the Capitol and businesses downtown. (The attorney general did not delve into the number of businesses that had "White Only" signs posted at their entrances.)

Daniel's direct examination was workmanlike and matter-of-fact. Marshall's cross-examination of Woodward focused on the 13th street building itself:

> MARSHALL: Could you put the library of the Law School of the University of Texas in that whole building?
>
> WOODWARD: Certainly not.
>
> MARSHALL: So, that brings us to the next question. Where are you going to put your library?
>
> WOODWARD: When the library is acquired, it will consist of ten thousand volumes. The library of the Law School of the University of Texas consists of approximately 65,000 volumes, of which about half of them are duplicates. Nobody in his right mind would undertake to assemble 65,000 volumes in a law library in a building or law school just started. There is ample space in the building on which we have the refusal in which to store and provide the use of ten thousand volumes we have under order. We can put them there.
>
> MARSHALL: Then I understand you can put the 10,000 volumes in the present building?
>
> WOODWARD: That would be my judgment, yes.
>
> MARSHALL: Well, now, as to these standards of the Association of American Law Schools, do you have . . . the amount of space required for library use of students?

WOODWARD: As to that, I wouldn't be qualified to say because I don't know what the requirements are . . . Under the provisions of the statute, with the law library we have under order and with the accessibility to the Supreme Court Library of the State of Texas, we have abundantly sufficient library facilities and working space for the relator's pursuit of his course of law.

Woodward proved to be a much more effective witness for the state than Simmons. When Marshall asked him how the students' use of the Texas State Library differed from what was afforded to any other citizen of the state, Woodward answered that the students could withdraw books while other citizens could not. Of all the state's witnesses, Woodward was the best at defending the motives of the board of regents:

WOODWARD: What we set up there was a plant fully adequate to give the very best of legal instruction for the only man of the Negro race who had ever applied for instruction in law at the University in about sixty-three years of the life of the school. We are practical people. We made . . . provision [for a law school education] fully adequate for that purpose.
MARSHALL: What do you mean by "practical"? You mean within the money you had available?
WOODWARD: No, here is what we were trying to do, Counsel. We were trying very hard to, and are still trying, to set up for the Negro population of the State of Texas a University really of the first class, which down through the years will develop and grow to what we hope to be the greatest University for Negroes in the world.

Woodward's subsequent testimony inadvertently confirmed that, contrary to generations of claims of a Negro university never being "practicable," Texas always had the resources to create the "university of the first class for Negroes" that had been promised in the Constitution of 1876. He continued:

WOODWARD: We have the assets with which to do it, and the determination to do it, and that was a part of the plan to provide here, at the threshold of this undertaking, [an] opportunity identical with that which was afforded at the University, eight blocks away.
MARSHALL: Well, you didn't get the idea and that plan until after this lawsuit was filed, did you?
WOODWARD: It happens you are mistaken about that.
MARSHALL: I would like to know [when].

WOODWARD: On the 13th of January, 1946, the Board of Directors of Texas A&M University and the Board [Regents] of the University of Texas . . . met in joint session at Ft. Worth, Texas. They are the governing boards of the two principal state-supported schools. One of the questions on that agenda of that meeting was the consideration of the responsibility of those two schools for providing a comprehensive plan of higher education for members of the Negro race in Texas.

MARSHALL: Did that Board meeting discuss the very wide publicity, including the paper in your home town, the *Dallas Morning News,* concerning a meeting of Negroes who were insisting on their equal right to an education?

WOODWARD: When was that? What meeting do you have reference to?

MARSHALL: The meeting held in Dallas at the Y.M.C.A.

WOODWARD: What date do you mean? Held on the 8th of March of this year?

MARSHALL: No, prior to January of 1946.

WOODWARD: I do not—that meeting was not considered at all, and it was not in any way the occasion for our holding the joint session, or discussing that program.

Marshall was referring to the meeting in Dallas on June 2, 1945, sponsored by the NAACP. Maceo Smith had organized the event and seen to it that it received maximum press coverage. The headline of the June 5, 1945, edition of the *Dallas Morning News* was "Negro Plan Revealed to Enroll in UT." Woodward continued:

WOODWARD: Members of those two boards felt as officers and directors of the State's leading educational institutions that they owed it as a public duty to devise some means of providing for what they thought was a real need for members of the Negro race, and they implemented that by appointing a committee of six, three from each school, to make a study of that. That committee worked diligently for about six months, made its report to the Governor of Texas, the Hon. Coke R. Stevenson, who in turn appointed the Bi-racial Committee, with which I am sure you are familiar. It filed its report, and that report was the basis of Senate Bill 140. So that the undertaking of those two boards ante-dated the filing of the suit by the relator here, and was not actuated by any extent by the meeting, whatever meeting it was, one that I never heard of, in Dallas, though I live there.

So Woodward testified that the governing boards of the two Texas flagship universities did not acknowledge a "real need" for higher education for

African Americans until January 1946 and that their actions had nothing to do with external pressures from the Supreme Court (that is, *Gaines*), or the very public and widely covered demands of African American leaders, or the anticipated and inevitable application of an African American Texan. And again, he delivered this testimony after having admitted that the state of Texas had the resources to create the "greatest university for Negroes in the world."

There were other equally incredible moments in Woodward's testimony:

MARSHALL: [Mr. Woodward], how old is the University of Texas?
WOODWARD: We think of it as having started in 1883.
MARSHALL: Is it not true it is one of the finest schools in the country?
WOODWARD: It continues to try to be.
MARSHALL: About how long do you think it would take to build for Negroes a university equal to that?
WOODWARD: It would depend to a greater extent on the response of the members of the Negro race than anything else.

Woodward could have added, but did not, that under his plan, if the "Negro race" was going to build a university equal to the University of Texas, it would have to do so without access to the Permanent University Fund.

Although it was never clearly defined in testimony offered by the state, the foundation of the state's idea of equal was that if two separate courses of study produced the same result, they were equal: if two law schools produced graduates capable of passing the bar exam and becoming licensed lawyers, the courses of study offered by those schools could be considered functionally equal. That was what made the 13th Street school equal to the University of Texas Law School. The same would be true of elementary and secondary education: the end result for everyone, white and black, was graduation from high school with a diploma. Thurgood Marshall did not let Woodward off the stand before attacking such a notion of equality.

MARSHALL: Do you mean equal, or do you mean if you use both of them you can get the same thing? Isn't that what you really mean?
WOODWARD: I mean this: that the educational opportunity offered [the] relator by those facilities at that date was fully equal to those offered on the same day in the Law School of the University of Texas eight blocks away. That is exactly what I mean, because that is a fact.
MARSHALL: Do you know the curriculum of the law school of the University of Texas?
WOODWARD: In a general way. It is identical in both schools.

MARSHALL: Do they have the Law Club set up in this school?

WOODWARD: A Law Club is set up by the students. Perhaps if the relator came and other representatives of his race came, you could form one.

MARSHALL: You can't form it with one student, and you can't have moot court with one student, can you?

WOODWARD: No, you couldn't do it.

MARSHALL: And you couldn't have any of the interchange common in law schools with one student?

WOODWARD: I presume if there is a good faith desire on the part of the Negro youth of the State of Texas to attend law school, all of those facilities will be developed in a short time, just as I presume they are at Lincoln and Howard. You have to start somewhere.

MARSHALL: While this is going on it is true, is it not, that the students are not getting the same things they are getting at the University of Texas? Isn't that true?

WOODWARD: Are you talking about social contacts, or educational?

MARSHALL: Sweatt isn't interested in social contact. He is interested in getting the best legal education he can get.

WOODWARD: Why didn't he come on the 10th of March?

MARSHALL: Your lawyers will have the opportunity to ask Sweatt about that.

WOODWARD: If that is his only interest he is sitting there within one hundred yards of the Supreme Court of Texas, Court of Civil Appeals, and the Attorney General's office, and the Legislature, where the public legal business of the State of Texas is centered. He has an opportunity [unsurpassed] to acquaint himself with those facts.

MARSHALL: He is in the middle of everything but the Law School of the University of Texas!

WOODWARD: He is in the middle of the Law School provided by law for him.

Within minutes of the heated exchange, Judge Archer adjourned the session until 1:45. Woodward had been on the stand for nearly an hour and forty-five minutes, and he was a good witness for the state insofar as Marshall did not succeed in rattling him as he had D. A. Simmons the day before. Woodward's problem, and thus the state's problem, was that he was called to defend a patently absurd position: that a three- or four-room law school, less than three months old, that was set up to receive five to ten students, was equal to the University of Texas Law School.

Heman Sweatt's lawyers did not rest or relax during recesses; they often assembled in the Samuel Huston College classroom of Marcellus "Andy" Anderson to plan strategy and prepare witnesses. In the evenings after meals, the lawyers and witnesses gathered in the living room of Marshall's hosts, Lewis and Carolyn Mitchell. At one time or another, at least seven lawyers worked the *Sweatt* case as advocates of Heman Sweatt: Thurgood Marshall, W. J. Durham, Robert Carter, James Nabrit, Jr., C. B. Bunkley, Robert Ming, and Harry Bellinger. Years later, Sweatt recalled that as he watched the collection of brilliant attorneys plotting strategy, "you just know you're in something that's just way beyond what you thought when you went down there to file an application. I was just amazed."[22]

Indeed, if the NAACP's direct attack on segregation is what led to *Brown v. Board of Education*, planning for the "Lexington and Concord" of courtroom fights started in the living room of Dr. Lewis Mitchell on Robertson Hill in east Austin.

But Marshall did not spend all of his time working. In addition to being a dentist, Lewis Mitchell was an extremely talented musician. He counted Count Basie among his friends and was the probable inspiration for many of Basie's hit songs. Some of the evenings in the Lewis home included singing.[23]

When court reconvened on the afternoon of May 13, Price Daniel conducted a redirect examination of D. K. Woodward. Daniel asked Woodward to describe the regents' efforts to establish the Texas State University for Negroes in Houston. His testimony included a brief history of the Houston College for Negroes and its unique association with the Houston Independent School District and the University of Houston. Woodward also described the new building on the fifty-three-acre site and plans to construct others. With other questions about accreditation, budget, and the acquisition of property, Daniel sought to demonstrate the good-faith efforts of the state to fulfill its responsibilities to the African American population. Daniel then moved to budgetary questions, and at the very end of his redirect of Woodward, the attorney general gave a hint of what was to come.

DANIEL: Do you know of any meetings held by an organization of the Negro race and attended by any persons in this court room on March 8, 1947, in Dallas?
WOODWARD: Through public reports?
MR. DURHAM: If Your Honor please, may we have that stricken?
THE COURT: Only of his knowledge.
DANIEL: Do you know of your own knowledge?
WOODWARD: Only through public reports and conversation.

MR. DURHAM: We object to that as not being responsive and hearsay.
DANIEL: That is all.

The *Houston Informer* reported that both Simmons and Woodward left the courtroom immediately after they were excused as witnesses.[24]

Charles McCormick, the dean of UT Law and interim dean of the 13th Street school, appeared as the next witness. Daniel's initial questions concerned the comparability of the two law schools as measured by floor space per student. McCormick's testimony was that in those terms, the 13th Street school was more comfortable than the UT Law School. If the makeshift school were to have ten students, the space per student would be 106 square feet, compared to 53 square feet for each of the 886 students at UT Law. Then McCormick testified that the 886 students at UT Law were studying in a building designed to accommodate 400. Daniel then attempted to show that the curriculum of the new school was identical to the one offered at UT Law. He introduced bulletins and course offerings and asked McCormick to identify the items and confirm that the law-school experience for each school was substantially equal. The testimony included information on the faculty assigned to teach at the new school. McCormick emphasized that the teachers were not only substantially equal but the same persons at both institutions. At noon, Judge Archer called for a recess until two. When the trial resumed, Daniel asked McCormick a few more questions and then surrendered his witness for cross-examination.

The May 15 NAACP press account of the trial stated that during his entire testimony Dean McCormick avoided looking at the UT law students assembled to watch the proceedings.[25] That may not have been too surprising: their dean was testifying that much of what they were working for was irrelevant to the quality of their school, which was equivalent to a few empty rooms in what some considered the basement of a building owned by an engineering firm. McCormick's testimony on direct examination by Daniel was straightforward, fact filled, and at times barely audible. Square footage, budget, and the requirements of the Association of American Law Schools did not make for exciting testimony.

That is, until James Nabrit, Jr., rose to cross-examine the dean.

Nabrit v. McCormick

James Madison Nabrit, Jr., was born in Georgia in 1900. In 1936, he left a law partnership with Carter Wesley and joined the Howard University Law

School's faculty. He would later become the dean of the law school and then the university's president. By 1947, he had become an expert in law-school education.[26]

Nabrit's first target was the library:

NABRIT: Is it your opinion, Dean McCormick, that for law school students . . . the best use out of this library [is with] a librarian who is there to serve students and teachers, people who are engaged in study and research?
MCCORMICK: I think a librarian is, of course, necessary for the operation of a library for the benefit of students or anyone else.
NABRIT: Who was the librarian for the Negro Law School on March 10th of this year?
MCCORMICK: Well, we had not formally appointed a librarian, but Miss Hargrave (UT Law's Librarian), for a considerable period of time gave a great deal of service to the planning and provision of the library arrangement.

Then Nabrit moved to accreditation:

NABRIT: Under the standards of the American Association of Law Schools, it is stated that in order for a school to qualify it shall have been in operation for a period, usually, for approximately two years, and then upon inspection by the Association, if it meets their standards, it will be accredited?
MCCORMICK: Two years is the minimum time, as I understand it.

Nabrit's question was simple enough: is a law school accredited by the Association of American Law Schools equal to one that is not?

NABRIT: Now, is it your opinion that a law school that is not accredited is for the purposes of accreditment equal to the law school of the—to the University of Texas Law School.
MCCORMICK: I don't understand that question.

Nabrit wanted a straight answer and he would not give up until he got it from McCormick. He lectured McCormick in a manner that must have sounded condescending.

NABRIT: Well, let's put it another way. The Association of American Law Schools accredits certain law schools based upon those schools having reached certain accepted standards which are known to all people in the field of law in rating law schools on that basis. If I look in this book and see the University is listed as a member, I know it meets these minimum standards. Now, for the purpose of accreditment, that is, for that purpose, is a law school which is not accredited as a member of this Association equal to the University of Texas School of Law?

MCCORMICK: For the purposes of accreditment, why, obviously, a law school that is not accredited does not equal one that is accredited, but I still don't catch the significance of the question.

NABRIT: It will follow. Is this Negro Law School which was open on March 10th a member of the Association of American Law Schools?

MCCORMICK: No, it is not.

NABRIT: Is it accredited?

MCCORMICK: Not in that sense, no.

NABRIT: In what sense is it accredited?

Everyone in the courtroom knew the answer to the question, but Charles McCormick, the dean of one of the most prestigious law schools in America, gave an answer that today seems incredible.

MCCORMICK: Well, if you mean by accredited, the opinion of people familiar with the situation and with the law school, their opinion as to the value of the facilities and instruction, why, then, it is accredited in that sense, by those who hold the favorable estimate of it. If you mean accredited by the Association of American Law Schools, why, it is not.

NABRIT: I mean is it accredited in the sense in which educators in the field of law speak of accreditment of law schools?

MCCORMICK: Well, they usually speak of it in the sense of being a member of the Association of American Law Schools, and of being an approved school on that list of the American Bar Association.

In his zeal to defend the state, McCormick advanced a definition of "accreditment" that was oxymoronic. It is the raison d'être of an accrediting agency, such as the Association of American Law Schools, to use well-defined criteria to objectively evaluate the quality of a school. In general, these criteria involve precise measurements, such as the number of books in a library, the number of teachers, their office hours, their course loads, etc. McCormick alleged that there could be such a thing as an accredited school based on an undefined body of people and their opinions.

Nabrit moved to questions about the opportunity UT law students had to take undergraduate and graduate courses on the UT campus. McCormick readily admitted that the law students did have access to all courses provided they did not take more than fourteen semester hours. When Nabrit asked where the students of the 13th Street school were to go for similar courses, Price Daniel objected; he said the line of questioning was "wholly irrelevant and immaterial." Nabrit countered that it was the state that argued that the 13th Street school provided equal opportunities, and the option to enroll in other classes was one of those opportunities. Judge Archer responded, "I will let him answer it if he can."

"I could not answer that question," responded Dean McCormick. He added that the law school did not encourage such a practice.

Nabrit then moved into an area of equality that proved to be even more troubling for the state.

NABRIT: As a former President of the American Association of Law Schools, and as the Dean of several law schools, and as an outstanding authority in several fields of law, Dean McCormick, are you of the opinion that one of the basic elements in a great law school is the history and traditions which have been built up over years of time, including the graduates who have become famous in the State of Texas? Is that your opinion—that is an element in a great law school?
MCCORMICK: Yes, that is a source of pride to a law school that has that background.

Nabrit's point was that it was not possible to create a new law school that already had distinguished alumni and all the benefits that group can bring to their alma mater. The governor of Texas at the time, Beauford Jester, was a UT Law graduate, as well as the attorney general of the United States, Tom C. Clark. The School of Law of the Texas State University for Negroes could not have similar clout for years—if ever.

Nabrit then addressed the curriculum and how certain courses and activities could never be equal. The first example was moot court.

NABRIT: Now, where is the moot court in this Negro Law School? I see here [in the UT Law course offerings] the moot court. What arrangements under the faculty for the Negro Law School are there for this law group competition and the moot court?
MCCORMICK: Well, that, of course, has not been instituted. It can't be instituted until you get some students.

Maybe so, but Nabrit got McCormick to admit that even though first-year law students did not take the class that included a moot court (the class was entitled Legal Argument), those students could attend, observe, and learn from the proceedings.

Under "Honors and Aids," Nabrit asked McCormick about the Order of the Coif. "I think you will agree that it is one of, if not the highest, legal honorary societies, and honor students in the upper tenth or upper number of the graduating classes at the University of Texas School of Law are eligible for that, is that not so," Nabrit insisted. McCormick agreed, and then Nabrit established that an Order of the Coif (an honors organization of law students) chapter could not be organized in an unaccredited law school, which meant that the African Americans entering the 13th Street school would likely graduate without ever having a chance for membership. McCormick testified that the law review, the Order of the Coif, and scholarships and awards were tangential activities—things not organized by the law school per se. The implication, of course, was that the activities were, as Nabrit put it, "extraneous."

> NABRIT: So . . . you consider the University of Texas Law Review an extraneous matter?
> MCCORMICK: Yes; it was founded by the lawyers of Texas, not by the State of Texas, and is financed by their contributions.
> NABRIT: And you consider honors at the University of Texas School of Law as extraneous?
> MCCORMICK: Well, you mean the honors, the Order of the Coif and Texas Law Review?
> NABRIT: Yes.
> MCCORMICK: Yes, they are minor and extraneous.
> NABRIT: How about these cash scholarship awards; are they extraneous?
> MCCORMICK: They are in the sense that I have been speaking about. They are very microscopic influences. They are not large elements in the picture at all.
> NABRIT: So that so far as the University of Texas is concerned, it might as well get rid of all of those?
> MCCORMICK: No, certainly not.

Dean Charles McCormick was a Harvard Law School graduate who knew and understood what those "extraneous" activities meant to law students and their careers. For some of those students, it would mean employment with a prestigious law firm doing exciting things in exciting places with powerful people.

Nabrit had made his point: some of the elements of great law schools had to develop over time and could never be replicated in a three- or four-room makeshift law school with three teachers on the ground floor of an office building.

McCormick's testimony continued until 4:35 and for some time during the next day's session. Nabrit methodically reviewed each of the requirements of the American Association of Law Schools and challenged McCormick to explain how the 13th Street school could meet those accreditation standards. In nearly all of the exchanges between the two learned attorneys, McCormick emphasized that nothing really mattered if the school had no students: if Heman Sweatt wanted an equal law school education, he had to show up. Nabrit continued to emphasize that the school, as it was on March 10, 1947, was not equal to the University of Texas Law School. The one issue that both men could agree on was that the new law school could not meet the requirement that it be in operation for two years before it could be accredited. McCormick considered the period reasonable and inconsequential to the measurement of equality.

The dramatic exchange between Nabrit and McCormick did not change or even influence the outcome of the trial: Judge Archer knew he was going to rule against Heman Sweatt. As Joe Greenhill admitted, "Marshall and I knew we were creating a record to present to the Supreme Court." Indeed, Thurgood Marshall was making a record that separate was inherently unequal.

CHAPTER 14

"I Don't Believe in Segregation"

As with all our court trials during that period, this one was public theater. The courtroom was filled to overflowing with black spectators. The trial was of intense interest because of its attack on school segregation and because spectators would have the opportunity to see the legendary Thurgood Marshall in action. He did not disappoint.

ROBERT L. CARTER, *A MATTER OF LAW* (2005)

During the evening of May 13, 1947, probably in the living room of Lewis and Carolyn Mitchell's home, Thurgood Marshall decided that on the next day he had better question the next witness himself.[1] Nabrit's tendentious cross-examination of Dean McCormick had effectively discredited the state's case, but the same approach might produce a public relations backlash if it was used when cross-examining Miss Helen Hargrave, the librarian of the University of Texas Law School and acting librarian of the 13th Street school. Marshall reasoned that the South's "peculiar chivalry" needed to be considered, and a white female librarian needed to be treated in a more gentlemanly manner.[2]

The lawyers also spent a considerable amount of time and effort "wood-shedding" Heman Sweatt. "Woodshedding" is a term lawyers use to describe the process of preparing a witness for testimony. Nabrit role-played the attorney general and asked grueling rapid-fire questions. Sweatt must have wondered whether he was going to be treated in the same unpleasant way Nabrit had treated McCormick earlier in the day.

Sweatt had to be prepared for two difficult lines of questioning. First, why had he changed his mind from demanding an equal facility to demanding admission to the University of Texas Law School? Second, why was Thurgood Marshall in the courtroom, and what was the NAACP's role in this case? In other words, was this really about his desire to become an attorney, or was he a guinea pig in a New York–led conspiracy to end segregation.

The Librarian and the Registrar Testify

Helen Hargrave had been a member of the UT Law Library staff since 1929. Dean McCormick and the attorney general's office had assigned her the task of providing an inventory of books that, when secured, could be defensible as a law library equal or substantially equal to the UT Law Library. Jackson Littleton conducted direct examination for the state.

Littleton established that Hargrave had produced the list of 10,000 volumes that would stock the new library and that it was based on the requirements of the Association of American Law Schools (AALS). Littleton sought to introduce the list as evidence after Hargrave produced it, but William Durham objected: he said the list was "self-serving." Judge Archer overruled.

Hargrave testified that her priority was to secure volumes normally used by first-year law students, since that would be the classification of all entering students. The Texas State Library had the volumes necessary for AALS certification, with a few exceptions. The Texas State Library, she testified, was not a teaching library; for example, the UT Law Library contained more textbooks and legal periodicals, which had been collected over a longer period, than the governmental library. Some of the older periodicals would be impossible to secure for the 13th Street school.

But the Texas State Library had inventory that the UT Law Library did not. It was a repository for all reports produced by the United States government and the State of Texas. It also received all attorneys general's opinions and other significant legal documents from other states.

In addition to the AALS list, Hargrave had ordered other books she knew would be useful to the new students. When Littleton asked to submit the book requisition as evidence, Durham made a series of objections over which lists (originals or copies) could be entered into the record. After several minutes of confusion, Littleton gave up, announced that he would come back to it later, and surrendered the witness.

Marshall, gentlemanly but firm in his questioning, focused on the differences between the Texas State Library and the UT Law Library. He seized upon Hargrave's earlier testimony about the difference between a teaching library like the one at UT Law and a repository like the Texas State Library. He had Hargrave describe her duties as librarian and how she functioned as more than just a locator of materials. Weren't law librarians also teachers, since they assisted students and took on similar responsibilities, as well as professionals who catalogued and organized materials for retrieval? He pointed out, for example, that Hargrave taught a class in legal bibliography. Another of the librarians had graduated from UT Law and was in a position to locate materials and assist students in the subject of the law. Of course, it was simple for Marshall to show that the 13th Street school did not have such a staff on March 10, when the school opened for business.

Hargrave's recurring response to Marshall's persistent questioning about the equality of the library where she worked and the one she was asked to set up was that "equality" does not mean "identical." But Marshall did succeed in getting her to admit that one of the state's ways of measuring equality was seriously flawed:

> MARSHALL: My question is . . . as of March 10th and as of today [May 14, 1947], is it not true that if you use all of the books in the 13th Street school for Negroes, plus all of the books in the State Library, that those two groups of books, taken all together, do not meet the standards of the Association of American Law Schools, is that correct?
> HARGRAVE: That is true.

Hargrave also admitted that the Texas State Library was open to everyone, including UT law students, who might have to consult government reports and other items not available at the law school. For Marshall, this meant that the books either should not be counted in the test of equality or else counted for both schools.

> MARSHALL: Do you know of any accrediting agency recognized in the legal field that uses as the basis for accrediting one school, the law library of another school? Have you ever heard of that?
> HARGRAVE: As far as I can remember, that has never come to my attention.
> MARSHALL: Well, isn't it true that in evaluating law libraries and law schools you evaluate the law library that is in that school? Isn't that correct?
> HARGRAVE: Some law school libraries—I would think in general that that is the method that is used.

When Jackson Littleton redirected, he had Hargrave testify that the library she ordered for the new school corrected the deficiency of textbooks. Additionally, 500–600 surplus books from the UT Law Library were to be transferred to the 13th Street school. Finally, Littleton read from a UT board of regents' resolution that "authorized to supply on a loan basis books from the Law Library of the University of Texas which may be needed in the efficient conduct of the School of Law of the Texas State University for Negroes."

E. J. Matthews had been the registrar of the University of Texas for thirty-five years when Jackson Littleton called him to the stand. The registrar occupied a position in a university where academics meets business operations, so Matthews had responsibilities that affected every step of a student's college career. He was also responsible for nearly all the university's official publications; Matthews brought some of those publications with him to supplement his testimony. At UT, Matthews's formal title was "Registrar and Dean of Admissions," and so he also oversaw the operations of the Office of Admissions. Matthews had also been assigned registrar and admissions duties at the Texas State University for Negroes.

Before the trial, Price Daniel had notified Heman Sweatt that he was to produce his official letter of acceptance to the 13th Street law school. When Littleton presented it to him, Matthews identified it as authentic, and it was introduced as evidence. After Littleton read its contents aloud, he asked Matthews if Sweatt had made any response. The registrar replied, "No, sir. None at all."

Matthews testified that the 13th Street school received a total of fourteen inquiries from prospective students, twelve of which came in the first half of March. Two others received in April must have been about enrolling in the fall semester of 1947. Only one student inquired in person.

William Durham cross-examined Matthews and easily established why Sweatt was denied admission to UT Law.

DURHAM: The application of the Relator was presented to you at that time [February 26, 1946] as Registrar of the University of Texas for admission to the first year law class of the University of Texas School of Law. I believe you examined the application and determined his qualifications for admission?

MATTHEWS: Yes, sir.

DURHAM: Is that the same application that you referred to in paragraph 2 of the letter addressed to the Relator on March 3, 1947?

MATTHEWS: Yes.

DURHAM: That was the only application that you had had from the Relator, and he possessed the qualifications necessary for admission to the law class, first year law class, in the University of Texas School of Law?

MATTHEWS: The academic qualifications.

DURHAM: The academic qualifications. Now, I believe the application on the part of the Relator for admission to the University of Texas School of Law, first year class was refused?

MATTHEWS: Yes, sir.

DURHAM: Why was it refused, Mr. Matthews?

MATTHEWS: Because the Constitution of the State of Texas forbids us to accept as students members of the Negro race.

DURHAM: He possessed all other qualifications, except he wasn't a white student?

MATTHEWS: So far as I know, yes. Academic qualifications.

DURHAM: And you refused his application for admission to the first year law class of the University of Texas Law School solely on account of race and color?

MATTHEWS: The Constitution of Texas.

Durham then noted that the letter and the envelope Matthews sent to Sweatt were not marked with letterhead; he introduced the envelope as evidence. The stationery had typed headings that had been mimeographed onto letter-grade paper. Price Daniel made no objection to the introduction of the letter and envelope, and Matthews was dismissed as a witness.

Matthews was lucky. Compared to Woodward and McCormick, his testimony had been uneventful and mercifully short. Judge Archer called for a lunch recess with instructions to reconvene at two. Half of the second day of the trial had been completed.

When court reconvened, Jackson Littleton recalled Helen Hargrave, who had spent much of the lunch recess with Dean McCormick at the 13th Street school. Her impromptu charge was to determine whether the facility could house the 10,000 books that would eventually be secured for the new school. She testified that it had enough space to do so.

Marshall asked whether it was possible to put all of the books on the ground floor. His questions implied that there was not enough space for the books and the furniture and that it would be difficult to navigate the five steps that led to the ground-floor entrance. Hargrave stated that the furniture in the rooms could be moved out to make room for about 7,000 of the 10,000 books. But not all the books needed to be kept on the first floor. Indeed, they would most likely be spread throughout the building. On redirect, Littleton asked Hargrave whether the entire building could house the books comfortably, and she indicated that it could. Durham objected to her testimony about areas of the building that had not yet been leased by the state. Littleton insisted that the evidence had shown that the lease of the rest of the building had been ensured by the state and was inevitable. Judge Archer cautiously and conditionally allowed the testimony about the second and third floors as library space.

The ruling by Judge Archer to allow a discussion of the second and third floors as part of the school appeared to be a small victory for Littleton until Marshall rose to recross Miss Hargrave. He brought up a potential problem not anticipated by the State, one that could not be addressed immediately by anyone in court:[3]

MARSHALL: Did you make any test as to whether or not the second and third floors would hold stacks of law books?

HARGRAVE: I made no tests.

MARSHALL: So, you are not in a position to testify, as to whether or not you could put a library on the second and third floors, are you?

HARGRAVE: I presume in a brick building the walls [of which are] solid brick that the balance of the books could be so arranged around the walls that with the knowledge that I have about that, it would take care of those books.

MARSHALL: Do I understand your testimony to be that you would put the books around the walls, and you wouldn't have stacks in the middle of the floor?

HARGRAVE: On the ground floor, no. On the ground floor, it would take the space of the ground floor for stacks, as we usually find them in libraries, in order to handle the approximately 7,000 books that I figured on.

MARSHALL: And where would the reading room be? Downstairs?

HARGRAVE: No, you couldn't have the reading room downstairs. It would have to be on another floor because the ground floor would be filled with stacks of books.

MARSHALL: Miss Hargrave, as a matter of fact, are you familiar with the amount of space in a law school that is needed for class room instruction, Dean's office, faculty offices? Are you familiar with that, or just in a general way?

HARGRAVE: Just in a general way. I don't know much about that.

MARSHALL: So that when you testify that that building is adequate to house all of this, you are testifying just in a general way, are you not?

HARGRAVE: I don't see how it could be much otherwise.

Daniel recalled to the stand Dean McCormick, who testified that the 13th Street school contained plenty of space for law books. James Nabrit then asked him questions that were similar to those Marshall had asked

Hargrave. Sweatt's lawyers demonstrated that no scientific method had been used to compute space requirements for 10,000 books, rooms for instruction, and administrative offices, and that no one knew whether the building could support the weight of the books. McCormick and Hargrave testified that because books varied in size and weight no one could say exactly how much space would be needed. Fundamentally, they testified that there was plenty of room for 10,000 books and that their conclusion was based on having been surrounded by books during their long careers.

Undoubtedly, Hargrave and McCormick were right, but again, the question of the building, its location, and whether it was structurally sound enough to house 10,000 books was a diversion. The premise of the state's case was that constitutional and statutorily mandated segregation in Texas was clear and unambiguous—and legal. Under the state's premise, the test of legality was one of substantial equality as mandated by *Plessy* and *Gaines*, and that meant that Heman Sweatt could attend and graduate from the School of Law of the Texas State University for Negroes with a law degree that could be used in the same way as a degree earned at the University of Texas Law School. Graduates from both schools faced the same coursework and had the same burden of passing the bar exam. Successful students from either school could become lawyers in Texas.

The testimony and evidence in *Sweatt v. Painter* thus far had consisted of haggling over standards, accreditation, curricula, shelves, basements, windows, and buildings. The merciful close of arguments over physical facilities and printed materials preceded a dramatic turn in the trial. On the afternoon of May 14, 1947, Attorney General Price Daniel rose to address Judge Archer: "We would like to call the relator, Heman Marion Sweatt."

Sweatt Takes the Stand

Seated upright, dressed impeccably, and speaking so softly his own lawyer had to ask Judge Archer to instruct him to talk louder, Heman Marion Sweatt didn't look like a revolutionary who was feared by Texas segregationists. He was a haunting, younger version of his father, James Leonard Sweatt, who was now deaf from decades of working on rattling trains. The son had inherited his father's sense of moral certainty. While James Leonard Sweatt is remembered by family and friends for being stern but fair in the affairs of family, church, and community, his son Heman is remembered for the strength of his conviction. He must have wondered what he had gotten himself into as he sat on the witness stand in a hot and humid courtroom, and was interrogated in public by the attorney general of Texas, knowing his every word was to be scrutinized by history. For the moment, he alone seemed to be bearing the weight of ending racial segregation in America.

DANIEL: You applied for entrance into the University of Texas on February 26, 1946, is that correct?
SWEATT: That is right.
DANIEL: I will ask you if it isn't true that on or about March 20, 1946, you were furnished a copy of an opinion by the Attorney General of Texas stating that if you desired and made a demand on Prairie View University, that that school was under mandatory duty to furnish you an equal law training with the University of Texas Law School?
SWEATT: Yes.
DANIEL: You read that opinion, did you?
SWEATT: I did.
DANIEL: Did you make demand or give any notice to Prairie View University, or any of its officers, that you wanted to attend a law course there?
SWEATT: I did not.
DANIEL: Did you ever apply to Prairie View University or to any official of that school, or of A&M College for a law course?
SWEATT: No.
DANIEL: You didn't, then, follow the Attorney General's opinion as to what was the legal procedure by which you were entitled to an equal law course?
SWEATT: No.

Heman Sweatt rigidly followed the instructions he had been given the night before. His answers were responsive, direct, and short. Sweatt also admitted that he was present when Judge Archer heard the resolution of the Texas A&M board of directors setting up a law school in Houston. When Daniel asked whether Sweatt knew that a law school had been set up in the Milam Street law offices of two black attorneys, Sweatt answered, "I knew some rooms were there." He also admitted to going to the Milam Street offices to see what they looked like, but he never spoke to the "faculty" and never intended to register. Sweatt testified that he decided not to attend the law school after talking to his attorney, William J. Durham.

Price Daniel then directed questions to his real concern:

DANIEL: Did you have Mr. Marshall, attorney for the National Association for Advancement of Colored People, as one of your attorneys at that time [during the first hearings in the 126th District Court on December 17, 1946]?
SWEATT: December 17th?

DANIEL: Right.

SWEATT: I didn't have—I never have had Mr. Marshall as my attorney.

DANIEL: You have not?

SWEATT: That is right.

DANIEL: You know Mr. Marshall, sitting right here, do you not?

SWEATT: Yes.

DANIEL: You know, of course, having sat through the case[,] he is participating here in the case and cross examining witnesses?

SWEATT: Yes, sir.

DANIEL: He is signing the papers as one of your attorneys of record?

SWEATT: Yes.

DANIEL: Didn't you authorize him to do it?

SWEATT: I authorized Mr. W. J. Durham to represent me, and in a conference with him, I left it with him to secure what aid he found it necessary to.

Apparently, Daniel still believed that Sweatt, and thousands of African American Texans, who had spent months raising funds to finance *Sweatt v. Painter*, were the malleable tools of a New York conspiracy to end the southern way of life. Sweatt continued by admitting that he never intended to enroll in the Milam Street school, even though it was less than three miles from his Delano Street home in the Third Ward in Houston.

Daniel followed with the same line of questions about the 13th Street school in Austin. Again, Sweatt candidly admitted that he had received the letter offering admission and knew all about the creation of the school. He also testified that, after receiving the letter, his first action was to bring it personally to Durham in Dallas.

DANIEL: Didn't you send the letter to Mr. Marshall, the letter that you saw him take out of his brief case, before we introduced it? Didn't you send that to Mr. Marshall?

SWEATT: No, I did not.

DANIEL: Who did you send it to?

SWEATT: I took it on the train to Mr. W. J. Durham.

DANIEL: When did you make up your mind not to go to the school?

SWEATT: When Mr. W. J. Durham told me it wouldn't give me equal law training as [at] the University.

Sweatt explained that he had made up his mind on the day he brought the letter to Durham. Sweatt had stayed in Dallas for about a week, which would have been from about March 4 or 5 to about March 11 or 12.

It was during that week, on March 8, that the Texas Council of Negro Organizations met in Dallas to consider actions by the State of Texas to provide equal educational facilities in graduate and professional schools.

DANIEL: Then you were there on March 8th when the National Association for the Advancement of Colored People and other organization representatives met to decide whether or not to support or not to support this separate Negro Law School, weren't you?

MR. DURHAM: We object to it; first, upon the assumption that the National Association for Advancement of Colored People met. That is the first assumption. The question assumes that he was there at the meeting. Both assumptions are without any evidence on the matter in the record.

JUDGE ARCHER: I think you had better ask him if he was there.

DANIEL: Were you in Dallas on March 8th, 1947?

SWEATT: I was there.

DANIEL: Are you acquainted with a meeting—do you know anything about a meeting held in Dallas on that date at which this lawsuit was discussed?

SWEATT: I know nothing of the meeting.

Clearly, William Durham was concerned about Daniel's emphasis on the TCNO meeting of March 8, 1947, and Sweatt's admission that he was in Dallas at the time. When Sweatt added that he did not even know of the meeting, Durham sought to short-circuit that line of questioning.

DANIEL: Did you while you were in Dallas read a report in the *Dallas News* about what took place in that meeting?

SWEATT: I did not.

MR. DURHAM: We object to it as being hearsay.

JUDGE ARCHER: He says he didn't.

DANIEL: You did not. Isn't it true that you knew before the date of registration down here, March 10th, at the new Negro Law School, that certain leaders who were helping you in this case opposed this separate law school?

MR. DURHAM: We object to that about "certain leaders." There is no evidence in the record. It is purely an assumption.

JUDGE ARCHER: He can ask him if he did.

SWEATT: I don't know anything about—I don't know what leaders—I don't know anything about the leaders.

DANIEL: Do you know Joseph J. Rhoads, President of the Texas Council of Negro Organizations?

SWEATT: Yes, I do.

DANIEL: Did you discuss this law school with him while you were in Dallas?

SWEATT: No, I didn't.

DANIEL: Did you hear about the action his organization took against the school while you were in Dallas?

SWEATT: No.

MR. DURHAM: We object to it as hearsay.

THE COURT: He says he never heard it.

In short, Heman Sweatt stretched his credibility by testifying that while a guest at William Durham's Dallas home, he was never made aware of and knew nothing of a TCNO meeting in Dallas, which Durham almost certainly attended with Texas's African American leadership, to discuss the 13th Street law school.

Price Daniel's questions placed Thurgood Marshall and the NAACP on trial. In American jurisprudence, the attorney-client privilege is so sacred that communications in that context are protected by the Constitution. One of the reasons why lawyers are given such unconditional protection is the presumption, by everyone, that an attorney is representing his client *and no one else.* Price Daniel was coming uncomfortably close to demonstrating that Sweatt's attorneys were not concerned about their client of record but about a larger movement: the NAACP's crusade to end segregation. Marshall said as much in the meeting room of the Ebenezer Baptist Church in Austin on March 25 when he mocked Price Daniel at a public rally: "I was deeply surprised that certain parties have just now found out that the NAACP is trying to abolish all segregation. Will you please tell them that the NAACP will only stop when segregation stops."[4] The Austin newspapers published the remark the next day, and Price Daniel saw it. During the direct examination of his real client, Heman Sweatt, Thurgood Marshall probably regretted having made that statement.

In his analysis of the NAACP's legal strategy against segregated education, Mark Tushnet wrote: "Lawyers who use litigation only to advance their personal goals, rather than the goals of their clients, are usually thought to act unethically."[5] Heman Sweatt's value as a plaintiff was never more clearly demonstrated than at this moment in the story of *Sweatt v. Painter:* his dedication to the cause of the NAACP was unselfish and unflappable, and when the NAACP decided to replace its equalization strategy with a direct attack on segregation, he willingly followed and did what his lawyers told him to.[6] Now he was taking the heat for it during Daniel's direct examination.

To a certain extent, Sweatt himself was also on trial, because some believed that he was never serious about becoming a lawyer; and they weren't all white racists.[7] If Daniel could expose such a scheme, Heman Sweatt could be shown to be acting in bad faith.

> DANIEL: Now, your deposition was taken in this case on June 15, 1946, wasn't it?
>
> SWEATT: There was a deposition taken in Houston a little before the first hearing.
>
> DANIEL: Did you state in your deposition at that time, and as you have stated here, your attorney was Mr. Durham, is that right?
>
> SWEATT: Yes.
>
> DANIEL: At the time you filed this suit Mr. Marshall wasn't in the case at all representing you, was he?
>
> SWEATT: No.
>
> DANIEL: At the time we took your deposition on June 15, 1946, he was not in the case, was he?
>
> SWEATT: No.
>
> DANIEL: You had not known him, and he had not been brought into the case at the time your deposition was taken, had he?
>
> SWEATT: Not from me, no.
>
> DANIEL: From anybody else, your attorney or anybody else?
>
> SWEATT: Not that I know of.
>
> DANIEL: Isn't it a fact that in your deposition taken on June 15, 1946 that this question was asked to you, and you gave the following answer; this is the question: "Isn't it a fact that you would not attend the Prairie View University if legal training were provided for you there?" And didn't you give this answer?
>
> "That is not true. I will attend Prairie View University or a first class law school equal to the University of Texas." Isn't that true?
>
> SWEATT: I gave that answer.

During the June 15, 1946, deposition, Sweatt was giving answers his lawyers had instructed him to give. Eleven months later, on May 14, 1947, Sweatt's answers reflected a change in the NAACP's legal strategy to a direct attack on segregation.

> DANIEL: At that time, on June 15, 1946, you said that you would have attended a law school at Prairie View University if it was equivalent to that at the University of Texas?
>
> SWEATT: If it was equivalent.

DANIEL: In other words, you have no objection to a separate law school for Negroes if it is equivalent?

SWEATT: I will have to answer that question in this way. I don't believe in segregation. I don't believe equality can be given on the basis of segregation. I answered that question, in that it stated that it would be—if it would be given at Prairie View, I still do not believe that segregation will give equal training.

DANIEL: That is exactly the point I am getting at. On June 15, 1946 you were willing to accept segregation and a separate law school at Prairie View if it was on an equal basis, weren't you?

SWEATT: Assuming that it would be equal.

DANIEL: That is what I say. Is this your signature to the deposition that was taken on June 15th?

SWEATT: That is mine.

DANIEL: Now then, after June 15th, 1946, and after you had sworn in your deposition that you would go to a separate law school if it furnished equal facilities; after that time, Mr. Herbert Marshall—I mean Mr. Thurgood Marshall, Attorney for the National Association for the Advancement of Colored People, came into this case, and has been helping on it since then?

Throughout that line of questioning, William Durham objected that Daniel's questions did not represent the facts of the case, but Daniels did not let up on Sweatt: "After June 15, 1946, after you swore to that in this deposition, is when you made up your mind you were not for segregation at all?"

Thurgood Marshall had been sitting quietly while Daniel grilled Sweatt, but as the attorney general came uncomfortably closer to establishing bad faith on Sweatt's part, Marshall could sit no longer:

DANIEL: Have you changed your mind?

SWEATT: Yes.

DANIEL: And you changed it after June 15, 1946?

SWEATT: No, I changed it after studying the situation after filing the suit, after learning more facts about education.

DANIEL: After you swore that you would attend one on June 15, 1946, isn't that right?

SWEATT: That is the date of the deposition?

DANIEL: That is the date of the deposition.

SWEATT: After that.

DANIEL: After that date?

SWEATT: Yes.

DANIEL: And it was after that date that Mr. Thurgood Marshall of the
N.A.A.C.P. came into this case?

MARSHALL: I didn't object in the beginning, but I object at this stage to
cluttering up the record, and I wish, if the Court would permit me to take
up a case on all fours.[8] It is *State, ex rel. Bluford vs. Canada,* 153 S.W. (2d),
page 12. That is in regard to the Journalism School at the University of Missouri, and that case ruled against the same things we are urging in this case.
However, in that case the Attorney General of Missouri put up the same
type of smoke screen to the effect that the case wasn't the plaintiff's case,
but [instead] belonged to a public organization. And to put the case further
on all-fours, the organization is the National Association for the Advancement of Colored People, and the Supreme Court, although ruling against
us, had this to say: "In our view, if appellant has the legal right and actually
expects to attend the University, her motives for doing so are immaterial."
On that basis, we object to the continuation of this line of testimony.

JUDGE ARCHER: I think he has answered it, as far as we need on it.

DANIEL: If the Court please, I would like to say to the Court that our purpose here is not to show his motive for wanting to attend a law school. Our
purpose is to lead up to a connected chain of events motivating him not
to attend the separate school that has been offered to him, and, therefore,
showing bad faith on the part of the relator.

DURHAM: He had a right to change [his mind] one minute before ten
o'clock on the [March] 10th. That is an individual right and the fact that he
did change can't be questioned.

JUDGE ARCHER: I think he had a right to change his mind.

DANIEL: Yes, sir.

Judge Archer's ruling had a double edge. Stopping Daniel from pursuing
the bad-faith angle mattered little in a court that, no matter what, was going to rule against Sweatt. But it was still beneficial to Sweatt because, as
Marshall put it, the record would not be "cluttered" with Daniel's conspiracy theories.

But, of course, Daniel's line of questioning allowed Durham, Marshall,
and Sweatt to lapse into delusions. In much the same way that McCormick and Woodward had insisted that a couple of rooms in the basement
of a petroleum-engineering firm was equal to the University of Texas Law
School, Sweatt claimed to know nothing about the meetings, financing, or
involvement of the NAACP in his case.

Daniel continued his questioning by turning to the March 25 meeting at
Austin's Ebenezer Baptist Church:

DANIEL: Were you in Austin on March 26, 1947, about the time of the last hearing in the Court of Civil Appeals in this case?

SWEATT: I was here at the last hearing in the Court of Civil Appeals.

DANIEL: Isn't it true that you attended a meeting here in Austin the night of March 25th, at which Thurgood Marshall, the attorney here, spoke to a group of Negro citizens.

DURHAM: We object to that as completely immaterial and not germane to any issue.

JUDGE ARCHER: I don't see how it could assist us, Mr. Attorney General.

DANIEL: I want to prove as to what was said and done about that matter about finances for this case, for the purpose of showing that the National Association for the Advancement of Colored People had as much control and management of this case, and what happened in this situation about this law school as he does himself, and that they have the further purpose of following that up with a concerted program to boycott this law school and keep other students out. Your Honor, we were careful not to bring up the point about no students over there. Only Marion Sweatt, did we, on direct examination show, was not in that school. The relator on every possible occasion has pointed to the fact that there were no students there, and we feel like we can show that chain of events and it is his fault and the people supporting the lawsuit that they don't have students, and that is a material issue in this case.

JUDGE ARCHER: Anything he would testify to would be hearsay, wouldn't it? It would be what somebody said, wouldn't it?

DANIEL: No, sir; I believe, Your Honor, that I can refresh his memory as to knowledge of money which has been spent in this case by N.A.A.C.P. I am trying to refresh his memory. I am also trying to—I will also try to impeach him in the fact that he said he doesn't know anything about the expenses paid by N.A.A.C.P., and show that he does know about it, and knew about it at this meeting where $20,000.00 was asked for.

The NAACP Papers in the Library of Congress show conclusively that Daniel was correct. For months, Thurgood Marshall had battled for the complete supremacy of the national association over the local chapters in all areas of civil rights litigation. Marshall's courtroom response was that even if the attorney general could prove all of what he was alleging, it didn't matter. Sweatt was the plaintiff, and how he made decisions and paid for his legal representation was his business and not relevant to whether he was to attend the University of Texas Law School.

Contrary to his testimony, Sweatt knew everything about his case and how it was being financed. To believe otherwise is to think he was a fool.

He was approving and cooperative. He understood what his attorneys were doing and that it was more for the greater good of justice for African Americans than for his personal benefit. Unlike Lloyd Gaines of Missouri, who craved blandishments, made demands for money, and ultimately disappeared before his case could be completed, Sweatt courageously faced the perils of being an NAACP soldier. But he didn't admit to it while on the witness stand.

DANIEL: Isn't it true that at that meeting you attended [March 25] you heard Mr. Marshall say that this case had already cost $6,000.00, and that the N.A.A.C.P. was helping finance it.

SWEATT: I don't remember.

MR. DURHAM: That is immaterial.

JUDGE ARCHER: He said he didn't hear it.

DANIEL: Did you hear Mr. Marshall tell the crowd you needed to raise $20,000.00 for this lawsuit.

MR. DURHAM: That would be hearsay, what the attorney said. It is purely hearsay.

DANIEL: Are you paying Mr. Marshall a salary or fee for assisting you in this case?

SWEATT: I am not.

DANIEL: The National Association for the Advancement of Colored People is furnishing his services?

SWEATT: I don't know.

DANIEL: You don't know how he came into the case?

SWEATT: He came into the case—in a conference with Mr. Durham, he said he would get assistance in the case, and how he got it and who is paying him, I don't know.

DANIEL: Do you know whether or not the National Association for the Advancement of Colored People have encouraged this lawsuit, and encouraged people to support it?

DURHAM: We object to it.

DANIEL: I asked if he knew.

DURHAM: We object to that as irrelevant and immaterial.

JUDGE ARCHER: If it was communicated directly to him, I expect it would be helpful.

SWEATT: I don't know.

Moments later Price Daniel completed his direct examination of Heman Sweatt by having him state that he consulted W. J. Durham about whether the "basement school" provided a law-school education equal to that of the

University of Texas. According to Sweatt, he decided not to enroll in the basement school "after talking to somebody who could judge a law school. I could not do that."

> DANIEL: If it is thought that the separate Negro Law School in Austin offers you absolutely equal facilities, you wouldn't attend it, would you?
> MR. DURHAM: We object. It is a supposition.
> JUDGE ARCHER: I believe in that case he would have a right to answer if, in his opinion, this school was absolutely equal.
> SWEATT: It depends upon an assumption that I can not agree with.
> DANIEL: If you could agree with it, let's say that, let's say we leave it to other judges, and some judges, somebody who knows about it, found it to be so, and we assume it is so, that the new Negro Law School is absolutely equivalent to the University of Texas Law School, but it is a separate school for Negroes, you wouldn't attend it, would you?
> SWEATT: I would not.
> DANIEL: That is all.

In some ways, Daniel's direct examination of Heman Sweatt was similar to Nabrit's cross-examination of Dean McCormick: they were both fast, loud, and gratifying to supporters of each side's cause. The difference was that Daniel successfully showed that the NAACP was behind both *Sweatt v. Painter* and a boycott that caused the failure of two makeshift law schools to attract a single student. Everyone already knew that, and it didn't matter as long as Heman Marion Sweatt was willing to be a plaintiff. Sweatt was the only person with the standing to complain that his lawyers were not representing him—and he was not about to do that. On the other hand, Nabrit showed that the 13th Street school was makeshift and that representing it as equal to the University of Texas Law School was utter nonsense. Everyone knew that, as well, but it mattered because it supported both legal approaches to improving education for African Americans: equalization and integration.

During the first round of hearings the previous December, Carter Wesley had written in the *Houston Informer* that "any impartial spectator would admit that the lawyers for Sweatt were the best lawyers in the court."[9] In May 1947, in the same courtroom, nothing had changed. And yet it was during this period, in letters widely circulated from late 1946 through nearly all of 1947, that Carter Wesley viciously attacked Thurgood Marshall for his handling of NAACP-sponsored litigation.

Carter Wesley was a complicated man.

CHAPTER 15

The Sociological Argument

There is no understandable factual basis for classification by race.
THURGOOD MARSHALL, BEFORE THE 126TH DISTRICT COURT
OF TRAVIS COUNTY, TEXAS, MAY 14, 1947

Heman Sweatt's testimony made a favorable impression on opposing counsel, Assistant Attorney General Joe Greenhill. During the 10:30 recess on May 14, 1947, Greenhill approached Thurgood Marshall and congratulated him on his "masterful job" of preparing Sweatt as a witness.

"Well, you know we woodshed our witnesses pretty well. Matter of fact, I expected him to do well. We went out early this morning and filled him full of gin."[1]

Of course the remark was a joke: no witness with gin in his system could have handled Price Daniel as well as Sweatt did. The comment is a good example of Marshall's affability. As Greenhill said decades later, "You couldn't help but like him."

That might have been one reason why Daniel, after questioning Sweatt, told Judge Archer, "Your Honor . . . I was just thinking, they have some witnesses they are in a hurry to put on, so I suppose it would be all right for us to stop our testimony, and come back to it later." Judge Archer recessed for ten minutes, and testimony resumed at 3:15.

Dr. Robert Redfield was an attorney as well as a professor and chairman of the Anthropology Department at the University of Chicago. He specialized in "problems between racial and color groups." For twenty years, he had conducted research on group differences, including those among school children. Thurgood Marshall quickly got to the reason for Redfield's appearance: "Well, Dr. Redfield, as a result of your studies, are you still in a position to give your opinion on the general subject? I will give you more specific ones later, but I wish on the general subject of, one, the inappropriateness of segregation to the purposes of education, [two,] the inappropriateness of segregation in education to the interests of public security end of it, and [three,] to the general welfare of the community?"

Before Dr. Redfield could respond, Daniel objected: "Your Honor, we object because this lawsuit involves only education in law and procedure. We object to . . . any other questions [not] along that line." Daniel's objection and Marshall's reply was a pivotal moment in American legal history. What became known as the "sociological approach" had been attempted previously in a California case involving Mexicans and Mexican Americans, but as Marshall later remembered, "it really came out in *Sweatt* and *McLaurin*."[2]

The sociological approach, largely the brainchild of Marshall's assistant Robert L. Carter, claimed that measures of equality should not be limited to inanimate objects like buildings, books, and money. A comprehensive measure of educational equality should include social and cultural capital as well (the accoutrements of privilege).[3]

When applied to segregation, the sociological approach added another dimension to inequality: racial separation in schools meant that whites had available to them a social network not available to blacks, producing a false sense of superiority in whites and an equally false sense of inferiority in blacks, neither of which had any scientific support or rational basis in fact. Inequality could not be remedied by merely cloning the buildings, books, teachers, and money invested in separate white schools. The only logical remedy was the integration of schools. Blacks could then have access to and exploit the same contacts as whites.[4]

Criticism of the introduction of the sociological approach in a court of law was not limited to segregationists like Price Daniel. In his memoirs, Robert Carter recalled: "The proposed use of social scientists' testimony came under fierce attack from the outset. A number of the most influential members of the committee [the NAACP's advisory committee on legal strategy] scorned social science data as without substance, since it was not hard science, proved by tests in the laboratory, but merely the reactions of a group of people." Professor Thomas R. Powell of Harvard, a lawyer and political scientist, called the idea the "silliest thing he had ever heard of." Carter and Marshall responded that if segregation was to be directly attacked, it had to be proved to be an unreasonable and irrational practice. The sole purpose of segregation was to subjugate one race to another—a public policy in violation of the Fourteenth Amendment.[5]

For Thurgood Marshall, the idea must have been reminiscent of a teaching of his mentor, Charles Houston: "A lawyer is either a social engineer or he is a parasite on society."[6]

The sociological approach contributed greatly to the cause of civil rights—all the way to *Brown v. Board of Education*—but in Austin in 1947 there was no guarantee that it would be heard, much less accepted as a courtroom tactic. It was against that background that Price Daniel's objection, Thurgood Marshall's response, and Judge Roy Archer's ruling became a major turning point in the civil rights movement. To Daniel's objection, Marshall responded:

> MARSHALL: May it please the Court . . . in our original petition we
> claimed that the refusal to admit the relator was in violation of the
> 14th Amendment, and in all of the pleadings filed by the State of Texas,
> no question has ever been raised as to the qualifications of relator other than
> his race or color . . . Then follows the allegation that the refusal to admit
> the relator in this case was not arbitrary at all . . . but was in keeping with
> the segregation statutes of the State of Texas . . . So, I think that the lines
> are drawn in this case, and the direct attack has been made that the statutes
> requiring segregation, the general statutes which prohibit this relator from
> attending the University of Texas, we claim are unconstitutional, and we
> have the right to show their unconstitutionality . . . *They haven't shown any*
> *line of reasoning for the statutes.* I imagine they are relying on the presump-
> tion that the statutes are constitutional. If they are relying on that, we have
> a right to put in evidence to show that segregation statutes . . . have *no line*
> *of reasonableness. There is no understandable factual basis for classification by*
> *race.* (emphasis added)[7]

During this argument, Marshall admitted that he was pursuing the "reasonableness" approach for the first time. He continued:

> And under a long line of decisions by the Supreme Court, not on the
> question of Negroes, but on the 14th Amendment, all courts agree that if
> there is no rational basis for the classification, it is flat in the teeth of the
> 14th Amendment.

In what, in retrospect, was a historic ruling, Judge Archer responded: "I will let you offer your testimony."

As stated earlier, Assistant Attorney General Greenhill always believed that Judge Archer granted Sweatt's lawyers a great deal of leeway in order to avoid a reversal on appeal. If so, this ruling proved to be extremely generous. Marshall and Durham could hardly have condemned Judge Archer for not allowing the sociological approach when, as Robert Carter said, "some of the most influential members" of the NAACP's own legal advisory committee thought it lacked substance.

Judge Archer, however, attached a disclaimer to allowing the testimony: "We are presumed to act only upon what is admissible testimony in the last analysis, anyhow. So I am going to hear it, and if in my opinion it is material and admissible testimony, I will consider it. If it isn't, I will not." Judge Archer had no trial jury to dismiss, so the proffered testimony needed to be presented only once.

"Not considering" something proffered in court is rather fictitious: to the nonlawyer, Judge Archer did consider it because he allowed it in his court. He did not give weight to the sociological evidence in his ultimate decision, but that did not matter: Marshall got it in the record for the U.S. Supreme Court to consider.

Marshall returned to his questioning of Dr. Redfield with a direct question: "Dr. Redfield, are there any recognizable differences as between Negro and White students on the question of their intellectual capacity?" Price Daniel objected immediately, complaining that the testimony went beyond the issue at hand, which was the admission of one Negro to a law school. Daniel also objected to Redfield stating conclusions without first describing how those conclusions were reached.

Redfield offered to describe the studies he had used to reach his conclusions, and Judge Archer allowed the testimony.

> REDFIELD: We . . . have been working in the field in which we began with a rather general presumption among our common educators that inherent differences in intellectual ability of capacity to learn existed between Negroes and Whites, and have slowly, but I think very convincingly, been compelled to come to the opposite conclusion . . . Perhaps at this point it is sufficient to say that the general conclusion to which I come, and which I think is shared by a very large majority of specialists—
> DANIEL: We object to that as hearsay, Your Honor.
> JUDGE ARCHER: I think so.
> REDFIELD: The conclusion, then, to which I come, is differences in intellectual capacity or inability to learn have not been shown to exist as between Negroes and Whites.

When Marshall asked the effect of segregation on schoolchildren, Redfield responded that the policy was "unfavorable to the full realization of the objectives of education" for both whites and Negroes because neither group can come to a full realization of the other—and they will all have to live together. Indeed, segregation fostered suspicion and distrust that "are not favorable conditions either for the acquisition and conduct of an education, or for the discharge of the duties of a citizen." Segregation, Redfield continued, denied students a "complete and natural representation of the full community" and accentuated "imagined differences between Negroes and Whites." At the University of Chicago, where he worked, integration was beneficial to everyone, Redfield insisted. At Marshall's prompting, Redfield testified that there were no ill effects—only benefits, like the improvement of relations between racial groups.

Before Daniel cross-examined Redfield, he addressed Judge Archer: "I want to be sure that my exceptions and objections have gone to the entire testimony."[8] Judge Archer assured him that they had.

Daniel began with a series of questions challenging the validity of Redfield's conclusions, which he [Redfield] had testified were based on science. Interestingly, the focus of Daniel's challenge was not whether segregation was good or bad, but whether it should be ended immediately or gradually. Daniel tried to get Redfield to admit that "gradualism" was better for blacks and whites than "immediacy."

> DANIEL: In other words, do you recognize or agree with the school of thought that, regardless of the ultimate objective concerning segregation, that if it is to be changed in southern communities where it has been in effect for many years, if it is to be changed successfully, it must be done over a long period of time, as the people in that community change their ideas on the matter?
>
> REDFIELD: That contention, I do not think, will be my opinion on the matter scientifically.

Daniel's ambition to expose the NAACP as the real source of the movement to desegregate Texas included his branding of Redfield as a political descendant of an infamous post–Civil War group.

> DANIEL: You are acquainted with the history of the carpet bagger days in the Civil War?
>
> REDFIELD: I feel better acquainted with it today, sir, than anybody.

The courtroom erupted in laughter. After an initial pause, Price Daniel laughed as well, but he clearly did not think Redfield's remark was funny, because he followed with serious questions that Redfield dodged.[9]

DANIEL: Dr. Redfield, let me get you clearly on that. You are not talking about your own trip down here, are you, to Texas? You say you are acquainted with it today?

REDFIELD: It just drifted into my mind.

DANIEL: You recall the carpetbaggers, where they packed up and came down here from out of the state. You didn't mean to be talking about your trip down here, did you? You are the only witness from out of the state that we have had on, so far. You didn't mean to be talking about the trip down here?

REDFIELD: I am afraid the idea has come into my mind now.

Robert Redfield wasn't laughing anymore. The attorney general positioned him into admitting that the last time the North had tried to impose integration on Texas, it failed. Daniel returned to the carpetbagger questions, and this time Redfield did not make any jokes.

DANIEL: Are you acquainted with the history of the carpetbagger days in the South?

REDFIELD: In a very general way.

DANIEL: You know, do you know, from that history, that the attempt to force the abolition of segregation in the South just didn't work?

REDFIELD: Yes, of course.

DANIEL: Do you feel like the social attitudes and beliefs of the people in that day had some bearing on whether or not it would work?

REDFIELD: Oh, yes.

DANIEL: Of both races?

REDFIELD: Oh, yes.

Daniel then followed with what was probably a jab at Thurgood Marshall and James Nabrit, Jr., a graduate and the dean of Howard University Law School, respectively.

DANIEL: Would you undertake to testify here, Dr. Redfield, that students attending that separate Law School for Negroes at Howard University do not receive equal educational opportunities in law with those attending a similar white school?

REDFIELD: In my opinion, deprivation of opportunity to exchange professional and intellectual matters with members of the other major groups in their nation is one of the short-comings of the school.

DANIEL: You have never made any check, though, as to students who have come out of that school, and [whether] that has been a handicap on them, have you?

REDFIELD: No, I never have.

DANIEL: It is just your idea it is a handicap, without having checked to see whether or not it is?

REDFIELD: That is right.

The Attorney General continued hammering Redfield: "I am simply trying to ask you, since you have testified that a certain amount of doing away with segregation is necessary, I want to know . . . how far it must be done away with in order to accomplish the best for the individual, the school and the community." Most of Redfield's replies were unresponsive, because, of course, he had no answer for that question.

When Daniel asked about social integration, Marshall objected, saying that Redfield's testimony should be limited to education benefits. For the most part, Judge Archer sustained Marshall's objections, but Daniel was making the point that Redfield's theme of desegregation serving the public good could not be applied in a consistent and uniform way. What was the limit of segregation? Daniel insisted on an answer. Redfield replied: "That general limit will be defined in my particular conclusion, as [to] the particular circumstances." What Redfield advocated appeared rather arbitrary.

Daniel was not the only person to question the ideas that Redfield's testimony put forth. Daniel's goal, as a matter of fact, was to make the same point that a dissenting group on the NAACP legal advisory committee had warned about when they opposed the use of the sociological approach: social science was not "hard science, proved by tests in the laboratory, but merely the reactions of a group of people."

Interrogating a Lawyer

When prompted to call his next witness, Price Daniel announced, "I want to call W. J. Durham." Testimony from a lawyer for one of the litigants is quite rare. But Daniel wanted to show, first, that the NAACP was behind the entire *Sweatt v. Painter* suit and, second, that no students had enrolled in the law schools the state set up for African Americans because of a boycott organized by the NAACP.

The record does not make clear whether Durham consented to taking the stand, but he was sworn in late in the afternoon of May 14. His answers were as short and direct as those Heman Sweatt had delivered. With only one exception, which brought an objection from James Nabrit, Jr., Daniel steered clear of asking questions that would violate the attorney-client privilege.

Daniel's direct examination of Durham focused on how much control the NAACP's national office had over the *Sweatt* suit and how the suit was being financed. Durham testified that to date the NAACP had paid $100 for the record on appeal. Far more valuable to the *Sweatt* case was that the services of Thurgood Marshall were being supplied free of charge.

Daniel's questioning also sought to connect Durham to the March 8 meeting of the Texas Council of Negro Organizations in Dallas. Durham admitted that during that week Heman Sweatt was his guest, but he never admitted that he or Sweatt attended the meeting. Instead, he explained that in the past he had attended many meetings with similar agendas and that he could not specifically recall being at that particular one. With a newspaper clipping (probably from the *Dallas Morning News*) in hand to "refresh" Durham's memory, Daniel pressed Durham to admit to attending the meeting. Durham stuck to his answer: he didn't remember.

Daniel also got Durham to admit that he advised Sweatt not to enroll in the 13th Street law school and that he had done little or nothing to check out the facility or the faculty assigned to teach there. Most of his information came from a report he requested of Maceo Smith, the secretary of the NAACP's Texas State Conference.

Thurgood Marshall's cross-examination of Durham cleared up the differences between the national office of the NAACP and the Texas State Conference. The money contributed by the NAACP to Heman Sweatt's cause came from the conference, which was a membership organization of about 40,000 black and white Texans.

William Durham was the last witness on May 14. It had been a long and memorable day.

Two More Deans Heard From

The next day's testimony began with James Nabrit, Jr., calling the dean of the University of Pennsylvania Law School, Earl G. Harrison, to the stand. Harrison, who was also the vice chairman of the American Bar Association's Committee on Continuing Education, was called to comment on segregation as public policy. It didn't take long for Harrison to get to the point of his testimony.

HARRISON: In my opinion, it is mistaken, even absurd, to speak of any
institution that has one student as a law school.
NABRIT: Why?
HARRISON: Because the system, the modern system of instruction used in
a law school is what is known as the case system: the case method. That is
to be contrasted with the former method of the lecture system, in which the
professor of law merely sat and lectured to the class, in which case it didn't
make much difference how many or how few students there were in the
class.

The lecture and textbook methods require students to work with "predigested" material from an author or expert in the field. When those methods
are used, students are treated like passive receptacles and are tested on the
amount of information they can regurgitate.

In the case method, by contrast, students become teaching tools for one
another.

HARRISON: That system merely means that the students go to the original
sources for their materials, namely, the decisions of the courts, and under
that system the professor does very much less talking than he did under the
lecture system. He calls on some member of the class to make a report on a
given case which has appeared in the case book, and right at that point, the
professor usually calls for comment from the other members of the class,
and from there on it is largely a matter of discussion in which the members
of the class participate to a large extent, one commenting on the recital
made by the previous; another criticizing his statement, either the facts of
the case or the decision arrived at by the Court, and it is first and foremost a
class discussion.

Harrison explained how the case method was impossible to use in a school
with one student; even with a class of ten, the method would be so restricted
that it would be meaningless. Large law schools have the advantage of using
students as teaching tools: the larger and more diverse the student body, the
more powerful the teaching tool.

And even if a black law school had a large number of students, segregation neutralizes a key component of the case method. Implied in the method
is the value of gaining experience with the diversity of people attorneys will
face in the practice of law. In 1947, every Texas judge was white. The 1940
census showed that there were 7,701 white lawyers and 23 black ones in the

state. African American law students securing their training in a segregated law school were effectively quarantined from 99.3 percent of the members of their profession.

The disadvantage of a small law school such as the 13th Street school was more than just a lack of racial diversity. Even with a "full" class of ten students, the school would have no upperclassmen. Harrison testified: "It would have a very material bearing upon the legal training the student would receive. In other words, work in a law school outside of regular class room hours is exceedingly important. Rubbing elbows with the other students in the law school, taking part in small discussion groups, discussion with advanced students, all are very important considerations, equally so, in my opinion, with the actual class room work itself."

Harrison explained that in studies he reviewed, a "small" law school had from 50 to 150 students. Those schools were less likely to produce a well-educated, well-rounded attorney. Such small schools were also less likely to offer students the opportunities and teaching tools, such as moot court and law review, that Dean McCormick had characterized as "extraneous"; Dean Harrison characterized them as "extremely important."

Nabrit guided Harrison's testimony through a point-by-point refutation of McCormick's assertions that the black and white law schools were substantially equal. Full-time professors and immediate access to a certified program were necessary, especially for students who might want or need to transfer credits from one law school to another, something that was not possible if the original school was not certified.

During cross-examination, Price Daniel sparred with Harrison over the advantages of having smaller classes, even when using the case method of teaching. Harrison did agree that in smaller classes a student was more likely to give recitations, comment on other students' recitations, and cover more cases, but he qualified his answer: in larger classes, a student will certainly hear more varied recitations and comments. Further, even if smaller classes resulted in the advantages Daniel alleged, black students would still be denied access to the ideas of more than 99 percent of the future lawyers of Texas.

After Harrison's testimony, Thurgood Marshall hoped to use testimony from Charles H. Thompson to provide the court with an overview of educational opportunities throughout Texas. Thompson was dean of the Graduate School of Howard University and a former editor of the *Journal of Negro Education*. He was active in many professional associations, including the Southern Association of Colleges and Secondary Schools, an accrediting agency. He had been in Austin for about two weeks researching educational opportunities for African American Texans. Before coming to Austin, he had spent a month "exhausting" similar data at the Howard University Library and government sources in the Washington, D.C., area. Thompson's trip to Texas included self-guided tours of the University of Texas and Prairie View A&M University.

Marshall took longer than usual to establish Thompson's credentials. Daniel did not challenge the witness's qualifications as an expert. He did, however, argue that the right Sweatt was contesting was an individual one involving two schools only—the one he was offered and the one he was applying to—which made testimony about other schools irrelevant and inadmissible. Again, Judge Archer ruled that unless the testimony had a final bearing on *Sweatt*, he would not "consider" it; he allowed Marshall to continue. And again, Marshall got what he wanted in the record.

Dean Thompson identified five criteria commonly recognized as measures of educational quality. First, he spoke of "institutional assets," a combination of physical facilities, which he called "plant assets," and the general total assets of an institution, including endowments. Second was the operational budget at the disposal of the institution; third, the curriculum, especially the courses of study offered; fourth, the quality and prestige of the faculty; and fifth, the library, including its staff. He added that the reputation of the institution "in the educational world and in the community" should be considered as well.

When Marshall prompted Thompson to compare Prairie View to UT and all other schools available to white students, Daniel renewed his objection; he said the testimony had no bearing on the extant case. Again, Judge Archer admitted he did not see a connection to the matter at hand, but he allowed the testimony to continue.

Using a number of state and federal surveys and government reports on higher education, catalogues from all of Texas's four-year colleges (except Texas Tech), and audit and annual reports, Thompson compared white institutions with Prairie View (the only recipient of Texas's public investment in Negro higher education) using the five criteria.

Thompson applied the provisions of the Second Morrill Act of 1890 as a measure of what should have been Texas's allocation of resources to Negro higher education: African Americans made up 14.4 percent of the population and so should have gotten that portion of state expenditures.

In fiscal year 1945–1946, the value of state-owned facilities at four-year institutions was approximately $72,790,097. Prairie View, the only campus accessible to African Americans, had plant assets of $2,170,910. Even after adding in $2,000,000 from sb 140, the figure was far less than half of the

Table 15.1. Comparison of the Number of Professionals to the Populations They Serve, by Race, in the State of Texas

Profession	White		Black	
	Number	Ratio	Number	Ratio
Physician	6,076	1/903	164	1/5,637
Dentist	1,901	1/2,886	81	1/11,412
Engineer	8,961	1/612	6	1/154,065
Lawyer	7,701	1/712	23	1/40,191

Source: U.S. Census, 1940

$10.5 million share that should have been apportioned to "Negro education" in Texas. Thompson then translated the figures into ratios: the state was spending $12.88 on higher education for every white citizen, but only $4.71 for every black Texan.

Thompson testified that the sum of "institutional assets" for Texas public institutions of higher education was $162,039,628. Prairie View's share, including $3,350,000 from SB 140, equaled $5,918,554. So Texas owned $6.40 of assets for higher education for each African American; the figure for whites was 4.47 times higher, $28.66 per person. A large portion of this difference was due to the Permanent University Fund. In 1945, the value of the PUF was $61,277,162. Prairie View's entire endowment consisted of $26,000 in U.S. government securities.

Marshall guided Thompson through even more shameful statistics: during the 1943 legislative session, the appropriation for higher education was $1.98 for each white person, but just 23 cents for each black Texan.

Judge Archer allowed Marshall to "expose" Texas's legacy of neglect of its duty to educate its African American population—a neglect that resulted in a quality of life significantly below that enjoyed by whites. That, Marshall argued, was in violation of the equal protection clause of the U.S. Constitution. In his testimony, Thompson expressed the differences in both raw counts and ratios of professionals to racial populations. The ratios of black professionals to their Texas constituents compared unfavorably even with figures from other black populations, such as those that benefited from black professional schools like Meharry Medical School and Fisk University (both in Nashville) and Howard University in Washington, D.C.

Throughout Thompson's testimony, Daniel objected that the entire line of questioning was immaterial and irrelevant: all that was relevant was whether the 13th Street law school offered Sweatt an equal or substantially equal educational experience as that provided to whites by the University of Texas. Repeatedly, Judge Archer allowed the testimony but cautioned that he would not consider any irrelevant parts of it when making his ruling.

Thompson then addressed differences in curriculums between the white universities and Prairie View. No one in the courtroom should have been surprised to learn that the white universities had three times as many academic departments, offering twice as many majors, as Prairie View. The difference was also qualitative: Prairie View offered courses in mattress making, dry cleaning, broom making, shoe repair, and plumbing. Graduate-school opportunities were even bleaker. From 1940 to 1945, Texas universities awarded 212 doctorates to whites and none to blacks. In separately funded research, white universities received $2,753,809, whereas Prairie View got nothing.

Gifted African American Texans wanting legal, dental, or medical training were given only one option: the out-of-state tuition-assistance program, which had already been ruled constitutionally insufficient in *Gaines*. Thompson's figures showed that Texas spent about $1,500 a year for every white dental student, but the most money a black student could receive to leave Texas for a dental-school education was $400. For medical students, the figures were $1,900 and $500, respectively.

The gross underfunding of African American education took its toll on Prairie View's ability to attract, compensate, and retain a qualified teaching force. Thompson explained that in five years Prairie View had lost twenty-five faculty members, eleven of whom had terminal degrees, to better-paying institutions outside of Texas.

The differences in the salaries of white teachers and what Prairie View could offer was stunning. As Thompson testified: "Except for one white teacher in thirteen white State-supported higher institutions, holding comparable positions in comparable departments, the highest salary paid a full professor in Prairie View is lower than the lowest salary paid a white professor in any one of these thirteen institutions, on a nine months basis." Until *Gaines* and *Sweatt*, the State of Texas made no attempt at even a semblance of dignity for Prairie View professors and administrators. The school's chief executive was not even designated as president—he was the "principal."

Thompson finished his overview of Texas's neglect of its African American citizens by comparing the libraries of Prairie View with those of other Texas colleges. White schools of comparable size had roughly two to three times as many books. UT's library, one of the finest in the world, had approximately thirty times more books.

When Daniel rose to cross examine Thompson, the attorney general may have known that Judge Archer would not consider Thompson's testimony. That could explain Daniel's rather lackluster line of questioning. Daniel did get Thompson to admit that his figures were historic—that is, they did not reflect what the state intended to do—and that he had not figured the allocations by number of students but by total population.

Daniel ended with contentious questions about whether black students would be "unhappy" in white schools. It was reminiscent of Grover Sellers's assertion during the first trial that he had nothing but the "tenderest feeling" for Heman Sweatt.

One Who Had Been There

Following the testimony of educational experts, Marshall called a witness with personal experience of the desegregation of an all-white law school. Donald G. Murray, an Amherst graduate who returned to his hometown of Baltimore with the goal of becoming an attorney, was also the plaintiff in Marshall's first major civil-rights court victory. At the time of Murray's graduation in 1934, African American Marylanders wanting to become attorneys were expected to take a train to Washington, D.C., and attend Howard University Law School. Instead, Thurgood Marshall and Charles Houston represented Murray and petitioned a Maryland court for a writ of mandamus ordering officials of the University of Maryland Law School to admit him. The district court granted the writ, and Murray enrolled in September 1935.

While Murray matriculated at the University of Maryland, Attorney General Herbert O'Conor and Assistant Attorney General Charles T. Le-Viness III filed an appeal arguing that Murray's enrollment would cause a severe disruption, even violence, on Maryland Law's campus.

As with Charles Thompson, Price Daniel objected to Donald Murray as a witness and his testimony as being irrelevant and immaterial.

> JUDGE ARCHER TO MARSHALL: Tell me your purpose of it. I don't quite see.
> MARSHALL: The whole purpose of it is that in the State of Maryland they have segregation statutes similar to the State of Texas. He was refused admission, and a lawsuit was filed, and they said if he was admitted to the school it would wreck the University, and he was admitted, and everybody got along fine.

JUDGE ARCHER: How is he going to prove what the State said except by hearsay?

MARSHALL: We have here a document from the Court of Civil Appeals, and motion to advance a case, signed by the Attorney General, and the Assistant Attorney General, from the State of Maryland. That is the only piece of evidence we are going to introduce as to what the State of Maryland said.

JUDGE ARCHER: Might not that be the attorney's contention?

MARSHALL: He was representing it as the official attorney of the State of Maryland.

JUDGE ARCHER: I will let you have it on your bill. You can offer it on your bill.

MR. MARSHALL: Thank you, sir.

Murray testified that none of Attorney General O'Conor's predictions of "dire consequences" came true. He was not ostracized, segregated, or mistreated in any way. Murray added, "My experience, briefly, was that I attended the University of Maryland Law School for three years, during which time I took all of the classes with the rest of the students, and participated in all of the activities in the school, and at no time whatever did I meet any attempted segregation or unfavorable treatment on the part of any student in the school, or any professor or assistant professor."

Marshall closed his direct examination of Murray by asking him to relate how Maryland's attorney general later became governor and was the official who handed Murray his law-school diploma during commencement exercises; the assistant attorney general was the first to hire Murray, as an attorney for the Board of Liquor License.

Price Daniel declined to cross-examine Donald Murray, so Thurgood Marshall quickly called J. B. Rutland to the stand. Rutland was the current director of education for Negroes at the Texas Department of Education. He was also the executive secretary of the scholarship committee that awarded state funds for African Americans to attend out-of-state graduate and professional schools. While Marshall did not ask Rutland for a direct opinion whether the program provided equal opportunities for postgraduate work, the figures spoke for themselves. Since the program's inception in 1939, its expenditures had never exceeded $24,000 in a single year, and in that time only eleven Negroes had been able to accept any money to go to law school.

The next witness, Henry Doyle, according to earlier testimony by Registrar E. J. Matthews, was the only African American prospective student to actually go to the school and make an inquiry. He spoke to an assistant registrar but ultimately decided that he was not yet ready to attend.

Henry Doyle was a teacher and grocery-store owner in his midthirties who wanted to be a lawyer. Price Daniel called him to the stand in yet another attempt to show that the failure of the 13th Street school to enroll students was due to the interference of the NAACP. It seemed important to Daniel to establish that Doyle was a participant in the March 8 meeting in Dallas that had been called by the Texas Council of Negro Organizations. Clearly, however, he had not woodshedded Doyle.

> DANIEL: How long did you stay there at the meeting in Dallas?
>
> DOYLE: I am not sure, approximately two hours.
>
> DANIEL: Were other officers of the National Association for the Advancement of Colored People there?
>
> DURHAM: We object to that as assuming that he knows them.
>
> JUDGE ARCHER: Unless he knows of his own knowledge.
>
> DURHAM: We object to it for the reason that he presupposes that he knows, and it is an assumption not based upon any facts.
>
> DOYLE: I do not.
>
> DANIEL: You do not know. What was the name of the group that held that meeting?
>
> DURHAM: We object to that as assuming that he knows.
>
> JUDGE ARCHER: If he knows.
>
> DOYLE: I do not know.
>
> DANIEL: Who notified you to come to the meeting?
>
> DOYLE: I was notified by circular letter.
>
> DANIEL: From whom?
>
> DOYLE: I don't recall the signature.
>
> DANIEL: Was the support of this lawsuit pending here by the National Association for the Advancement of Colored People mentioned at that meeting by anyone?
>
> DURHAM: We object to that.
>
> JUDGE ARCHER: Of course, it would not be admissible unless the relator was there, and unless he made it.
>
> DURHAM: And unless it was by his authority, and we object to it as not being binding upon the relator, unless he shows that connection.
>
> JUDGE ARCHER: That is right.
>
> DANIEL: Did you see Heman Marion Sweatt there?
>
> DOYLE: I did not.
>
> DANIEL: Did you see Mr. Durham, the man that just made the objection, any time during that meeting?

DOYLE: I saw him.

DANIEL: Did he appear before the meeting?

DOYLE: He did.

DANIEL: Before that meeting concluded, did you announce to that meeting that you would not enter the law school, Negro Law School on March 10, 1947?

DURHAM: We object to that as being irrelevant and immaterial as to what he would do.

JUDGE ARCHER: I believe I will let him answer it, in view of our prior rulings of that. We may strike it all later.

DANIEL: Did you make such statement to the meeting before it adjourned?

DOYLE: I said I was seeking information relative to making up my mind whether or not I would enter the law school.

DANIEL: Did you announce before the meeting was over that you would not enter the law school the next Monday morning?

DOYLE: I did not.

Doyle's denial stunned Daniel.

DANIEL: Didn't you tell me that you did?

DURHAM: We object to him arguing with his own witness.

JUDGE ARCHER: That is right.

DANIEL: Did you enter the Negro Law School on March 10, 1947?

DOYLE: I did not.

DANIEL: That is all.

Durham declined to ask Doyle any questions so that he could be dismissed as a witness. In an understatement, Judge Archer announced, "I think the testimony is perhaps not relevant," and ruled that it be stricken from the record. Doyle's testimony was a severe setback for Daniel, who seemed determined to show what everyone knew: the NAACP was behind the *Sweatt* case and the boycott of the state's attempts to open a Jim Crow law school to keep black students out of UT Law. It was also embarrassing: the Attorney General put a witness on the stand without knowing what that witness was going to say. The next day, Texas's big-city dailies reported on Daniel's unsuccessful attempts to "wring" testimony from Doyle.[10]

At four twenty, Daniel announced that he had no more witnesses for the day. Judge Archer called a recess until nine the next morning.

CHAPTER 16

The House That Sweatt Built

To keep Heman Sweatt out of its white college, Texas builds one for him, but he won't go to it.

LIFE, SEPTEMBER 29, 1947

The debate over whether the case method was appropriate for teaching law in very small classes continued when the state called UT Law professor A. W. Walker to the stand and Assistant Attorney General Joe Greenhill made his début as a questioner. But Walker's testimony was little more than a rehash of previous testimony provided by both the state's and Sweatt's witnesses about the law-school teaching experience. Greenhill, however, proved himself to be more adept than Price Daniel at handling the vigorous cross-examination of James Nabrit, Jr. He even used it to the state's advantage.

> GREENHILL: Judge Walker, these thought-provoking questions that [James Nabrit, Jr.] is asking you about; I will ask you whether or not it is often that the professor himself asks those [kinds of] questions?
> WALKER: Oh, yes.

Nabrit declined to recross, and Walker was dismissed as a witness.

Following Walker's testimony, Greenhill called Benjamin Floyd Pittenger, a professor of educational administration at UT's College of Education. Pittenger had been at the university since 1911 and had served as dean of the college since 1926. More recently, he had served as chairman of the steering committee of Governor Coke Stevenson's Bi-Racial Conference on Negro Education. His testimony reflected the conference's report, which concluded that African Americans did not favor, and would not be "happy" in, predominantly white institutions. Greenhill used Pittenger to challenge a key point that Sweatt's team of attorneys had tried to document for the record: that separate was automatically unequal.

> GREENHILL: Now, in your judgment, are there advantages to the Negro in being taught in a separate institution?
> PITTENGER: Yes.
> GREENHILL: What are they?
> PITTENGER: I think that the educational value of . . . an education to a student at any level is determined by the total college situation . . . It isn't merely a question of classroom teaching and study, or of laboratory activities or of library activities . . . an increasing part of the value of education at any level is in the total influence [and] the total contact of the student with the institution.
> GREENHILL: I will ask you whether or not you think the Negro student would have the same opportunity to develop leadership in a mixed institution, or at a separate institution?
> PITTENGER: I think that normally, ordinarily, he would have a better opportunity to develop leadership in a separated institution than in a mixed institution, and I make that statement because the whole life of the institution would then be open to the Negro's participation. My judgment is that particularly in the South, that the Negroes' opportunities in institutions patronized in the great majority by Whites would be limited to the classroom facilities and the regular educational activities almost wholly.

Pittenger argued that much of the value of a college education came from the social interaction of students outside of the classroom. Curiously, he indirectly acknowledged the NAACP's argument that the absence of intellectual intercourse among the races made the classroom experience of segregated institutions unequal. Incredibly, Pittenger took the idea one step further, insisting that African Americans attending a predominantly white institution would likely segregate themselves outside the classroom and thus not benefit from the rich social scene in which students learned social graces and emerged as leaders. In a segregated school, these same African American students would be the leaders of "their own" school's social scene. In all, the segregated setting provided a better educational experience for a black student.

Many integrationists, like Thurgood Marshall, had been insisting for decades that African Americans were not interested in social equality, only in access to educational opportunities. Pittenger's testimony blurred those distinctions by including social commingling in the curriculum, an idea likely to create concern among many moderate and liberal whites.

Pittenger also confronted another concern the white establishment harbored: if Heman Sweatt prevailed, how was the South to maintain segregation in elementary and secondary schools? "I am unable to see how segregation could be constitutionally maintained below the college level and be unconstitutional at the college level," he said. Then he launched into a remarkable interpretation of Texas educational history: he believed that the development of Texas public schools had been "aided" by the segregation of the races; without segregation, public education would have been "much more retarded." Public education was a "long way from having reached anything like the national standard as a whole, and we are still in the formative period." The forced integration of higher education would ultimately spread to lower education, and when that happened, "it would [become] a bonanza to the private white schools of the State, [in] that it would mean the migration out of the [public] schools and the turning away from the public schools."

Pittenger provided a historical context by explaining that private education and tutoring had always been strong in the South and that public education for whites, always retarded by the "plantation system," was a relatively new phenomenon. He suggested that segregation made public education acceptable to middle-class whites and that without it, public education was imperiled. Then he extended his fearmongering to African Americans: "There are some nine or ten thousand colored public school teachers in Texas. If segregation were abandoned, I can't help asking myself what would become of that body of Texas teachers, our colored teachers in Texas . . . Teaching is a principal outlet of service for the educated colored man and woman."

The attorneys and law students in the room must have been wondering why Marshall, Durham, and Nabrit had not made objections during Pittenger's testimony. Finally, Marshall raised an objection.

MARSHALL: May it please the Court, we have waited as we have been doing all along to see just where the testimony was going. At this time we move to strike everything said about lower schools. The reason I do, sir, is that although Dr. Pittenger is an expert in the field, I think his original statement was assuming that you can't have unconstitutionality at the graduate level without affecting the lower level, and he isn't a legal expert, and he doesn't have a right to draw that conclusion.

JUDGE ARCHER: He doesn't have a right to draw a conclusion as to constitutionality.

MARSHALL: All of his testimony was based on that, and we move to strike it.

GREENHILL: Their witness yesterday on the stand testified that in his opinion—

JUDGE ARCHER: Are you abandoning your theory that it is only higher education and only one man involved in this case?

GREENHILL: Oh, no, sir.

JUDGE ARCHER: Then, this would not be admissible.

GREENHILL: Sir?

JUDGE ARCHER: This would not be admissible as to the others, would it?

GREENHILL: On the stand yesterday, over our objection, their witness testified that the time was ripe now to just throw off segregation entirely from the graduate school to the kindergarten.

MARSHALL: No, he didn't. He said just the opposite, that the time was ripe for the graduate school.

JUDGE ARCHER: That is what I understood, was for the graduate school.

DANIEL: Yesterday we objected to all of the testimony concerning schools in general.

JUDGE ARCHER: Yes.

DANIEL: That was overruled, and we preserved a bill. We offer this simply in rebuttal to that, in case the Court allows that yesterday to stand.

JUDGE ARCHER: In so far as any evidence has been received here affecting the secondary schools or less than graduate schools, I am not considering it.

And yet again, Judge Archer took great time and patience to listen to and allow evidence he never intended to consider.

The final Sweatt witness was another professor from the University of Chicago, Malcolm P. Sharp, who also served as the chair of the Curriculum Committee of the Association of American Law Schools. The group's function was to consider the curriculum of its member schools for the purpose of recommending changes and improvements to the overall educational environment. During his testimony, Sharp addressed a point that was becoming a more prevalent part of Sweatt's legal argument: law school was more than a place to become an attorney—it was also a training ground for public service. To meet that mission, Sharp insisted, a law school needed a "stimulating large student body," a criterion that clearly could not be met by a school with an enrollment of one, two, or ten.

Under Marshall's questioning, Sharp also testified that the use of the case method with only one student was nothing more than a lecture. And even if such a condition could remotely be considered equal to a class of eager students, the overall educational experience of the 13th Street school would still be unequal because of what occurred outside of the classroom.

Sharp and Pittenger were saying the same thing about the importance of learning outside of the classroom; the difference was that Pittenger believed that black students were likely to segregate themselves and not reap that benefit.

Sharp also described an atmosphere in which much learning comes from competition among students. Two of the highly prized products of friendly competition and free association were participation in the law review and membership in the Order of the Coif. Sharp did not understand how anyone could believe that such coveted achievements could be considered extraneous to a law-school experience. He went a step further: such lofty achievements by a law student not only gave the student an edge after graduation, they also contributed to the prestige of the school.

> MARSHALL: Is the reputation of a law school of any value to the student, its reputation in the legal field?
> SHARP: To the student while he is a student?
> MARSHALL: To the student while he is a student?
> SHARP: I think it is; it gives him confidence, pride, interest; it is a good deal of difference to the student if he feels he is in a good school, running well.
> MARSHALL: Is the reputation of a law school of any value to the student after he graduates?
> SHARP: Well, we all know it may be of importance getting a job for a time.

For the most part, Marshall's direct examination of Sharp brought out nothing new, but Price Daniel's cross was different from earlier questioning in that he challenged the idea that separate could not be equal by focusing on gender segregation. Was a university for women providing an inherently inferior education to that obtainable at a coeducational institution? Sharp asserted that segregation by gender was a weakness of the institution.

Daniel followed by trying to get Sharp to admit that a Negro college student in the South would get a better education in a culturally acceptable (that is, segregated) institution than in an integrated university, where resistance would surely disrupt the educational process. When Sharp refused to accept the idea, Daniel asked a series of questions that forced Sharp to admit that he had never studied and did not have any expertise in education in the South.

After Daniel's cross-examination of Sharp, Judge Archer called for a lunch recess. When court reconvened at two on the afternoon of May 16, Price Daniel rose to ask William Durham if the relator, Sweatt, had rested his case. "Yes," Durham answered, and with that Daniel presented "authorities" for the court to reconsider its decision to not take account of the testimony by Henry Doyle. Daniel again insisted that since Sweatt's attorneys argued strenuously that the 13th Street law school was not equal to UT Law because it had no students, it was relevant that Sweatt, Durham, and, especially, Marshall were connected to an association, the NAACP, that encouraged a boycott of the school and intimidated anyone from applying. Daniel admitted that he had no direct evidence to support his claim, but the authorities he cited—three rules of evidence as well as court precedents—not only allowed for the consideration of circumstantial evidence, they required it. Judge Archer did not change his original ruling, but noted the state's exception for the record.

JUDGE ARCHER: Have you anything further?
DANIEL: That is all, Your Honor.
MARSHALL: We are through.

And with that exchange, at a few minutes after two on May 16, 1947, trial-court testimony in the matter of *Heman Marion Sweatt v. Theophilus S. Painter et al.* ended.

The Ruling

As a remanded district-court trial, *Sweatt v. Painter* had been quite a show. Sweatt's attorneys displayed an impressive level of skill. Marshall was a first-rate lawyer—and a showman. The thunder he brought into the courtroom not only served his client, but also infused the African American community in Texas with a sense that the euphoria of the 1944 white-primary victory could happen again—this time in higher education. Even certified black professional teachers who preferred segregation because it allowed them to teach in Negro schools they could control had to admit that if Sweatt wanted to go to the University of Texas Law School, he should be able to.[1] That was how Sweatt, the plaintiff, became a unifying force among fractious groups within the African American community in Texas.

Although William Durham was Sweatt's attorney of record and all of the other lawyers taking up every seat at the plaintiff's table were technically just resources for Durham, the record clearly shows that Marshall called the shots. That was by design and prior agreement with the NAACP's Texas State Conference of Branches, which had retained Durham.

Both Daniel and Marshall waived their rights to present closing arguments because they both wanted Judge Archer to hand down a ruling during the afternoon of May 16, 1947.[2]

"This case has been ably and adequately and splendidly produced," Judge Archer began. "It is a matter in which we are all greatly interested. I have been greatly impressed with the type of people who have come here and testified as witnesses." He added that the press coverage had been "fair, instructive, and constructive."[3]

Archer's formal ruling came on June 17, 1947, exactly one year after the original *Sweatt* ruling. After the customary historical overview of the case, including how it had been remanded, Judge Archer described his finding of facts and opinion:

> Upon this rehearing, having heard the Pleadings, evidence and arguments, this Court is of the opinion and finds from the evidence that during the appeal of this cause and before the present hearing, [President Painter and the other Respondents], pursuant to the provisions of Senate Bill 140, Acts of the 50th Legislature, 1947, have established the School of Law of the Texas State University for Negroes [that is, the 13th Street law school] in Austin, Texas, with *substantially equal* facilities and with the same entrance, classroom study, and graduation requirements, and the same courses and the same instructors as the School of Law of The University of Texas; that such new law school offered to [Heman Sweatt] privileges, advantages, and opportunities for the study of law *substantially equivalent* to those offered by the State to white students at the University of Texas. (citations removed; emphasis added)

Judge Archer's findings were consistent with all arguments and evidence produced by the state during the trial. Then the judge addressed Sweatt's rejection of the "substantially equivalent" educational opportunity the state had provided him:

> [Heman Sweatt], although duly notified that he was eligible and would be admitted to said law school March 10, 1947, declined to register; that from his own testimony, [Sweatt] would not register in a separate law school no

matter how equal it might be and . . . the facts in this case showing that [Sweatt] would be afforded equal if not better opportunities for the study of law in such separate school, the petition for Writ of Mandamus should be denied.

Judge Archer chose not to break any legal ground and relied on prior federal precedents, like *Gaines,* that acknowledged that separate could be equal, as well as on the Texas Constitution of 1876, which mandated separation of the races.[4]

For most plaintiffs, such a ruling would have been a defeat, but for Heman Sweatt, it was a step in the right direction. Remarkably, Carter Wesley reported that Judge Archer had been "absolutely fair" during trial, not because of his ruling, but because he allowed a full presentation by Sweatt's team of lawyers.[5]

Now Heman Sweatt looked forward to losing again, this time in the Third Court of Civil Appeals and the Texas Supreme Court. The U.S. Supreme Court was the intended destination, and as the *Dallas Morning News* reported two days after the trial, "extreme care was exercised in preparation of the record during trial as it is designed as a test case to be taken to the Supreme Court."[6]

From the date of Judge Archer's final ruling, Sweatt had sixty days to file an appeal.

Harassment

From the beginning of his lawsuit, Sweatt had been harassed by white supremacists—and even a few blacks whose social and economic security depended on segregation. "To many [black professionals] who understood [the litigation]," Sweatt remembered years later, "this was a threat to their employment, to being identified with me."[7]

During the course of the litigation, Sweatt received 528 letters, 57 of which were threatening. At the time of the Supreme Court's adjudication of his case in 1950, Sweatt was asked whether he had ever been threatened with physical violence. He answered no. In interviews nearly thirty years later, he told very different stories. While on his postal routes, for example, he recalled harassment and threats to his life. At his home on Delano Street, vandals defaced his house and broke his windows with rocks. Some of the rocks had obscene and threatening notes attached.[8]

The abuse Sweatt endured was probably best described in a letter Thurgood Marshall wrote to Carl Murphy, an African American journalist from Baltimore: "Sweatt is taking a terrific punishment from a few critics in Texas, and it would be most helpful if you would send him a little note of encouragement, not that I am afraid that he is weakening because I know that he is not, but every little bit helps."[9] Marshall would not have asked Carl Murphy for protection from a mob. If the "punishment" he referred to had included threats of physical violence, Marshall would certainly have gone public and demanded protection for his client, and Carter Wesley would have printed headlines in the *Houston Informer*.

Some of the stress Sweatt endured might have been the result of the polarizing private writings and public editorials of Carter Wesley. Using his "Ram's Horn" column in the *Houston Informer*, Wesley's ferocious attacks on NAACP leaders must have grieved Sweatt. He and Wesley remained close personal friends, and Wesley is never known to have attacked Sweatt in any way, but it could not have escaped Sweatt's attention that the *Informer* vehemently opposed the crux of his testimony: that there could not be separation and equality. Nor could Sweatt ignore the merit of Wesley's point: were African Americans supposed to oppose what they were witnessing with their own eyes, namely, the construction of a university in their neighborhood. Instead, as Amilcar Shabazz wrote, were they to "keep their children in ignorance until the NAACP and the Supreme Court got white schools opened to blacks? What would it materially hurt to improve black schools now?"[10]

Wesley's editorial warfare was directed at Thurgood Marshall, however, rather than Sweatt. Through much of 1946 and 1947, Marshall made no significant public response—until the eleventh annual meeting of the NAACP's Texas State Conference of Branches, held in Denison, Texas.

Marshall Strikes Back

The meeting started on Friday evening, September 5, 1947, about three months after Judge Archer's ruling, at the Hopewell Baptist Church in the Texas-Oklahoma border town of Denison. The elite of the Texas African American civil rights movement attended, including Dallas's R. A. Hester, the conference's director of political action and the leader of the group that had accompanied Heman Sweatt to his now-infamous meeting with President Theophilus Painter. Sweatt's former Wiley College teacher James H. Morton, of Austin, now the NAACP's state lobbyist, attended as well. The event, a celebration of NAACP goals, was best described by its theme: "Separate Equality . . . A Judicial Myth."[11]

Thurgood Marshall dominated the meeting for a number of reasons. Texas was a battlefront, but it was also a source of manpower and financing. The dissenters, especially Carter Wesley, had to be converted or confronted. Marshall chose confrontation.

At the opening of the meeting, Marshall lashed out at everyone who was less than fully committed to the unconditional end of racial segregation. At eight in the evening, he took the stage and bellowed that any black person not accepting the NAACP's decision to drop equalization suits should just "wear a bandana." His historical analysis, legal reasoning, and passionate call for the realization of the American ideal of equality must have inspired the audience. But in a speech in which he pummeled Carter Wesley, Marshall also engaged in shocking demagoguery that could have further fractured the African American community in Texas.[12] Perhaps Marshall had tired of Wesley's abusive letters and scathing editorials or maybe he figured he had nothing to lose because the Texas black community could not be further divided. Whatever Marshall had on his mind, he used the meeting to get his concerns off his chest.

African American Texans had been pursuing separate equality for more than eighty years, he said, and in that time, no progress had been made. The irony was that at that moment a substantial new university called the Texas State University for Negroes was being constructed in Houston only a few blocks from the homes of Heman Sweatt, Lulu White, and Richard Grovey in the Third Ward. Marshall acknowledged that, but dismissed the event, saying that any African American who accepted the legitimacy of the university was a sellout.

> It no longer takes courage to fight for mere equality in a separate school system . . . I think everyone knew that when the state legislature in Texas agreed to advance more than $3 million for a Jim Crow University there would be Negroes who would be willing to sell the race down the river in order to either get jobs in the school, or to determine who should build the school, or to determine where the school should be built, or any other method whereby the individual could get personal gain . . . You realize that Negroes have been fighting for equality in separate schools for more than eighty years and have not obtained a semblance of equality.[13]

It made no sense to ask for more segregation, Marshall shouted. Carter Wesley and those like him were looking for "the easy way out" by asking whites for "Jim Crow Deluxe."

But Marshall knew he was speaking to a sympathetic crowd. In other places and on other occasions, audience members might have asked him whether he fully understood what he was asking of African American Texans—to turn down a chance to be taught by learned black professors and earn a college degree in a new, albeit segregated, university. Was that not progress? And what would a black university mean to the uneducated? How many new jobs were to be created for groundskeepers, carpenters, electricians, plumbers, custodians? How many new educated black citizens would be infused into a black middle class in places like the Third Ward in Houston? Such was the schism of thought among African American Texans.

Marshall's evening sermon was a keynote address. The rest of the conference focused on solidifying the membership's commitment to desegregation. The next day, Heman Sweatt led a discussion entitled "The Sweatt Case: No Compromise on Segregation." The panel included Thurgood Marshall and William Durham. On that day, Marshall, Roy Wilkins, and Gloster Current, delivered a forty-five-minute presentation on the activities of the association.[14]

The meeting ended on Sunday, September 7, 1947, with what was undoubtedly a rousing address by Sweatt's former teacher Melvin B. Tolson, who had recently been appointed poet laureate of the Republic of Liberia.[15] The meeting must have been a satisfying event for Heman Marion Sweatt.

Sweatt was becoming a celebrity of sorts, and so was his counterpart north of the Red River. During the Ninth Annual Youth Conference of the NAACP, hosted by Lulu White's Antioch Baptist Church, Sweatt and Ada Lois Sipuel, of Oklahoma, were the featured speakers. Sweatt was a frequent participant at other NAACP events. During a Founders Month observance at the Greater Zion Baptist Church in Houston, Sweatt gave a response to a presentation by Gloster Current, the national director of NAACP branches.[16]

TSUN and the 13th Street School

On September 8, 1947, only three days after Thurgood Marshall condemned African American Texans who accepted the Texas State University for Negroes as having sold "the race down the river," more than 2,300 young black applicants formed lines outside Fairchild Hall to register for classes. The next day, the *Dallas Morning News* reported that the very first registrant was a seventeen-year-old boy from St. Louis, Missouri, named Hyland Grayson Stuart. The young man was apparently not conscious of the historic nature of his registration when he admitted that his father was the campus's head electrician and that he had cut in line by entering the building through a side door. By the end of the registration period, one week later, TSUN was the largest African American university in the South.[17]

Even before Marshall's thunderous call for boycotting the school, the Texas State Conference of Branches had made it known that the opening of a black university in Houston would not satisfy their demands for a university equal to the University of Texas.[18]

Dissuading a few prospective law students from enrolling in makeshift schools in the office of a divorce lawyer or the basement of a building run by a petroleum-engineering firm proved to be easier than preventing the opening of a university that African Americans had been hungering for since 1876. Lulu White wrote to Maceo Smith: "I heard a minister say yesterday that Texas would soon have the best educational system in the United States for Negroes because the first unit of it would open in Houston."[19] The preacher's optimism and the eager new college students who enrolled at TSUN represented what Carter Wesley called a "practical approach" to achieving full citizenship: "Those students represent a lot of sentiment in favor of the practical approach of making the best of what is available, while you fight for better circumstances . . . The NAACP doesn't have the courage to carry its stupid theory to its logical conclusion where they know that the people would not follow them."[20]

Wesley emphasized what everyone knew: "Even if Sweatt enters the University of Texas, we will not close nor want to get rid of Texas State University for Negroes."[21] As long as Heman Sweatt's court battles continued, the state of Texas had to make some effort, however insincere, to build a university for its African American population. Wesley insisted that "in addition to the Sweatt case we have got to file suits for equalization of educational opportunities if we expect our children to get the benefit of improved education in our time."[22] Within two weeks, the NAACP's Texas State Conference of Branches backed off its uncompromising boycott when James H. Morton admitted that the NAACP would no longer fight the establishment of TSUN: "We regard it as a necessary evil," he said.[23]

In 1950, Texas was home to 12 of the nation's 108 predominantly black institutions. Of those twelve, TSUN had 2,043 of the 8,812 enrolled students—almost 25 percent.[24]

When the school opened on September 8, 1947, the property and governance had not yet been transferred to TSUN's board of regents. There was little material difference between the old Houston College for Negroes and TSUN. The only semblance of parity between what was offered to blacks and whites in higher education might have been in the College of Education. In all other areas, the differences were shameful. The temporary chief educational officer was Allen E. Norton, who had taken leave from the Houston Independent School District to serve as acting president. In July 1948, Raphael O'Hara Lanier, a former minister to Liberia and former dean of the Houston Colored Junior College, was appointed president. At the time, he had a faculty of eighty-five.[25]

On September 8, 1947, the African American students and the parents who sent them to the school were not attracted to TSUN by Fairchild Hall or the barracks-like outbuildings that had been recently relocated from a military outpost in Galveston, but by the construction going on all around them. The bulldozed soil, fresh concrete, and other signs of construction represented the promise of a real public university for Texas's African American population. How could a neglected population of talented and education-hungry citizens not be excited by such development?

For Heman Sweatt, the thousands of students in the registration lines were a somber development. He was as close to being a universally lauded hero as Texas blacks had, and many congratulated him for his courage and the good he had already done. They credited him with the ongoing construction of the new university—a development that would have been unheard of only a decade earlier. The unsettling truth looming over all the euphoria was that the University of Texas at Austin and other white universities were still closed to African Americans. And, rightly or wrongly, TSUN would become known as "the House that Sweatt Built."[26] The compliment was flattering, but *Sweatt v. Painter* was not over, and even if TSUN were to become everything the African American community wanted it to be, it was still Jim Crow and it was still wrong. Thurgood Marshall called it a "Jim Crow Dump."[27]

Within a year, reality set in for the new TSUN students. TSUN became a splendid example of what Thurgood Marshall and Heman Sweatt's legal team had been arguing all along: it was not possible to create a university equal, or substantially equal, to the University of Texas out of thin air. Lost in the developments were the displaced students of Houston College for Negroes: their school had been taken over, and according to Lulu White, they were not pleased.[28]

TSUN offered programs of study in a College of Arts and Sciences, a School of Vocational and Industrial Education, a Graduate School, and soon, the 13th Street law school would be transferred to the TSUN campus. In the beginning, however, the school was much like the Houston College for Negroes it replaced, and acting president Norton admitted that a large percentage of the students were carryovers. The campus offered four fully equipped shops for training in dry cleaning, shoe repair, tailoring, and auto mechanics. There was one small chemistry classroom, and the physics department had no laboratory.[29] If the 13th Street law school, officially called the Texas State University for Negroes School of Law, were considered part of the university, then TSUN had the distinction of having a law school before having a mathematics department.

But Norton beamed on opening day: "This school will furnish a great opportunity for Negro youths to get their education at minimum cost. This is no makeshift affair here. We have fine equipment for our vocational training classes, and our liberal and fine arts schools will have as fine a faculty as it is humanly possible to obtain." He seemed unaware of what the school was supposed to be—a university of the first class, comparable to the University of Texas—when he fingered the lapels of his finely tailored checked suit and told reporters, "Our people turn out good work. This suit of mine was turned out by a Houston College student tailor last year."[30]

TSUN's reputation was not helped by Governor Beauford Jester's appointment of W. R. Banks, the retired principal of Prairie View, to the position of vice chairman of the TSUN board of regents. "Among the Negro members of the Board," Ira B. Bryant wrote, "W. R. Banks was the most widely known because of his connection with education in the state over a long period of time, but Negroes generally did not trust him."[31]

Indeed, TSUN struggled. In September 1948, on the first anniversary of its opening, administrators had to announce that its enrollment had fallen by 15 percent, from 2,303 to 2,009. Banks blamed both blacks and whites for the drop, saying that the "NAACP and some other groups" were discouraging the development of the new university, and that it was widely believed that many Texas whites considered the new university a "joke."[32]

Meanwhile, with the blessing of the 126th District Court in Travis County, university officials set out to establish a temporary law school at 104 East 13th Street in Austin. The course announcement for the 1947 winter semester (the university was still under the wartime schedule) indicated that a program of instruction was to begin on September 22, 1947. In a memo to the faculty on September 9, Dean Charles McCormick indicated that the enrollment was expected to be from one to five students and that an instructor for a course in personal property had already been assigned. One week later, McCormick scaled down his enrollment estimate to only one, and that student was the same prospective student who had proved to be such an unreliable witness for Attorney General Price Daniel—Henry Doyle.[33]

Thurgood Marshall knew of Henry Doyle from the *Sweatt* trial. When his registration became known, James H. Morton and Lulu White sent

Marshall more information about the man who was breaking the NAACP boycott. Doyle was a graduate of Austin's Samuel Huston College, circa 1932, and had been a teacher in the local school system. After the war, he opened what Morton described as a "first-class restaurant" and then ran a grocery store. He sold the store to apply for law school. It was Morton's personal observation that "Mr. Doyle is not a stable person."[34]

Henry Doyle understood the significance of his groundbreaking registration. In fact, to the chagrin of the NAACP, he was keeping the School of Law of the Texas State University for Negroes alive. To those who would condemn him, he asked only for the right of self-determination when it came to his own education. His choice brought about personal hardship, he said.

On September 24, 1947, Doyle informed law professor Kenneth Woodward that he wanted a job at the school. Undoubtedly, his need for a job was legitimate, since he was a thirty-seven-year-old man. The 13th Street location had to be kept open from eight in the morning to eleven each night to match the hours of availability of the UT Law School, and so Woodward wrote to McCormick that "it might be desirable to give Doyle some such title as 'secretary' although I am sure he will be willing to take care of the janitorial work also."[35] The job would hardly be burdensome for the young man, since the 1,000-square-foot facility was so small and there were so few people involved in the operations of the "school." In early October, Doyle was appointed "secretary and custodian" and paid $25 a week for his services. At the time of Doyle's request, only three keys were being issued to the facility: one for Woodward, one for Doyle, and one for the school's second registered student, Heaullan E. Lott. On September 27, 1947, the last day of registration, a third applicant, named Fannie Ussery Brown, registered. The 13th Street school had a student body of three.[36]

Helen Hargrave's responsibility for the new library at the 13th Street school had become an extension of her duties, and Dean McCormick felt that her pay should be increased by $200 a month. President Painter met with Vice President James Dolley and, deciding that Hargrave was being paid too much already, denied the pay raise. But like a good administrator, McCormick met directly with Painter and tied Hargrave's salary to standards set by the American Association of Law Schools. She got her raise.[37]

Sweatt and Doyle

Back in Houston, Heman Sweatt returned to his job as a mail carrier. For all practical purposes, his "job" as a plaintiff was over. He would not be called upon to testify unless the Third Court of Civil Appeals sent the case back to district court—and that was very unlikely, since each side was satisfied that it had been allowed to present its case before Judge Archer. Nevertheless, Thurgood Marshall, remembering the Lloyd Gaines fiasco, took care to encourage Sweatt. "None of us knew Lloyd Gaines in the Missouri Case very well and we took a chance," Marshall wrote to Sweatt. Marshall went on to say that the *Gaines* case cost the NAACP more than $25,000, and when they needed him the most, Lloyd Gaines disappeared.[38]

Marshall must have been gratified at how solidly committed Sweatt had become to the cause of rejecting equalization and ending racial segregation. While Sweatt maintained good relations with Carter Wesley, he nonetheless had become deeply entrenched in the NAACP camp. In late September 1947, in a letter to Marshall, he described Wesley as "typically void of tact," and Wesley's *Houston Informer* editorials as "psychopathic squeals." In his reply, Marshall encouraged Sweatt's line of thought by lamenting that the *Sweatt* case was handicapped because they could not rely on the *Informer* newspapers.[39]

Both Marshall and Sweatt had to be concerned about the developments in Austin at the 13th Street law school. The makeshift school might have only three students, but it was still open and classes were being held. African American Texans who were qualified to enroll were being asked to put their personal ambitions aside—no one knew for how long. There was a real chance that Henry Doyle was going to become a lawyer in three or four years while others, like Sweatt, waited. In an Austin newspaper interview, Doyle used an unfortunate analogy to describe his decision to enter the 13th Street school: "It's just like having a steaming plate of chicken in a box in the backyard. I'd rather have it in the house, but chicken is chicken and it's better in the backyard than none at all." In the postscript of his letter to Sweatt, Marshall called the 13th Street school "Uncle Tom's Cabin," adding that Henry Doyle's chicken was nothing but the "neck and feet."[40] Marshall went on to draw a stark and brutal comparison between Sweatt and Doyle: "On the one side we have a Negro American and on the other side we had the remnants of a Negro slave."[41]

For the top administrators at the University of Texas, the makeshift law school on 13th Street quickly became an unwelcome burden. Within two months, Dean McCormick wrote to President Painter: "It appears that we shall have to plan to provide instruction at the Negro Law School here both in the spring semester and in the summer of 1948. This will necessitate heavy additional burdens upon the time of our faculty, but it seems to be inescapable."[42]

Indeed, a spring semester at 13th Street could involve a little less than half of the UT Law faculty for the instruction of six to ten students—for a student-teacher ratio of approximately 1:1. Painter's reaction was to put pressure on the TSUN regents to accept custody of the law school as soon as possible. Craig F. Cullinan of the regents wrote: "We would like very much to start our school at the beginning of the next semester, but I am afraid that we shall not be ready before September, 1948 semester."[43]

The summer of 1948 proved to be a stressful time for the three students of the 13th Street school. Each indicated that they would like to attend summer school in Austin, but they also had to prepare to move themselves and their families to Houston. None of them had the money to relocate, so they appealed to Dean McCormick for assistance. Whether he had a genuine concern for the students' plight or was making an attempt to keep the students from dropping out, McCormick sent a request for donations to a number of Texas law firms on April 30. Hoping to have a fund of about $1,000, he was willing to personally donate the first $50. Responses varied from genuine support to grudging contempt and racism. Leon Jaworski (who later became famous as a Watergate special prosecutor), of the Houston firm Fulbright, Crooker, Freeman and Bates, sent in a donation, adding, "We recognize this as a most worthy project and appreciate your thoughtfulness in calling it to our attention." On the other hand, Frank G. Coates, of Baker, Botts, Andrews and Parish in Houston, asked, "Is this law school project being pressed by earnest Negroes who really want a legal education or by racial zealots and idealists?" In a separate letter, Rex Baker wondered, "Perhaps I am a little bit reactionary, but I doubt whether there is a real need for a Negro law school and have further doubt as to the proficiency of a Negro lawyer." Nonetheless, Baker donated $100.[44]

Of the three law students that matriculated at the 13th Street school, only one, Henry Doyle, transferred to the law school at the Houston campus. Heaullan Lott could not move to Houston, and Fannie Brown had withdrawn from the school.[45]

The establishment of the 13th Street school and Texas State University for Negroes came at a time when Texans demonstrated a surprising lack of confidence in their ability to govern themselves or follow the law. Fear and bigotry rendered meaningless the many eloquent invocations of equality and equal protection, and promises of first-class universities. To the well-meaning whites and blacks who believed that segregation was necessary to keep the peace, Tillotson College's president William H. Jones said: "Laws are an expression of the people's will; and law crystallizes the will of people who have not made up their minds on a subject. They are trained to follow a law, and will not trespass it, even though they are opposed to it. If laws gave the Negro civil rights, most people would be inclined to accept them."[46]

The U.S. Constitution and the Texas Constitution of 1876, along with virtually all laws and court rulings, had been written by white men, but in Texas in 1947, it was African Americans who respected the ideals expressed in them.

CHAPTER 17

"Don't We Have Them on the Run"

*Please remember that I ask for education—not Negro education. And the facts
will unquestionably demonstrate a vast difference between the two. In fact,
sufficient difference to guarantee that [Prairie View A&M] will never find itself
faced with an entrance application from a normal White student.*
HEMAN MARION SWEATT, "WHY I WANT TO ATTEND THE
UNIVERSITY OF TEXAS," *TEXAS RANGER,* SEPTEMBER 1947

In September 1947, the *Texas Ranger,* a University of Texas student magazine,
published its largest issue ever, both in size and circulation—20,000 copies
and sixty-four pages. The issue launched the magazine's editorial page and
its first color cover. Below the cover-story title, an editor noted: "The *Ranger*
believes that the racial problems in education should be openly discussed by
all intelligent people."

"Why I Want to Attend the University of Texas" had been written by
Heman Marion Sweatt, and it identified two issues foremost on his mind:
the racist and insulting notion that African Americans were not really interested in education, but in an opportunity to mix socially with whites, and
the impossibility of the state to craft an acceptable "Negro education" for
him that could replace the University of Texas Law School.[1]

> Several months following my application to enter The University of Texas
> Law School, one individual who interpreted this action as one suggesting
> the Negro's claim to equal national achievement, raised the question: "If
> Negroes think themselves equal to the White man, why doesn't one of them
> make an atomic bomb?" . . .
>
> Too many people of today have permitted themselves to shape distorted
> pictures of life in this country as: The Labor movement being composed
> of innumerable prisoners chained to a few labor leaders hell-bent upon

stealing management's last shirt; as New Dealers assuredly seeking political dictatorship; and as White men sleeping with one eye open to protect their homes from the assumed ravish nature of Negroes, while thirteen million Negroes are viewed as incapable of harboring any ambition higher than dancing at the Waldorf-Astoria in the embrace of Lana Turner . . .

It is thoroughly consistent with this consistency, then, to find that my application to enter The University of Texas Law School had similarly picked up its fair share of dogmatists who have not only refused to view my action in terms of anything other than an abstract racial crusade, but have denied the most remote possibility that the application is one of good faith.

It cannot be denied that the implications of this matter are destined to affect the lives of many other Negroes, but I am responsible only to the extent of this application—and there were hundreds of entrance requests made at the date on which mine was filed . . .

I have already consented to explore this subject in the *Texas Ranger* for several reasons . . . As an initial reason and in keeping with my legal ambition, I welcome this opportunity to plead my own case. However, I hasten to attribute any error in my technique to the fact that events thus far have forced me to the reversed training schedule of taking my laboratory experience *before* I have had the privilege of training [in] any basic theory . . .

Indeed, as far as attitudes regarding the problem of segregated education are involved, unanimity of opinion does not exist anywhere. Very assuredly, I did not find such a state at Michigan University during my study there toward the master's degree . . .

The very fact that the state provides funds (though tragically inadequate) for Negroes to study the professions in northern and eastern schools justifies my conclusion that their reason for doing so is wholly void of the social fears often expressed. This is to say that the race or color of the student who is to sit beside them up there is obviously of no concern, but the dollars and cents saved by sending them there is . . .

I can now give you my reason for wanting to study law at [the University of Texas].

My answer simply and conclusively is: For the same reason that there are other Texans studying there. It is the best law school in Texas, and the only one that can offer me equal training to that available for other students.

Please remember that I asked for Education—not *Negro education*. And the facts will unquestionably demonstrate a vast difference between the two. In fact, sufficient difference to guarantee that [Prairie View A&M] will never find itself faced with an entrance application from a normal White student.[2]

A Parallel Reality in Oklahoma

The NAACP had been active throughout the southern and border states in cases like *Sweatt v. Painter*. In Oklahoma, Ada Lois Sipuel's application to the University of Oklahoma Law School brought about a U.S. Supreme Court ruling in January 1948 that rocked segregated states. The oral arguments in *Sipuel* were instructive to states like Texas. Justice Robert H. Jackson asked Oklahoma's counsel if he *really* believed that a school with a single student could afford an acceptable education in the law. Ada Lois Sipuel remembered that when the state's attorney, Maurice Merrill, answered yes, the astounded justice responded that such foolishness was neither reasonable nor equitable.[3]

Only four days after oral arguments, the Supreme Court's decision in *Sipuel* added to the duties that states had to take in order to provide equality for their African American citizens. *Gaines* required a state to provide for equality within its own borders; *Sipuel* further required the state to "provide it . . . in conformity with the equal protection clause of the Fourteenth Amendment *and provide it as soon as it does for applicants of any other group*" (emphasis added).[4]

Oklahoma responded by hastily creating a makeshift law school. In an apparent attempt to avoid a "basement school" type of controversy, the "school" was set up in the Capitol in Oklahoma City as an adjunct of Langston University. Like Sweatt, Sipuel refused to enroll, announcing, "No matter how it is advertised, it still does not give us the equality of treatment for which we have been fighting for two years."[5]

The response in Oklahoma mirrored Texas's efforts to circumvent *Sweatt*. The governor formed biracial committees, and the legislature increased funding for makeshift and Jim Crow schools. But in January 1948, six black Oklahomans applied to the OU Graduate School, causing the Board of Regents of Higher Education to investigate what it would have to do to ensure separate equality for those applicants.

In March 1948, a committee of academic deans from several Oklahoma colleges issued a report that forced diehard segregationists to face a stark reality: even if separate could be made equal, it was going to cost a lot of money. Duplicating existing OU and Oklahoma State University graduate programs would cost twelve million dollars for the basic physical plant alone. The effort would require four to five years of construction plus a minimum annual outlay of half a million dollars. Even assuming that the necessary facilities were made available, staffing the campuses would be a near impossibility. In 1947, only eight African Americans in the entire United States earned PhDs, and those available as teachers were highly recruited by hundreds of institutions seeking diversity for their faculties. Moreover, the mere creation of entire academic departments and colleges for African Americans did not guarantee their use all year, every year—making it probable that expensive departments and facilities would be left empty much of the time. The deans, ashamed that such madness was even being considered for an estimated enrollment of twenty to thirty students, concluded that all of Oklahoma's higher-educational institutions should be opened to all of its students.[6]

In June 1948, six months after the *Sipuel* ruling, George W. McLaurin, a sixty-eight-year-old black man with a master's degree from the University of Kansas, filed suit in federal court, and on September 29 won the right to be admitted to OU's Graduate School of Education. The OU regents followed the court's order, and on October 13, 1948, McLaurin became the first African American to matriculate at OU. The university's regents followed the court order but, to comply with the state's segregation laws, assigned McLaurin seating for all four of his classes in the anteroom of Room 104 of the Carnegie Building; the setup was reminiscent of the "basement school." Thurgood Marshall called McLaurin's seating area a "broom closet."[7] To further ensure segregation, while McLaurin was in the library, he was required to sit at a designated desk outside of the reading room, and he was assigned a designated table in the school cafeteria. In other areas of the campus, he was separated from others by railings made of two-by-fours. Oklahoma argued, as if to demonstrate its enlightenment, that McLaurin could converse with students while waiting in line in the cafeteria. As Ada Lois Sipuel recalled years later in her autobiography, "Oklahoma had given Marshall the perfect circumstances to challenge separate but equal. Everything was equal in every way except McLaurin was separated."[8]

The Multistate Compact

As *Sweatt, McLaurin,* and *Sipuel* moved through the courts, the segregated border and southern states realized that maintaining constitutionally acceptable separate school systems was going to be an overwhelmingly expensive proposition. To address this political reality, the governors of fourteen states resurrected an implausible and unworkable plan to pool their resources to establish regional graduate, professional, and technical schools. They signed a regional compact for something to be called the Board of Control for Southern Regional Education. The governors sought congressional sanction for their proposal through House Judiciary Committee hearings. Not surprisingly, the NAACP arrived to voice its opposition. The House bill, which was introduced by Representative Sam Hobbs (D-AL), was success-fully steered through the House Judiciary Committee. As it awaited a date for consideration on the House calendar, however, its companion bill in the Senate Judiciary Committee stalled. A two-man subcommittee composed of Senators Alexander Wiley (R-WI) and J. Howard McGrath (D-RI), held hearings for two days: one day for the southern governors, the other for the NAACP.[9]

The proponents of the legislation disingenuously testified that their com-pact's goal was to go beyond "Negro schools" to a multitude of colleges and professional schools. The NAACP told the Senate subcommittee that if the regional-school bill were to pass, the NAACP's attempts to realize equal edu-cational opportunities for African Americans would be set back one hun-dred years.

The segregationists hoped that a congressional charter for regional Jim Crow schools would make it politically difficult for the Supreme Court to force the University of Texas to enroll Heman Sweatt. That ambition was fanciful for two reasons. First, such an endeavor would have required vol-untary cooperation among states so completely married to the states'-rights creed that they could do no better than form a confederacy during the Civil War. Second, as Benjamin Pittenger testified during the *Sweatt* trial, the states involved had never religiously adhered to the concept of mass public education, even for the bulk of their white citizens.[10]

In a law school designed for as many as fourteen states, where would the Napoleonic Code, which was the basis for state law only in Louisiana, fit in the curriculum? Its study would be essential for a student planning to practice law in Louisiana, but it would be a historical curiosity, at best, for any other prospective lawyer. And if such an institution were to provide an equal educational experience for African American students, it would have to be equal to the best public law school in the fourteen participating states. Under such a condition, African American law students would be getting a better education than the white students of the other thirteen states. And finally, for such a regional concept to work, as mentioned earlier, colorful southern governors and other politicians would have to heavily invest state funds in the schools but, for all practical purposes, relinquish the kind of political patronage that fed their power.

Texas governor Beauford Jester was one of the fourteen southern gov-ernors who signed the regional pact, but Texas was never an enthusiastic supporter of the interstate agreement. Jester set up a board in June 1949, and the enabling legislation passed the state Senate but was never brought to a vote in the House.[11]

The regional school concept went nowhere. As early as October 1947, Lulu White, as if amused by yet another attempt by bumbling southern politicians to preserve segregation, wrote to Thurgood Marshall: "Don't we have them on the run?"[12]

Then there was what the *Dallas Morning News* called the "Arkansas Solution." On January 30, 1948, Arkansas university officials announced that they would admit qualified African American graduate students to the University of Arkansas System. This made UA the first white southern university since Reconstruction to admit black students. Three days later, an African American Arkansan named Silas Hunt, a severely wounded veteran of the Battle of the Bulge, appeared at the University of Arkansas Law School to register for the spring semester. Hunt had already been accepted by the University of Indiana School of Law, but he decided instead to break the color barrier at UA.

Hunt met with Dr. Robert A. Leflar, dean of the law school, on February 2, 1948, and after a brief review of Hunt's academic record, Leflar admitted him to the law school. The event was not as enlightened as it may have appeared. Hunt was assigned to a segregated class in the basement of the law school, where he studied alone until several white students discovered that they were not restricted from attending the classes with Hunt. Soon, each of Hunt's classes included from three to five whites who descended into the basement so that Silas Hunt would not be alone.[13]

In Austin, the long fight by Dr. Everett Givens and attorney Kenneth Lampkin to force the UT board of regents to establish the Negro university first described in the Texas Constitution of 1876 and authorized by voters in 1882 effectively came to an end when the Third Court of Civil Appeals rejected Givens's argument that regental action setting up the new university was mandated. In the trial court ruling in February 1947, Judge J. Harris Gardner of the 53rd District Court had declared: "We do not maintain that Texas Negroes are not entitled to a school, but we do say that the (UT) Board of Regents does not have the authority to establish one." Establishing a constitutional university for Negroes was solely within the province of the legislature, "when deemed practicable." The appeals court agreed.[14]

W. Astor Kirk

On September 5, 1947, a young assistant professor at Tillotson College named William Astor Kirk inquired about doctoral work in government at TSUN. By the Thanksgiving holidays, he had decided he wanted a PhD in political science. For personal and professional reasons, he wanted to earn his terminal degree in Texas.

As a young boy, Kirk had grown up doing grueling farmwork in Marion County in East Texas. At the age of fourteen, while navigating a mule and plow through the rich soil of his father's forty-two-acre cornfield, he heard a "loud and clear" voice: "If you accept the existing circumstances of your life, then that means denying your God-given ability to visualize something radically different and much better."[15]

One of the "existing circumstances" Kirk was not willing to accept was the limited educational opportunities available to African Americans in Texas. As a boy, he had walked five miles to and from school each day because the public school district did not provide transportation for blacks.

Kirk spent the first two years of his college career at Wiley College in Marshall, where three of his professors, one being Melvin Tolson, encouraged him to "think some new thoughts, critically examine old ideas and develop new premises."[16] For financial reasons Kirk's time at Wiley lasted only two years. Shortly afterward, he moved to Washington, D.C., where he completed his undergraduate studies at Howard University. During his senior year, he observed a series of meetings attended by Thurgood Marshall, James Nabrit, Jr., and Charles Thompson as they developed the legal strategy for *Sweatt v. Painter*. He followed his undergraduate degree by earning a master of arts in government.

With a master's in hand, he was offered teaching positions at Morehouse College in Atlanta and Tillotson College in Austin. He preferred the more prestigious and lucrative Morehouse offer, but the convenience of being near his and his wife's families in Texas prompted him to accept an assistant professorship in political science at Tillotson.[17]

In an autobiography published more than sixty years after he reported for Tillotson's 1947–1948 academic year, Kirk remembered that Austin "was far more progressive in race relations than East Texas, [but] it was still a segregated city."[18] Jim Crow Austin, Kirk explained, was more like Washington, D.C., than Marshall, Texas. His remembrance is supported by contemporaneous accounts such as a *Daily Texan* student poll conducted during the *Sweatt* litigation: 56.6 percent of UT students favored the admission of African Americans to the Graduate School. The sentiment on campus contrasted with the results of Joe Belden's Texas polls, which from 1948 through 1950, showed that only about one-third of all white Texans favored the integration of UT.[19]

Upon Kirk's arrival in Austin, he joined the NAACP. The president of the

Austin chapter, James Morton, asked him to chair the local Legislative Liaison Committee, which monitored the state legislature and the governor's office.

Kirk brought excitement and action into his classroom and extracurricular activities. He infused activism and a sense of civic responsibility into his lessons. One activity of the Ralph Bunche Political Science Club (for which Kirk was a faculty sponsor) was to uncover the legal basis for racial segregation in Austin. One of the club's guest speakers, Carter Wesley of the *Houston Informer*, was so impressed with the activity that he donated $250 to cover expenses the students might incur while researching the answer.[20]

Kirk's pursuit of a doctorate was sincere, and it began when he contacted TSUN and requested an application for the fall semester of 1947. Of course, he knew that TSUN did not offer what he was applying for, and so it was no surprise that on September 10, 1947, he received a letter from the acting president, stating, "We are sorry we can not serve you this year in your chosen field."[21]

Having missed the fall semester, Kirk turned to James Morton and the Austin NAACP chapter for assistance. Morton promised to place Kirk's request on the agenda of the first chapter meeting in 1948. In a letter to Thurgood Marshall, Morton supported Kirk's cause by reminding Marshall that "there is no training available for [Negroes] who seek to do work beyond the Master's degree."[22]

A. Maceo Smith supported Kirk's efforts as well, but with *Sweatt* making its way through the courts, he asked the Austin chapter to assume all costs for Kirk's support at least until 1949. William Durham was more cautious; he worried that setting up another makeshift Jim Crow school for Kirk would be easy for the UT regents. Thurgood Marshall saw the merits of Durham's logic and legal reasoning, but he was also undoubtedly pleased to see a young, handsome, and articulate plaintiff take action with the active support of the once-dormant Austin NAACP chapter. Kirk also provided the NAACP with an attractive backup in case something should go wrong with the *Sweatt* litigation. (Marshall undoubtedly remembered that during the white-primary fight he had had to drop *Hasgett* and champion Lonnie Smith of *Smith v. Allwright*.) After a review of Kirk's transcripts, Marshall wrote to Durham: "It looks as though the case of Mr. W. Astor Kirk is shaping up and I hope that it can be pushed so that we can get started on legal action."[23]

As a courtesy, on December 3, 1947, Kirk informed UT officials that on the next day he would be in the registrar's office for the purpose of applying for admission to the Graduate School. On December 4, he entered the University of Texas Main Building and Tower and walked into the same room Heman Sweatt had entered in February 1946.

The circumstances were different. Kirk brought along only one person to serve as his witness, J. A. Elmore, who was his friend and colleague as well as the dean of women at Tillotson College, but reporters were there as well. (In his memoirs, Kirk revealed that he did not alert the press to his impending visit. He does not know how the press knew to be there.)[24]

Kirk and Elmore met with associate registrar Max Fichtenbaum, who counseled Kirk to make an application to TSUN. When Kirk answered that he had done so and been informed that TSUN currently had no graduate programs in government, Fichtenbaum told Kirk to apply for an out-of-state scholarship. A polite but determined Kirk answered that such an arrangement was "unacceptable." The interview ended when Fichtenbaum informed Kirk that "under no circumstances" would he be admitted to the University of Texas Graduate School.[25]

Coverage of Kirk's application hit the newsstands later the same day. The *Austin American* reporter referred to Kirk as "the nattily dressed assistant professor." As a result of Fichtenbaum's refusal of the application on December 4, Kirk submitted another one by mail the next day, along with a letter that sought a confirmation of his denial. The university took the unusual step of having President Painter reply. On January 21, 1948, UT offered Kirk the coursework he requested on the "Forty Acres" campus, but at the 13th Street law school set up for Heman Sweatt.[26]

William Durham was proved right: it was easy for the UT regents to set up a makeshift school, but it didn't really matter. Like Sweatt, Kirk refused the offer of admission and never attended a class at the 13th Street school.

On April 12, 1948, Durham and C. B. Bunkley, Jr., filed a lawsuit in Judge Archer's 126th District Court on behalf of W. Astor Kirk. Ten days later, Painter wrote to Dudley Woodward: "It is fairly obvious that the Negroes are determined to make it as embarrassing as possible for us to maintain separate institutions for the two races."[27]

Painter had no idea how right he was.

At the Third Court of Civil Appeals

Heman Sweatt presented more than 2,000 pages of legal arguments and exhibits to the Third Court of Civil Appeals on September 30, 1947. The mass of material included photographs of the University of Texas Law School and the makeshift "basement" school on East 13th Street. The clerk announced that President Painter had until November 1 to answer.

Sweatt's appeal argued that the district court had failed to recognize that the "separate but equal" doctrine was an "invalid hypothesis." Equality, Marshall and Durham's brief argued, could be attained only by allowing Sweatt to enroll in the University of Texas Law School. Prairie View and TSUN could never become the equal of a premier university like UT Austin, but even if equal facilities could be built, the opportunities could never be the same; segregation per se was a violation of the Fourteenth Amendment.[28]

During arguments before the appeals court, Marshall expanded on the fiction of separate but equal by pointing out that the state never specifically held that the makeshifts they created were "equal." Instead, he continued, "They say it is 'substantially equal.' You can have either equality or you don't. You can't have 99 percent equality. There is no such thing as 'separate but equal' anyplace in the United States."[29] He knew, of course, that such an argument would go nowhere in a state court in Texas; he was asking a Texas appeals court to overrule decades of U.S. Supreme Court precedents.

In a voice dripping with sarcasm, Marshall called the UT School of Law the "big law school training" and the 13th Street school the "basement education." He continued: "The modern law school is operated so the student can understand ideas of all stratas of society, so he can go out and be of service to his community, his state and his nation . . . In today's school you have all groups except one. You tell him, 'You go over there by yourself. You don't have a chance to exchange ideas with anybody.'"[30]

The appeals court issued a 5,000-word opinion by Chief Justice James McClendon on February 25, 1948. The direction of the ruling was apparent from the start: "At the outset it should be borne in mind that the validity of state laws which require segregation of races in state supported schools, as being, on the ground of segregation alone, a denial of due process, is not now an open question. The ultimate repository of authority to construe the Federal Constitution is the Federal Supreme Court. We cite chronologically, in a note below, the unbroken line of decisions of that tribunal recognizing or upholding the validity of such segregation as against such attack."[31] The court, like others before it, relied on *Plessy v. Ferguson*'s infamous declaration, "The object of the [Fourteenth] amendment was undoubtedly to enforce the absolute equality of the two races before the law, but, in the nature of things, it could not have been intended to abolish distinctions based upon color, or to enforce social, as distinguished from political, equality, or a commingling of the two races upon terms unsatisfactory to either."

The appeals court then addressed the legal and intellectual foundation of the NAACP's direct attack on segregation: "Although separate school laws have been enforced by several states, an examination of the cases in the United States Supreme Court and lower courts will demonstrate that these statutes have never been seriously challenged *nor their validity examined and tested upon a record adequately presenting the critical and decisive issues such as presented by the record in this case*" (emphasis added).

In three quotations from the NAACP's brief, the court enumerated the association's main arguments: there was no rational basis for racial classifications, "separate but equal" in both theory and fact was consistently unequal and discriminatory, and it was impossible to have the equality required by the Fourteenth Amendment in a school system that relegated citizens of a disadvantaged racial minority group to separate schools. The court replied: "This assertion in effect impeaches the soundness of the various decisions of the contrary, as being predicated upon a purely abstract and theoretical hypothesis, wholly unrelated to reality. To so hold would convict the great jurists who rendered those decisions of being so far removed from the actualities involved in the race problems of our American life as to render them incapable of evaluating the known facts of contemporaneous and precedent history as they relate to those problems."

To Thurgood Marshall's assertions, in the brief and in oral argument, that "substantial equality" was not "equality" and that "99 percent equality" was unconstitutional, the appeals court answered that such an argument was true in a purely mathematical sense. But there was a difference between theoretical and applied mathematics. "Equality" was an abstraction requiring context or an understanding of the setting in which it was employed. In the *Sweatt* case, equality did not mean that what was separate had to be verified as equal by measuring a number of standard units. "Equations in nature are manifestly only approximations . . . We are not dealing here with abstractions but with realities," and so, in the context of education, "substantially equal" and "equal" were synonymous.

The court showed even less patience with the sociological approach. To the notion that *Sweatt* showed that there was "no rational justification for segregation," the court replied that the sociological evidence was "outside the judicial function."

The sole question before the Court, Chief Justice McClendon wrote, was whether what the State of Texas provided for Heman Sweatt satisfied the equal protection guarantees of the Texas and U.S. constitutions. "The evidence shows, on the part of the State of Texas, an enormous outlay both in funds and in carefully and conscientiously planned and executed endeavor, in a sincere and earnest *bona fide* effort to afford every reasonable and adequate facility and opportunity guaranteed to Relator [Heman Sweatt] under the Fourteenth Amendment, within the State's settled policy (constitutional and statutory) of race segregation in its public schools. We hold that the State has effectually accomplished that objective." The judgment of the 126th District Court was affirmed.

Justice McClendon attached a 2,100-word appendix of supporting facts describing the faculty, curriculum, classrooms, library, and physical facilities of the University of Texas Law School and the School of Law at TSUN.

The next stop on the long road to justice for Heman Sweatt was for his team of attorneys to file a motion in the Third Court of Civil Appeals for a rehearing. "We presume it will be overruled, and in that case, we will immediately file an application for a writ of error in the Texas Supreme Court," Durham explained to reporters.[32]

On March 11, 1948, Durham filed the motion for a rehearing in the appeals court and argued that the court had merely adopted Texas's brief without making an independent evaluation of the record. Six days later, the court denied the motion and reminded Durham and Marshall that appeals courts were not finders of fact.[33]

On April 14, 1948, the Texas Supreme Court received a writ of error from Sweatt's attorneys. By refusing the writ with a one-sentence ruling on September 29, the Texas Supreme Court bypassed the arduous process of calling for briefs and listening to oral arguments.[34] A motion for a rehearing in the Texas Supreme Court by Sweatt's attorneys was a mere formality. On October 27, the court overruled the motion.[35]

The official record of *Sweatt v. Painter* took more than a month to prepare for transmittal to the U.S. Supreme Court. It included more than two years of hearings, trials, and appeals. The State of Texas had won in its own courts, but Thurgood Marshall had also gotten what he wanted: a record, crafted with mastery, that would serve him well in the U.S. Supreme Court.

Wearing Down the Segregationists

For white segregationists, developments in *Sweatt* and other civil rights cases were unsettling. The more-rational southern lawmakers understood that victory for their side would be enormously costly. Each of the southern states defended segregation by offering their funding efforts as evidence of meeting the "separate but equal" mandate. Simply allowing Sweatt into the

UT Law School would have been far cheaper than spending millions of dollars to build a new university with a law school. On July 4, 1948, the *Dallas Morning News* reported that the NAACP boasted that "when and if the *Sweatt* case is won, from that moment on segregation will begin to crumble." The same article included an astonishingly candid interview with Donald Jones, the secretary of the Dallas-based regional office of the NAACP. He revealed that in addition to four active lawsuits, including cases to open high schools in La Grange and Hearne to black students, there were plans for six more court filings in Texas alone. It was a "well-organized legal battle." A few weeks later, James Morton admitted that he knew of "four or five Negroes" who indicated they were ready to apply for admission to UT.[36] Jones, perhaps to Thurgood Marshall's chagrin, went so far as to give some hypothetical examples: "Suppose, for example, a Negro applied to the College of Mines and Metallurgy at El Paso. That institution probably cost the state fifteen million dollars, at least. To set up a separate school for that Negro, it would cost at least five or six million dollars. That is why we believe the various cases we have filed will finally convince the authorities that it is economically sound to avoid segregation."[37] Whether a civil rights suit was for equalization or improved facilities or a direct attack on segregation, Texas had to defend itself in the same way—by showing separate equality. In a case like *Sweatt*, the state had to do so even if defeated African Americans were getting a new university in Houston.

For segregationists, the news outside of Texas was not good either. Oklahoma's resistance to desegregating graduate and professional education was wearing down as Ada Lois Sipuel came closer to enrolling in the University of Oklahoma Law School. Unlike UT president Theophilus Painter, OU president George Lynn Cross understood the folly (and immorality) of continued resistance. In her memoirs, Ada Lois Sipuel Fisher clearly saw President Cross as being sympathetic to her cause.[38] Arguably, Painter could not have shown such support, because his position was much more untenable: for much of this period, he was still acting president, serving at the pleasure of the regents. He had also succeeded an administrator, Homer Rainey, who had been acrimoniously fired.

In early April 1949, President Joseph Rhoads of Bishop College summoned a number of students to discuss an application to the UT medical school by Herman A. Barnett, a gifted black student from Samuel Huston College. As president of the Texas Council of Negro Organizations, Rhoads was in an extraordinary position to give direction to civil rights efforts. He complemented Maceo Smith, who was more of a strategic and organizational genius, with his gift for motivation and direct action. Smith, for example, in a letter to James Morton on October 27, 1948, suggested that as many qualified black students as possible should be encouraged to apply for admission to the University of Texas in as many different areas as possible. The task of actually getting the students to apply and engage in public demonstrations, however, fell to Rhoads, Morton, and Astor Kirk.[39]

On April 5, 1949, Smith informed Thurgood Marshall of a "program of action" and plans for "mass applications [of African Americans] to UT . . . with the blessings" of James Rhoads. "A bus will be chartered," Smith continued, "to pick up these students at the various [Texas Negro] colleges to transport them to Austin on a date to be designated for the purpose of filing these applications in person."[40] The date and timing mattered because the group intended to follow their mass applications at the UT Main Building and Tower with a short march southward to the Capitol, where the legislature would be in session.

On April 27, 1949, students from Bishop, Wiley, and Jarvis colleges arrived in Austin, and were joined by others whom James Morton and Astor Kirk had organized from Samuel Huston and Tillotson Colleges. The national office of the NAACP encouraged and supported the event; Marshall thought the dramatic show would have "wholesome repercussions," but he also warned that the affair should be tightly controlled. There was no way to know for sure whether picketing students would be arrested once on the Capitol grounds. Always conscious of the stain of communist influence, Marshall added, "Please also be careful that the Comrades don't take it over as they did in Oklahoma."[41]

Indeed, the event was carefully planned for maximum exposure. The Houston NAACP chapter leaked the plans to the *Houston Post* and the Associated Press, but when the *Daily Texan* asked James Morton whether it was true that a large group of black students planned a march on UT, Morton slyly replied, "There will possibly be someone on campus Wednesday, but I don't know for sure."[42] The cryptic reply, of course, only heightened anticipation of the event.

The buses arrived in Austin at seven fifteen on the morning of April 27 and proceeded to Tillotson College, where the students were fed breakfast. James Morton and Astor Kirk briefed the students on logistics. They also emphasized to the groomed and well-dressed students the importance of conducting themselves as mature young adults. Astor Kirk, only a few years older than most of the students, led by example: "I tried at all times to really remain faithful to my belief that we have a moral obligation to do whatever we can to achieve openness of mind and heart, civility, and mutual respect as we interact with one another in dealing with highly controversial issues of the human condition."[43]

After the briefing, the buses left Tillotson College, crossed East Avenue, and proceeded to 21st Street and University Avenue, where the Littlefield Fountain greets visitors entering the UT campus from the south. From the fountain, the students made an orderly march up the shaded walkways of the South Mall past statues of Confederate officials like Robert E. Lee and Jefferson Davis. (The statues had been placed there during the World War I era, along with likenesses of George Washington and Woodrow Wilson, to signify a nation united against the Central Powers of Europe.)[44]

The *Houston Informer* reported that the protesters had favorable comments about their reception by white students—some even joined the march. Once the group reached the upper terrace of the South Mall, they entered the Main building and proceeded to the Office of the Registrar. Accounts differ, but between thirty-five and forty-two students crowded the hallway outside of Room 1 on the ground floor—the same room Heman Sweatt and W. Astor Kirk had entered during their unsuccessful attempts to become UT students.

Astor Kirk was already familiar with associate registrar Max Fichtenbaum. Their second conversation was nearly identical to the first, five months earlier: "We have some students here from senior colleges who would like to make applications for graduate work," Kirk said.

"You know, I'm sure, that the Texas State University for Negroes was set up for Negroes in Houston. The law provides that you apply there. We cooperate with that university in providing courses they do not have. You'll have to file there. That's the law in Texas," Fichtenbaum replied.

Simpson Tate of the NAACP regional office in Dallas followed with questions about applications to the medical and dental schools; Fichtenbaum replied that regardless of who provided the courses, the students would still have to apply at TSUN. The associate registrar could only repeat: "That is the law in Texas."[45]

The confrontation in the registrar's office had ended by eleven, so the students marched out double file through the east door and back to the Littlefield Fountain, where they reboarded the buses to return to Tillotson for a brief lunch. On the way, however, they stopped to have their picture taken. Many carried signs with slogans such as "Regional Education is Unconstitutional" and "Separate and Equal Education is a Mockery." One white student carried a poster saying "Civil Rights are Everyone's Rights."[46]

By three, the protesters were seated in the galleries of the Capitol. It is customary for a legislator to recognize such groups, but no member in either the House or the Senate acknowledged the students. Instead, while in the Senate, the sergeant at arms approached those with pickets and told them that their signs were not allowed in the Senate Chamber. "We will follow your rules, of course," Astor Kirk replied calmly, and the signs were stacked in the hallway without incident.

Toward the end of the march, the group received word that Governor Jester had agreed to meet with a delegation from the group. Two students, David Williams and Sheffield Quarles, were selected by the other students to be spokesmen. The only hint of disrespect directed at anyone was when David Williams walked up to Jester's desk, then put one hand in a jacket pocket and a fist on the governor's desk. "We represent 300 of the 1000 Negro seniors in Texas colleges who have evidenced their desire to extend their preparation into professional fields. We come to you, Governor, not as beggars seeking alms but as free citizens of the State of Texas claiming those things rightfully ours, but which we have long been denied . . . Our business here today is to ask you . . . to help us enter the graduate schools of the University of Texas."[47] When Governor Jester replied that he and the legislature were taking drastic steps to ensure that Negroes had separate and equal educational opportunities, both Quarles and Williams argued that integration was the only solution. One of the problems was the time it would take to reach the equality the governor envisioned. "Time is not the whole answer," Jester replied. Then he added that the meeting was over.[48]

The governor, the legislature, and university officials knew many more applications would be coming. The day after the march on Austin, Donald Jones of the Southwest Regional Office of the NAACP announced that suits would be filed by each of the students refused on the previous day. Jones understood the value of the applications. Earlier in the year, he had written to James Nabrit, Jr., of Howard University and asked, "Is there any Texas student at Howard interested in atom smashing?"[49]

CHAPTER 18

A Shattered Spirit

The Sweatt Case is the most important case in the lives of Negro Americans in this century. Heman Marion Sweatt is the champion of this great cause.
A. MACEO SMITH TO J. M. TOLBERT, MARCH 16, 1950

As the *Sweatt* case moved forward, the Texas Legislature felt pressured to show progress in building a "university of the first class for Negroes." In the fall of 1948, President Raphael O'Hara Lanier and the TSUN regents submitted a proposed budget of $10,269,233 to the legislature for a two-year expansion program; roughly 75 percent of the budget was for new construction. Shortly into the 1949 regular legislative session, Lanier saw his budget proposal cut almost in half.[1]

From its inception, the Texas State University for Negroes was a tormented institution. Many white elites saw it as the result of a judicial shakedown—not just "the House That Sweatt Built" but also "the House That Sweatt Forced Us to Build." The Texas Legislature grudgingly appropriated funds to keep TSUN running in order to keep the University of Texas white.

But for the African American community, TSUN presented even more complex issues—and painful choices. Sweatt's application to the UT Law School had galvanized black churches and civic groups throughout Texas into action. Sweatt's lawsuit would ultimately cost the NAACP about $40,000, and even after three years of litigation—and adverse rulings at each step—African American Texans seemed ready to raise more. Even so, leaders like Carter Wesley foresaw the ultimate consequence of a *Sweatt* victory. As long as *Sweatt* posed the threat of integrating UT, the state of Texas would continue to be pressured to show it was providing substantial equality in the form of TSUN and the expansion of Prairie View A&M. That translated into real money. According to Gale Leslie Barchus, "during the prosecution of the *Sweatt* case, the State in fact appropriated more funds for Negro higher education than had been provided in its entire history."[2]

If Sweatt were to win his case and enter UT, the state would be relieved of its burden to deliver substantial educational equality in predominantly black institutions. If that happened, what would become of funding for TSUN, which was already one of the largest African American universities in the United States?

In the spring of 1949, Governor Beauford Jester gave the TSUN commencement address, telling the crowd that "custom makes 95 percent of both our white and Negro citizens in Texas prefer separate schools."[3] He presented no evidence to support such a statement, and in fact, it was not true outside of Jester's own worldview.

By that time, Heman Marion Sweatt's world had developed into one of fatigue, fear, and tension. On at least one occasion he felt as if he were being left out of the NAACP inner circle. "It embarrasses me to no end to realize that I have not kept you up to date on your own case," Thurgood Marshall wrote apologetically after Sweatt asked what was going on. Even more troubling to Sweatt, however, were the divisions within the African American community over whether to embrace the establishment of TSUN. In a letter to Marshall, he blasted toasts and speeches of appreciation by African American Texans for Governor Jester's "first class Negro University." He was especially galled at the spectacle of young black choral groups singing for the governor, and at some of his own friends (whom he did not identify) for accepting "cash lollipops." During this period, Sweatt noted an increase in anonymous and harassing phone calls telling him that he was "on a limb" by himself. He had, in his own words, a "shattered spirit."[4]

Sweatt also despaired when people spoke of his case in the past tense. Even before the U.S. Supreme Court agreed to hear *Sweatt v. Painter*, grateful African Americans commented about what great good had come from the case and how he was a hero to thousands of TSUN students and their families. From his office in New York City, Marshall felt a need to write encouraging and supportive letters, but he knew Sweatt was strong enough to last through a final adjudication. When Sweatt assured Marshall that he was "staying put, in spite of all of this," Marshall knew, once again, he had an ideal client.[5]

The long road to justice for Heman Sweatt also took a physical toll on him. In late January 1950, after yet another postponement of oral arguments before the Supreme Court, Sweatt became seriously ill. He had been plagued by a series of illnesses since his time at the University of Michigan, but at this point some observers believed that he had become sick in "mind and body." Connie Sweatt admitted to reporters that he had "worried himself sick over the case." She was overheard asking, "I wonder if it's worth it?"[6]

Sweatt's illnesses lasted through much of January and February. In early March, he wrote to Marshall that he had "just returned to work after several weeks illness, the cost of which is an excellent argument for Truman's national health program."[7] His mail route served a white neighborhood of blue-collar railroad workers who seemed to like him: "They have been very kind to me," Sweatt said.[8] But his health prospects for the immediate future were not good. If his job as a mail carrier and the physical stamina it required contributed at all to his frail health, he could not have looked forward to the approaching brutally hot and humid summer months in Houston.

Although some thought the *Sweatt* case was over, the fight for educational equality was moving forward, even as Sweatt waited. Attorney General Price Daniel had urged the U.S. Supreme Court to deny Sweatt's writ of certiorari (the writ asking the Court to hear the appeal) on the grounds that the establishment of the Texas State University for Negroes and an expansion of programs at Prairie View provided substantial equality of educational opportunities for Texas's African American population. Separately, the Court had been presented with *McLaurin v. Oklahoma* (1950), which dealt with whether a state could segregate by race within a school or classroom, and *Henderson v. United States* (1950), which involved racial segregation in railroad dining cars.[9]

The Supreme Court granted certiorari for *Sweatt v. Painter* on November 7, 1949. "Please notify everyone in Texas[,] Supreme Court granted certiorari in Sweatt Case today," Marshall telegraphed Maceo Smith. Marshall also took care to telegraph Sweatt individually.[10]

Within a few days, Marshall and Assistant Attorney General Greenhill were working out the details of the record to be presented to the Court. The two men had grown to respect each other, and Greenhill considered himself one of Marshall's friends. For his part, Marshall clearly appreciated Greenhill's easygoing and professional manner. While preparing the record, he wrote to Greenhill of their "spirit of cooperation."[11]

The people Marshall selected to receive copies of the printed record of the *Sweatt* case illustrated whom he considered key to victory. Besides Heman Sweatt, Marshall sent a copy to Dr. Robert Redfield of the University of Chicago, the anchor witness supporting the sociological approach, and Austin dentist Dr. Lewis Mitchell and his wife Carolyn, writing to the latter: "As you know, both of you played a most important part in this case and I believe that you should have the record for whatever use you care to make of it other than throw it away."[12]

To Thurgood Marshall, who was doing a job that required 50,000 miles of travel each year to areas that had no acceptable accommodations for a professional black man (or no accommodations at all), Lewis and Carolyn Mitchell represented something as important as a well-written brief or a cogent legal argument: they reminded him and his lawyers that the people they were representing deserved the investment, sacrifice, and pain they endured. Carolyn Mitchell, who was on the faculty of both Samuel Huston and Tillotson Colleges, would have had to leave Texas to earn a doctorate if she decided to study for one. To improve his skills as a dentist, Lewis Mitchell had to travel to Tuskegee, Alabama, for professional development. But perhaps even more important was the fact that the Mitchells made Marshall as comfortable as he could be made in a state that did not want him; they made him laugh during a time where almost nothing was funny. He sipped their whiskey, ate their food, and sang songs with them. For Marshall, a man who often seemed on the verge of physical exhaustion and who had fainted three times over the past ten years from overwork and a lack of sleep, the Mitchells were more than just gracious hosts. Before the end of the *Sweatt* case, Marshall was calling Carolyn Mitchell his "Mama."[13]

Preparing for the Supreme Court

While Joe Greenhill did most of the legal work for the State of Texas on the *Sweatt* case, Attorney General Price Daniel continued to try to convince the public that Heman Sweatt was merely a tool of the NAACP. "If Sweatt had been really interested in obtaining a legal education," Daniel told a Texas court, "he could have his license by now."[14] In January 1950, he called upon state attorneys general from across the South to come together and file briefs in defense of the right of states to maintain racial segregation. If Texas lost in *Sweatt,* Daniel wrote to Eugene Cook, of Georgia, "your office and my office will be deluged with law suits for entry of Negroes into white colleges, high schools and grade schools." Attorney General Harry McMullan of North Carolina publicly stated that *Sweatt* was the most important Supreme Court case to come out of the south since the days of the Civil War. Most of McMullan's colleagues in the South agreed and so filed amici curiae (friends of the court) briefs in support of Texas. They included the attorney general or assistant attorney general of Arkansas, Florida, Georgia, Kentucky, Louisiana, Mississippi, North Carolina, Oklahoma, South Carolina, Tennessee, and Virginia. The collective legal talent of the group, however, descended into a "peculiar chivalry" mode when it asserted that

"Negro men do not want their daughters, wives, and sweethearts dancing, dating, and playing with white men any more than white men want their women folk in intimate social contact with Negro men."[15]

Other groups from across the country filed amicus briefs. The American Veterans Committee, a group of progressive World War II veterans that counted Franklin Roosevelt, Jr., and Hollywood actors like William Holden and Ronald Reagan among its members, supported Sweatt's cause. They argued that if Texas prevailed in *Sweatt*, the GI Bill of Rights would be made meaningless for Negro veterans, since there would be no graduate or professional schools for them to attend. Throughout America, respect and encouragement for returning veterans was sacrosanct, and the American Veterans Committee reminded the Court that both whites and African Americans served honorably during the war. Service during war transcended racial segregation even for some southerners. One letter in support of the application of Herman Barnett, a Tuskegee Airman who applied to the UT medical school, came from a physician who wrote to President Painter that "[Barnett] was enough of a citizen to dodge bullets in World War II."[16]

When the American Council of Churches of Christ announced it would submit a brief to the Court supporting Sweatt, it proudly announced that it was the first time the church leadership had ever intervened in a court case. "Segregation in matters of the mind and spirit means second class citizenship," the ecclesiastical organization noted. The brief, however, lost much of its moral force when Joe Greenhill challenged the group to include the fact that the member churches were themselves segregated—and so were the schools under their control.[17]

Attorney L. N. D. Wells, Jr., filed a brief for the Texas Council of Negro Organizations. It attacked the state's argument that integration would lead to social unrest and violence. Wells discussed with Thurgood Marshall the possibility of including an affidavit from Ada Lois Sipuel, which would confirm that she was well treated by her University of Oklahoma classmates; the students had taken the initiative of removing the Reserved for Colored signs placed to segregate her from others.[18]

The amicus carrying the most intellectual power, however, resulted from a request Marshall made to law professors Thomas I. Emerson of Yale and John Frank of the Indiana Law School to develop a brief to be signed by as many law-school teachers as possible. Eventually, more than 200 law school deans and professors from more than forty schools signed it. The brief, called the "Committee of Law Teachers Against Segregation in Legal Education," branded makeshift Jim Crow law schools in places like Missouri, Oklahoma, and Texas "a mockery of legal education and of the equal protection of the laws." The professors also argued that Congress had intended the Fourteenth Amendment to outlaw all forms of segregation, and even if Congress had intended to allow a condition like "separate but equal," it did not apply to education. Finally, the brief argued that even if segregation in education was reasonable under *Plessy*, the TSUN and UT law schools were not equal.[19]

Attorney General Price Daniel rendered a predictably political, rather than legal, reply to the committee of law teachers: it was not the first time, he insisted, "northern professors have tried to tell us how to run our schools in Texas."[20] Joe Greenhill, in contrast, went to work on the question of congressional intent as it related to school segregation and the passage of the Fourteenth Amendment. The product of his research represented the best legal work presented by the attorney general's office throughout the *Sweatt* litigation.

Greenhill reminded the Court that in the District of Columbia, the only jurisdiction in which Congress had complete control, Congress set up segregated schools in 1862, kept those schools segregated throughout the Civil War and Reconstruction, and maintained them as segregated in 1950 as *Sweatt* was being argued. Greenhill argued that the Fourteenth Amendment and the Civil Rights Act of 1866 were meant to give everyone equal civil rights, which never included school integration. Greenhill showed that during congressional debates over the Fourteenth Amendment in May 1866, Congress donated land to segregated Negro schools, and they later addressed the method of tax support for the schools.[21]

Greenhill's brief reported that in the late 1860s and early 1870s, when the Radical Republicans held tight control over Capitol Hill, Massachusetts senator Charles Sumner made repeated attempts to insert measures for the integration of schools into legislation; he was defeated each time. Congress was able to require the southern states to ratify the Fourteenth Amendment in order to be readmitted to the Union, but no evidence existed that school desegregation was connected with that compliance. Indeed, eleven of the northern and border states that ratified the Fourteenth Amendment maintained white and nonwhite school systems, as did all the former Confederate states. Greenhill also pointed out that as of 1950, at least five state courts outside the South had ruled that the Fourteenth Amendment did not mandate integrated schools.[22]

For seventy-five years after the Civil War and Reconstruction, Congress had done nothing to make school desegregation a condition for any service or money provided by the federal government. On the contrary, guidelines explained how money should be divided among the races, such as the

"A&M" money provided for in the Morrill Acts and the housing units paid for by federal funds.[23] Greenhill's research and conclusions were later independently verified by Justice Felix Frankfurter's law clerk Alexander M. Bickel during the 1952 term. After months spent researching the legislative history, Bickel reported that it was "impossible" to establish any connection between school desegregation (or any other racial separation) and congressional intent regarding the Fourteenth Amendment. He added that Congress had not even foreseen the abolition of school segregation.[24]

Carter Wesley thought that the most significant of the amici was submitted by Philip Perlman, the solicitor general in Harry Truman's Justice Department. His brief labeled all segregation unconstitutional and called for the outright overturning of *Plessy*. It reinforced the sociological approach in that it called for the Court to consider the immorality of segregation, since there was no logical or scientific reason for it.[25]

As the time drew near for oral arguments, Heman Sweatt again became the focus of attention. In early 1950, several African American civic groups began to raise money for Heman and Connie Sweatt to travel to Washington, D.C., to witness the trial. In a letter to Thurgood Marshall, Sweatt wondered whether such a solicitation, which was called the "Sweatt Travel Fund," was the best use of the money raised. Maceo Smith reassured Sweatt: "Your presence at the trial will be another manifestation of your determination to lead the movement of fifteen million Negroes to obliterate the vicious practices of segregation in order to make democracy work."[26]

The Sweatts made the trip to Washington, D.C., and to show its appreciation for his dedication to and patience in the struggle for full citizenship for African Americans, the NAACP arranged for J. M. Tolbert, the president of the Texas Club, to entertain the couple while they were in the capital.[27]

For Joe Greenhill, the night before oral arguments was almost as memorable as his appearance before the Court. At a social gathering, Sam Rayburn, the legendary Speaker of the House of Representatives, insisted that Joe and Mrs. Greenhill join him for a drink. It was a pleasant evening for the couple, but Greenhill was understandably distracted. The next day, he and Thurgood Marshall would be arguing over the future of racial segregation in America. "Actually, we and Marshall thought that we were trying . . . the *Brown v. Board* [of Education] case."[28]

Thurgood Marshall arrived in Washington on Friday, March 31, and checked into the Charles Hotel on R Street. On the next day, he and William Durham went through a grueling and arduous daylong rehearsal and discussion of the case. The Howard Law School tradition and ritual involved an actual presentation of the arguments before an assembly of faculty, gifted law students, and outside attorneys. During the mock hearing, nine professors sat at a long table and role-played being specific justices. The exercise was meant to be more punishing than the Court appearance itself.[29]

The Big Day at Last

When Heman and Connie Sweatt arrived at the Supreme Court building on Tuesday, April 4, 1950, a long line of people were waiting for tickets to hear the oral arguments. Shortly after the Sweatts took their seats, the justices, all of whom had been appointed by Franklin Roosevelt or his successor, Harry Truman, entered the chambers. Seated left to right were Justice Tom C. Clark, of Texas, Harry Truman's former attorney general and a graduate of the University of Texas Law School, whom Truman had appointed in August 1949; Justice Robert H. Jackson, of New York, appointed by FDR in 1940; Justice Felix Frankfurter, an Austrian immigrant from New York appointed by FDR in 1939; Justice Hugo Black, of Alabama, FDR's first appointment, in 1937; Chief Justice Fred M. Vinson, of Kentucky, Truman's former secretary of treasury, appointed in June 1946; Justice Stanley F. Reed, of Kentucky, appointed by FDR in 1938; Justice William O. Douglas, of California, appointed by FDR in 1939; Justice Harold H. Burton, of Ohio, appointed by Truman in 1945; and Justice Sherman Minton, of Indiana, appointed by Truman in October 1949.[30]

As the first order of business, Chief Justice Vinson admitted eleven attorneys to the Bar of the Supreme Court. The chief justice then called for arguments in the *McLaurin* case. Thurgood Marshall's young assistant Robert L. Carter, representing McLaurin, delivered the NAACP's argument that any separation of the races, even in the same building or classroom, was unconstitutional. He was followed by Oklahoma's first assistant attorney general, Fred Hansen, who defended the separate-but-equal doctrine and described Oklahoma officials as "thoughtful men and good men" who were doing the best they could to deal with a true dilemma.[31]

When the matter of *Sweatt v. Painter* came before the Court, it was William J. Durham, of Dallas, who reviewed the long history of legal proceedings that had led to the present hearing—perhaps because Marshall was sensitive to past complaints that Texas attorneys should litigate Texas cases. Once Durham finished, Marshall, who at age forty-one was appearing for the eighth time before the Supreme Court, approached the advocate's lectern to present the legal argument for ending segregation.

Marshall said that today all segregation laws were being attacked in the Court. Furthermore, Sweatt's testimony that he would not attend any law school so long as it was segregated had crystallized the issue before the Court: was Heman Sweatt correct in his assertion that separate could not be equal? Marshall drove home the point: "Now, Texas argues that they were relying on decisions of the Supreme Court [but] they didn't put in any evidence to justify the reasonableness of this statute." He added that if a state chooses to treat racial groups differently, it has the burden of showing the differences between them. The sociological evidence rejected by Texas courts showed that there were no differences between blacks and whites.[32]

Separate but equal was not possible, Marshall emphasized: "They can build an exact duplicate of the University of Texas Law School in brick, mortar, desks, and libraries, but it will make no difference as long as it is segregated." Indeed, he continued, Texas attorney general Price Daniel argued during trial that the basement law school on 13th Street was even better than the University of Texas, and the state had prevailed. Then the state built a new law school for Negroes in Houston that, if it were superior, would give white students cause to file complaints. "How can it be," bellowed Marshall, "that this law school, which does not have any alumni, can be equivalent to the University of Texas, which has so many members in the state House of Representatives, so many members in the state Senate, [and] one member of this Court?"[33]

Marshall counseled the Court that the fear of unrest as a result of Heman Sweatt's enrollment at UT Law School was unfounded for a number of reasons. First, no such unrest had yet occurred in other graduate and professional schools that had been integrated. To believe that violence would be directed at Heman Sweatt was to believe UT law students were "hoodlums." Second, such unrest would most likely happen in common schools and public facilities like swimming pools, and that was irrelevant to the *Sweatt* case. Third, dire predictions of unrest because of Negroes voting in formerly all-white Democratic primaries never materialized: "Now Negroes vote and there is no trouble." But even if some law-school students found Heman Sweatt's presence uncomfortable or unsettling, the students did not have to associate themselves with Sweatt in any way. They could merely leave him alone: "We want to remove governmental restriction. If [the white students] want to, they can keep their prejudices." The removal of the governmental restriction was a constitutional right that was owed to Heman Sweatt: "It makes no difference if every Negro and every White wants separate schools . . . treatment of [Sweatt] cannot be conditioned upon the wishes of any other citizen."[34]

Attorney General Price Daniel approached the advocate's lectern and, for about thirty minutes, argued that the U.S. Supreme Court had already settled the reasonableness of racial classifications. To Marshall's contention that education was the foundation of all rights, the attorney general replied that under the U.S. Constitution the state was under no obligation to provide anyone an education. And even if it did, the state clearly had the right to determine the conditions under which the service would be rendered.

To Marshall's argument that *Plessy* should be reexamined because its precedent was based on cases adjudicated before the ratification of the Fourteenth Amendment, Daniel emphasized that the Court was being challenged to overrule not just *Plessy v. Ferguson* but a host of other cases, over a period of almost six decades, in which the Court cited *Plessy* as precedent.

For justices and observers who rely on precedent and a literal interpretation of the Constitution when forming their opinions, Daniel's oral arguments were well taken. Then Daniel fell into his old habit of presuming to speak for African American Texans: neither whites nor Negroes wanted to cross the racial lines of demarcation. "It is a reality you have to face—that some people have feelings that lead to conflict when a relationship is forced," he insisted. The natural racial order was not the result of hatred or prejudice, he explained. The American Council of Churches of Christ was a good case in point: the group advocated the integration of public institutions while representing racially segregated congregations in the South.

And so it was always with carpetbaggers (a term Daniel did not specifically use), the agitators from the north who would deprive Texas of its right as a state to decide its own destiny. Separate schools had been upheld by courts in many northern states. Heman Sweatt was merely a tool being used to have courts eliminate segregation in areas where states had determined it to be necessary.[35]

Joe Greenhill presented a much more workmanlike argument, citing a list of precedents supporting the right of states to handle issues like education and transportation as they saw fit. *Cumming v. Richmond County Board of Education* (1899) meant "the education of the people in schools maintained by taxation is a matter belonging to the respective states"; *Chesapeake and Ohio Railway v. Kentucky* (1900) upheld segregated intrastate commerce in Kentucky; from *Berea College v. Kentucky* (1908), Greenhill quoted Justice Harlan, "Of course what I have said has no reference to regulations prescribed for public schools, established at the pleasure of the state and maintained at public expense"; and *Chiles v. Chesapeake and Ohio Railway* (1910) upheld reasonable regulations of a private carrier that segregated passengers by race.[36]

Greenhill's most impressive argument was that the Fourteenth Amendment had never been intended to integrate the races. His documentation and logic was strong enough for Marshall to concede that the history and intent of the amendment could be used to support either side of the school-integration argument, but Marshall argued that it was undeniable that the amendment was meant to guarantee full citizenship rights, which were what Texas sought to deny Sweatt.[37]

Both Daniel and Greenhill argued that sociological evidence had been appropriately ignored by the Texas courts because it was the job of state and local legislators and executives to evaluate such data. It was not the job of any court to formulate policy for a state. Moreover, since Sweatt had changed his mind about attending a substantially equal law school that might have been set up at Prairie View A&M, then the testimony regarding equal facilities was irrelevant as well. So as far as Daniel and Greenhill were concerned, the question before the Court was whether Texas had the right, as a state, to control its schools. Their position was supported by the U.S. and Texas constitutions, history, case law, and the social order of the time. Daniel and Greenhill also insisted that the state had acted in good faith to provide an equal or substantially equal opportunity for Sweatt to become a licensed attorney.[38]

At the end of the session, everyone posed for pictures. The next day, Charles Thompson of Howard University wrote Marshall a letter of congratulations: "I have heard you upon numerous occasions in the lower courts and several times before the Supreme Court. But I think that your presentation yesterday surpassed all of your past performances."[39]

Unfortunately, Marshall had more on his mind than just the *Sweatt* case. His mentor and teacher, Charles Hamilton Houston, who had insisted to his students that they were parasites as lawyers unless they became social engineers, had been hospitalized in late 1949 for chronic chest pains and shortness of breath. Like Marshall, Houston had spent his career seeking full citizenship for the descendants of African slaves. His decades-long habit of fourteen- to eighteen-hour workdays caught up with him. During the early afternoon of April 22, 1950, less than three weeks after his star pupil appeared before the Supreme Court to argue *Sweatt,* Charles Houston's eyes brightened when he recognized a friend at the door of his hospital room. He raised his hand and said, "Hi, Joe," took a final breath, and died almost instantly in his bed at Freedmen's Hospital in Washington, D.C.[40]

Justice Tom Clark

Justice Harold Burton's clerks thought *Sweatt* was a good case for reconsidering *Plessy,* and they wrote a long memorandum to that effect.[41] The views of another justice, however, were eagerly anticipated.

It was natural for Justice Tom Campbell Clark to take a special interest in *Sweatt v. Painter.* Clark was born in Dallas on September 23, 1899, and graduated from UT Law School in 1922. After practicing law and serving as a local district attorney in Dallas, Clark joined the Justice Department in 1937; President Harry Truman appointed him U.S. attorney general in 1945. He took his oath as a Supreme Court justice on August 24, 1949.[42] In a memorandum to the brethren, as the justices were known until Sandra Day O'Connor joined the Court in 1981, he said, "Since these cases arise in 'my' part of the country it is proper and I hope helpful for me to express some views concerning them."[43]

Clark dismissed the prospects of unrest and violence, which he called "horribles." "Oklahoma was frank enough to admit this," Clark continued, and as a native of Dallas and an alumnus of UT, he understood the difference between Austin and much of the rest of Texas. But there was another reason why he felt confident that Heman Sweatt could attend UT without incident: "There would be no 'incidents' in my opinion, if the cases are limited to their facts, i.e., graduate schools." Clark thought there could be trouble if the ruling would be extended to elementary and secondary schools. "Certainly this is not required now. I would be opposed to such extension at this time and would vote against taking a case involving same."[44]

Tom Clark thought that the Texas courts should be reversed in *Sweatt.* One way was to overrule *Plessy,* but Clark was not willing to go that far. *Sweatt* could easily be distinguished from *Plessy,* since the latter did not involve education, and the measures for what was "equal" in the two cases were clearly not the same. Clark also thought that it was unclear that black and white elementary and secondary schools were as obviously unequal as UT Law and what was being offered to Sweatt. He steered the Court away from the tediousness of counting books, desks, and bricks to a discussion of what every justice knew: those tangibles were not all a law school was about.

(1) white schools have higher standing in the community as well as nationally . . . ; (2) the older and larger college has more alumni, which gives the graduate more professional opportunities; (3) the larger and older school attracts better professors; (4) competition among schools is much keener in the older and more established school . . . ; (5) the larger and older institution attracts a cross section of the entire State in its student body—affords a wider exchange of ideas—and, in the combat of ideas, furnishes a greater variety of minds, backgrounds and opinions . . . ; (6) it takes years and years to establish a professional school of top rank, affording law reviews, competitions, medals, societies . . . ; (7) acquaintance is important in the profes-

sions and segregation prevents it . . . These and other reasons are those
which I am sure have led all but nine of the States to abandon the 'separate
but equal' doctrine at the graduate level.[45]

None of Justice Clark's seven points could be measured in a standardized
fashion or placed on a common scale. No two independent researchers
would ever quantify Clark's points and achieve identical results. Gone were
the tedious arguments about square footage per student, or numbers of volumes dealing with English common law or the Napoleonic Code. And yet
Clark was obviously speaking the truth. As a UT Law student observed
during the *Sweatt* trial, "Hell, anyone can see that the Negro school isn't
equal or even substantially equal to our law school."[46]

Justice Clark helped move the Court from considering equality only as
a measurable mathematical construct, such as equalized pay for African
American teachers, to what would become known as "intangibles." He
closed his memorandum with "If some say this undermines *Plessy* then let it
fall, as have many Nineteenth Century oracles."[47]

Clark did not want to overrule *Plessy;* he wanted to "undermine" it. It was
the compromise the justices were looking for.

UT's Continued Unwillingness to Admit
Astor Kirk and Herman Barnett

During the first half of 1950, W. Astor Kirk quietly continued his efforts
to be admitted to the UT Graduate School's doctoral program in political
science. In mid-January, Kirk had been invited to a discreet meeting at the
Capitol with Attorney General Price Daniel and his assistants Joe Greenhill
and E. "Jake" Jacobson. In his memoirs, Kirk remembered that the cordial
meeting lasted about half an hour. Daniel offered Kirk a PhD in "an unusu-
ally short period of time," but Kirk insisted that UT Graduate School was
where he wanted to earn a doctorate.[48]

For Kirk, the meeting was instructive in another way: "I did come away
from that meeting with one distinct impression: the strong feeling that if
the State of Texas lost the *Sweatt* case in the U.S. Supreme Court, the Attorney General's office would not support the [UT] Board of Regents in
continued resistance to desegregate the Graduate School and its other professional schools."[49] If Kirk's impression was accurate, it would indicate that
Daniel, Greenhill, and Jacobson had already resigned themselves to probable defeat in *Sweatt.*

After Kirk's first attempt to enroll in the UT Graduate School, the regents entered into a contractual agreement with the Texas State University for Negroes in which UT would provide African Americans with classes not offered on the Houston campus. It was through this arrangement that Kirk was accepted as a TSUN student, but offered two classes in Austin taught by UT professors. On January 30, 1950, Kirk went to the UT Department of Government, registered for two courses, and paid $26 in tuition. The classes were to begin on February 6, but Kirk was to report to the YMCA building on Guadalupe, across the street from campus. He soon learned that he was to be the only student in the class.[50]

On February 6, 1950, Kirk reported to room 7 of the YMCA, which had been rented by the University for use as Kirk's class. As soon as a Bible-study class adjourned, Dr. Charles Timm of the Department of Government greeted Kirk. The two men talked for about forty-five minutes. Kirk calmly and firmly let Dr. Timm know that the arrangements were not acceptable. He emphasized that he had no personal animosity toward Dr. Timm and departed with a "no hard feelings attitude." As Kirk recalled years later, "Because of the way I responded to University administrators, to the Texas Attorney General, and to representatives of the print and broadcast media, those faculty members 'understood' and treated me as a decent, honorable, ethical, and professionally-motivated human being."[51]

As Kirk left the "classroom," Dr. Timm said, "I probably would take the same course of action if I were in your shoes."[52]

From the YMCA building, Kirk went to the office of UT vice president J. C. Dolley, who told [Kirk] that under current Texas law, the university had "no discretion" in the matter of Kirk's integrating the UT Graduate School. Reporters had been alerted to the developments, and Kirk told them that he "had hoped that arrangements could be made which would not make him or the university look ridiculous. I am prepared to meet them half way on an on-campus arrangement."[53]

On March 2, 1950, the Texas State University for Negroes issued a refund check to W. Astor Kirk in the amount of $26.[54]

Herman Barnett, the medical-school applicant from Samuel Huston College who had inspired the march on the UT campus in April 1949, had scored so high on the medical-school aptitude test that he could have been admitted to any medical school in the country. Donald Jones of the regional office of the NAACP in Dallas marveled at the extraordinary loyalty Barnett had for African American Texans. Barnett had already been accepted to the medical schools of Meharry and the University of Chicago, but the Lockhart native chose to stay in Texas and fight for his rights as a citizen. His official application was dated May 11, 1949, and in August, President Painter informed him in a letter that he had been admitted to the medical school through the same contractual arrangement that had been offered to Astor Kirk. Segregating Herman Barnett in the same way that UT had tried to segregate Kirk, however, was just not possible. Makeshift labs and medical facilities could not be established in Galveston, where the UT medical school was located. As Donald Jones explained to his NAACP regional advisory board, "Technically, Mr. Barnett is being registered as a student at the Texas State University for Negroes at Houston, and will be a contract student at the medical school. But actually the wall is breached; the decisive first thrilling step had been made."[55]

A decision about whether Astor Kirk could cross Guadalupe Street to join the white graduate students on the main UT campus or whether Herman Barnett would be required to attend medical school under the cover of a sham contract between UT and TSUN would soon be made by nine white men in black robes in Washington, D.C.

CHAPTER 19

The Big One

Now, the state will have to age law schools like good whiskey.
THURGOOD MARSHALL TO HEMAN MARION SWEATT,
JUNE 5, 1950

Many American cities register temperatures warmer than Houston, Texas, during the summer months, but few can claim to be more uncomfortable. The heat is less like that produced by an oven, as in Phoenix or Las Vegas, than like the hot, cloudy flush of moisture escaping from an opened dishwasher while flatware and utensils are being "sanitized." The month of June, which has average high temperatures of 91 degrees, is the second wettest in the city, which receives nearly fifty inches of rain a year. June is the beginning of three months of unforgiving and unrelenting discomfort.[1]

Carrying the U.S. mail in such conditions was hard on a man as physically frail as Heman Marion Sweatt; such work would tax the strength of anyone. Sweatt was certainly tired and hot after completing his route on Monday, June 5, 1950. He returned to his Delano Street home to encounter his excited wife, Connie. She told him that the Supreme Court had issued its ruling in his case. Area radio stations were providing complete coverage.[2]

The news was good. The justices had given him a comprehensive victory—at least that was what it sounded like. Then the phone rang. It was Thurgood Marshall. In what was surely a booming and euphoric voice, Marshall said, "We won the big one!" During his abbreviated explanation of the ruling, Marshall said, "Now, the state will have to age law schools like good whiskey."[3]

The Supreme Court Ruling

The ruling was by a unanimous Court, and Chief Justice Vinson wrote the opinion. He first made clear that the Court was not yet ready to make a sweeping ruling on the issue of the inherent constitutionality of racial segregation: "This case and *McLaurin v. Oklahoma State Regents* present different aspects of this general question: To what extent does the Equal Protection Clause of the Fourteenth Amendment limit the power of a state to distinguish between students of different races *in professional and graduate education* in a state university? Broader issues have been urged for our consideration, but we adhere to the principle of deciding constitutional questions only in the context of the particular case before the Court" (emphasis added).[4]

The decision to narrow the question in that way eliminated much of the evidence presented by both the state and the NAACP: "Because of this traditional reluctance to extend constitutional interpretations to situations or facts which are not before the Court, much of the excellent research and detailed argument presented in these cases is unnecessary to their disposition." Neither the NAACP's sociological approach nor Joe Greenhill's masterly research into congressional intent regarding the Fourteenth Amendment was given weight by the Court.

After the usual historical overview of the case history, Chief Justice Vinson wrote of the objective measures of quality of the University of Texas Law School. The Court seemed to be going down the tired and familiar path of counting books, teachers, and expenditures. By the end of the paragraph, however, the comparison included subjective assessments: "The school's alumni occupy the most distinguished positions in the private practice of the law and in the public life of the State. It may properly be considered one of the nation's [top ranked] law schools."

For the next two paragraphs, Vinson contrasted UT Law with the law school proposed for TSUN, both at the time Sweatt had been offered admission and at the time of the oral arguments. Again, the chief justice counted volumes, students, faculty, and accreditation status. He concluded: "Whether the University of Texas Law School is compared with the original or the new law school for Negroes, we cannot find substantial equality in the educational opportunities offered white and Negro law students by the State. In terms of number of the faculty, variety of courses and opportunity for specialization, size of the student body, scope of the library, availability of law review and similar activities, the University of Texas Law School is superior."

The opinion seemed to be headed for a straight finding of unequal treatment according to measurable and objective criteria. Had the opinion stopped there, Texas and the rest of the South would have had an opening to engage in more makeshift enhancements in order to argue that their new and improved "schools" now provided a substantially equal learning environment for nonwhite students and thus were in compliance with *Sweatt*. Such a limited decision would have required the NAACP to engage in new lawsuits and years of litigation. *Sweatt* itself had taken more than four years to reach the U.S. Supreme Court.

But the Court did not stop with measurable and objective criteria: "What is more important, the University of Texas Law School possesses to a far greater degree those *qualities which are incapable of objective measurement* but which make for greatness in a law school. Such qualities, to name but a few, include [the] reputation of the faculty, experience of the administration, position and influence of the alumni, standing in the community, traditions and prestige. It is difficult to believe that one who had a free choice between these law schools would consider the question close" (emphasis added).

"Qualities which are incapable of objective measurement" came to be known as "intangibles." How could the State of Texas create a law school for Negroes, where none had existed before, with alumni of "position and influence"—and one that was equal to the sixty-seven-year-old UT Law School? The Court did not say; it did not have to. The Court consciously undermined *Plessy v. Ferguson,* as Justice Tom Clark had suggested, in graduate- and professional-school education by setting an impossible subjective standard for equality. Justice Clark was even more emphatic years later in an interview: "In fact, not in *Brown [Brown v. Board of Education,* 1954] as people say, did we overrule *Plessy.* We implicitly overruled *Plessy . . .* in *Sweatt* and *Painter*."[5]

As if to hammer the theme of the impossibility of equality in a segregated setting, Vinson lectured Texas, and by implication all of the southern attorneys general supporting Price Daniel, about the realities of a legal education: "Moreover, although the law is a highly learned profession, we are well aware that it is an intensely practical one. The law school, the proving ground for legal learning and practice, cannot be effective in *isolation* from the individuals and institutions with which the law interacts. Few students and no one who has practiced law would choose to study in an academic vacuum, removed from the *interplay of ideas and the exchange of views* with which the law is concerned" (emphasis added).

The opinion became the most valuable precedent for explicitly ending legal racial segregation in the United States, because it had already implicitly done so. In the context of education, what was the material difference between "isolation from . . . individuals and institutions" and enforced segregation? Moreover, a law student could be exposed to the "interplay of ideas and exchange of views" under only one condition: a racially integrated setting. Racially, Texas wanted to separate Heman Sweatt from 85 percent of the population of the state and all but about two to three dozen of the thousands of lawyers and judges in the state. As the Court noted: "With such a substantial and significant segment of society excluded, we cannot conclude that the education offered petitioner is substantially equal to that which he would receive if admitted to the University of Texas Law School." Chief Vinson's scolding continued: "It may be argued that excluding [Heman Sweatt] from that school is no different from excluding white students from the new law school. This contention overlooks realities."

For four years, Heman Marion Sweatt had been appearing before courts to secure, in the chief justice's words, "personal and present" rights guaranteed him by the Fourteenth Amendment. *Missouri ex rel. Gaines v. Canada* (1938) mandated that states provide equal protection within their own borders. *Sipuel v. Board of Regents* (1948) added that such protection had to be provided to formerly excluded minorities at the same time it was provided to others. Vinson pointed out that "these are the only cases in this Court which present the issue of the constitutional validity of race distinctions in state-supported graduate and professional education," then drew the inescapable conclusion that Sweatt had a full constitutional right to a legal education in Texas immediately because such was being offered to white students. *Plessy* was irrelevant because the Negro law school was not, in fact, equal to UT Law. And so, "We hold that the Equal Protection Clause of the Fourteenth Amendment requires that petitioner be admitted to the University of Texas Law School."

On the same day, the Court delivered its ruling in *McLaurin v. Oklahoma State Regents*. During the course of the litigation, the University of Oklahoma had allowed George W. McLaurin to move from the anteroom that Thurgood Marshall had called a "broom closet" to an area inside the classroom where the seat assigned to him was labeled "reserved for colored" and surrounded by a "railing" made of pine two-by-fours. He was also assigned a table in the library and the cafeteria.[6] Chief Justice Vinson again wrote for a unanimous Court: "In this case, we are faced with the question of whether a state may, after admitting a student to graduate instruction in its state university, afford him different treatment from other students solely because of his race. We decide only this issue."

The importance of *McLaurin* was that, indeed, the Court was faced only with the question of separate and different treatment. Unlike the ruling in *Sweatt*, this one contained no discussion of the quality of facilities or the quantity of faculty, library volumes, or capital outlay. McLaurin was inside the classroom with whites, but he was still treated differently solely because of his race. In the separate-but-equal context, it was about as "equal" as a state bent on segregation could provide.

Vinson applied the same reasoning he used in *Sweatt* to declare that separate was incompatible with equal: "These restrictions were obviously imposed in order to comply, as nearly as could be, with the statutory requirements of Oklahoma . . . The result is that [George W. McLaurin] is handicapped in his pursuit of effective graduate instruction. Such restrictions impair and inhibit his ability to study, to engage in discussions and exchange views with other students, and, in general, to learn his profession." The separation that Chief Justice Vinson declared unconstitutional in *Sweatt* and *McLaurin* was the separation not from white students, but from ideas and points of view. What other remedy could there be but the integration of the races in graduate and professional schools?

In *McLaurin*, the Court went even further. Vinson added that it was in the public interest, that is, there was a compelling interest, to prepare future leaders for an "increasingly complex" society: "Appellant's case represents, perhaps, the epitome of that need, for he is attempting to obtain an advanced degree in education, to become, by definition, a leader and trainer of others. Those who will come under his guidance and influence must be directly affected by the education he receives. Their own education and development will necessarily suffer to the extent that his training is unequal to that of his classmates. State-imposed restrictions which produce such inequalities cannot be sustained." An inescapable extension of that reasoning was that McLaurin's separation was unconstitutional because it represented the unequal treatment of African American leaders, which would inevitably have the effect of denying equality to African Americans as a group.

In *McLaurin*, Chief Justice Vinson drew a clear line between state imposed discrimination and individual socializing: "There is a vast difference—*a Constitutional difference*—between restrictions imposed by the state which prohibit the intellectual commingling of students, and the refusal of individuals to commingle where the state presents no such bar" (emphasis added).

By the time the justices finished reading the opinions in *Sweatt*, *McLaurin*, and *Henderson* on June 5, 1950, legally enforced racial segregation was facing extinction.[7] The cold reality was that if Texas chose to continue to exclude blacks from its white graduate and professional schools, it would have to attempt to meet an impossible standard. If Texas could not provide for separation and immediate equality, and if it therefore allowed Heman Sweatt through the doors of UT Law, then, under *McLaurin*, it had to let him in without any conditions related to his race. He could not be kept separated even within the confines of a white institution.

Finally, *Gaines* and *Sipuel* provided legal conditions for what was "acceptably" separate. In *Gaines*, for example, the separate facilities had to be within the borders of a state. In *Sipuel*, separate facilities had to be offered at the same time. *Sweatt* was the first to define acceptable separate equality.[8] But separate equality under the *Sweatt* guidelines was impossible. If the desegregation of graduate and professional schools was necessary because students could not be treated equally when separated from 85 percent of the people they would eventually have to work with, then under what other circumstances in life could racial segregation be acceptable? How could such logic not be applied to elementary and secondary education, business, and all levels of government? As Juan Williams wrote in his biography of Thurgood Marshall, "The ruling meant that for the first time in American history an all-white school was being compelled to admit a black student *despite* the separate-but-equal laws."[9] Robert L. Carter believed the *Sweatt* ruling left *Plessy* "moribund."[10]

The value of *Sweatt v. Painter* as a precedent for future civil rights cases cannot be underestimated. (It is still used today in affirmative-action litigation.) Thurgood Marshall understood *Sweatt* to mean that "a major modification in the pattern of American life is in the making" and that "the complete destruction of all enforced segregation is now in sight."[11]

The Immediate Aftermath

Oklahoma newspaper publisher Roscoe Dunjee immediately sent Marshall a letter: "What I read seems too good to be true." Indeed, as Amilcar Shabazz argued, the *Sweatt* decision was a "Great Awakening." "All of our state conferences are being alerted to make a survey of the change in admissions policies in their state universities," announced the NAACP national office. On the regional level, Donald Jones cautioned that while the *Sweatt* decision was to be celebrated, the Court had not yet specifically overturned *Plessy* and the separate-but-equal doctrine.[12]

Word of Heman Sweatt's victory spread quickly through Houston's Third Ward, and soon his Delano Street home was crowded by friends and fans who wanted to congratulate him. The *Dallas Morning News* reported that the humble mail carrier quietly said, "I shall enroll in the University of

Texas in September without malice toward anybody in spite of the four year delay. I am happy over having won entrance. I think this is a milestone in the progress of democracy. And that is all I care to say at this time."[13]

Among Carter Wesley's first printed words on the *Sweatt* victory were that Thurgood Marshall was a "pinhead." Wesley followed with his usual bravado: "But beforehand I'd like to remind my readers of my score in predicting what would happen in the three segregation cases." Then he came very close to taking credit for the milestone victory: "The Sweatt case was begun in my office in the *Dallas Express* at Dallas." On the other hand, amid the euphoria of victory, Carter Wesley was the first to caution that "Negroes get a chance to get their people prepared and their students qualified."[14]

Within a week, Sweatt received a letter from Thurgood Marshall: "You are entitled to the fullest credit for a job well done and if it had not been for your courage and refusal to be swayed by others, this victory would not have been possible."[15]

In Austin, Price Daniel sat fixed to a telephone and listened intently as the *Sweatt v. Painter* opinion was read to him. His first interpretation was that Sweatt was immediately entitled to enter the University of Texas Law School and that the state's separate-but-equal system for lower education was surely going to be "upset." Almost immediately, however, Daniel began to backtrack: "The Supreme Court has left undisturbed its previous decisions that separate schools are constitutional if they are in fact substantially equal . . . It appears that the Court confined its opinion strictly to Heman Marion Sweatt and its belief that the separate Negro law school heretofore established by the state [is] not equal to the University of Texas Law School."[16]

The attorney general explained that Thurgood Marshall had argued that separate schools should be declared unconstitutional even if those schools were found to be equal. By omission, the Court seemed not to agree. Daniel was technically correct, but he did not volunteer an opinion about how it was possible for segregated schools to "be found to be equal" given the Court's inclusion of "qualities which are incapable of objective measurement." In a much more candid interview twenty-nine years later, Daniel admitted that the ruling was a "legal calamity" for segregationist Texas.[17]

The Response at the University of Texas and Elsewhere

The lead defendant, President Theophilus Painter of the University of Texas, announced that Heman Sweatt would be admitted to the UT Law School "if that is the order of the U.S. Supreme Court as interpreted by Attorney

General Price Daniel." When asked to elaborate, Painter added, "If Price Daniel says to enroll him, we will."[18] UT regents chairman Dudley Woodward, Jr., issued a statement that "the University of Texas, of course, will observe the law announced by the Supreme Court of the United States as interpreted by its able counsel, Attorney General Price Daniel."[19] Shortly afterward, Painter clarified by announcing that the university's policy on admitting Negro students was to determine whether the graduate or professional program was offered in segregated state institutions, that is, Prairie View A&M or TSUN. If it was (except for the law school), the application would be rejected.[20]

Within a few days, George McElroy, a journalism major from TSUN, challenged that policy. McElroy's earlier application to UT's journalism school had been rejected by the registrar; the rejection letter stated that a comparison of the UT and TSUN catalogues indicated that the courses McElroy sought were offered at TSUN. McElroy wrote back and acknowledged that the courses were offered at TSUN, but claimed that little else was equal. "We [TSUN students] have no opportunity for electives, no daily newspaper, no radio station, or other component parts of the field of journalism that the University of Texas offers . . . I must take issue with your statement that the work is offered at TSUN. I wish to take journalism with all modern appliances. Plus the rich tradition, prestige, and other intangible qualities obtained only at a well established school of journalism," he said.[21] While McElroy's application was for an undergraduate and not a professional school, which was the subject of *Sweatt*, how could he lose such a legal challenge with *Sweatt* now serving as a precedent?

In Texas, there was almost nothing in the way of graduate or professional schools for African Americans, so the doors of Texas's white graduate schools had to be opened. On the morning of June 7, 1950, two days after the *Sweatt* decision, John Sanders Chase, a twenty-five-year-old African American veteran of World War II and a native of Austin, signed up for classes at UT. He had been admitted to a master's program in architecture. The completion of his registration, however, was delayed by the discovery of a possible deficiency in his high school credits. While the registrar's office evaluated Chase's deficiency, Horace Lincoln Heath, a fifty-year-old native of Waco who had been admitted to the graduate program in government, became the first African American to complete his registration and pay his fees. Shortly afterward, five women and one man were admitted to the Graduate School for the second term of the summer of 1950. They were W. D. McClennan, L. June Harden Brewer, and Wilhelmina Perry, of Austin; Mabel Langrum, of Crockett; Emma Harrison, of Waco; and Bessie Randall, of Houston.[22]

Heman Marion Sweatt formally reapplied to the law school on July 17, 1950; he was accepted on July 20. The *Austin American* quoted Registrar H. Y. McCown as saying that Sweatt was the fourth African American law-school student and the twelfth African American overall scheduled to attend classes on the UT campus in the fall of 1950. By October 2, the university had received thirty-two applications to sixteen different programs. Ten were denied: three because they were undergraduates, five because the programs were available at TSUN, and two because of academic deficiencies in their high school records.[23]

The reaction among southern leaders and educators was varied. Dr. George Cross, the president of the University of Oklahoma, who had never been a segregationist, used the *Sweatt* ruling to announce that the decision "apparently knocks out all segregation in graduate schools at Oklahoma University." In Tennessee, the commissioner of education insisted that "the particular instances cited in [*Sweatt*] are not applicable to Tennessee because . . . we have an excellent Negro state college . . . [and] therefore no Negroes have been admitted to the University." North Carolina faced four pending desegregation lawsuits, one of which demanded access to the University of North Carolina Law School. In Florida, six pending lawsuits called for the desegregation of various graduate and professional schools at the University of Florida; the Florida superintendent of public instruction was moved to say that "the ramifications of those decisions are of such [a] vital nature it's difficult for me to foresee the results."[24]

Without question, the shrillest reaction to the *Sweatt* decision came from Georgia, where Governor Herman Talmadge shouted publicly, "As long as I am governor, Negroes will not be admitted to white schools. The line is drawn; the threats that have been held over the head of the South for four years are now pointed like a dagger ready to be plunged into the very heart of southern tradition."[25] Talmadge had cause for concern: his state was facing two lawsuits demanding equality in public schools, and his own state superintendent of education estimated that equalizing Negro public schools would likely cost $100,000,000. Charles Harper, the secretary of the Georgia Negro Education Association, eagerly called for a special session of the legislature to fund school improvements.[26]

The *Sweatt* victory galvanized black activists. On July 4, 1950, Joseph Rhoads pushed a resolution through the Texas Council of Negro Organizations to widen its battle against discrimination from education to housing, health, and political rights. Thurgood Marshall, who had once argued that the *Sweatt* case was limited to graduate and professional schools, announced the beginning of an attack on segregation in all levels of education, "from law school to kindergarten."[27] In New York City, Walter White of the NAACP's national office announced that Heman Sweatt's court battle had cost $40,000—and the association expected to raise more funds for future court battles.[28]

Since September 1949, Herman Barnett had been attending classes with white students at UT's medical school in Galveston. Technically, he was a TSUN student receiving instruction under a contract between the UT regents and TSUN. During the 1949 regular session of the Texas Legislature, $350,000 had been appropriated for a medical school for African Americans, but the TSUN regents took no action because the funds were grossly insufficient. It became apparent that a school equal to the UT medical school could not be created under *Sweatt* guidelines and that Barnett's special status as a contract student was likely unconstitutional under *McLaurin*. Complicating Barnett's case for the State of Texas were regulations related to veterans' benefits that Barnett had earned as a Tuskegee Airman. On October 17, 1950, NAACP attorney Donald Jones euphorically wrote to Herman Barnett that the University of Texas board of regents had nullified the UT-TSUN contract and that Barnett was officially a student at the University of Texas medical school.[29]

In 1953, Herman Barnett graduated with honors and received a standing ovation when handed his diploma.

For more than two years, W. Astor Kirk had refused the opportunity to earn a PhD in the YMCA across the street from other students on the UT campus in Austin. While *Sweatt* was making its way to the U.S. Supreme Court, Kirk's suit was in limbo. After a few weeks of classes during the fall of 1950, Kirk wrote Maceo Smith: "I am pleased to advise you that I am now enrolled in the graduate school of the University on a basis of complete equality. That is satisfactory to me. In reference to the suit filed two years ago on my behalf, I advise dismissal of same."[30]

Kirk completed his degree requirements for a doctor of philosophy degree in August 1958. In a 2004 interview with the Austin History Center, when Dr. Kirk was asked how he had been treated by UT students, he replied, "Oh, they were fine." [31]

Sweatt Enrolls

Sweatt v. Painter and its companions *McLaurin* and *Henderson* were not the only rulings issued by the U.S. Supreme Court on June 5, 1950. In *United States v. Texas*, 339 U.S. 707, the Court ruled that nearly 2.5 million acres of submerged tidelands in the Gulf of Mexico belonged to the United States and not Texas. Arguably, this case was of even greater concern to the Texas political establishment. As *Sweatt v. Painter* was making its way through Texas courts of appeals, a 1949 opinion poll found that the public considered the tidelands controversy a more important issue than the integration of the University of Texas Law School.

Texans considered the tidelands controversy to be important because the revenue produced by severances had been dedicated to the Permanent University Fund. The disputed tidelands sat over billions of dollars of oil pools and natural-gas reserves. Ownership of such unimagined wealth could determine whether Texas was to be rich or poor. In a state without a history of personal taxation, in many ways the future of Texas higher education for both blacks and whites was at stake.[32]

Writing for a 4–3 majority (Justices Tom Clark and Robert Jackson did not take part in the deliberations), Justice William O. Douglas conceded Texas's ownership of the disputed Gulf bottoms during its days as an independent republic. When Texas became a state, however, the clause of the U.S. Constitution that requires all new states to be admitted on an "equal footing" meant a transfer of national sovereignty over the tidelands from the Republic of Texas to the United States.[33] (Congress restored all states' tidelands claims in 1953.)

During the summer of 1950, Heman Sweatt celebrated his victory and prepared to enter the University of Texas Law School in the fall. Less than a week after the *Sweatt* ruling, Maceo Smith telegraphed Thurgood Marshall about a statewide Sweatt Victory Rally to be held in Dallas on the Fourth of July. Marshall agreed to attend, arriving in Dallas on the third. The Sweatt Victory Dinner at the Moorland YMCA in Dallas was a huge success. The event coincided with Joseph Rhoads's announcement that the Texas Council of Negro Organizations was to expand its war on segregation to all areas of American life. Marshall announced that the NAACP would continue to lead the way in courts of law.[34]

The Houston NAACP was planning a similar event later in the year, perhaps because Carter Wesley suggested that the dinners and fund-raising events should wait until the fall, when Sweatt was going to need assistance to attend UT Law. There was never a doubt that Heman Sweatt was going to need financial assistance if he was going to attend law school. He was not wealthy. He had not attended college since his year in Michigan in the 1930s, and if he was to have any chance of success, he would have to concentrate on his studies. During the Christmas holidays of 1950, the Houston Committee of Victory for Sweatt hosted a banquet at Houston's Club Matinee. Carter Wesley reported in the *Houston Informer* that Sweatt accepted a large check from the committee "in the light of the understanding that freedom is everyone's job."[35]

Donations to the Sweatt Victory Trust Fund represented more than just donations of gratitude. On January 23, 1951, under A. Maceo Smith's signature, the NAACP's Texas State Conference of Branches entered into a three-page contract with Heman Sweatt in which it agreed to pay Sweatt $11,500 for his living expenses and legal education while enrolled in UT Law. In 1956, Carter Wesley told the Associated Press that he was the one who had insisted that Sweatt and the NAACP enter into a formal agreement. "It was estimated Sweatt would need $11,000 to $11,500 to go through three years at the university," Wesley said. "Apparently the NAACP verbally agreed to pay this money to him but wasn't able to raise all the money."[36]

In 1950, the UT Law School did not offer summer classes for entering first-year students, so everyone knew that Heman Sweatt was going to report for registration in September. On September 19, Sweatt and five other African Americans joined "scores of white boys" to enroll.[37] Watching closely was the new dean of UT Law, W. Page Keeton.

Dean Keeton may have been the most qualified administrator in America to oversee the desegregation of the University of Texas Law School. From 1946 to 1949, he had been dean of the University of Oklahoma Law School during Ada Lois Sipuel's attempts to enroll; like the OU president, George Cross, he supported her desegregation efforts. Keeton had even testified as one of Thurgood Marshall's witnesses during the *Sipuel* trial. Only three days after the *Sweatt* decision came down, Thurgood Marshall counseled Heman Sweatt that he should "get in touch with Dean Page Keeton of the Law School. Dean Keeton is a very decent person and while the Dean of the Law School of the University of Oklahoma, testified for us . . . I am sure that you will have no trouble with him."[38]

With such a resounding endorsement from his trusted attorney, Sweatt was probably taken aback when Keeton said to him, "As far as I am concerned, you are just another student and I hope you make good. I think that, as far as you and the school are both concerned, the less publicity the better." Clearly, Dean Keeton did not want things to get out of hand. Historian Michael Gillette characterized Keeton as "demonstrating his hostility" when he warned Sweatt against any "NAACP showmanship."[39] But there is no contemporaneous record of Sweatt alleging any hostility directed to him by anyone. Three days after registration, James H. Morton reported to Maceo Smith that "except for the enormous representation of the newspapers and magazines, the registration might be considered as routine."[40]

Of greater concern to Dean Keeton was the conduct of the throngs of reporters and photographers gathered in the hallway of the law-school building. He was concerned enough to call President Painter for guidance on how to handle the reporters. The president decided that reporters and photographers should be allowed in the commons area of the building, which was the hallway where the students waited in line, but not inside classrooms and offices, where business was conducted. Years later, Keeton recalled that reporters insisted on taking pictures of him enrolling Sweatt. When Keeton rejected the request, "some of them indicated that they might do it whether I wanted them to or not. I said, 'I've got a lot of law students around here who say you're not going to. You'll get thrown out.'"[41]

Throughout the registration process, Heman Sweatt conducted himself honorably and with dignity. He was easily the best dressed of the law students, arriving in a light-colored suit, a white shirt, and a wide, dark necktie. A gold chain hung from his belt to his right hip pocket. It was hot; all of the young men standing around him had rolled up their sleeves. Soon, the September heat forced him to remove his coat, which he held draped over his left forearm. He stood silently with pursed lips and looked straight ahead as photographers took his picture. Finally, he approached Kenneth Woodward, the assistant law dean, presented his paperwork, and signed up for a full load of six first-year law classes.[42]

Most of the questions on the Permanent Record Data card Sweatt had been asked to provide were more appropriate for much younger matriculants. He had graduated from Jack Yates High School twenty years earlier and had not lived at his father's Chenevert Street house in Houston for many years. But of course, he answered the questions anyway. He listed the Wesley Chapel AME, where he had volunteered to become a plaintiff, as his church. Finally, in an ironic twist, on the bottom of the card he pledged on his honor not to "encourage or participate in hazing" other students during his attendance at the university.[43]

Hard Truths from the Texas Legislative Council

As the Texas Legislature prepared to meet for its 1951 regular session, the leadership was faced with determining the future of Texas higher education. One interpretation of the *Sweatt* decision was that the State of Texas was no longer required to provide separate and equal graduate- and professional-school opportunities for its black citizens, since the new criteria for equality could never be met. In November 1950, the Texas Legislative Council released a study entitled *Staff Monograph on Higher Education for Negroes*. The principal author, Graham Blackstock, forced the legislature to face some cold facts about any decision to continue funding segregated higher education. Blackstock quoted an Oklahoma report stating that staffing first-class black institutions was an impossibility: there were not enough African American PhDs to form a faculty. Politicians in Texas and across the South had painted themselves into a corner. By the end of 1949, the states that had long pretended to be providing "separate and equal" higher education for Negroes had failed to produce a single doctoral graduate.[44]

Higher Education for Negroes continued that even if all was equal and "even if the State should embark upon a program of spending millions of dollars in an attempt to provide Negro graduate and professional training programs equivalent to those supplied to white students, the efforts may be insufficient." The problems were Chief Justice Vinson's "intangibles." The legislature could not legislate or buy intangibles, and even if it attempted to do so, it would cost so much that "every other school in the state [would] suffer." Texas had three options. First, it could continue its attempts to provide separate but equal graduate and professional school education, an effort that had already failed to satisfy the Supreme Court in *Sweatt;* second, it could provide separate facilities for African Americans and not make any pretense about equality; or it could integrate all graduate and professional schools. Option three, the report concluded, was the least expensive of the state's choices.[45]

Apparently no longer feeling the pressure to provide for separate equality or a "university of the first class for Negroes," the legislature cut the budget of TSUN by 39 percent, from $1,570,000 to $958,672.[46]

It was an "I told you so" moment for Carter Wesley.

At the annual meeting of the NAACP's Texas State Conference later that year in Austin's new Ebenezer Baptist Church, Thurgood Marshall told the crowd of more than two hundred: "When we get through in Texas, we'll have two universities of Texas—one in Austin and one in Houston." He made clear, however, that his vision of two UTs would be realized through continued efforts at integration. "If Price Daniel doesn't make up his mind to let all qualified Negroes into the university at all levels, we've got the lawyers and the money to do it—our way." Continued resistance to the integration of higher education at all levels was "silly"; there had been no serious acts of lawlessness since the desegregation of the graduate and law schools. Marshall also had a message for African Americans in Texas: more Negroes should put aside their "inferiority feelings" and apply for entrance to the University of Texas.[47]

CHAPTER 20

Why Sweatt Won

I am tired of trying to save the white man's soul.
THURGOOD MARSHALL, MAY 1951

The American experience with race is replete with irony. After the ratification of the Constitution in 1789, the abolitionist movement of the John
Adams era largely nested within the northern Federalist faction. As the
nation's factions evolved into political parties, namely, Alexander Hamilton's Federalists and Thomas Jefferson's Republicans, the Federalists—the
group widely believed to embrace antidemocratic elitism and even monar-
chy—fought to end slavery. At the same time, while Jeffersonian Republicans and their heirs, the Jacksonian Democrats, claimed to have empowered
and brought democracy to commoners, they vigorously excluded women
and staunchly defended slavery.

During and immediately after the Civil War, Congress drew up the
Thirteenth, Fourteenth, and Fifteenth Amendments, which were intended
to end slavery and give full citizenship rights to freedmen, including voting
rights for black men. But after the end of Reconstruction in 1876, hostile
court rulings gutted the force of the laws. The twentieth-century irony re-
lating to racial politics is that the "lesson in the progress of Democracy" that
Heman Sweatt associated with his court victory came about through intervention by the least democratic of the three branches of the federal government. Justice Hugo Black once stated: "If we [the Supreme Court] have to
decide the question, then representative government has failed."[1] Justices of
the Supreme Court dress in robes, are called "Your Honor," work in majestic, palatial surroundings, and enjoy a monarchist's tenure, since they are
appointed for life by the president. Justices' appointments are ratified by
the Senate, the congressional house set up to check the passions of what

Alexander Hamilton called the "public beast." And yet it was the federal judiciary in the 1940s and 1950s—when Congress lacked the political will to protect or extend basic civil rights—that restored the meaning of the Civil War amendments and first made African Americans adults and citizens. "We couldn't get a damn thing through Congress," Thurgood Marshall bitterly recalled. "You can't name one bill that passed in the Roosevelt Administration for Negroes. Nothing. We couldn't even get the anti-lynching bill through. So you had to go to the courts."[2]

The presidential elections of 1932 through 1948 made *Sweatt v. Painter* possible. In a twenty-year period, Presidents Franklin Roosevelt and Harry Truman appointed twelve justices to the Supreme Court, eleven of whom voted consistently to undermine racial segregation in education. The other justice, James F. Byrnes, served only one year and was never presented with a significant civil rights case. Nearly all of the justices were young New Dealers who believed in the power of the federal government to address serious national challenges, such as the Great Depression. Franklin Roosevelt may not have succeeded in packing the Supreme Court through legislation, but he far exceeded his aspiration to create an activist court. For all practical purposes, Harry Truman "packed" it a second time, with unintended help from Eisenhower's appointments of Earl Warren and William Brennan.

As a group, the New Dealers had diverse ideas about civil liberties, and the liberals and conservatives on the Court were easily identifiable. But in the area of civil rights, the FDR and Truman appointees voted unanimously and consistently to break down the walls of segregation.[3]

Using *Gong Lum* (1927), the Mississippi case in which a Chinese American unsuccessfully tried to enroll his daughter in a white high school, as a benchmark, the measured change in the Court's attitude toward school segregation makes the NAACP's victory in *Sweatt,* and later in *Brown v. Board of Education,* more understandable. It also shows, as Mark Strasser later wrote in the *Howard Law Journal,* "The 'separate but equal' jurisprudence in the education context . . . had evolved greatly over that period (from *Plessy* to *Brown*). While *Brown* would have represented a radical shift from some of the earlier cases, it was a predictable and sensible development in light of later ones."[4]

When it considered *Gong Lum,* the Taft Court included seven Republican appointees, only one of whom had not been appointed by Harding, Taft, or Coolidge—all firm believers in limited government. The other two members were Democrats who had been appointed by President Woodrow Wilson. Although Wilson is often considered a progressive by historians, his record on segregation resembled that of a southern conservative. As president of Princeton University from 1900 to 1910, he presided over the only major northern university that excluded African Americans. As governor of New Jersey and president of the United States (his administration was called, with unintentional irony, "New Freedom"), he oversaw increased segregation of federal facilities and a nearly complete neglect of what were called Negro schools and institutions.[5]

In October 1927, the Taft Court heard arguments in *Gong Lum v. Rice*. Taft, writing for a unanimous Court, declared that segregation was a decision "within the discretion of the state in regulating its public schools, and does not conflict with the Fourteenth Amendment." Though not as egregious as *Dred Scott* or *Plessy, Gong Lum* represented a low point in the judicial history of civil rights in the twentieth century. It was a unanimous vote against access to education.

By 1948, the year the Supreme Court ruled unanimously for progress toward greater access in *Sipuel,* seven justices had been appointed by Franklin Roosevelt and two by Harry Truman. Two years later, the 1950 *Sweatt* decision came from a Court with five FDR- and four Truman-appointed justices. Here is a closer look at those nine men.

During the summer of 1946, President Truman appointed Fred Vinson as chief justice to replace the recently deceased Harlan Fiske Stone, who had been elevated to chief justice by Franklin Roosevelt. Vinson's vote in *Sipuel* and his majority opinion in *Sweatt* were landmark precedents for *Brown v. Board of Education* and the affirmative action cases of *Bakke* (1978) and *Grutter* (2003).

Justice Hugo Black was a fifty-one-year-old Alabama populist and rabid New Dealer when FDR appointed him to the Court. In his first case as a lawyer, he defended an African American convict who had been made to do hard labor for fifteen days beyond his court-imposed sentence. As a district attorney in Alabama, he prosecuted the Bessemer Police Department for beating confessions out of black suspects in a torture chamber. In 1923, Black joined the Ku Klux Klan, but dropped out after two years. When former president Herbert Hoover heard of Black's appointment, he said that the Court was now "one-ninth packed."[6] Black joined the Court in August 1937 and cast pro-civil-rights votes in *Gaines, Sipuel, Sweatt,* and *Brown.*

A lifelong New Deal liberal, Justice William O. Douglas, who would become the longest-serving Supreme Court justice in American history, was appointed to the Court in April 1939 at the age of forty-one. He replaced Justice Louis D. Brandeis, a legal legend, who had an inconsistent civil rights voting record. He had voted to sustain the right of a state to segregate its schools in *Gong Lum,* but he also held Missouri accountable for providing Lloyd Gaines with a separate and equal law school education within its borders. Justice Douglas compiled a much more activist civil rights record. He voted to undermine segregation in *Sipuel, Sweatt,* and *Brown.*[7]

Justice Stanley Reed, another of FDR's young New Dealers, was appointed at age fifty-three. Generally considered a centrist on most issues, he could nonetheless be counted on to "attack the scandal of Negro inequality." Chief Justice Harlan Stone assigned the writing of the *Smith v. Allwright* opinion (which ended the white primary) to Reed because, like Hugo Black, he was a populist southerner. Reed was appointed to the Court in January 1938, and later voted for the NAACP's position in *Gaines, Sipuel, Sweatt,* and *Brown.*[8]

Justice Felix Frankfurter was appointed by President Franklin Roosevelt in January 1939; he was fifty-seven years old. Few nominees ever had a more impressive pro-civil-rights resume: he had served as a legal advisor for the NAACP. He replaced Justice Benjamin Cardozo, a conservative Herbert Hoover appointee who had voted to uphold the white primary in the *Grovey* case. Justice Frankfurter cast pro-NAACP votes in *Smith, Sipuel, Sweatt,* and *Brown.*[9]

Justice Robert Jackson did not consider himself a New Dealer, but he came to be identified as a crony of the left-wingers of the Roosevelt administration. In July 1941, he took a seat on the Supreme Court that had been occupied by Republican appointees since the days of Abraham Lincoln, when the seat was created. Justice Jackson replaced Justice Harlan Fiske Stone, who had been promoted to chief justice. Jackson overcame his devotion to precedent to provide a consistent pro-civil-rights vote on the Court. He supported the NAACP in *Sipuel, Sweatt,* and *Brown.*[10] Notably, he took a leave of absence from the Court to serve as a chief prosecutor at the Nuremberg war crimes trials.

Justice Harold Burton was a Republican appointed by Democratic president Harry Truman in October 1945, but Burton's subsequent votes would never differ significantly from those cast by FDR's appointees or Truman's future Democratic appointments. Burton occupied a seat once held by Justice Owen Roberts, a conservative Hoover appointee who had authored *Grovey* and had been the lone dissenter in *Smith v. Allwright.* Burton was a dependable civil rights advocate who concurred with the majorities in *Sipuel* and *Sweatt.*[11]

Justice Tom Clark, a native Texan and graduate of the University of Texas Law School, was a veteran of the Truman administration's civil rights initiatives. His office in the Justice Department submitted an amicus curiae in *Shelley v. Kraemer* (1948), the case that outlawed state enforcement of restrictive covenants.[12] Tom Clark's Supreme Court appointment did not alter the direction of the Court, since he replaced Justice Frank Murphy, an FDR appointee who had cast a pro-NAACP vote in *Sipuel*. Murphy, however, had replaced Justice Pierce Butler, a conservative Harding appointee.

In the 1930s, Sherman Minton was known as a "militant and outspoken New Dealer." He was one of the floor leaders of Franklin Roosevelt's ill-fated "Court-packing" plan. As a United States senator, he shared a desk with Harry Truman, and the two became close friends. He was widely considered a conservative insofar as he believed that individuals had a right to discriminate, but he had no such belief as far as government agencies.[13] Minton was a third-generation FDR-Truman appointee, replacing Justice Wiley Rutledge, an FDR appointee who had voted for the NAACP's position in *Sipuel*. (Rutledge had replaced James Byrnes, another FDR appointee, who served only one year.) When *Gaines* was heard, the seat was held by James Clark McReynolds, a conservative Wilson appointee.

The Role of Thurgood Marshall and the NAACP

Sweatt v. Painter ended as it did because FDR and Truman appointed New Deal supporters who also unanimously supported civil rights for minorities. If Thurgood Marshall had argued *Gong Lum* before Chief Justice Vinson and his Court, he would have won and Martha Lum would have attended school with white children; if he had argued *Sweatt* in 1927 before Chief Justice Taft and his Court, he would have lost and Sweatt would have studied law in the basement of the 13th Street law school.

It would, however, be a serious mistake to marginalize the remarkable accomplishments of Charles Houston, Thurgood Marshall, James Nabrit, Jr., Robert Carter, and the hundreds of civil rights lawyers who fought the judicial battles leading to victories in *Sweatt* and *Brown*. These gifted men fought the good fight and gave Americans a great historical gift. As Nelson Mandela said in his inaugural address as South Africa's president in 1994, "Out of the experience of an extraordinary human disaster that lasted too long, must be born a society of which all humanity will be proud." The men who fought for voting and educational rights for all Americans presented us with a vision of a society that all humanity could be proud of, one based on America's own oft-stated lofty principles described in the Declaration of Independence and the Constitution and its subsequent amendments. In 1941, Ralph Bunche wrote: "It is the Constitution and the ideals of the American Revolution which gave the Negro the persistent belief that he was entitled to equality of rights."[14]

Thurgood Marshall understood that rights, above all, had to be guaranteed by law and the power of unambiguous words, such as those found in many court rulings. Lawlessness guaranteed nothing: "The only thing you get out of a race riot is that no guilty person ever gets hurt. The innocent people get hurt."[15] A necessary prerequisite to such a belief in the law is acceptance and confidence in existing governmental institutions, such as the judiciary. In her memoirs, Ada Lois Sipuel recalled that Marshall and Oklahoma civil rights activist Roscoe Dunjee never allowed her to lose faith in the U.S. Constitution.

Years later when Marshall was consulted on the creation of a new constitution, he observed: "When I did the constitution for Kenya, I looked over just about every constitution in the world just to see what was good. And there's nothing that comes close to comparing with this one in the U.S. This one is the best I've ever seen."[16]

A large part of Marshall's professional life was dedicated to getting the U.S. Supreme Court to write, "Separate educational facilities are inherently unequal." In 1954, those words became law—as powerful and enforceable as a constitutional amendment.

There was also a personal element to Marshall's success: in all the press coverage of the litigation of *Sweatt v. Painter,* no memorable bigoted or stereotypical descriptions of Thurgood Marshall can be found. Opposing counsel never accused him of being a sloppy, lazy, or inferior lawyer. Joe Greenhill recalled: "He was an excellent lawyer in the courtroom. He was courteous. He didn't rant and rave, and he asked good questions." Robert Figg of South Carolina said that Marshall was "an able lawyer and a skillful advocate. His appeals gain power from this dedication to the cause which he represents." Taggart Whipple, a renowned New York attorney, said that Marshall "was eminently fair. Certainly he was one of the top civil liberties lawyers in the country."[17] James Nabrit, Jr., recalled that he had "been all over the country with Thurgood Marshall and . . . never known any situation where after two or three days he was not liked by the very people he was opposing. . . . It is almost his most important contribution because everywhere he has gone he has made friends for us."[18]

It must not have been easy for Marshall to maintain his sense of respect and affability; even his own staff sometimes questioned his willingness to associate with the "enemy." During the litigation of *Brown,* Marshall accepted an invitation to lunch from opposing counsel, John Davis. Marshall explained to his colleagues: "We're both attorneys, we're both civil. It is very important to have a civil relationship with your opponent."[19]

And so in the courtroom, Marshall disarmed his opponents with genuine legal talent, civility, and hard work. (He once said, "I never filed a paper in any court with an erasure on it.") He never answered racism with more hatred, nor did he ever believe his opponents were fools. That would have prevented him from seeing what was going on in their minds. As Marshall himself once said about the Supreme Court, "I ain't no fool when it comes to those boys."[20]

Which is another reason why Sweatt won: the defense of a racist policy or position requires intellectual dishonesty and delusion. To advance his case that the makeshift 13th Street law school was equal to the University of Texas Law School, the attorney general of Texas stood before a court and argued that UT Law attached no value nor had any pride in its traditions or its accomplishments. The logical and inescapable extension of that absurdity had to be a belief that in almost seventy-five years UT Law had not grown to anything beyond the equivalent of a first-year law school set up in a few weeks for an estimated enrollment of ten. As Joe Greenhill admitted in 2005 during an interview for this book, "It sounds impossible, and it was impossible to create a substantially equal law school in a few months." Thurgood Marshall observed that witnesses like Charles McCormick and Dudley Woodward were "intelligent, well-educated, and otherwise honest men."[21] And yet as Marshall's assistant Robert Carter noted in his autobiography, defending the segregationist view required limiting one's own vision and mental reach. How could these men deny the admonition of the dean of the University of Pennsylvania Law School: "It is mistaken, even absurd, to speak of any institution that has one student as a law school."[22]

Finally, the ultimate folly of the segregationist worldview was, of course, the false sense of superiority. Throughout the South, Marshall and his legal teams stunned judges and attorneys. As William H. Jones, the president of Tillotson College, said in 1948, shortly before the *Sweatt* case made it to the Texas Supreme Court: "Southern people are not accustomed to seeing trained Negro lawyers as in the Heman Sweatt case. Law students attending the hearings saw what they will be up against the next ten years when brilliant Negro minds clash with those of white lawyers."[23] And as Carter Wesley editorialized on June 10, 1950, "As to the *Sweatt* case, [Price Daniel] had nothing to argue but Southern tradition."[24]

NAACP-sponsored legal strategy and courtroom performances have been studied and documented as brilliant pieces of social engineering that long outlived the New Dealers on the Court. We are still living with their work in affirmative-action cases like *Bakke* (1978) and *Grutter* (2003). Charles Houston and the cadre of African American attorneys he inspired gave receptive Supreme Court justices what they needed to change America. But it was not only, as Heman Sweatt contended, a lesson in democracy. It was also a lesson in how the limits of democracy can be overcome and how the rights of minorities can be protected in a government that values the concept of majority rule.

Heman Sweatt at UT

Eleven days after the Supreme Court issued its opinion in *Sweatt*, a poll taken on the University of Texas campus indicated that only 5 percent of UT students opposed the decision to admit Heman Sweatt to the Forty Acres. In Texas, the UT student body was second only to the NAACP in its acceptance of integration. Some students had joined the all-white campus NAACP chapter and marched through the South Mall into the Main Building and Tower with African Americans during protests. A few African Americans who had enrolled in graduate school the previous summer actually preceded Heman Sweatt's arrival for the fall semester of 1950. These students attended classes without incident.[25]

But unlike those other African American students, Heman Sweatt was a celebrity, even though he spoke little and minded his own business. He gave every indication that he was a serious law student with a singular objective of earning a degree and passing the bar. During his time in Austin, there was little or no coverage of his being an activist or someone seeking to capitalize on his celebrity status. In a letter to Thurgood Marshall, Sweatt indicated that he had classes with two of Price Daniel's witnesses: Helen Hargrave, who taught bibliography, and Charles McCormick, who taught contracts. His favorite classes, however, were torts and property.[26]

Reports of race-based abuse Sweatt supposedly endured are not as clear. Dramatic differences exist between primary historical accounts of Sweatt's time in Austin and more recent secondary sources and oral-history projects. One month after he enrolled as a student, Sweatt wrote to Thurgood Marshall that UT students had been "very agreeable" and that he had been appointed to the social committee. He also made it clear that he had no difficulty using restrooms, fountains, or lounges.[27] Almost at the same time, from his second-floor office in the Main Building, President Theophilus Painter wrote to an acquaintance that "the admission of Negroes to the graduate and professional schools (law and medicine) had not caused any trouble as yet on our campus."[28] Both Sweatt's and Painter's comments were written only a few days after an incident that is most often cited as part of the terror Sweatt faced on the Forty Acres.

On Tuesday, October 17, 1950, at about 10:45 p.m., near the southern corner of the law building, unknown individuals used stolen scaffolding from a nearby construction site to prop up a six-foot-tall wooden cross made from four-by-fours. The base of the cross had been shaved to a point in a way that suggested that its builders wanted to plant it in the ground. (If they had tried to plant such a cross, they would have encountered solid rock at a very shallow depth.) The cross had been wrapped with kerosene-soaked rags and set afire. It burned for about fifteen minutes until a fire truck from the 13th Street station arrived and doused the blaze. "KKK" had been scrawled on the steps of the law building. According to *Daily Texan* reporters at the scene, a single policeman investigated the incident and could not determine who started the blaze. "The policeman looked at the cross and mumbled, 'Students!'"[29]

Apparently contacted at home by telephone later that night, Sweatt could think of no incident that day that he could link to the incident: "I spent one of the most cordial days yet in law school. In fact, several of the fellows were especially nice to me, and we had some interesting conversations about some of the problems that came up in class." Eleven days later, in a letter to Thurgood Marshall, Sweatt downplayed the incident and even indicated that it resulted in other students going out of their way to be kind.[30]

Sweatt told a quite different story in the 1970s. He incorrectly recalled that the incident happened on the first Friday after he enrolled. He also recalled that he witnessed the cross burning, that there was a large KKK demonstration, and that a white classmate walked him to his car only to find that his tires had been slashed.[31] If his memory served him well twenty-five years after the incident, it is truly remarkable that in 1950 he made no such report to anyone who would have come to his defense, like the NAACP or Austin's African American community, which would not have tolerated such a naked threat to Sweatt's safety. Undoubtedly, James Morton, Kenneth Lampkin, and Everett Givens would have organized and led marches on the UT campus to protest.

There are other inconsistencies in accounts separated by about twenty-five years. In 1950, James Morton reported to Maceo Smith that Sweatt's registration was "routine" except for the throngs of reporters and photographers chronicling his every move. But in the mid-1970s, Sweatt was quoted as saying, "The hostility was terrifying. I think I was in the law school five minutes before I was pulled out of the registration line and cussed out."[32] None of the assembled members of the media, who undoubtedly hungered for something to report, witnessed such an event, and if it happened outside of their view, Sweatt reported the incident to no one at the time.

In October 1974, Heman Sweatt visited the University of Texas Law School and told the assembled students that he would "leave the law school each day right after classes for the black ghetto for fear of personal harm."[33] While in Austin, Sweatt's mailing address was 1209 East 12th Street, which was a dwelling directly across the street from Dr. Lewis Mitchell's dental practice. It was less than a hundred yards from the Lewis home where Thurgood Marshall had stayed during the *Sweatt* trial and only a couple of blocks from James Morton's home on San Bernard Street.[34] The neighborhood was, and still is, a neighborhood of great character that was not, and would never become, a ghetto.

Perhaps the accumulated frustration brought about by the slow pace of progress for African Americans explains the differences between Sweatt's 1950s and 1970s accounts of the difficulties and personal dangers he faced in Austin. In 1950, Sweatt entered the doors of the UT Law School at a time when he and the NAACP were announcing that the end of enforced racial segregation was in sight. It was a euphoric time of promise, progress, and victory. When he returned to Austin in 1974, even though UT welcomed him as a hero, he had to have noticed that the University of Texas was only slightly more integrated than when he had matriculated as a law student. And elsewhere, twenty years after *Brown*, southern elementary and secondary schools were only beginning to desegregate. His 1970s reminiscences might have been influenced by the decades of turmoil and race riots that accompanied the opening of other flagship universities in the South, like Alabama and Ole Miss. Perhaps by the 1970s, the euphoria of the *Sweatt* and *Brown* cases, and the promises they held, had given way to the bitter disappointment of persistent legal and de facto segregation. In Austin, East Avenue was still a line of demarcation between the races.

The folklore connected to Sweatt's legacy might also be needed to adequately illustrate the sacrifice a truly courageous young man made to the progress of democracy. Even so, the Sweatt legend has more than its share of truth. Dean Keeton remembered an incident in which a few students, whom Keeton referred to as "these rednecks," came to him and refused to use the same restrooms as the African American law students.

> Now there was a group of students who came to me and said, "We don't want to go to the same restroom . . . as these blacks are going to. We object to them. We want you to have a separate 'black only' restroom." So that type of segregation they wanted within the law school. That might've been lawful at that time, I don't know, but I wasn't about to do it. But we did have two restrooms—two men's restrooms, fortunately, and not just one.

And so I called the blacks in. I said, "Look, I've got a group of rednecks here that object to using the same restroom you use. Now, they wanted me to set up a 'For Blacks Only' restroom. Well, I refused. But, will you voluntarily use just one of those men's rooms, instead of both of them. We won't put up any signs or anything." They said they would. And so I told these rednecks that they could use this other one. And they didn't have much complaint then.[35]

Dean Keeton clearly intended to portray himself as having stood up to the "rednecks" by refusing to place Jim Crow signs over the restroom doors. The incident reveals the dean's priorities: he supported the black students, but he did not want any trouble either. It also reveals the priorities of the African American students: they wanted a law-school education and were willing to voluntarily stay out of one of the restrooms in order to get it.

Sweatt and the other blacks may even have taken some measure of satisfaction from knowing that Price Daniel's dire prediction of trouble was not going to come true—at least not over access to all the law school's urinals. The sad part of this episode is that Keeton could have shown courage. He could have used the opportunity to educate a small group of bigoted whites by giving them a stern lesson in manners—and the law. Those young men should have been made to research and recite *McLaurin v. Oklahoma* (1950) so that they could have learned for themselves that what they were asking for had been ruled unconstitutional the previous summer. They could have been made to respect the law.

While historians can review the contemporaneous primary documentation and conclude that Heman Sweatt's 1970s reminiscences of abuse are exaggerated, it does not follow that his fears were neither justified nor real. As Thurgood Marshall wrote in a letter to Sweatt on November 6, 1950, "As you know, the case is now over and the entire burden is on your shoulders."[36] For years, southern white attorneys general and governors had been warning state and federal judges that violence—even bloodshed—would surely result if the federal government forced the integration of all-white institutions. There were other first-year African American law students, but when Heman Sweatt walked through the doors of the UT law school in September 1950, he was, in some sense, alone. He must have felt like Ada Lois Sipuel, who wrote in her memoirs: "I realized I was still the guinea pig . . . I was alone." And as Joe Greenhill recalled nearly sixty years later, "Sweatt was in no danger but he didn't know that."[37]

Indeed. As Sweatt calmly faced the possibility of violence directed toward him because of his race, he may well have felt terrorized. It matters not that the 1953 Ashmore Project, a survey reported in the *Journal of Negro Education,* concluded that the cross-burning episode on the UT campus in October 1950 was "half-playful."[38] The fact that actual violence did not happen does not diminish his courage or assuage the fear he must have felt. As Alfred Hitchcock, a master of suspense, is said to have explained the principle: "There is no terror in the bang, only in the anticipation of it."

Some Problems of Equality

In November 1950, Sweatt admitted having regrets that the progress he and the NAACP had been fighting for had to begin with graduate and professional schools rather than in the elementary grades: "We should start with the younger minds and condition them for the improvements ahead. Instead we are forced to take the more practical step and work from the top down, knowing that it is not right, but the only thing to do." He continued, "The books are full of statistics. What we need is the courage to put into effect the necessary measures to correct these wrongs." And yet he appreciated his role in the most significant civil rights breakthrough of the time, and he refused to discard optimism: "The other day I was walking by the flagpole in front of the Main Building. I looked up and saw the American Flag and it hit me for the first time—that here I was, a human being, not just a beast to be stared at through the bars of a cage."[39]

In his office in Houston, only a few days after the *Sweatt* ruling, Carter Wesley wrote: "Now both white and colored have a chance to adjust to the impact of the *Sweatt* decision on the upper level, and to condition their thinking to the inevitable changes that must come on the lower levels."[40] For years, Wesley had warned that there would be consequences, not so much from separateness—because given a chance, African Americans could take quite good care of themselves—but from inequality. He saw the need for a transitional period of separateness and equality in order to prepare black students to compete in an integrated academic setting. He and Thurgood Marshall fought openly and bitterly for months over whether prerequisite equalization had any place in the struggle for full citizenship rights. The crux of the Wesley-Marshall debate was over the transition from Jim Crow to full integration: Carter Wesley saw the need for a transition.

Marshall's position was summarized by John P. Frank in the *Journal of Negro Education* two years after the *Sweatt* ruling: "The basic hypothesis of those who have supported the attack on segregation . . . is an assumption that Negro applicants to these graduate schools would be capable of carrying on the work."[41] Carter Wesley did not dispute Marshall's facts—that segregation did damage to those who were segregated and that it prevented them from gaining an equal education—only the time line of his remedy. Many African American students were not prepared for immediate access to the highest levels of established and privileged white educational institutions. Frank added that some African Americans "are failing out of white law schools solely because of inadequate pre-law training and, I am morally certain without any discrimination against them whatsoever."[42]

In the period between the *Sweatt* and *Brown* rulings, even Thurgood Marshall cryptically admitted that African American graduate- and professional-school students were severely disadvantaged academically. He could hardly have argued otherwise, since he initiated and carried forward the argument that separate was inherently unequal. If, as Marshall wrote in 1952, "most Negroes who have received their early education in segregated schools are handicapped because their early training was inadequate and inferior," what other result could there be but a high attrition rate among those pioneering African American students?[43] Even so, when Carter Wesley had anticipated such a problem, Thurgood Marshall called him an "Uncle Tom" during a statewide conference of NAACP branches.

Studying the attrition rates of the first group of African American students to walk through the doors of formerly all-white institutions is problematic. First, there were very few of them, so each dropout represents a large percentage of the cohort. Second, conducting such a study of attrition rates from the 1950s through the mid-1970s at the University of Texas, and many other institutions, is not possible because racial and ethnic data were never collected. (For example, there is nothing in Heman Sweatt's official UT record to indicate that he was African American.) In a 1986 interview with H. W. Brands, Dean Page Keeton remembered that five other African Americans entered UT Law with Heman Sweatt and that two successfully completed their studies—which would indicate a dropout rate of 67 percent. At the time, however, the entrance requirements for UT Law were minimal, and according to Keeton, the dropout rate for whites was about 50 percent. Patricia Lefforge Davis estimates that from 1950 through 1968, thirty-seven black students enrolled in UT Law and that only ten (27 percent) graduated. At least fifteen of the dropouts were unable to maintain good academic standing.[44]

Heman Sweatt struggled academically, and Dean Keeton attributed his difficulties to inadequate preparation: "He was a fine person, but he didn't have the educational background the white students had." More specifically, Keeton remembered that Sweatt's problem was his writing: "Sweatt was impossible. He couldn't write a simple sentence."[45] Keeton's assessment was not that of a racist administrator determined to see Sweatt fail. J. Frank Dobie, an outspoken UT "campus radical" and strong supporter of everything Heman Sweatt tried to accomplish, communicated as much to Sweatt directly but more diplomatically. In early 1947, Sweatt sent Dobie a draft of the first two chapters of a novel entitled *No Hiding Place*. It was a story of a mythical Jackson family that was clearly based on the Sweatts of Chenevert Street in Houston. "I would appreciate your most rigid criticism," Sweatt requested of Dobie. Dobie obliged by marking up the manuscript and sending it back to Sweatt. Sweatt acknowledged problems such as tenses changing within sentences and candidly admitted, "I am thoroughly aware of a grossly inadequate background for writing." Dobie concluded his correspondence with Sweatt by sending him a small manual on the technique of writing.[46]

By June 1951, Sweatt had been barred from readmission to the law school for poor academic performance. He was allowed to complete his 1951 summer classes, but he dropped one and failed the other four. He took reexaminations in February and May 1952, but did not score high enough to be readmitted.[47]

Tragically, Sweatt's most serious problems were not academic. His health was failing, and his personal life had become a nightmare. A combination of persistently troubling stomach ulcers and an appendectomy in November 1951 took Sweatt away from six weeks of developmental activities intended to provide him with the remedial education he needed in order to retake the classes he had failed. As Sweatt put it decades later: "What was really driving me [to drop out] was just reliving the hell that was going on inside of [my home] all the time I was in school [and] all the time I was fighting the case."[48]

After more than four years of having their home life disrupted, Connie and Heman Sweatt's marriage began to fall apart. In Heman's version: "I'd come in from work and say, 'This is what happened today,' and she'd say, 'See, it ain't the only damn thing that's gonna happen to you.'" He added that he and Connie were "constantly at each other."[49] Making matters worse was the unreliable receipt of financial aid that had been promised to him by the Sweatt Victory Fund. Connie Sweatt found the financial hardships particularly difficult.[50]

The effect on his studies can be illustrated by what happened the night before he was to take his first law school exam. In Sweatt's words: "A most traumatic thing happened. I was going off with a group of students to study, and my wife just became outraged. And she performed. Her performance was such that we never lived together a day after that. She was on the train going home [to her mother] the next day while I was taking my first examination at the school—and I failed it."[51]

On July 8, 1952, Heman Sweatt announced to the *Dallas Morning News* that he had "flunked out." After six years, he was a physical and emotional wreck: "There were no incidents. I may have lost my personal ambition but I think the manner in which the other [black students] are getting along in their relations with the white students proves that it can work. The fear that the abolition of segregation would result in a great turmoil has proved unfounded. I think the experiment is working successfully." When asked for a comment, Dean Keeton replied that it was likely that Sweatt suffered the "handicap of having been out of school for a long period before taking legal study."[52]

When asked about his future plans, Sweatt announced that he intended to further his education, possibly in biological sciences, where he enjoyed "much better academic success." For the time being, he would return to Houston and likely be under medical care for the rest of the summer of 1952.

Sweatt after Austin

While Heman Sweatt was recuperating from serious health problems during the summer of 1952, Whitney Young, who would shortly become the dean of the School of Social Work at Atlanta University, invited Sweatt to enroll as a graduate student on a full scholarship. In 1954, Sweatt earned a master's degree with an emphasis in community organizations. Afterward, he moved to Cleveland, Ohio, and worked in the Urban League office. After eight years, he relocated to the Urban League's Atlanta office, where he served as the assistant regional director responsible for organizing new chapters. During his service, the number of affiliates tripled. He also worked in voter-registration drives and programs assisting southern African Americans wishing to move north.[53]

During an Urban League picnic, Heman Sweatt met Katherine Gaffney. In 1963, Heman and Katherine married, and he adopted Katherine's daughter, Edwina. Shortly afterward, Katherine gave birth to Heman's only child, a daughter they named Hemella, who would come to be called Mellie. The family lived in a neat and comfortable home in southwest Atlanta that, one journalist wrote, reflected a "near obsession with order and symmetry."[54]

Today, Mellie remembers the Sweatt home as being in a typical lower-middle-class black neighborhood. She also remembers how her father spoke kindly of Thurgood Marshall and Whitney Young, and that he seldom spoke about *Sweatt v. Painter.* Instead, he insisted on talking about what interested her and what she wanted out of life. Over and over again, he insisted, education was the key to her dreams.

In April 1972 during a visit to Houston, Sweatt made the news with a controversial statement, apparently in response to false information about Texas Southern University and the University of Houston. Sweatt, the symbol of the integration of higher education in Texas, reacted surprisingly to the idea of merging the predominantly white (U of H) and predominantly black (TSU) institutions. One of the ironies of the NAACP victory in *Sweatt* was that the state of Texas was no longer pressured to provide any semblance of separate equality for its African American graduate and professional students. During the first legislative session after the *Sweatt* ruling, the legislature did not appropriate any money for new buildings for what would shortly become Texas Southern University. What was intended to be a "university of the first-class for Negroes" still had no dormitories. In August 1951, approximately 90 percent of TSU students were commuting from the Houston metro area.[55] The state's neglect of TSU angered Sweatt, who told the *Houston Post:* "I believe in integration. I had believed in it all my life. But I don't believe in it today, not in the prostituted form we've had. Not when it's based on us giving up everything so that black institutions can be absorbed and controlled by people who don't understand what [we] are all about."[56] Carter Wesley had died three years earlier; he must have turned over in his grave.

On September 24, 1974, twenty-four years after he first entered the doors of the University of Texas Law School, Heman Sweatt returned to the Forty Acres as a guest of honor. It was the first time he had visited the law school since leaving in 1952. He delivered an address to a conference sponsored by the African and Afro-American Studies and Research Center. The theme was "Black Americans in Texas History." The highlight of his two-day trip to the campus, however, was an informal gathering he held with about one hundred law students in the Tom Clark Lounge.[57]

Heman Sweatt worked for the Urban League for twenty-three years. His office was in a downtown Atlanta building. Each day he left for work, smartly dressed, carrying a briefcase packed with business papers and a banana. One of Mellie's childhood memories is of the scent of the briefcase— an odd combination of banana and cologne.[58]

Sweatt's health eventually deteriorated to the point that he required regular dialysis treatments. He took Mellie's departure for college particularly hard: on September 2, 1982, he wrote, "No barbeque to cook on Labor Day. Who is left to enjoy it with?"[59] After nearly twenty years of marriage, Katherine and Heman Sweatt separated, and Heman moved in with a friend named Kenneth Crooks.

In late August 1982, Sweatt's physician "launched some technical innovation in [Sweatt's] dialysis routine which seemingly complemented" his coronary-artery bypass surgery. During an interview for this book, Sweatt's nephew, Dr. James Leonard Sweatt III, a cardiac surgeon who had occasional contact with his uncle, recalled that the dialysis treatments "tore up" his blood vessels.[60] A lifetime of health problems seemed to be catching up with Heman Marion Sweatt, who had not yet reached his seventieth birthday.

By the fall of 1982, Sweatt was a physically and emotionally exhausted man. He had retired only one year earlier, likely because of the rigors of dialysis and constant chest pains. The light of his life was Mellie, who was now an undergraduate at Duke University enrolled in a premedical program. On September 30, 1982, Sweatt enclosed a check and wrote to her:

Hemella, My Dearest Daughter:
This is to get you your funds for the coming month. Of course, without the need for saying so, it is to demonstrate for you my support for your study efforts . . .

Thankfully, since my heart operation, I have not had any of those painful chest pains that I have encountered so frequently. I had a flair-up in the stomach last week that put me in the hospital several days; but the doctors solved that problem and generally now I am feeling so very much better.

In the letter, Sweatt encouraged his beloved Mellie to do her best to not allow his marital and health problems to interfere with her academic responsibilities. She was to concentrate on her studies and grow intellectually. As for his own future, Sweatt wrote, "As soon as I regain my strength, I am going to join some church and try to find for myself the happiness I have known in my life years before having to be upset by some of the experiences of my present day-to-day life . . . I am going to get out and live differently for the happiness I still hope to find again."[61]

Three days later, on Sunday, October 3, 1982, Heman Marion Sweatt died of a massive heart attack in the home of his friend Kenneth Crooks.

CHAPTER 21

Epilogue

Heman Sweatt was a courageous man.
CHIEF JUSTICE JOE GREENHILL, FEBRUARY 28, 2005

Lonnie Van Zandt lives in a simple white frame house at 1193 San Bernard Street in Austin, Texas. Because of a stroke he suffered more than twenty years ago, his speech is slightly slurred and his step is not what it once was. But his eyes are clear and his posture is erect. He looks directly into my eyes with the confidence of a proud black man. Having witnessed much in seventy-eight years, he is not easily impressed or surprised these days.

San Bernard Street is located on Robertson Hill. Despite Austin's designation of it as an historic district, many of the neighborhood's old homes are weathered and in a sad state of disrepair, including Van Zandt's. His large wooden house sits behind a small front yard covered with lush St. Augustine grass. Sections of the walls and floors sag noticeably above concrete blocks that have settled unevenly over the decades. An oak tree, rooted too close to the house, has lifted and cracked the concrete steps in front of a screened porch; above these steps are wooden ramps, originally built for his mother, which now make it easier for Van Zandt to go inside.

Robertson Hill was a different place in the 1940s, when the house belonged to Dr. Lewis Mitchell and his wife, Carolyn. Thurgood Marshall stayed here during the *Sweatt v. Painter* trial and on other visits to Austin. Just around the corner at 1209 East 12th Street is where Heman Sweatt lived when he entered the UT Law School, and across the street from that was where Dr. Mitchell had his dental practice.

Robertson Hill is now valuable real estate, not because of this rich history, but because the Robertson Hill summit overlooks downtown Austin and some of the most prized possessions of the people of Texas. East Avenue, once the racial line of demarcation in Austin, is now Interstate Highway 35. Due west is the Texas Capitol. A short distance north is the University of Texas.

As of September 23, 2008, there was nothing to signify 1193 San Bernard Street as the place where, every evening, from May 11 through May 16, 1947, in the spacious living room that is today covered with a worn green shag carpet, Thurgood Marshall and other lawyers prepared witnesses and formulated legal tactics. James Nabrit, Jr., Robert L. Carter, and W. J. Durham were among the many lawyers who met in the Mitchells' living room and ate in the connecting dining room as they prepared for *Sweatt v. Painter*.[1]

From their home on San Bernard Street, the Mitchells could not have foreseen that on Friday, April 15, 1988, at three in the afternoon, the portion of the main UT Austin campus known as the Little Campus, on the southeast corner of 19th and Red River streets, would be renamed the Heman Sweatt Campus. The ceremony was part of the Second Annual Heman Marion Sweatt Symposium on Civil Rights, an event that is still hosted each year by the Division of Diversity and Community Engagement of the university. The largest building on the Sweatt Campus is John Hargis Hall, which houses the Freshman Admissions Center. In June 1955, John Hargis became the first African American undergraduate applicant admitted to the University of Texas.[2]

John Saunders Chase, one of the first two African Americans to register as a student at the University of Texas, became one of the first black graduates of the university in 1952. He earned a master's degree in architecture. He founded the National Organization of Minority Architects and taught architectural drafting at Texas Southern University, where he designed the Thurgood Marshall School of Law and several other buildings. He also designed one of UT's major parking facilities; it is where I park whenever I drive to campus.[3]

Sweatt's housemate at 1209 12th Street (after Connie and Heman separated), George Washington, Jr., who had registered at UT Law on the same day as Sweatt, became, in 1954, the first African American graduate of the UT Law School. In 1968, Washington returned to teach the first African American history course ever offered at UT. Of the thirty-five students enrolled, five were black. When asked if he was disappointed at the small number of minority students taking the class, Washington replied, "No . . . I think it's a representative number of those enrolled in the University."[4]

In May 1964, W. W. Heath, the chairman of the University of Texas board of regents, on the occasion of the integration of the dormitories, announced, "The whole University of Texas System is integrated now—in every respect."[5]

Theophilus S. Painter resigned as president of UT in 1952 but continued to teach in the Department of Zoology until his retirement in 1966. He died in Fort Stockton, Texas, on October 5, 1969. He is buried in Austin Memorial Park in Austin. Painter Hall houses Honors Research and International Studies and other programs.[6]

Painter's predecessor, Homer Rainey, died at the age of eighty-nine on December 19, 1985, in his home in Boulder, Colorado.[7] Rainey Hall on 21st Street houses the Department of French and Italian.

Today, UT Austin ranks sixth in the nation in producing undergraduate degrees for minority students.[8]

Houston

More than 150 miles southeast of Austin, an energetic woman named Betty Joyce Gilmore lives in a small house at 3402 Delano Street in Houston. Gilmore is sixty-seven years old and, like Lonnie Van Zandt, has had a stroke. She walks with a cane, on wooden access ramps built over the original concrete steps of a house that measures only twenty-eight by thirty-eight feet—not counting a six-foot-wide screened front porch.

This neighborhood is still in the Third Ward and is similar to Robertson Hill. It, too, was once the center of an African American intellectual circle. Ruby Overton, a neighbor and cousin of Gilmore's, remembers a time when the area housed teachers, lawyers, professors, and doctors. Today, the urban poor living there stubbornly struggle against gangs, crime, and poverty.

Visitors enter Gilmore's Delano Street house through her front door. The dark center-matched hardwood floors, original to the house, creak with age. Straight ahead is the kitchen, and on the left, French doors open to a hallway leading to two small bedrooms separated by a bathroom. Like Lonnie Van Zandt's house, 3402 Delano is in a sad state of disrepair now but was an important part of the *Sweatt v. Painter* story: Heman Sweatt lived there with his wife Connie. In the fall of 1945, this house hosted strategizing African American leaders after Heman Sweatt agreed to become an NAACP plaintiff.

In the summer of 2005, three or four houses down Delano Street, while sitting in a rocker on her front porch, Ruby Overton remembers Heman as a small but handsome man and Connie as a beautiful woman. The Sweatts were not rich, but he had a good, steady job as a mail carrier, and Connie taught elementary school a few blocks away. They had their own, new house, which was more than most African American families in the postwar South had. They could have left well enough alone.

In her living room, Connie watched Heman put it all at risk for a cause greater than himself. And like Carolyn Mitchell, Connie Sweatt was a teacher who could not have known then how the Sweatt name would eventually become revered by many in Texas. As a well-read, educated person, however, she was keenly aware of the danger of such an undertaking. She must have looked at those living-room walls and feared losing that neat little house. After four years of struggle—she did. When her marriage to Heman ended in 1950, she returned to her parents in Houston. She died in the Third Ward in Houston in August 1993.

A few blocks from Heman Sweatt's old house, where the Houston College for Negroes once stood, stands the "House That Sweatt Built." In February 1951, Carter Wesley ran an editorial denouncing the name "Texas State University for Negroes." As a result, a delegation of students testified before a legislative committee, demanding that "for Negroes" be dropped because it implied inferiority. UT president Theophilus Painter, however, opposed the name change, testifying against it until a compromise was reached. The passage of House Bill 82 changed the name to Texas Southern University (TSU) on June 1, 1951. TSU is now the second-largest predominantly black institution in the United States. Its 150-acre campus has forty-five buildings serving more than 11,600 students—of whom more than 600 are enrolled in the school of law that Sweatt refused to attend.[9]

Today the TSU law school is called the Thurgood Marshall School of Law. It was named after the NAACP attorney who did everything in his power to fight the idea of building "equal" educational facilities for African Americans. The law school's name was changed during a luncheon ceremony at the Imperial Ballroom of the Hyatt Regency Hotel in Houston on February 14, 1976. Heman Sweatt attended, and was incorrectly identified by many news organizations as an attorney. At first, Thurgood Marshall refused to allow his name to be associated with the school and declined to attend the ceremony. It took the personal intervention of the Texas Supreme Court's chief justice to convince Marshall to agree to the name change and to attend the ceremonies. Ironically, Chief Justice Joe Greenhill gave the address during the ceremony. When Marshall rose to speak, he gazed at the young black law students, and with a glare that would have made his mentor Charles Hamilton Houston proud, he said, "For every fourteen hours [your opponent] puts in, you must put in fifteen."[10]

The number of African American attorneys in Texas more than doubled from 1940 to 1960.[11]

At the time of the law school's name change, Thurgood Marshall was serving as a justice of the Supreme Court, the first African American ever appointed. He had been appointed by President Lyndon B. Johnson, a Texan, to replace Justice Tom C. Clark, another Texan, who had voted with the majorities in both *Sweatt* and *Brown*.

Thurgood Marshall died of heart failure at Bethesda Naval Medical Center on Sunday, January 24, 1993. He was buried in an area of Arlington National Cemetery near a number of other justices of the Supreme Court.[12]

Joe Greenhill

Shortly after arguing *Sweatt v. Painter* before the Supreme Court, Joe Greenhill resigned as Price Daniel's assistant attorney general and cofounded the law firm of Graves, Dougherty, and Greenhill. Seven years later, he was appointed to a seat on the Texas Supreme Court and was elected to a seat in 1958. (His opponent was Dallas judge Sarah T. Hughes, who would become iconic for administering the oath of office on Air Force One to Lyndon Johnson on the day of the assassination of John F. Kennedy.) He served on the court for twenty-five years, the last ten as chief justice. He joined the law firm of Baker Botts, LLP, in Austin, where he still works today—at the age of ninety-five.

Greenhill is a man whose conscience is clear: "I'm not a segregationist. I wasn't in *Sweatt v. Painter* to be for or against segregation. I was in there as a lawyer with a client to represent. My client was Dr. Painter and the University of Texas. Either I could do my best or quit."[13] On October 28, 1997, he was the guest of a law class studying civil rights. "They began with the opinion that I was a bad guy—segregationist," Greenhill recalled. During an interview for this book, he also seemed greatly saddened when, during the rededication of the Travis County Courthouse where Judge Archer presided over the trial of *Sweatt v. Painter,* it was suggested that the attorney general forced Heman Sweatt to sit on the floor during the proceedings. Perhaps that is why Greenhill is quick to tell the unrelated story of how he was a guest of Thurgood Marshall during the reading of the *Brown v. Board of Education* ruling: "I was the first to shake his hand and congratulate him."[14]

And perhaps Greenhill has a point. But another irony of the Heman Sweatt story is that on the Baker Botts website, when accessed on July 16,

2008, Greenhill's page lists as honors his membership in the Order of the Coif and his editorship of the *Texas Law Review*. In 1950, Price Daniel's witnesses argued that those were "extraneous" distinctions that did not add to the quality of a law-school education.

During his six years as Texas attorney general, Price Daniel disposed of more than 5,000 lawsuits, composed more than 2,000 bills for the legislature, and successfully defended more money and land claims than any other attorney general in the history of Texas. In 1952, he was elected U.S. Senator, but returned to Texas during his first term to run for governor. He won the gubernatorial elections of 1956, 1958, and 1960. During his career, he served on at least twenty-five boards and agencies, and is identified by *The Handbook of Texas* as having held more offices of public trust than anyone else in Texas history. He died on August 25, 1988, at the age of seventy-seven.[15] Today, the Price Daniel, Sr., Building houses the Third Court of Appeals of Texas and several state-agency offices, including the Office of the Attorney General. In yet another irony in Texas's history of race relations, in *Fisher v. Texas* (2008) the attorney general is defending UT's use of affirmative action in its freshman admissions process. On August 17, 2009, federal judge Sam Sparks upheld UT's policy, ruling that the university had a compelling interest in diversifying its student body and that its policy was narrowly tailored to achieve that end. On September 14, 2009, attorneys for the plaintiffs served UT administrators with a notice of intent to appeal the ruling to the U.S. Court of Appeals for the Fifth Circuit.[16]

Finalities

If there is an "Arlington Cemetery" for African American civil rights legends from Houston, it is Paradise North. It is an enormous expanse of flat grassland. Near the entrance, Lulu and Julius White lie side by side. On June 1, 1957, Lulu White had to be taken to a hospital for chronic heart problems. On July 7, she died at her home on Tuam Street, where she had become known for her Sunday-afternoon teas. Thurgood Marshall read a tribute during her funeral at Antioch Baptist Church. Julius White, her fearless underworld husband, died three years later on October 18, 1960. His obituary in the *Houston Informer* included a picture of him with heavyweight boxing champion Joe Louis—they were both "Champions."[17]

One of the more prominent markers in Paradise North is the Perry family monument. Heman Perry, who was Heman Sweatt's uncle and namesake, is buried there with his family. In the immediate area lies Ella Rose

Sweatt, Heman Sweatt's mother. She died on April 18, 1963, of cancer. Next to her in an unmarked plot lies the man Carter Wesley called "the Great Prophet," Heman's father, James Leonard Sweatt, Sr. He died in February 1954 of heart failure. At the time, Leonard was one of the last surviving founders of the National Alliance of Postal Employees—the president of the organization attended the funeral.[18]

Next to his parents lies Heman Marion Sweatt. His daughter Mellie eventually had his cremated remains interred there. Heman would have been proud of Mellie; she graduated from Duke University and Howard Medical School and is today a physician in Cincinnati, Ohio. She is the mother of two handsome boys; her oldest son is named Heman.

The Reverend Albert A. Lucas, described by Thurgood Marshall as a cleric who carried a gun as well as a Bible in his car, in case the Bible did not work, died in 1963 and is buried in the Lucas family plot.

Nearby in an unmarked grave lies Richard Randolph Grovey, the militant barber and plaintiff in the ill-fated *Grovey v. Townsend* case that represented the low point in the white-primary fight. Cemetery records indicate that he was buried in early October 1960.

A few feet away is the Richardson family plot. Here, the memorial identifies the family as the founders of the *Houston Defender,* "Houston's community minded newspaper." Below is the inscription: "Trims no sail to catch the passing breeze: flies no doubtful flag." Clifton F. Richardson, Sr., who also founded Carter Wesley's *Houston Informer,* died suddenly in 1939. His son, Clif Richardson, Jr., the eyewitness reporter who gave the most complete account of Sweatt's application to the University of Texas Law School in February 1946, is buried there as well; he died in 1983.

Far away from the Richardsons and Lulu White, as if to keep his distance from those he bitterly fought with while alive, lies Carter Walker Wesley. True to form, his headstone is unlike any other; it is glossy black marble with a white inscription. He died at home after a long illness on November 10, 1969.[19]

In Dallas, A. Maceo Smith, the organizational brains behind many civic groups, including the NAACP's Texas State Conference of Branches, retired in 1973 after a long career with the U.S. Department of Housing and Urban Development. He died on December 19, 1977. A. Maceo Smith High School in Dallas is named for him. Even today, students there call him "the man."[20]

Joseph J. Rhoads, the activist president of Bishop College who headed the Texas Council of Negro Organizations, continued to serve as Bishop's president until his death in 1951. In 1947, he established a Dallas branch of

Bishop College that set the stage for the school's relocation there in 1961. He is buried in McJohnson's Cemetery in his hometown of Marshall.[21]

Dr. Lonnie Smith, the Houston dentist who became plaintiff in *Smith v. Allwright*, the successful suit ending the white primary, retired from his dental practice in 1968. He died at the age of sixty-nine on March 6, 1971.[22]

Melvin Tolson, the Wiley College speech and debate teacher whom Heman Sweatt identified as one of the two most influential men in his life, died on August 29, 1966, in St. Paul's Hospital in Dallas. He is buried in the Summit View Cemetery in Guthrie, Oklahoma. In 2008, actor Denzel Washington released a movie entitled *The Great Debaters*, a dramatization of Wiley's defeat of the national champion debate team at the University of Southern California (although in the movie the champions were from Harvard).

W. Astor Kirk, the Tillotson College teacher who refused to attend classes in a YMCA across the street from the UT campus, earned a PhD from the University of Texas in the summer of 1958. He has just published his autobiography, entitled *One Life: My Civil Rights Story*. It is a story from a wise and kind man who knows how each of us can achieve healing and peace: "I kept in the forefront of my consciousness day after day the fundamental truth that one cannot achieve and sustain wholeness of mind, body, and soul without forgiving those who inflict pain, cause misery and sow seeds of discord—even when one is unable to forget what these others do."[23] Kirk now lives in Maryland.

The Santa Rita No. 1 oil rig in West Texas continuously produced oil for sixty-seven years, greatly enriching the Permanent University Fund, until it was finally capped in 1990. In 1940, the original rig was moved to the UT Austin campus. Reassembled in 1958, it can be seen on the corner of Trinity Street and Martin Luther King Boulevard, within sight of Hargis Hall on the Heman Sweatt campus. It deserves monument status: on February 1, 2008, the *Chronicle of Higher Education* reported that UT's endowment had a market value of $15.6 billion. It ranked fifth among all American universities and was the largest among public institutions.

Things Come Full Circle at the Courthouse

Today, the Travis County Courthouse on Guadalupe Street in Austin is still located about nine blocks south of UT's "drag" (Guadalupe Street). It is an old building that was once fashionable, but today bears the scars of years of modernization and increasingly stringent building codes. The fourth-floor hallways that lead to room 436, the courtroom for the 126th District, are dark and dank. The courtroom, which is on the southwest corner of the main hallway, was once presided over by Judge Roy Archer. Today, the judge is Darlene Byrne.

On February 28, 2005, a plaque hanging on the wall to the right of the black double-door entrance of the courtroom was dedicated. One of the speakers was retired chief justice Joe Greenhill, who has doubts about whether that was exactly where the *Sweatt v. Painter* trial was held. "Maybe it was; that was a long time ago," he said.

Later the same year, on Friday, October 21, Travis County Commissioners hosted another dedication ceremony. This time the courthouse itself was being renamed. Above the main entrance is inscribed:

HEMAN MARION SWEATT
TRAVIS COUNTY COURTHOUSE
COURAGE   PERSEVERANCE   SACRIFICE

I went to the courthouse that day to witness the dedication and hear the guest speaker, Vernon Jordan, one of America's most famous attorneys and a former president of the Urban League. The badged hostesses greeted my wife and me on the third floor and escorted us to a nearly empty room with a midsized movie screen. There were three of us in the room, and I realized that the ceremony was being held somewhere else. The video screen guaranteed that I would not miss a word of anyone's presentation; I had more room to myself than the spectators inside. In every way it was "separate but equal," but it didn't matter. I wanted to be with everyone else. "You'll see everything in the overflow room," I was assured.

It was almost as if Heman Sweatt were talking to me and preparing me for this book: "This is why I didn't go to the basement school—it is not the same, is it?" I heard him say. So I returned to the hostesses and politely asked, "May I go to the room where the dedication is actually being held?"

She replied, "I'm sorry, you need a VIP invitation for that."

Notes

Introduction

1. Throughout this book, I grappled with the use of the terms "desegregation" and "integration." Professor Lodis Rhodes of the Lyndon Baines Johnson School of Public Affairs at the University of Texas at Austin gave me the best advice on this by arguing that "desegregation" is more accurate because it is a "descriptive term for a desired legal/constitutional outcome—a unitary, indivisible nation [begetting] systems of public and common goods equally available to and shared by all." Historically, however, the NAACP, especially its counsel Thurgood Marshall, referred to the creation of such an indivisible state as "integration." I agree completely with Dr. Rhodes's distinction between the two terms, but solely for purposes of clarity, in this book I will use the two terms interchangeably, as Thurgood Marshall did from the 1930s through the 1960s.

2. See Hugh Kennedy, *When Baghdad Ruled the Muslim World.*

3. See W. E. B. Du Bois, *The Souls of Black Folk,* 4; the text of the book is also online at http://www.bartleby.com/114/index.html (accessed April 26, 2006).

4. *The American Heritage Book of English Usage* online states: "*Black* is sometimes capitalized in its racial sense, especially in the black press, though the lowercase form is still widely used by authors of all races . . . On the other hand, the use of lowercase *white* in the same context as uppercase *Black* will obviously raise questions as to how and why the writer has distinguished between the two groups. There is no entirely happy solution to this problem." While acknowledging the absence of a "happy solution" to this usage question, in this book I have lowercased "black(s)" and "white(s)" throughout, whether used as nouns or adjectives. (Capitalized forms appearing in quoted material were left that way.) This seems to be in keeping with both the current general trend regarding this matter and the usual practice of the University of Texas Press.

Chapter 1

1. *Houston Informer,* December 28, 1946.

Chapter 2

1. *The Handbook of Texas Online,* s.vv. "Juneteenth" and " Gordon Granger," http://www.tshaonline.org/handbook/online/articles/JJ/lkj1.html and http://www.tshaonline.org/handbook/online/articles/GG/fgr10.html (accessed March 5, 2006).

2. The story is from Wendell Sweatt and was reported in the *Fort Worth Star Telegram,* October 10, 1982.

3. See the 1870 and 1880 U.S. Census Records for the Waxahachie precinct of Ellis County, Texas.

4. Michael Lowery Gillette, "The NAACP in Texas, 1937–1957," 51–53. An abbreviated version of this dissertation is Michael L. Gillette, "Heman Marion Sweatt: Civil Rights Plaintiff," in Alwyn Barr and Robert Calvert, eds., *Black Leaders: Texans for Their Times.*

5. Those comments were made by Carter Wesley, the editor of the *Houston Informer,* in his column "Ram's Horn," February 20, 1954.

6. Gillette, "NAACP in Texas," 51–53; James Sweatt first appears in the *Houston City Directory* in the 1897–1898 edition. A copy is housed in the Houston Metropolitan Research Center (IIMRC) in the Houston Public Library.

7. William Joseph Brophy, "The Black Texan, 1900–1950: A Quantitative History," 35. The ratio between black and white teachers' salaries in Texas went from .83 in 1900, about three years after James Leonard Sweatt left teaching, to .58 in 1930, about the time he would have retired.

8. Prairie View A&M University does not have any official record of James Leonard Sweatt's matriculation there, but the catalogue for the school year 1900–1901 has a list of the members of the class of 1890, where he is listed with his fellow graduates; Heman Marion Sweatt, quoted in the *Dallas Morning News,* May 20, 1979.

9. Howard Beeth and Cary D. Wintz, eds., *Black Dixie: Afro-Texan History and Culture in Houston,* 22.

10. *Houston City Directory,* 1897–1898, 1899, and 1900–1901.

11. Beeth and Wintz, *Black Dixie,* 23. Gillette maintains that the Sweatts were isolated from the bulk of Houston's Negro community ("NAACP in Texas," 51–53). That can hardly be true. Other blacks lived on Chenevert as late as 1946, and Dowling Street, the center of the Third Ward's black business district, was only a few blocks away.

12. This is from copies of death notices generously provided to me by Dr. Hemella Sweatt and from conversations with Anna Sweatt, Heman Sweatt's sole surviving sister-in-law.

13. Wendell Sweatt, quoted in the *Fort Worth Star Telegram,* October 10, 1982.

14. "Jack" is an unusual nickname for "James," but he was named Jack because he was born on July 4, 1910, the day boxer Jack Johnson defeated James Jeffries in a fifteenth-round knockout—an occasion for great celebration among American blacks.

15. Beeth and Wintz, *Black Dixie,* 89; Gillette, "NAACP in Texas," 51–53.

16. Heman Marion Sweatt, quoted in the *Dallas Morning News,* May 20, 1979. For convenience I will not refer to Heman Sweatt as "Bill."

17. Unidentified newspaper clipping dated March 3, 1946 ("Heman Sweatt" ver-

tical file, Dolph Briscoe Center for American History [DBCAH], University of Texas at Austin).

18. Heman Sweatt to Walter White, September 3, 1948 (NAACP Papers, *Sweatt v. Painter* files, 1945–1950); Gillette, "NAACP in Texas," 51–53. I consulted the microfilm collections of the NAACP Papers kept in the Perry-Castañeda Library and the Tarlton Law Library, both located at the University of Texas at Austin.

19. Gillette, "NAACP in Texas," 53.

20. Ibid. I based my measurements on the *Houston City Directory* for 1922, when Sweatt would have been old enough to walk alone to school. Locating 2415 Chenevert, the Longfellow School, which in the 1920s was at 2209 Chartres Street, and Frederick Douglass Elementary School, which was at 3000–30 Trulley St., or where Hadley and Trulley meet, the route is nine-tenths of a mile. It is not my intention to suggest that Heman Sweatt deceived anyone. It does illustrate, however, how unreliable oral interviews can be. I conducted interviews while preparing all my previous books, but I did so with skepticism. It is my observation that stories of emotional topics like victimization, discrimination, and bigotry are organic and grow with time. We will see much more of these kinds of inconsistencies throughout this book.

21. *Houston City Directory*, 1918.

22. Clifton F. Richardson, Sr., "Houston's Colored Citizens: Activities and Conditions among the Negro Population in the 1920s," in Beeth and Wintz, *Black Dixie*, 129.

23. Lorenzo Greene, "Sidelights on Houston Negroes as Seen by an Associate of Dr. Carter G. Woodson in 1930," in Beeth and Wintz, *Black Dixie*, 143.

24. National Urban League, *A Review of the Economic and Cultural Problems of Houston, Texas: As They Relate to the Conditions in the Negro Population, April–May, 1945*, 17–18, 59. Richardson, "Houston's Colored Citizens," 129; "Negro History," vol. 1, 4 (this is a collection of ephemera compiled into scrapbooks by the HMRC).

25. Beeth and Wintz, *Black Dixie*, 87.

26. Ibid., 24–27; *Historic Highlights: The Antioch Baptist Church* (this was a souvenir publication printed around 1976 for a centennial celebration of the church; a copy is in the HMRC).

27. *Houston Post* survey, cited in National Urban League, *Economic and Cultural Problems of Houston*, 160; William Edward Terry, "Origin and Development of Texas Southern University," 13; *Antioch Baptist Church*.

28. National Urban League, *Economic and Cultural Problems of Houston*, 17–18, 59; Gillette, "NAACP in Texas," 51–53.

29. See James M. SoRelle, "Race Relations in 'Heavenly Houston,' 1919–45," in Beeth and Wintz, *Black Dixie*, 175, 188.

30. Casey Edward Greene, "Apostles of Hate: The Ku Klux Klan in and Near Houston, Texas, 1920–82," 25, 126. The second period was the 1960s, when the KKK targeted threats of communism and integration, and the third was the 1970s, when it targeted immigration.

31. Ibid., 33.

32. Ibid., 34.

33. Ibid.

34. Ibid. 34–36; *Houston Post*, May 2, 1921.

35. Ibid.

36. Ibid.

37. Unidentified physician, quoted in the *Houston Post*, May 2, 1921; SoRelle, "Race Relations," 178; Greene, "Apostles of Hate," 34–36. It was not Mayor Oscar Holcombe's last clash with the Klan. The next year he earned its enmity when he refused to fire three employees of his administration because they were Catholic; see *The Handbook of Texas Online*, s.v. "Oscar Holcombe," http://www.tshaonline .org/handbook/online/articles/HH/fho21.html (accessed March 9, 2006).

38. James Leonard Sweatt, quoted in Gillette, "Heman Marion Sweatt," 163.

39. Jackson Davis, "The Outlook for the Professional and Higher Education of Negroes."

40. Robert M. Farnsworth, *Melvin B. Tolson*, 31; current information about Wiley College was taken from the school's website, www.wileyc.edu (accessed March 11, 2006); David A. Williams, "The History of Higher Education for Black Texans, 1872–1977," 81.

41. Gillette, "NAACP in Texas," 51–53; Gillette, "Heman Marion Sweatt," 163; *The Handbook of Texas Online*, s.v. "James Leonard Farmer," http://www.tshaonline .org/handbook/online/articles/FF/ffa30.html (accessed March 11, 2006).

42. Robert M. Farnsworth in Melvin B. Tolson, *Caviar and Cabbage: Selected Columns by Melvin B. Tolson from the "Washington Tribune," 1937–1944*, 1; Joy Flasch, *Melvin B. Tolson*, preface.

43. Quoted in Farnsworth, *Tolson*, 31.

44. Tolson, *Caviar and Cabbage*, 99.

45. Quoted in Flasch, *Melvin B. Tolson*, 24.

46. Farnsworth, *Tolson*, 32.

47. Gillette, "Heman Marion Sweatt," 163.

48. See Heman Sweatt's official transcript as an enclosure of W. J. Durham to Thurgood Marshall, January 28, 1946 (NAACP Papers, *Sweatt v. Painter* files, 1945–1950); for an example of a report identifying Sweatt as an honor graduate, see Jonathan L. Entin, "Desegregating the American Law School: The Road to *Brown*."

49. Heman Sweatt, quoted in Gillette, "NAACP in Texas," 54–56.

50. *Sweatt v. Painter*, no. 74,945, Relator's Third Supplemental Petition, filed May 12, 1947, and Application for Writ of Mandamus, filed May 16, 1946, 126th District Court of Travis County Texas.

51. Gillette, "NAACP in Texas," 54–56; unidentified clipping, March 3, 1946 ("Heman Sweatt" vertical file, DBCAH).

52. *Daily Texan*, clipping dated December 18, 1946 ("Heman Sweatt" vertical file, DBCAH).

Chapter 3

1. National Urban League, *Economic and Cultural Problems of Houston*, 9; Charles William Grose, "Black Newspapers in Texas, 1868–1970," 111; *The Handbook of Texas Online*, s.v. "Charles N. Love," http://www.tshaonline.org/handbook/ online/articles/LL/floac.html (accessed April 22, 2006).

2. Grose, "Black Newspapers in Texas," 19.

3. Ibid., ix.

4. *Houston Informer,* January 13, 1945.

5. See *Love v. Griffith,* 266 U.S. 32 (1924).

6. Grose, "Black Newspapers in Texas," 127–137; http://www.jimcrowhistory .org/scripts/jimcrow/press.cgi?state=Texas, accessed April 21, 2006.

7. Information on the threatening note and the exchange between Richardson and Goodson is in James M. SoRelle, "The Darker Side of 'Heaven': The Black Community in Houston, Texas, 1917–45," 74, 178.

8. Merline Pitre, *In Struggle against Jim Crow,* 13–15.

9. Quoted in Darlene Clark Hine, *Black Victory: The Rise and Fall of the White Primary,* 160–161.

10. Ibid.; for an example of Julius White's philanthropy, see the program for the Fifth Annual Art Exhibit at the Colored Carnegie Library, June 27–July 6, 1937 ("Negro History," vol. 1, 12 [HMRC]). Julius White is listed as a patron.

11. Grose, "Black Newspapers in Texas," 138–142.

12. Richardson, "Houston's Colored Citizens," 131.

13. *The Handbook of Texas Online,* s.v. "Carter Walker Wesley," http://www .tshaonline.org/handbook/online/articles/WW/fwe28.html (accessed April 22, 2006); Robert V. Haynes, "Black Houstonians and the White Democratic Primary, 1920–45," 197–198; Hine, *Black Victory,* 161.

14. Grose, "Black Newspapers in Texas," 138–142; the quotation is from Hine, *Black Victory,* 161.

15. Grose, "Black Newspapers in Texas," 138–142.

16. Ibid.; *The Handbook of Texas Online,* s.v. "Carter Walker Wesley."

17. Haynes, "Black Houstonians," 197–198; Hine, *Black Victory,* 161; Grose, "Black Newspapers in Texas," 138–142.

18. The suit was dismissed in early 1931 when the litigators failed to appear for trial.

19. Haynes, "Black Houstonians," 197–198; Hine, *Black Victory,* 161; Grose, "Black Newspapers in Texas," 138–142.

20. Grose, "Black Newspapers in Texas," 175.

21. *Houston Informer,* March 2, 1940.

22. Carter Wesley to Thurgood Marshall, July 2, 1940 (NAACP Papers, legal files, "Carter Wesley/*Houston Informer,* 1940–1947"); *Houston Informer,* May 18 and 25, 1940.

23. Quoted in the *Houston Informer,* March 16, 1940.

24. Haynes, "Black Houstonians," 198; Darlene Clark Hine, "Blacks and the Destruction of the Democratic White Primary," 43–59; Hine, *Black Victory,* 164; Pitre, *Struggle against Jim Crow,* 23–25.

25. Quoted in the *Houston Informer,* March 16, 1940.

26. Hine, *Black Victory,* 164, 194.

27. Amilcar Shabazz, *Advancing Democracy: African Americans and the Struggle for Access and Equity in Higher Education in Texas,* 75.

28. Grovey, quoted in Haynes, "Black Houstonians," 198.

29. Pitre, *Struggle against Jim Crow,* 10, 14–15; *The Handbook of Texas Online,* s.v. "Lulu Belle Madison White," http://www.tshaonline.org/handbook/online/ articles/WW/fwh75.html (accessed April 23, 2006); Hine, *Black Victory,* 29, 31;

Ira B. Bryant, *Texas Southern University: Its Antecedents, Political Origin, and Future*, 1.

30. Pitre, *Struggle against Jim Crow*, 25, 37; Hine, *Black Victory*, 28; Gillette, "Heman Marion Sweatt," 177.

31. Thurgood Marshall to Lulu White, telegram, November 5, 1945 (NAACP Papers, legal files, "Carter Wesley/*Houston Informer*, 1940–1947"); Lorenzo Greene, "Sidelights on Houston Negroes," 138–141; *The Handbook of Texas Online*, "Lulu Belle Madison White"; Merline Pitre, foreword to Hine, *Black Victory*, 30; Pitre, *Struggle against Jim Crow*, 28; Gillette, "NAACP in Texas," 173.

32. See Booker T. Washington, *Up from Slavery*. Washington included the speech in full beginning on page 218. It is also posted at http://www.africawithin .com/bios/booker/atlanta_compromise.htm.

33. Ibid.

34. Raphael O'Hara Lanier, "The History of Higher Education for Negroes in Texas, 1930–55, with Particular Reference to Texas Southern University," 2; *Frontline: The Two Nations of Black America*, http://www.pbs.org/wgbh/pages/frontline/ shows/race/etc/road.html (accessed April 25, 2006).

35. Du Bois, *Souls of Black Folk*, 30; Du Bois's remark about "full manhood rights" is quoted in James W. Marquart, Sheldon Ekland-Olson, and Jonathan R. Sorensen, *The Rope, the Chair, and the Needle: Capital Punishment in Texas, 1923–1990*, 8.

36. Du Bois, *Souls of Black Folk*, 56.

37. Ibid., 58–59.

38. Lanier, "Higher Education for Negroes," 2; Warren D. St. James, *The National Association for the Advancement of Colored People: A Case Study in Pressure Groups*, 36, 156; Hine, *Black Victory*, 104. There are conflicting reports about why the Niagara Movement's first meeting was held on the Canadian side of the falls. The first was that Du Bois and his guests were not allowed in an American hotel: "The meeting had originally been planned to take place on the American side of the falls, but the delegates were denied accommodations by racially prejudiced hotel managers. They crossed over to the Canadian side where they were welcomed and received rooms without incident" (*The Rise and Fall of Jim Crow: Jim Crow Stories*, http://www.pbs.org/wnet/jimcrow/stories_events_niagara.html [accessed April 26, 2006]). However, according to William Evitts of the Buffalo and Erie County Historical Society: "Originally the group planned to meet at a hotel in Buffalo. This arrangement fell through, although whether because of racial discrimination (as some maintain) or because of the crush of a huge convention of Elks in town at the same moment, is not perfectly clear in the record. We don't know the name of the hotel. But for whatever reason, the group transferred to Fort Erie at the last minute" ("The Niagara Movement," http://www.buffaloah.com/h/niag.html [accessed August 18, 2009]). Neither of the explanations are plausible, because both assume Du Bois arrived in Buffalo without having made prior hotel arrangements for what he hoped would be a meeting of about fifty of America's African American elite. He would never have taken such a foolish and irresponsible chance. The Niagara Movement meeting took place precisely where Du Bois wanted it to: in the Erie Beach Hotel, a resort in Fort Erie, Canada. The University of Buffalo hosts an excellent website called *Uncrowned Queens*, which is dedicated to promoting research into the history of notable women of color. One biography is that of Mary B. Talbert, who, along

with her husband, assisted Du Bois in making arrangements. The Talberts also hosted planning and preliminary meetings for the event in their home. *Uncrowned Queens* conclusively cites Du Bois's papers and his autobiography to confirm the obvious: he planned carefully for the event, looked closely at hotels in the area, and chose to meet in Canada (see http://wings.buffalo.edu/uncrownedqueens/C/history/niag_mov/mystery_solved.html [accessed August 18, 2009]).

39. St. James, *National Association for the Advancement of Colored People*, 39.

40. Ibid.

41. Ibid., 33–39; Juan Williams, *Thurgood Marshall: American Revolutionary*, 23; Mark V. Tushnet, *The NAACP's Legal Strategy against Segregated Education, 1925–1950*, xi, 1.

42. St. James, *National Association for the Advancement of Colored People*, 159.

43. Melvin James Banks, "The Pursuit of Equality: The Movement for First Class Citizenship among Negroes in Texas, 1920–1950," 178. Banks does not identify the young woman; he incorrectly lists "Heman Sweatt, Sr." as a member of the first Membership Committee. Of course, it had to be James L. Sweatt. The other members were E. O. Smith, John Adkins, Tad Scott, Duke Crawford, Julius White, Dick Thomas, L. H. Spivey, Miles Jordan, W. L. D. Johnson, and R. T. Andrew, Sr.

Chapter 4

The quotation used in the epigraph is taken from Genna Rae McNeil, *Groundwork: Charles Hamilton Houston and the Struggle for Civil Rights*, 84.

1. "Chief Counsel for Equality," undated and unidentified article (likely to be Oliver Allen, "Chief Counsel for Equality," *Life*, June 13, 1955, which was a profile of Marshall) in the papers of Joe Greenhill (hereafter, Greenhill Papers), which were provided to the author.

2. "Dummy's retreat" is from Thurgood Marshall, "Tribute to Charles H. Houston," *Amherst Magazine*, Spring 1978, reproduced in *Thurgood Marshall: His Speeches, Writings, Arguments, Opinions, and Reminiscences*, 272; Robert L. Carter, *A Matter of Law: A Memoir of Struggle in the Cause of Equal Rights*, 24.

3. Felton G. Clark, "The Development and Present Status of Publicly-Supported Higher Education for Negroes"; Douglas O. Linder, "Before *Brown:* Charles H. Houston and the *Gaines* Case," http://papers.ssrn.com/sol3/papers.cfm?abstract_id=1109108 (accessed August 18, 2009).

4. Charles Houston, quoted in Genna Rae McNeil, *Groundwork: Charles Hamilton Houston and the Struggle For Civil Rights*, 45; Gillette, "NAACP in Texas," 1–2.

5. Ibid.; Howard University Law School website, http://www.law.howard.edu/19 (accessed June 3, 2006).

6. For an example of Howard Law being "admirable," see McNeil, *Groundwork*, 64.

7. The Charles Houston quotations are from Houston, "The Need for Negro Lawyers," 49; Marshall, "Tribute to Houston," in *Marshall: Speeches*, 273; Linder, "Before *Brown.*"

8. Houston, quoted in Tushnet, *NAACP's Legal Strategy*, 18.

9. Juan Williams, *Thurgood Marshall*, 75–76; "'With an Even Hand': *Brown v. Board* at Fifty," Library of Congress website, http://www.loc.gov/exhibits/brown/brown-segregation.html (accessed June 4, 2006).

10. For an excellent overview of the Margold Report, see the summary at the Loyola Law School of Los Angeles website, http://classes.lls.edu/archive/manheimk/civrts/strategy1.html.

11. McNeil, *Groundwork*, 111–121; Darlene Clark Hine, "Destruction of the Democratic White Primary"; Marshall, "Tribute to Houston," in *Marshall: Speeches*, 274; Hine, *Black Victory*, 212; Juan Williams, *Thurgood Marshall*, 94.

12. See *State of Texas v. NAACP*, cause 56-469 (unreported), district court of Smith County, Texas, 7th Judicial District, 1957.

13. Juan Williams, *Thurgood Marshall*, 29; "Chief Counsel for Equality," Greenhill Papers; Marshall, "The Reminiscences of Thurgood Marshall," in *Marshall: Speeches*, 415.

14. See *Pearson v. Murray*, 169 Md. 478 (1936).

15. Ibid.

16. Ibid.; Albert P. Blaustein and Clarence Clyde Ferguson, Jr., *Desegregation and the Law: The Meaning and Effect of the School Segregation Cases*, 106.

17. *Pearson*, 169 Md. 478.

18. Linder, "Before *Brown*."

19. Daniel T. Kelleher, "The Case of Lloyd Lionel Gaines: The Demise of the Separate but Equal Doctrine"; Sidney Redmond, interviewed by Richard Resh and Franklin Rother for the Black Community Leaders Project, July 6, 1970, transcript archived at the Western Historical Manuscript Collection, University of Missouri–St. Louis, Oral History T-025, http://www.umsl.edu/~whmc/guides/t025.htm (accessed September 4, 2009).

20. Thurgood Marshall to Heman Sweatt, September 30, 1947 (NAACP Papers).

21. Juan Williams, *Thurgood Marshall*, 97–98.

22. Linder, "Before *Brown*."

23. *Missouri ex rel. Gaines v. Canada*, 305 U.S. 337 (1938); the text of the opinion is available from FindLaw, http://caselaw.lp.findlaw.com/scripts/getcase.pl?navby=CASE&court=US&vol=305&page=337 (accessed August 18, 2009).

24. Ibid. at 350.

25. Ibid. at 352.

26. Portions of the letter are quoted in Linder, "Before *Brown*."

27. Ibid.; Kelleher, "Lloyd Lionel Gaines."

28. Quoted in the *St. Louis Riverfront Times*, April 4, 2007.

29. Kelleher, "Lloyd Lionel Gaines"; Marshall to Sweatt, September 30, 1947; *St. Louis Riverfront Times*, April 4, 2007. Gaines simply vanished. During World War II, not even the Selective Service could find him. In early 2007, the NAACP petitioned the FBI to investigate the disappearance of Lloyd Lionel Gaines.

30. Quoted in Linder, "Before *Brown*."

Chapter 5

1. At the time, it was possible to become a lawyer in one of two ways: a person could either earn a degree at a law school or study law under the supervision of an

experienced attorney. In either case, an aspiring attorney had to pass the state's bar examination.

2. *The Handbook of Texas Online,* s.v. "Alexander Watkins Terrell," http://www.tshaonline.org/handbook/online/articles/TT/fte16.html (accessed April 28, 2006); Haynes, "Black Houstonians," 194. An excellent and definitive history of the disenfranchisement of African American Texans is Hine, *Black Victory;* no discussion of the topic is possible without depending heavily on this work.

3. Ibid.

4. James Jackson Kilpatrick, *The Southern Case for School Segregation,* 33–34.

5. Ibid.; *The Handbook of Texas Online,* s.v. "Election Laws," http://www.tshaonline.org/handbook/online/articles/EE/wde1.html (accessed April 28, 2006).

6. *Newberry v. U.S.,* 256 U.S. 250 (1921).

7. Haynes, "Black Houstonians," 194; Thurgood Marshall, "The Rise and Collapse of the White Democratic Primary"; Texas Legislature, regular session, 1923, Senate Bill 44, introduced by Mr. Bowers; Hine, *Black Victory,* 70; Conrey Bryson, *Dr. Lawrence A. Nixon and the White Primary,* 11.

8. The *Dallas Express* quotations are included in Grose, "Black Newspapers in Texas," 93–94, 99.

9. Hine, *Black Victory,* 113 114; *The Texas Handbook Online,* s.v. "Lawrence Aaron Nixon," http://www.tshaonline.org/handbook/online/articles/NN/fni10.html (accessed July 23, 2006).

10. This exchange is my reconstruction based on Bryson, *Lawrence Nixon,* 18.

11. See *Nixon v. Herndon,* 273 U.S. 536 (1927); Bryson, *Lawrence Nixon,* 18; Haynes, "Black Houstonians," 195.

12. *Nixon,* 273 U.S. 536.

13. Ibid. at 540–541. The quotation cited by Holmes is from *Buchanan v. Warley,* 245 U.S. 60 (1917), in which the Court struck down as unconstitutional a Louisville, Kentucky, ordinance that required residential segregation based on race.

14. *Nixon,* 273 U.S. at 541.

15. *Nixon v. Condon,* 286 U.S. 73 (1932).

16. Ibid. at 91.

17. Ibid. at 88, 84. Another example of the Supreme Court instructing states on how to make a particular practice constitutional occurred in *Furman v. Georgia* (1972). In *Furman,* the Court struck down death-penalty laws—certainly a victory for death-penalty opponents—but also provided instructions on how to make executions constitutional. Within a few years, the result was more, not fewer, executions.

18. *Smith v. Allwright,* 321 U.S. 656–657 (1944).

19. Hine, *Black Victory,* 144; Darlene Hine, "The Elusive Ballot: The Black Struggle against the Texas White Primary, 1932–45."

20. Marshall, "White Democratic Primary"; Hine, *Black Victory,* 193.

21. Ralph Bunche, "The Negro in the Political Life of the United States"; Hine, "Elusive Ballot"; Haynes, "Black Houstonians," 201.

22. Banks, "Pursuit of Equality," 223; Haynes, "Black Houstonians," 197–198, 201; *Dallas Morning News,* May 20, 1979 (in a feature article, Heman Sweatt recalled how his family knew Grovey, Wesley, Smith, et al.); Hine, *Black Victory,* 160–165, 194–195, 210; Pitre, *Struggle against Jim Crow,* 23; *The Handbook of Texas Online,* s.v. "White Primary," http://www.tshaonline.org/handbook/online/articles/WW/wdw1.html (accessed June 28, 2007).

23. Grovey, quoted in the *Houston Post,* July 1, 1934.

24. See *Grovey v. Townsend,* 295 U.S. 45 (1935), and *Smith v. Allwright,* 321 U.S. 649 (1944).

25. *Grovey,* 295 U.S. 45.

26. *Houston Informer,* March 2, 1935; the quotation is also in Hine, "Destruction of the Democratic White Primary."

27. Hine, *Black Victory,* 196.

28. *Grovey,* 295 U.S. 50, 54–55.

29. Evans and Nixon are quoted in Hine, *Black Victory,* 198.

30. Quoted in Haynes, "Black Houstonians," 202.

31. Ibid.; Hine, "Destruction of the Democratic White Primary."

32. Quoted in Banks, "Pursuit of Equality," 232.

33. Ibid.

34. Haynes, "Black Houstonians," 203–204; Hine, *Black Victory,* 218.

35. Banks, "Pursuit of Equality," 232; Pitre, *Struggle against Jim Crow,* 23–25; Hine, *Black Victory,* 173, 202–225.

36. Lampkin quoted in Pitre, *Struggle against Jim Crow,* 32–33.

37. White quoted in ibid., 33.

38. "Negro History," vol. 1, 17 (HMRC)

39. Ibid.; Haynes, "Black Houstonians," 204.

40. Marshall, "Reminiscences," 509.

41. *Houston Informer,* January 1, 1944.

42. Quoted in Banks, "Pursuit of Equality," 190.

43. Details of the fight were recounted by Carter Wesley in the *Houston Informer,* March 30, 1940. It should be considered highly biased. For the next several weeks, Wesley relentlessly attacked Alphonse Mills in the *Informer;* see Gillette, "NAACP in Texas," 17–23.

44. *Houston Informer,* May 11, 1940; Haynes, "Black Houstonians," 204; Patricia Lefforge Davis, "*Sweatt v. Painter:* Integration in Texas Higher Education," 46.

45. Frank Hamer's statement to the governor is posted on the Texas State Library and Archives Commission website, http://www.tsl.state.tx.us/governors/personality/moody-hamer-1.html (accessed July 1, 2007). *The Handbook of Texas Online,* s.vv. "William J. Durham" and "Sherman Riot of 1930," http://www.tshaonline.org/handbook/online/articles/DD/fdu46.html and http://www.tshaonline.org/handbook/online/articles/SS/jcs6.html (accessed July 1, 2007).

46. *The Handbook of Texas Online,* s.vv. "William J. Durham" and "Sherman Riot of 1930"; Gillette, "NAACP in Texas," 14; Wade quoted in the *Dallas Morning News,* May 20, 1979.

47. *The Handbook of Texas Online,* s.v. "Antonio Maceo Smith," http://www.tshaonline.org/handbook/online/articles/SS/fsm61.html (accessed July 3, 2007); for a reference to Smith as "the Man," see http://www.dallasisd.org/schools/hs/amsmith/amsman.htm (accessed July 3, 2007).

48. Effie Kaye Adams, *Tall Black Texans: Men of Courage,* 22–23; *The Handbook of Texas Online,* s.v. "Antonio Maceo Smith."

49. Shabazz, *Advancing Democracy,* 26.

50. Gillette, "NAACP in Texas," 7.

51. Banks, "Pursuit of Equality," 157, 189; Adams, *Tall Black Texans,* 22–24; *The Handbook of Texas Online,* s.v. "African Americans and Politics," http://www

.tshaonline.org/handbook/online/articles/AA/wmafr.html (accessed July 3, 2007); Haynes, "Black Houstonians," 202; Hine, *Black Victory*, 207; Gillette, "NAACP in Texas," 4–5, 14.

52. Gillette, "NAACP in Texas," vii; *The Handbook of Texas Online*, s.v. "National Association for the Advancement of Colored People."

Chapter 6

1. *Houston Informer*, May 11, 1940; Juan Williams, *Thurgood Marshall*, 104; Gillette, "NAACP in Texas," 18–23.

2. Thurgood Marshall to Walter White, May 14, 1940 (NAACP Papers); Marshall is also quoted in Hine, *Black Victory*, 220, and Gillette, "NAACP in Texas," 17–23.

3. Carter Wesley to Thurgood Marshall, July 2, 1940 (NAACP Papers).

4. Haynes, "Black Houstonians," 204–205; Hine, *Black Victory*, 223; *Houston City Directory*, 1946–47.

5. Haynes, "Black Houstonians," 204–205.

6. Ibid.; Grose, "Black Newspapers in Texas," 191; Juan Williams, *Thurgood Marshall*, 109; Hine, *Black Victory*, 224.

7. In Texas, the state court system begins with municipal courts, justice of the peace courts, county-level courts, and district-level courts. The first-level appellate courts are fourteen geographically based courts of appeal. The final courts of appeal are the Texas Supreme Court and the Court of Criminal Appeals.

8. *U.S. v. Classic*, 313 U.S. 299 (1941).

9. Marshall, "White Democratic Primary."

10. *U.S. v. Classic*, 313 U.S. at 313–314. In excerpts from Supreme Court decisions, I have removed any citations to other cases.

11. Unidentified Texan quoted in Marshall, "Reminiscences," 426–427.

12. Ibid.; Hine, *Black Victory*, 228–230; Hine, "Destruction of the Democratic White Primary."

13. Grose, "Black Newspapers in Texas," 198; *Houston City Directory*, 1946–47; "Lonnie Smith" vertical file (HMRC); Roger Goldman and David Gallen, *Thurgood Marshall: Justice for All*, 51; *Smith v. Allwright*, 321 U.S. 649 (1944).

14. Hine, "Destruction of the Democratic White Primary"; *Smith*, 321 U.S. 649.

15. The conversation is recounted in Marshall, "Reminiscences," 426–427.

16. *Smith*, 321 U.S. at 658; Hine, "Destruction of the Democratic White Primary."

17. *Smith*, 321 U.S. at 652.

18. Ibid. at 661–662, 666.

19. Lulu White, quoted in Gillette, "NAACP in Texas," 25–30; Daisy Lampkin, quoted in the *Houston Informer*, April 8, 1944.

20. Marshall, "Reminiscences," 512.

21. Robert E. Martin, "The Relative Political Status of the Negro in the United States"; National Association for the Advancement of Colored People, annual report for 1947, 65.

22. Grose, "Black Newspapers in Texas," 198.

23. "Lonnie Smith" vertical file (HMRC); Beeth and Wintz, *Black Dixie*, 158.

24. Shabazz, *Advancing Democracy*, 44.

25. Gillette, "NAACP in Texas," 25–30.

26. *Alcalde*, July–August 2005.

27. National Urban League, *Economic and Cultural Problems of Houston*, 211; Graham Blackstock, *Staff Monograph on Higher Education for Negroes*, Texas Legislative Council, November 1950, 1.

28. Blackstock, *Higher Education for Negroes*, 1–2. I am indebted to Lee S. Smith of the University of Texas for his counsel on the conditions for the readmission of Texas to the Union. See also Office of the Attorney General of Texas, Opinion No. V-31, 1947, on the Constitutionality of Senate Bill No. 140, establishing a statutory university for Negroes, and related questions (hereafter cited as AG Opinion V-31); Shabazz, *Advancing Democracy*, 10.

29. Banks, "Pursuit of Equality," 349.

30. An unamended Texas Constitution of 1876 is posted at http://tarlton.law .utexas.edu/constitutions/text/1876index.html; for commentary, see National Urban League, *Economic and Cultural Problems of Houston*, 34; Brophy, "Black Texan," 26; Patricia Lefforge Davis, "*Sweatt v. Painter*," 34; Joe Greenhill, notes for oral arguments in *Sweatt v. Painter*, Greenhill Papers; Shabazz, *Advancing Democracy*, 23, citing Frederick H. Eby, *The Development of Education in Texas*.

31. AG Opinion V-31.

32. Ibid.; Alton Hornsby, Jr., "The 'Colored Branch University' Issue in Texas— Prelude to *Sweatt v. Painter*"; Blackstock, *Higher Education for Negroes*, 2.

33. Again, I am grateful to Lee S. Smith of UT Austin for his valuable insights into the nuances of the early history of higher education in Texas.

34. Hornsby, "'Colored Branch University'"; David A. Williams, "Higher Education for Black Texans," 87; Greenhill, notes for oral arguments in *Sweatt v. Painter*, Greenhill Papers; Thomas Sears Montgomery, *The Senior Colleges for Negroes in Texas: A Study Made at the Direction of the Bi-Racial Conference on Education for Negroes in Texas*, 22.

35. Provisions of the Second Morrill Act are quoted in Robert Bruce Slater, "The First Black Graduates of the Nation's 50 Flagship State Universities"; Jacqueline A. Stefkovich and Terrence Leas, "A Legal History of Desegregation in Higher Education"; and Rufus B. Atwood, "The Origin and Development of the Negro Public College, with Special Reference to the Land Grant College."

36. Blackstock, *Higher Education for Negroes*, 4.

37. Shabazz, *Advancing Democracy*, 18; Brophy, "Black Texan," 52; David A. Williams, "Higher Education for Black Texans," 30; Hornsby, "'Colored Branch University,'" 57.

38. Hornsby, "'Colored Branch University,'" 57. The 1915 vote was 50,318 for and 81,658 against.

39. "Heman Sweatt" vertical file (DBCAH); *Daily Texan*, December 18, 1946.

40. Heman Sweatt to Walter White, November 11, 1946 (NAACP Papers); National Urban League, *Economic and Cultural Problems of Houston*, 43; unidentified clipping dated March 3, 1946 ("Heman Sweatt" vertical file, DBCAH); "Negro History," vol. 1, 71 (HMRC); *Houston City Directory*, 1946–47.

41. Heman Sweatt to Walter White, September 3, 1948, and transcript of press

conference with Heman Sweatt, September 3, 1948 (both in NAACP Papers); Gillette, "Heman Marion Sweatt," 165.

42. Martin D. Jenkins, "The Availability of Higher Education for Negroes in the Southern States"; Henry Allen Bullock, "The Availability of Education in the Texas Negro Separate School."

43. William H. Gray, Jr., "Trends in the Control of Private Negro Colleges"; Leon A. Ransom, "Legal Status of Negro Education under Separate School Systems."

44. Montgomery, *Senior Colleges for Negroes in Texas*, 37.

45. Clark, "Publicly-Supported Higher Education for Negroes"; Aaron Brown, "Graduate and Professional Education in Negro Institutions"; Preston Valien, "Desegregation in Higher Education: A Critical Summary"; Louis Shores, "Library Service and the Negro"; Montgomery, *Senior Colleges for Negroes in Texas*, 63–64.

46. Bunche, "The Negro in the Political Life of the United States," 567, 583, 584, 581.

47. Ibid., 577.

Chapter 7

1. Naomi Goldstone, "'I Don't Believe in Segregation': *Sweatt v. Painter* and the Groundwork for *Brown v. Board of Education*," 19–24; Adams, *Tall Black Texans*, 24–25.

2. Banks, "Pursuit of Equality," 249.

3. Ibid.

4. Du Bois, *Souls of Black Folk*, 3.

5. *Plessy v. Ferguson*, 163 U.S. 537 (1896).

6. Ibid.; David W. Bishop, "*Plessy v. Ferguson:* A Reinterpretation." For a good discussion of New Orleans's unique combination of white, African American, Cajun, and Creole cultures, see Harvey Fireside, *Separate and Unequal: Homer Plessy and the Supreme Court Decision That Legalized Racism*.

7. In *Plessy*, the U.S. Supreme Court briefly discussed the "colored blood" issue, citing the following cases: *State v. Chavers*, 5 Jones [N.C.] 1; *Gray v. State*, 4 Ohio 354; *Monroe v. Collins*, 17 Ohio St. 665; *People v. Dean*, 14 Mich. 406; and *Jones v. Com.*, 80 Va. 544 (see *Plessy*, 163 U.S. at 552).

8. See *Dred Scott v. Sandford*, 60 U.S. 393 (1857), which stated that a slave was property and thus could never be a citizen; Linder, "Before *Brown.*"

9. *Plessy*, 163 U.S. at 544.

10. Ibid. at 551; for a good discussion of *Plessy* in the context of school desegregation, see Jonathan L. Entin, "Desegregating the American Law School: The Road to *Brown.*"

11. *Plessy*, 163 U.S. at 551; Entin, "Desegregating the American Law School."

12. *Plessy*, 163 U.S. at 562; Bishop, "*Plessy v. Ferguson*"; see also Thurgood Marshall, "An Evaluation of Recent Efforts to Achieve Racial Integration in Education through Resort to the Courts," included in *Marshall: Speeches*, 145–156 (subsequent citations are to this volume); Douglas J. Ficker, "From *Roberts* to *Plessy:* Educational Segregation and the 'Separate but Equal' Doctrine."

13. Patricia Lefforge Davis, "*Sweatt v. Painter,*" 3–4.

14. Milton R. Konvitz, "The Extent and Character of Legally-Enforced Segregation."

15. See *Gong Lum v. Rice,* 275 U.S. 78 (1927).

16. Ibid.

17. Ibid. at 85.

18. Quoted in *Cumming v. Richmond County Board of Education,* 175 U.S. 528 (1899) at 533.

19. Ibid.; Mark Strasser, "Was *Brown*'s Declaration of Per Se Invalidity Really out of the Blue? The Evolving 'Separate but Equal' Education Jurisprudence from *Cumming* to *Brown*"; Patricia Lefforge Davis, "*Sweatt v. Painter,*" 18.

20. *Kentucky Acts 1904,* chapter 85, 181; see also the Berea College website: http://community.berea.edu/EarlyBlackBerea/daylaw.html.

21. *Berea College v. Kentucky,* 211 U.S. 45 (1908) at 58.

22. Strasser: "*Brown*'s Declaration of Invalidity"; Patricia Lefforge Davis, "*Sweatt v. Painter,*" 18; Joe Greenhill, Brief of Argument before the U.S. Supreme Court.

23. Strasser, "*Brown*'s Declaration of Invalidity," 775; Blackstock, *Higher Education for Negroes,* 20; Blaustein and Ferguson, *Desegregation and the Law,* 108.

24. Montgomery, *Senior Colleges for Negroes in Texas.*

25. Ibid., 22; Shabazz, *Advancing Democracy,* 36.

26. Quoted in Montgomery, *Senior Colleges for Negroes in Texas,* 14.

27. Ibid.

28. Ibid., 14, 63–64, 85–86, 91, 94; Shabazz, *Advancing Democracy,* 37–39.

29. Montgomery, *Senior Colleges for Negroes in Texas,* 83–85.

30. Ibid.

31. Homer P. Rainey, *The Tower and the Dome,* 3.

32. Patricia Lefforge Davis, "*Sweatt v. Painter,*" 82–83.

33. Marian Wynn Perry to Martin Popper, January 27, 1946 (NAACP Papers).

34. W. Page Keeton, interviewed by H. W. Brands for the University of Texas Law School, June 2, 1986; available online at http://www.houseofrussell.com/legalhistory/sweatt/docs/koh.htm (accessed August 19, 2009).

35. Quoted in George Norris Green, *The Establishment in State Politics: The Primitive Years, 1938–1957,* 94.

36. Rainey, *Tower and Dome,* 7; *The Handbook of Texas Online,* s.v. "Homer Price Rainey," http://www.tshaonline.org/handbook/online/articles/RR/fra54.html (accessed August 25, 2007).

37. M. L. Fleming to T. S. Painter, April 5, 1949; E. M. Biggers to board of regents, January 1, 1948; L. D. Fretwell to T. S. Painter, February 15, 1948; for an example of a letter of support for liberal activists, see Tom Neal to T. S. Painter, March 28, 1949 (all correspondence in the President's Office Records, DBCAH).

38. Banks, "Pursuit of Equality," 422.

39. *The Handbook of Texas Online,* s.v. "James Frank Dobie," http://www.tshaonline.org/handbook/online/articles/DD/fdo2.html (accessed August 25, 2007); the Coke Stevenson quotation is from an unidentified newspaper clipping in "J. Frank Dobie, September 1947" folder, box VF 19/A.B., President's Office Records, DBCAH.

40. Ibid.
41. Ibid.
42. Marshall, "Recent Efforts to Achieve Racial Integration," 146.
43. Blackstock, *Higher Education for Negroes,* 3; AG Opinion V-31.
44. *Alcalde* 93, no. 6 (July–August, 2005), 46–50; *The Handbook of Texas Online,* s.v. "Santa Rita Oil Well," http://www.tshaonline.org/handbook/online/articles/SS/dos1.html (accessed December 29, 2005).
45. "Some Pertinent Facts Which Must Be Taken into Account When Considering Institutions of Higher Learning for Negroes in the State of Texas, 1939–1952" a white paper in the "Negroes in College 1939–52" folder, box VF 20/B.a., President's Office Records, DBCAH; Bullock, "Availability of Education."
46. Shabazz, *Advancing Democracy,* 170; Gillette, "NAACP in Texas," 43–45; Gillette, "Heman Marion Sweatt," 170.
47. Hornsby, "'Colored Branch University' Issue"; Patricia Lefforge Davis, "*Sweatt v. Painter,*" 14, 52; Blackstock, *Higher Education for Negroes,* 9.
48. Maceo Smith to Thurgood Marshall, May 4, 1945 (NAACP Papers).

Chapter 8

1. *Dallas Morning News,* June 5, 1945 (clipping in "*Sweatt v. Painter*" file, NAACP Papers).
2. *Dallas Morning News* editorial, quoted in W. E. B. Du Bois, Phylon 5, no. 2 (1944): 101–102, 165–188.
3. Banks, "Pursuit of Equality," 179.
4. Shabazz, *Advancing Democracy,* 36–39.
5. Maceo Smith to Thurgood Marshall, April 9, 1945 (NAACP Papers); Gillette, "NAACP in Texas," 39–40, 43–45; Gillette, "Heman Marion Sweatt," 159.
6. Entin, "Desegregating the American Law School"; Gillette, "NAACP in Texas," 46–51; Gillette, "Heman Marion Sweatt," 159–160.
7. Thurgood Marshall to J. J. Jones, June 12, 1945 (NAACP Papers); Entin, "Desegregating the American Law School"; Gillette, "Heman Marion Sweatt," 160.
8. Thurgood Marshall to Kenneth R. Lampkin, June 22, 1945 (NAACP Papers).
9. J. Mason Brewer, *A Pictorial and Historical Souvenir of Negro Life in Austin, Texas, 1950–51: Who's Who and What's What; Austin City Directory,* 1947.
10. Blackstock, *Higher Education for Negroes,* 11–12.
11. William H. Jones, "Desegregation of Public Education in Texas—One Year Afterward," 348; Alwyn Barr, quoted in the *Fort Worth Star Telegram,* October 10, 1982; Patricia Lefforge Davis, "*Sweatt v. Painter,*" 43; Banks, "Pursuit of Equality," 351.
12. Carolyn Jones, *Volma: My Journey,* 47.
13. W. Astor Kirk, interviewed by Anthony Orum ("W. Astor Kirk," box AF-Biography, Austin History Center).
14. Patricia Lefforge Davis, "*Sweatt v. Painter.*"
15. Tushnet, *NAACP's Legal Strategy,* 36; Marshall, "Recent Efforts to Achieve Racial Integration," 147–148; Patricia Lefforge Davis, "*Sweatt v. Painter,*" 29.

16. William Hastie, quoted in Tushnet, *NAACP's Legal Strategy,* 37.

17. Tushnet, *NAACP's Legal Strategy,* 88; Gillette, "Heman Marion Sweatt," 156–188; Gillette, "NAACP in Texas," 46–51.

18. W. J. Durham to NAACP, August 6, 1945 (NAACP Papers).

19. Maceo Smith to J. J. Jones, July 31, 1945; Maceo Smith to Thurgood Marshall, August 17, 1945; Thurgood Marshall to William Durham, August 21, 1945; William Durham to NAACP, August 6, 1945; C. B. Bunkley to Thurgood Marshall, August 30, 1945 (all in NAACP Papers); Entin, "Desegregating the American Law School"; Gillette, "NAACP in Texas," 46–51; Gillette, "Heman Marion Sweatt," 160–161.

20. Lulu White to Thurgood Marshall, October 10, 1945 (NAACP Papers), cited in Gillette, "NAACP in Texas," 46–51.

21. See Merline Pitre's observation in Hine, *Black Victory,* 37.

22. Pitre, *Struggle against Jim Crow,* 37, 110; Marshall, "Reminiscences," 509; *Antioch Baptist Church Centennial, Houston, 1866–1966* (HMRC).

23. Shabazz, *Advancing Democracy,* 67.

24. Gillette, "NAACP in Texas," 57–59.

25. Almost all secondary-source accounts of the Wesley Chapel AME meeting ultimately come from Michael Gillette's interview with Heman Sweatt ("NAACP in Texas," 54–59).

26. Ibid.

27. Carter, *Matter of Law,* 33.

28. Marshall, "Reminiscences," 439.

29. Heman Sweatt, quoted in the *Dallas Morning News,* May 20, 1979 ("Heman Marion Sweatt" scrapbook, DBCAH).

30. Texas Commission on Democracy in Education (Joseph J. Rhoads, chairman), "Advancing the Cause of Democracy in Education," 1951 (NAACP Papers); Gillette, "NAACP in Texas," 54–56; Gillette, "Heman Marion Sweatt," 166–167.

31. Kirk interview.

32. Ibid.

33. Heman Sweatt, quoted in the *Dallas Morning News,* May 20, 1979 ("Heman Marion Sweatt" scrapbook, DBCAH); Merline Pitre, "Black Houstonians and the 'Separate but Equal' Doctrine: Carter W. Wesley versus Lulu B. White," 27; *The Handbook of Texas Online,* s.v. "Carter Walker Wesley"; Gillette, "Heman Marion Sweatt," 166; Carter Wesley to Thurgood Marshall, October 8, 1947 (NAACP Papers).

34. William Durham to Thurgood Marshall, January 28, 1945 (NAACP Papers).

35. Thurgood Marshall to William Durham, January 30, 1945 (NAACP Papers); *Sweatt v. Painter,* no. 74,945, Application for Writ of Mandamus, filed May 16, 1946, in the 126th District Court of Travis County, Texas; Ada Lois Sipuel Fisher, *A Matter of Black and White: The Autobiography of Ada Lois Sipuel Fisher,* 84–85.

36. Entin, "Desegregating the American Law School"; Gale Leslie Barchus, "The Dynamics of Black Demands and White Responses for Negro Higher Education in the State of Texas, 1945–1950," 8; Juanita Craft, quoted in the *Fort Worth Star-Telegram,* October 10, 1982; Gillette, "Heman Marion Sweatt," 167; Gillette, "NAACP in Texas," 60–61.

Chapter 9

1. *The Handbook of Texas Online,* s.v. "Theophilus Shickel Painter," http://www.tshaonline.org/handbook/online/articles/PP/fpa10.html (accessed on November 17, 2007); Gillette, "NAACP in Texas," 41–42.

2. "Some Pertinent Facts Which Must Be Taken Into Account When Considering Institutions of Higher Learning for Negroes in the State of Texas, 1939–52" (President's Office Records, DBCAH).

3. Barchus, "Dynamics of Black Demands," 7; "Some Pertinent Facts"; *Daily Texan,* March 1, 1946 ("Heman Sweatt" vertical file, DBCAH).

4. Gillette, "NAACP in Texas," 60–61; the quotation is from Banks, "Pursuit of Equality," 409.

5. The most complete reporting of the February 26, 1946, meeting between Heman Sweatt, the NAACP delegation, and President Painter and his staff is from Clif Richardson, Jr.'s eyewitness account, which was published in the *Houston Defender* (March 9, 1946). Another account was published by the *Houston Informer* (March 5, 1946). In a request to Grover Sellers for an attorney general's opinion, President Painter gave his account of the meeting. All of my reporting of the meeting is from these three sources, and there is no significant disagreement among them. A clipping of the *Defender* article is in "Negro Question—Sweatt Case, 1946" folder, box VF 20/B.a, President's Office Records, DBCAH. There is no record of President Painter or anyone else at the university challenging the facts as Richardson presented them. For the rest of this chapter, unless additional sources are noted, my reconstruction of the meeting is from these three sources.

6. They are Homer, Herodotus, Aristotle, Cicero, Virgil, Dante, Shakespeare, Milton, Moliere, Goethe, Scott, Mark Twain, Cervantes, and Chaucer.

7. I am grateful to Gary Speer of the University of Texas Registrar's Office for providing me untitled documents describing the Main Building and Tower and other information regarding UT's history and academic programs and semesters.

8. My 70 percent figure is an estimate based on Shores, "Library Service and the Negro."

9. Banks, "Pursuit of Equality," 409.

10. Theophilus S. Painter to Grover Sellers, February 26, 1946 (*Sweatt v. Painter* and TSUN [Texas State University for Negroes] files, box I115, Charles T. McCormick Papers, Rare Books and Special Collections, Tarlton Law Library, University of Texas at Austin, and posted online at: http://www.houseofrussell.com/legalhistory/sweatt/ctm/ctm.html).

11. *Report to the President of the University,* Office of the Registrar, 1945–46, October 15, 1946; registrar E. J. Matthews wrote the report, though he is not identified on it as the author.

12. Heman Sweatt is quoted in Gillette, "Heman Marion Sweatt," 166–168.

13. *Houston Informer,* January 22, 1946.

14. Painter to Sellers, February 26, 1946 (McCormick Papers).

15. Ibid.

16. *Daily Texan,* March 1, 1946.

17. Heman M. Sweatt to James Clay Dolley, February 26, 1946 ("Negro Ques-

tion—Sweatt Case, 1946" folder, box VF 20/B.a, President's Office Records, DBCAH).

18. Quoted in Gillette, "Heman Marion Sweatt," 176.

19. *Daily Texan,* March 1, 1946.

20. William Durham to Thurgood Marshall, telegram, February 27, 1946 (NAACP Papers).

21. Ibid.; Maceo Smith to Carter Wesley, March 21, 1946 (NAACP Papers).

22. Quoted in the *Houston Defender* (clipping located in President's Office Records, DBCAH); Sweatt to Dolley, February 26, 1946.

23. Painter to Sellers, February 26, 1946 (McCormick Papers).

24. *Houston Informer,* March 1, 1946.

25. Ibid.

26. Painter to Sellers, February 26, 1946 (McCormick Papers).

27. *Daily Texan,* March 1, 1946, and unidentified clipping dated March 3, 1946 ("Heman Sweatt" vertical file, DBCAH).

28. Ibid.; *Houston Informer,* March 9, 1946.

29. Flasch, *Melvin B. Tolson,* chronology and preface; Tolson quoted in Farnsworth, *Tolson,* 104.

30. *Dallas Morning News,* May 17, 1946. By 1946, the Lincoln University School of Law had graduated fifteen students; thirteen passed the bar exam in Missouri, Illinois, and Michigan; two held positions with the federal government.

31. Ibid.

32. Fisher, *Black and White,* 84–85.

33. *Sipuel v. Board of Regents of the University of Oklahoma,* 332 U.S. 631 (1948); Fisher, *Black and White,* 82–85, 128–129; John T. Hubbell, "The Desegregation of the University of Oklahoma, 1946–1950"; Blackstock, *Higher Education for Negroes,* 21.

34. Fisher, *Black and White,* 62.

35. Greenhill, interviewed by the author, September 9, 2005.

36. *The Handbook of Texas Online,* "Texas since World War II," http://www.tshaonline.org/handbook/online/articles/TT/npt2.html (accessed December 2, 2007).

37. Unless otherwise noted, the source for the rest of this section is Grover Sellers to T. S. Painter, Opinion No. O-7126, March 16, 1946.

38. Patricia Lefforge Davis, "*Sweatt v. Painter,*" 48.

39. T. S. Painter to Heman Sweatt, March 16, 1946 ("Negro Question—Sweatt Case, 1946" folder, box VF 20/B.a, President's Office Records, DBCAH).

40. *Houston Post,* March 17, 1946, cited in Barchus, "Dynamics of Black Demands," 11.

41. Gillette, "NAACP in Texas," 63–65.

42. *Austin American-Statesman,* March 17, 1946; Heman Sweatt to Maceo Smith, March 19, 1946, and Carter Wesley to William Durham, March 22, 1946 (NAACP Papers); Carter Wesley, *Houston Informer,* March 23, 1946.

43. The unidentified Texas official is quoted in Bryant, *Texas Southern University,* 35.

44. Gillette, "NAACP in Texas," 63–65; Grover Sellers, quoted in the *Daily Texan,* January 8, 1947.

Chapter 10

1. Maceo Smith and Carter Wesley to "Friend," September 3, 1946 ("Carter Wesley/*Houston Informer,* 1940–47" file, NAACP Papers).

2. The SNCEEO flier is in the NAACP Papers along with a handwritten note from Lulu White to Walter White.

3. Thurgood Marshall to Carter Wesley, October 25, 1946 (NAACP Papers).

4. Carter Wesley to Thurgood Marshall, December 23, 1946 (NAACP Papers). Both Merline Pitre (*Struggle against Jim Crow,* 96–104) and Amilcar Shabazz (*Advancing Democracy,* 45–65) provide excellent analyses of the Carter-Marshall-White feud.

5. Walter White to Carter Wesley, December 27, 1946 (NAACP Papers).

6. Thurgood Marshall to Carter Wesley, December 27, 1946 (NAACP Papers).

7. Walter White to Thurgood Marshall, memorandum, December 30, 1946 (NAACP Papers).

8. Carter Wesley to John Jay Jones, January 2, 1947 (NAACP Papers).

9. Ibid.

10. Ibid.

11. Thurgood Marshall to Carter Wesley, January 7, 1947 (NAACP Papers).

12. Carter Wesley to [Houston NAACP branch], January 17, 1947 (NAACP Papers).

13. Carter Wesley to Thurgood Marshall, January 28, 1947 (NAACP Papers); Shabazz, *Advancing Democracy,* 53.

14. James W. Nabrit, Jr., to Carter Wesley, January 30, 1947, and Maceo Smith to Thurgood Marshall, May 27, 1947 (NAACP Papers).

15. Gloster Current to Walter White, memorandum, January 11, 1947 (NAACP Papers).

16. Barchus, "Dynamics of Black Demands," 6–7; Tushnet, *NAACP's Legal Strategy,* 147.

17. Carter Wesley, *Houston Informer,* August 16, 1947.

18. Walter White to Thurgood Marshall, undated memo (NAACP Papers).

19. Thurgood Marshall to Carter Wesley, October 3 and December 16, 1947 (NAACP Papers).

20. Pitre, "Black Houstonians," 23–36.

21. Carter, *Matter of Law,* 62–63; St. James, *National Association for the Advancement of Colored People,* 128.

22. George Wilfred Stumberg to C. T. McCormick, memorandum, March 26, 1941 (McCormick Papers).

23. Ibid.

24. Blackstock, *Higher Education for Negroes,* 22.

25. Stumberg to McCormick, memorandum, March 26, 1941, and Henry Witham to Charles McCormick, October 20, 1941 (McCormick Papers).

26. Ibid.; William H. Wicker to Charles McCormick, June 12, 1946 (McCormick Papers).

27. Stumberg to McCormick, memorandum, March 26, 1941, and Witham to McCormick, October 20, 1941 (McCormick Papers).

28. Guy B. Johnson, "Racial Integration in Public Higher Education in the South"; Blackstock, *Higher Education for Negroes*, 23.

29. Stumberg to McCormick, memorandum, March 26, 1941 (McCormick Papers).

30. William Durham to Thurgood Marshall, telegram, May 16, 1946 (NAACP Papers).

31. Painter to Sellers, May 20, 1946 (President's Office Records, DBCAH).

32. Patricia Lefforge Davis, "*Sweatt v. Painter*," 49; Vivé Griffith, "'Courage and the Refusal to Be Swayed': Heman Marion Sweatt's Legal Challenge That Integrated the University of Texas," http://txtell.lib.utexas.edu/stories/soo10-short.html (accessed August 19, 2009).

33. Garland Bailey to T. S. Painter, February 28, 1946, and George W. Willey III, undated telegram (President's Office Records, DBCAH).

34. *Sweatt v. Painter*, no. 74,945, Application for Writ of Mandamus, filed May 16, 1946, in the 126th District Court of Travis County, Texas.

35. *Dallas Morning News*, May 18, 1946.

36. Ibid., May 1, 1946.

37. Bullock, "Texas Negro Separate School," 432. The figure is repeated in Patricia Lefforge Davis, "*Sweatt v. Painter*," 48.

38. *Houston Informer*, March 9, 1946, quoting the *Daily Texan*, March 3, 1946; Heman Sweatt to Lulu White, July 25, 1946 (NAACP Papers).

39. *Alcalde*, June 1922. Dudley Woodward, Jr., is featured in this issue (available online at http://www.utsystem.edu/bor/former_regents/regents/Woodward/ [accessed August 19, 2009]).

40. *Daily Texan*, June 9, 1946.

41. *Austin American*, June 19, 1946.

42. *Austin American*, undated, 1947 (clipping in "Heman Marion Sweatt" scrapbooks, DBCAH).

43. Joseph J. Rhoads, quoted in *Austin American*, June 27, 1946.

44. On March 13, 1947, Rhoads, speaking as the president of the Texas Council of Negro Organizations, stated: "Texas Negroes do not accept creation of Texas State University and Prairie View Agricultural and Mechanical College as a satisfactory solution to their higher educational problem" (*Dallas Morning News*, March 14, 1947).

45. As stated earlier. On October 15, 1947, the *Dallas Morning News* opined: "The [NAACP's] tendency to stir up trouble is far more conspicuous in our view than its contribution to the advancement of interracial relations in this section."

46. *Austin American*, June 16, 1946.

47. Today, the 126th District Court of Travis County, Texas, is located in the southeast corner on the same floor.

48. Greenhill interview.

49. *Austin American*, June 18, 1946.

50. *Sweatt v. Painter*, no. 74,945, Judgment of the Court, filed June 26, 1946, in the 126th District Court of Travis County, Texas.

51. *Austin American*, June 18, 1946.

52. Barchus, "Dynamics of Black Demands," 9; *Houston Post*, June 18, 1946.

Chapter 11

1. "Report of Special Joint Committee on Higher Education for Negroes in Texas," July 5, 1946 (President's Office Records, DBCAH).

2. "Higher Education for Negroes in Texas," minute order no. 124-46 (McCormick Papers); Patricia Lefforge Davis, "*Sweatt v. Painter,*" 56.

3. Coke Stevenson to T. S. Painter, July 18, 1946 (President's Office Records, DBCAH).

4. Maceo Smith to Negro leaders in Texas, July 26, 1946, and meeting handout entitled "To: The Governor's Commission on the Higher Education of Negroes in Texas," August 8, 1946 (NAACP Papers).

5. *Austin American,* July 26, 1946.

6. "To: The Governor's Commission on the Higher Education of Negroes in Texas" (NAACP Papers).

7. *Dallas Morning News,* August 9, 1946; "To: The Governor's Commission on the Higher Education of Negroes in Texas"; the quotation from Smith is in Maceo Smith to Robert Carter, August 9, 1946 (all in NAACP Papers); J. N. R. Score to T. S. Painter, July 29, 1946; Texas Council of Negro Organizations presentation of August 8, 1946 (both in President's Office Records, DBCAH).

8. Maceo Smith to Robert Carter, telegram, and Robert Carter to Rev. A. A. Lucas, telegram, both on August 23, 1946 (NAACP Papers).

9. *Austin American,* July 26, 1946.

10. Terry, "Texas Southern University," 52, 76; Bryant, *Texas Southern University,* 3.

11. Bryant, *Texas Southern University,* 10, 13; Terry, "Texas Southern University," 79–80.

12. Brewer, *Pictorial and Historical Souvenir.*

13. *Dallas Morning News,* November 20, 1946 ("Heman Marion Sweatt" scrapbook, DBCAH).

14. Marian Wynn Perry to Martin Popper, January 27, 1946, and Thurgood Marshall to J. H. Morton, December 3, 1946 (NAACP Papers).

15. Gillette, "NAACP in Texas," 80–85.

16. *The Handbook of Texas Online,* s.v. "Juanita Jewel Shanks Craft," http://www.tshaonline.org/handbook/online/articles/CC/fcr59.html (accessed December 21, 2007).

17. Shabazz, *Advancing Democracy,* 71–73; *Austin City Directory,* 1947.

18. The groups included the Canterbury Club, Campus Guild Co-op, Wesley Foundation, Community Church Student Fellowship, Women's Independent Campus Association (WICA), YMCA, American Veterans Committee, Mortar Board, Lutheran Students Association, Baptist Student Union, YWCA, Latin American League, Common Sense, Alba Club, and Hillel Independents (*Austin American,* November 19, 1946).

19. Ibid.; *Dallas Morning News,* November 20, 1946; *Houston Informer,* November 23, 1946; *Dallas Morning News,* November 19, 1946; Gillette, "NAACP in Texas," 80–85.

20. "Slow and distinct" is from *Austin American,* November 19, 1946; *Daily Texan,* November 19, 1946.

21. "Easy and affable" is from *Austin American*, November 19, 1946.

22. *Daily Texan*, November 19, 1946; *Austin American*, November 19, 1946; *Houston Informer*, November 23, 1946.

23. Ibid.

24. *Dallas Morning News*, November 21, 1946.

25. NAACP memorandum, April 24, 1947; Gloster Current to James Morton, May 1, 1947; Maceo Smith to Gloster Current, June 12, 1947; Marion Ladwig to Thurgood Marshall, October 15, 1947; Roy Wilkins to James H. Morton, September 2, 1947 (all in NAACP Papers). The best treatment of the dissension and infighting of the university NAACP branch is in Gillette, "NAACP in Texas," 168–169; see also Shabazz, *Advancing Democracy*, 73.

26. Heman Sweatt to Lulu White, July 25, 1946 (NAACP Papers).

27. Mark McGee to Coke R. Stevenson, December 17, 1946, and "Report of the Bi-Racial Committee to the Governor," December 6, 1946 (both in President's Office Records, DBCAH).

28. Ibid.

29. Resolution of the board of directors of the Agricultural and Mechanical College of Texas, meeting held at Austin, Texas, November 27, 1946 (McCormick Papers); *Austin American*, November 28, 1946.

30. Heman Sweatt to Walter White, November 8, 1946 (NAACP Papers).

31. Juan Williams, *Thurgood Marshall*, 174–177.

32. John W. Stanford, Jr., to T. S. Painter, December 13, 1946 (President's Office Records, DBCAH).

33. *Daily Texan*, November 27, 1946.

34. *Houston Post*, June 18, 1946.

35. Unidentified newspaper clipping (NAACP Papers); *Houston Informer*, December 14, 1946; *Austin American*, December 15, 1946. Dorie Miller Auditorium was built in 1943 to provide recreational facilities for African American soldiers stationed at nearby Bergstrom Air Force Base.

36. Banks, "Pursuit of Equality," 422.

37. Ibid.

38. Jim Smith is quoted in the memorandum of a telephone conversation between Walter White and Thurgood Marshall, December 17, 1946 (NAACP Papers).

39. Heman Sweatt, quoted in Gillette, "Heman Marion Sweatt," 172–173.

40. Unidentified newspaper clipping (NAACP Papers).

41. Barchus, "Dynamics of Black Demands," 17; memorandum of telephone conversation between White and Marshall.

42. The best description of the courtroom atmosphere is in the *Daily Texan* December 18, 1946; see also the *Austin American*, December 18, 1946.

43. Something of a legend has grown around the fact that Heman Sweatt had to sit on the floor during the proceedings. It is commonly believed today that it was the result of a discourtesy or slight of some sort directed at him by Judge Archer or the state. There is no contemporaneous evidence to support the lore. At the time of the trial, neither Sweatt nor Marshall ever mentioned it, and it is difficult to believe that none of Sweatt's six lawyers would have objected to such treatment. Carter Wesley was present in the courtroom, and the *Houston Informer* reported innocuously that "all seats at the table were taken, and Sweatt sat on the floor just in-

side the bar" (December 21, 1946). Sweatt had to sit on the floor because he wanted to sit up front and his lawyers occupied all of the chairs at the relator's table.

44. The following account of the hearing is taken from coverage in the *Houston Informer, Dallas Morning News, Austin American,* and *Daily Texan.*

45. *Sweatt v. Painter,* No. 74,945, Judgment of the Court, filed in the 126th District Court of Travis County, Texas, December 17, 1946.

46. *Daily Texan,* December 18, 1946.

47. Ibid.

48. *Austin American,* December 18, 1946; *Daily Texan,* December 18, 1946.

49. Ibid.

50. Heman Sweatt, quoted in Bill Hughes, "Sweatt Background Is One of Education," *Daily Texan,* December 18, 1946.

51. Ibid.

52. Ibid.

53. Minutes of the meeting of the executive committee of the Texas NAACP, December 18, 1946 (NAACP Papers).

54. Ibid.

55. Carter Wesley, *Houston Informer,* December 21, 1946; Carter Wesley to Thurgood Marshall, December 23, 1946 (NAACP Papers).

Chapter 12

1. Gillette, "NAACP in Texas," 110; William Jones, "Desegregation of Public Education in Texas."

2. Marshall, "Recent Efforts to Achieve Racial Integration," 148.

3. "Heman Marion Sweatt" scrapbook (DBCAH); *Austin American,* March 22, 1947.

4. Ibid.

5. For biographical information about Beauford Halbert Jester, see Archie P. McDonald, "Beauford Jester," at TexasEscapes.com, http://www.texasescapes.com/AllThingsHistorical/Beauford-Jester-AM1104.htm (accessed August 19, 2009), as well as the entry on Jester in *The Handbook of Texas Online,* http://www.tshaonline.org/handbook/online/articles/JJ/fje8.html (accessed August 19, 2009).

6. The Railroad Commission of Texas does far more than its name suggests. Established in 1891, it is the oldest regulatory agency in state government. At first its constitutional mandate was to prevent discrimination in railroad charges, but it has grown to include several regulatory divisions that oversee the Texas oil and gas industry, gas utilities, pipeline safety, safety in the liquefied-petroleum-gas industry, and the surface mining of coal. Given the abundance of those natural resources in Texas, the Railroad Commission is one of the most powerful bodies in state government.

7. *Sweatt v. Painter,* no. 74,945, Statement of Facts, 126th Judicial District, Travis County, Texas, proceedings of May 12, 1947.

8. *Austin American,* November 28, 1946; *Houston Informer,* December 21, 1946; Barchus, "Dynamics of Black Demands," 16.

9. *Houston Informer,* December 21, 1946.

10. Ibid.; *Sweatt v. Painter*, Statement of Facts, May 12, 1947.

11. Carter Wesley, *Houston Informer*, December 21, 1946.

12. Ibid.; Patricia Lefforge Davis, "*Sweatt v. Painter*," 58; *Dallas Morning News*, February 25, 1947; *Sweatt v. Painter*, Statement of Facts, May 12, 1947; Barchus, "Dynamics of Black Demands," 18.

13. Quoted in Barchus, "Dynamics of Black Demands," 21.

14. Jenkins, "Higher Education for Negroes."

15. *Sweatt v. Painter*, Statement of Facts, May 12, 1947; Patricia Lefforge Davis, "*Sweatt v. Painter*," 66.

16. Quoted in the *Austin American*, February 11, 1947.

17. *General and Special Laws of the State of Texas*, Fiftieth Legislature, regular session, SB 140 (hereafter cited as SB 140), 36.

18. Ibid., 36–40.

19. Ibid.

20. *Houston Post*, February 12, 1947; *Austin American*, February 12, 1947.

21. D. K. Woodward, Jr., and Wesley quoted in the *Houston Informer*, February 15, 1947.

22. Unidentified speaker quoted in the *Daily Texan*, February 10, 1947.

23. Patricia Lefforge Davis, "*Sweatt v. Painter*," 89; Ward and Martin are quoted in the *Austin American*, February 25, 1947; *Austin American*, March 4, 1947; *Daily Texan*, February 10, 1947.

24. *Austin American*, February 25, 1947.

25. *Dallas Morning News*, March 5, 1947.

26. Patricia Lefforge Davis, "*Sweatt v. Painter*," 89; *Austin American*, February 25, 1947, and March 4, 1947; *Daily Texan*, February 10, 1947.

27. *Austin American*, February 25, 1947.

28. SB 140, 41; E. J. Matthews to Heman Sweatt, March 3, 1947 (President's Office Records, DBCAH); *Daily Texan*, March 4, 1947.

29. *Sweatt v. Painter*, cause no. 9619, motion no. 10,363, Mandate of the Court of Civil Appeals, filed March 28, 1947, in the Court of Civil Appeals for the Third Supreme Judicial District; *Austin American*, May 13, 1947; *Dallas Morning News*, March 27, 1947.

30. Blackstock, *Higher Education for Negroes*, 12–18; *Austin American*, March 27, 1947.

31. SB 140, 39–40.

32. Patricia Lefforge Davis, "*Sweatt v. Painter*," 59; D. K. Woodward to Price Daniel, February 26, 1947 (McCormick Papers); *Daily Texan*, March 4, 1947.

33. Minutes of a meeting of the faculty of the law school, February 28, 1947 (McCormick Papers).

34. Ibid.; minutes of a meeting of the Budget Council, February 28, 1947, and Charles T. McCormick to T. S. Painter, March 10, 1947 (both in McCormick Papers).

35. *Sweatt v. Painter*, no. 74,945, Respondent's First Amended Original Answer, filed May 1, 1947, in the 126th District Court of Travis County, Texas; D. K. Woodward to Price Daniel, February 26, 1947 (McCormick Papers).

36. E. J. Matthews to Heman Sweatt, March 3, 1947 (copies in NAACP Papers and McCormick Papers).

37. Ibid.

38. Heman Sweatt to William Durham, March 4, 1947 (NAACP Papers); Barchus, "Dynamics of Black Demands," 25.

39. Ibid.; *Austin American,* undated 1947 clipping in "Heman Sweatt" scrapbook (DBCAH).

40. Resolution of the Texas Council of Negro Organizations, March 8, 1947, and Maceo Smith to Thurgood Marshall, March 11, 1947 (NAACP Papers).

41. D. K. Woodward to T. S. Painter, February 22, 1947 (McCormick Papers).

42. *Sweatt v. Painter,* Statement of Facts, 126th District, May 13, 1947; *Austin City Directory,* 1947; *Daily Texan,* March 4, 1947.

43. *Sweatt v. Painter,* Opinion of the Court of Civil Appeals for the Third Supreme Judicial District, February 25, 1948, and Statement of Facts, 126th Judicial District, May 13, 1947; Barchus, "Dynamics of Black Demands," 24; Greenhill, interviewed by Brands, February 10, 1986, posted at http://www.houseofrussell.com/legalhistory/sweatt/docs/goh.html (accessed August 19, 2009); personal files of Joe Greenhill, provided to the author. In addition, the McCormick Papers contain a large body of primary-source materials on the establishment of the 13th Street law school.

44. See Griffith, "'Courage and the Refusal To Be Swayed.'"

45. Oliver Harrington to Thurgood Marshall, May 6, 1947 (NAACP Papers).

46. *Announcement of Courses for the Spring Semester, 1947, of the School of Law of the Texas State University for Negroes,* and Charles T. McCormick to T. S. Painter, March 10, 1947 (McCormick Papers).

47. *Dallas Morning News,* March 14, 1947; *Austin American,* March 18, 1947; Rhoads's claim to represent a combined membership of 500,000 is highly suspect. NAACP testimony during the *Sweatt* trial only a few weeks later established that the entire African American population in Texas at the last U.S. census (1940) was a little less than 925,000. Even accounting for white members, Rhoads was claiming his organizations accounted for more than the total adult black population in Texas. Undoubtedly, he did not account for duplicate memberships by individuals, and most likely he counted the entire congregations of many of the pastors serving as members of the TCNO.

48. Ibid.

49. Lulu White to Maceo Smith, July 11, 1947 (NAACP Papers).

50. *Sweatt v. Painter,* Statement of Facts, 126th Judicial District, May 14, 1947; *Dallas Morning News,* March 9, 1947; Gillette, "NAACP in Texas," 65–69.

51. *Austin American,* March 18, 1947.

52. Charles T. McCormick to T. S. Painter, March 19, 1947 (McCormick Papers).

53. Charles T. McCormick to postmaster, Austin, Texas, March 19, 1947 (McCormick Papers).

Chapter 13

1. *Dallas Morning News,* March 22, 1947.

2. *Austin American,* March 22, 1947; Patricia Lefforge Davis, "*Sweatt v. Painter,*" 61.

3. Quoted in *Time,* March 24, 1947.

4. National Association for the Advancement of Colored People, *Annual Report* (1947), 25; press release dated May 9, 1947 (NAACP Papers).

5. *Sweatt v. Painter,* 339 U.S. 629 (1950).

6. Quoted in Barchus, "Dynamics of Black Demands," 45, which cites the *Houston Post,* May 17, 1947.

7. George N. Red, "Present Status of Negro Higher and Professional Education"; Patricia Lefforge Davis, "*Sweatt v. Painter,*" 46, 55; Barchus, "Dynamics of Black Demands," 45; Thurgood Marshall to William Durham, January 30, 1947 (NAACP Papers); Charles Henry Thompson, "Separate but Not Equal: The *Sweatt* Case"; Michael D. Davis and Hunter R. Clark, *Thurgood Marshall: Warrior at the Bar, Rebel on the Bench,* 53; Gillette, "NAACP in Texas," 108.

8. *Daily Texan,* March 22, 1947.

9. Unidentified newspaper clipping, undated but probably March 25, 1946 (DBCAH).

10. Ibid.

11. The tidelands controversy was a court battle between Texas and the federal government over the ownership of 2,440,650 acres of submerged land in the Gulf of Mexico. Price Daniel argued that when Texas declared its independence from Mexico, it became the sole titleholder of the immensely valuable land. When Texas entered the Union in 1845, it reserved for itself all unsold public lands. Texas's ownership of the property had been recognized and conceded by the federal government for more than a century until massive oil pools were discovered beneath it. Holders of oil leases then advocated ownership by the federal government because federal leases were cheaper.

12. Greenhill, interviewed by the author, September 9, 2005; see also Greenhill's biography at http://www.bakerbotts.com/lawyers/detail.aspx?id=0ae17456-0e49-40ed-bd52-7a187601b7a8.

13. Greenhill interview; Joe Greenhill to Bill Pugsley, November 20, 2003 (Greenhill Papers).

14. *Sweatt v. Painter,* Statement of Facts, 126th Judicial District, May 12, 1947.

15. Thurgood Marshall to William Hastie, April 3, 1947 (NAACP Papers).

16. William Hastie to Thurgood Marshall, April 9, 1947 (NAACP Papers).

17. Davis and Clark, *Thurgood Marshall,* 142. A Texan who "draws a line in the dirt" or "a line in the sand" has made a do-or-die decision—the metaphor is the Texan version of "crossing the Rubicon." It originated in the legend of William Barret Travis, commander at the Alamo, taking his sword, drawing a line in the sand, and asking for volunteers to cross the line and join him in a final, fatal defense of the Alamo. All the volunteers are thought to have crossed the line, including James Bowie, who was so ill that he had to be carried across.

18. Thurgood Marshall to Carl Murphy, May 3, 1947 (NAACP Papers).

19. Thurgood Marshall to Ollie Harrington, telegram, May 7, 1947 (NAACP Papers).

20. Unless otherwise noted, my account of D. A. Simmons's testimony, along with all quotations, is entirely from *Sweatt v. Painter,* Statement of Facts, 126th Judicial District, May 12, 1947, which is available online at: http://www.houseofrussell.com/legalhistory/sweatt/docs/svptr1.htm#statements. In a few instances, I have made minor and inconsequential edits for clarity.

21. *Houston Informer,* May 17, 1947.

22. Quoted in the *Dallas Morning News,* May 29, 1979.

23. Gillette, "NAACP in Texas," 67; Ada Cecilia Anderson, interviewed by the author, March 10, 2006; Brewer, *Pictorial and Historical Souvenir.*

24. *Houston Informer,* May 24, 1947, quoted in Barchus, "Dynamics of Black Demands," 30.

25. NAACP press account of the proceedings of May 14, 1947 (NAACP Papers).

26. For a short biography of James Nabrit, Jr., see http://www.brownat50.org/BrownBios/BioJamesNabritJr.html (accessed August 19, 2009).

Chapter 14

1. As in the previous chapter, my coverage of *Sweatt v. Painter* in the 126th District Court is taken almost completely from the trial transcript, which is available online at: http://www.houseofrussell.com/legalhistory/sweatt/docs/svptr1.htm #statements. In a few instances, I have made minor and inconsequential edits for clarity.

2. Gillette, "Heman Marion Sweatt," 173–174.

3. Greenhill, interviewed by the author, September 5, 2005, and by H. W. Brands on February 10, 1986.

4. Unidentified newspaper clipping, undated but certainly March 26, 1946 (DBCAH).

5. Tushnet, *NAACP's Legal Strategy,* 146.

6. Gillette, "Heman Marion Sweatt," 172–173.

7. W. Astor Kirk, interviewed by Anthony Orum.

8. "All fours" is a metaphorical expression lawyers use to signify that a current case agrees in all its circumstances with another case, which should be used as precedent. It stands on all four legs, so to speak, as an animal does.

9. *Houston Informer,* December 21, 1946.

Chapter 15

1. Juan Williams, *Thurgood Marshall,* 180. Justice Greenhill repeated the story to me during my interview with him on September 5, 2005. He asked that I not repeat the story, but I told him that it was already widely known and already in print.

2. Marshall, "Reminiscences," 461–462.

3. For a brief discussion of the evaluation of human and cultural capital in college admissions, see my commentary in the *Chronicle of Higher Education Review* ("College Admissions as Conspiracy Theory," November 9, 2007).

4. Tushnet, *NAACP's Legal Strategy,* 119.

5. Carter, *Matter of Law,* 99; Marshall, "Reminiscences," 501. In this article, Marshall called Thomas Powell an "old mossback."

6. Charles Houston, "The Need for Negro Lawyers"; Marshall, "Tribute to Houston," 273; Linder, "Before *Brown.*"

7. Marshall's comments were much longer than the excerpt presented here.

They included his reading of long passages from briefs submitted by the state and by Sweatt's lawyers.

8. According to Richard Kluger: "Throughout the five-day trial of *Sweatt v. Painter* Price Daniel was a tiger. He objected every time Marshall or his two associates, James Nabrit, Jr. and Dallas Attorney W. J. Durham, blinked too hard. He went after the NAACP witnesses as if they were cattle rustlers" (*Simple Justice*, 261). After reading the trial transcript, I could not understand what Mr. Kluger meant or how that statement could be true. To test the statement, I electronically searched the trial transcript for the words "object" and "objection." After examining each instance, I concluded that Daniel made approximately thirty-five objections throughout the trial. William Durham, on the other hand, made approximately eighty-six, far more than twice as many as Daniel. Each of the other attorneys, including Thurgood Marshall, made about five or fewer objections.

9. *Austin American*, undated clipping, probably May 15, 1947 ("Heman Marion Sweatt" scrapbook, DBCAH).

10. For examples of newspaper coverage, see the *Houston Post* and *Austin American*, May 16, 1947; see also Barchus, "Dynamics of Black Demands," 40.

Chapter 16

1. Unidentified and undated newspaper clipping ("Heman Sweatt" vertical file, DBCAH).

2. *Austin American*, May 17, 1947.

3. Quoted in ibid.

4. *Sweatt v. Painter*, no. 74,945, Judgment of the Court, filed June 17, 1947, in the 126th District Court of Travis County, Texas.

5. Carter Wesley's reporting and the "absolutely fair" quotation are in Barchus, "Dynamics of Black Demands," 42.

6. *Dallas Morning News*, May 18, 1947.

7. Quoted in the *Daily Texan*, February 10, 1987.

8. For Sweatt's denial of having been threatened with physical violence, see the transcript of a press conference with Heman Marion Sweatt, April 4, 1950, held in the offices of the NAACP (NAACP Papers). Examples of Heman Sweatt's stories of harassment and threats can be found in the *Dallas Morning News*, May 20, 1979, and in Gillette, "Heman Marion Sweatt," 174–175.

9. Thurgood Marshall to Carl Murphy, September 30, 1947 (NAACP Papers).

10. Shabazz, *Advancing Democracy*, 62.

11. Materials from the meeting are found in the Byron and Rannie Cook Papers, Box 2.235/A124a (DBCAH), and in Banks, "Pursuit of Equality," 437.

12. By far the best account of the eleventh annual meeting of the NAACP's Texas State Conference of Branches is in Shabazz, *Advancing Democracy*, 62; see also Patricia Lefforge Davis, "*Sweatt v. Painter*," 88.

13. Quoted in Juan Williams, *Thurgood Marshall*, 182.

14. Byron and Rannie Cook Papers, Box 2.235/A124a (DBCAH).

15. Ibid.

16. Ibid.

17. *Dallas Morning News*, September 9, 1947.

18. Banks, "Pursuit of Equality," 437; Bryant, *Texas Southern University*, 39.

19. Lulu White to Maceo Smith, July 11, 1947 (NAACP Papers).

20. Carter Wesley, *Houston Informer*, September 20, 1947.

21. Carter Wesley, *Houston Informer*, September 13, 1947.

22. Ibid.

23. Quoted in the *Dallas Morning News*, September 26, 1948.

24. Blackstock, *Higher Education for Negroes*, 39.

25. Terry, "Texas Southern University," 78—according to this source, the transfer of the college took place on September 17, 1947; Bryant, *Texas Southern University*, 48; Jenkins, "Higher Education for Negroes"; Hornsby, "'Colored Branch University'"; *The Handbook of Texas Online*, s.v. "Texas Southern University," http://www.tshaonline.org/handbook/online/articles/TT/kct27.html (accessed April 25, 2008).

26. Patricia Lefforge Davis, "*Sweatt v. Painter*," 89.

27. Gillette, "Heman Marion Sweatt," 176–177; Thurgood Marshall to W. Astor Kirk, September 29, 1947 (NAACP Papers).

28. Bryant, *Texas Southern University*, 50; Lulu White to Maceo Smith, July 11, 1947 (NAACP Papers); Terry, "Texas Southern University," 77; Lanier, "Higher Education for Negroes in Texas," 222.

29. Bryant, *Texas Southern University*, 50; "Texas Southern University: The Stepchild of the Texas Higher Education System."

30. *Dallas Morning News*, September 9, 1947.

31. Quoted in Bryant, *Texas Southern University*, 50.

32. Terry, "Texas Southern University," 84; Banks quoted in the *Dallas Morning News*, September 30, 1948.

33. *Announcement of Courses for the Winter Semester, 1947, of the School of Law of the Texas State University for Negroes;* memo to the faculty, September 9, 1947; Charles McCormick to C. D. Simmons, September 17, 1947 (all in McCormick Papers).

34. Lulu White to Thurgood Marshall, telegram, September 23, 1947, and J. H. Morton to Thurgood Marshall, September 26, 1947 (NAACP Papers).

35. M. Kenneth Woodward to Charles McCormick, September 24, 1947 (McCormick Papers).

36. Charles McCormick to Harris Louis Walton, September 23, 1947; Charles McCormick to Ruth Norman, September 23 and 27, 1947; Charles McCormick to C. D. Simmons, September 25 and 27, 1947; Charles McCormick to M. Kenneth Woodward, September 24 and October 8, 1947 (all in McCormick Papers); Shabazz, *Advancing Democracy*, 70.

37. Charles McCormick to T. S. Painter, October 2, 1947, and T. S. Painter to Charles McCormick, October 9, 1947 (McCormick Papers).

38. Thurgood Marshall to Carter Wesley, October 3, 1947, and Thurgood Marshall to Heman Sweatt, September 30, 1947 (NAACP Papers).

39. Heman Sweatt to Thurgood Marshall, September 19, 1947, and Marshall to Sweatt, September 30, 1947 (NAACP Papers).

40. Marshall to Sweatt, September 30, 1947; unidentified clipping entitled "Lone Negro Law Student Resigned to Segregation" (both in NAACP Papers).

41. Marshall to Sweatt, September 30, 1947.

42. Charles McCormick to T. S. Painter, November 12, 1947 (McCormick Papers).

43. Craig F. Cullinan to T. S. Painter, November 12, 1947 (McCormick Papers); Gillette, "NAACP in Texas," 70–72.

44. The letters are in the McCormick Papers.

45. Barchus, "Dynamics of Black Demands," 54.

46. Quoted in the *Daily Texan*, March 19, 1948.

Chapter 17

1. *Austin American*, September 16, 1947; the *Texas Ranger* article was reproduced by the *Daily Texan* in its February 10, 1987 issue. The *Texas Ranger*'s last issue was published in the early 1970s.

2. The article is reproduced here in its entirety as it was reproduced by the *Daily Texan*, February 10, 1987 (courtesy of the University of Texas Publications).

3. Fisher, *Black and White*, 121.

4. *Sipuel v. Board of Regents of University of Oklahoma*, 332 U.S. 631 (1948).

5. Hubbell, "Desegregation of the University of Oklahoma," 373.

6. Ibid., 375.

7. Fisher, *Black and White*, 152.

8. *McLaurin v. Oklahoma State Regents*, 339 U.S. 637 (1950); Fisher, *Black and White*, 152; Hubbell, "Desegregation of the University of Oklahoma," 376; Whittington B. Johnson, "The Vinson Court and Racial Segregation, 1946–1953"; F. D. Moon, "Higher Education and Desegregation in Oklahoma."

9. Blackstock, *Higher Education for Negroes*, 61–63; *Austin American*, March 21, 1948.

10. Ibid.

11. Blackstock, *Higher Education for Negroes*, 61–63; Williams, "Higher Education for Black Texans," 13.

12. Lulu White to Thurgood Marshall, October 22, 1947 (NAACP Papers).

13. *Dallas Morning News*, February 4, 1948; *Encyclopedia of Arkansas History and Culture*, s.v. "Silas Herbert Hunt," http://encyclopediaofarkansas.net/encyclopedia/entry-detail.aspx?search=1&entryID=1676 (accessed May 18, 2008). Unfortunately, Silas Hunt did not live to become a lawyer. He died in a VA hospital in Missouri of tuberculosis, probably a complication of his war wounds, in 1949.

14. *Austin American*, February 12, March 18, and December 11, 1947.

15. W. Astor Kirk to the registrar at TSUN, September 5, 1947 (NAACP Papers); W. Astor Kirk, *One Life: My Civil Rights Story*, 5, 12, 105.

16. Kirk, *One Life*, 22.

17. Ibid., 44, 51.

18. Ibid., 51.

19. Unidentified newspaper clipping, *Daily Texan*, March 21, 1950 ("Heman Marion Sweatt" scrapbook, DBCAH). Interestingly, the portion of the Texas population most strongly opposed to the integration of the University of Texas was the group with the lowest level of educational attainment—those who had never been college students. For Joe Belden's polls, see William Jones, "Desegregation of Public Education in Texas," as well as the *Daily Texan*, March 21, 1950.

20. Barchus, "Dynamics of Black Demands," 52; Kirk, *One Life,* 52, 59, 71, 83. The students discovered that racial segregation in Austin was almost completely the result of custom and practice. State law required separation only in education and transportation, and it forbade miscegenation. There were no local ordinances requiring separation in restaurants, parks, or public services. In 1928, the City of Austin had adopted a development plan that designated East Austin as the "Negro District," but it apparently did not technically have the force of law.

21. W. Astor Kirk to the registrar at TSUN, September 5, 1947, and A. E. Norton to W. Astor Kirk, September 10, 1947 (NAACP Papers).

22. J. H. Morton to Thurgood Marshall, December 11, 1947 (NAACP Papers).

23. J. H. Morton to William Durham, December 5, 1947; Thurgood Marshall to William Durham, December 10, 1947; A. Maceo Smith to William Durham, December 18, 1947 (all in NAACP Papers); Shabazz, *Advancing Democracy,* 74.

24. Kirk, *One Life,* 106.

25. Kirk's contemporaneous account of the meeting of December 4, 1947, is in W. Astor Kirk to William Durham, December 4, 1947 (NAACP Papers). See also Kirk, *One Life,* 106.

26. W. Astor Kirk to Max Fichtenbaum, December 5, 1947 (NAACP Papers); *Austin American,* December 4, 1947; Shabazz, *Advancing Democracy,* 74.

27. T. S. Painter to Dudley Woodward, Jr., January 31, 1948 (President's Office Records, DBCAH).

28. *Daily Texan,* October 1 and 2, 1947; *Austin American,* August 16, 1947.

29. *Austin American,* January 30, 1948.

30. Ibid.

31. My discussion of the court of appeals decision will come from the opinion itself, which is available online at http://www.houseofrussell.com/legalhistory/sweatt/docs/svppldng.htm. Other sources will be noted as appropriate.

32. Quoted in *Daily Texan,* February 26, 1948.

33. *Sweatt v. Painter,* no. 10,502, Opinion on Appellant's Motion for Rehearing, filed March 17, 1948, Court of Civil Appeals for the Third Supreme Judicial District of Texas; Patricia Lefforge Davis, "*Sweatt v. Painter,*" 70; Barchus, "Dynamics of Black Demands," 52.

34. *Sweatt v. Painter,* no. A-1695, Judgment Refusing Application for Writ of Error, September 29, 1948, Supreme Court of Texas; *Daily Texan,* March 12, 1948; *Dallas Morning News,* April 15, 1948; *Austin American,* April 8 and September 30, 1948.

35. *Sweatt v. Painter,* no. A-1695, Order Overruling Motion for a Rehearing, October 27, 1948, Supreme Court of Texas.

36. *Dallas Morning News,* July 4, 1948, and September 26, 1948.

37. Quoted in *Dallas Morning News,* July 4, 1948.

38. Fisher, *Black and White,* 81–85, 92.

39. Maceo Smith to J. H. Morton, October 27, 1948 (NAACP Papers); Kirk, *One Life,* 84.

40. Maceo Smith to Thurgood Marshall, April 5, 1949 (NAACP Papers).

41. Thurgood Marshall to Maceo Smith, April 18, 1949 (NAACP Papers); Williams, "Higher Education for Black Texans," 59; Banks, "Pursuit of Equality," 443; Shabazz, *Advancing Democracy,* 75.

42. Quoted in Shabazz, *Advancing Democracy,* 75.

43. *Austin American,* April 27, 1949; Kirk, *One Life,* 120; W. Astor Kirk, interview with the author, June 13, 2008.

44. For more information on the statues on the South Mall of the UT campus, see the *Daily Texan,* October 12, 2005; even today, the university struggles with what to do with those statues; see also Shabazz, *Advancing Democracy,* 75–76.

45. *Austin American,* April 28, 1949; Kirk, *One Life,* 87–88; Shabazz, *Advancing Democracy,* 75–76.

46. Shabazz, *Advancing Democracy,* 75–76; *Houston Informer,* April 30, 1949.

47. Quoted in an NAACP press release of August 26, 1949 (NAACP Papers).

48. The best account of Jester's meeting with the protesters is Shabazz, *Advancing Democracy,* 75–77; see also the *Houston Informer,* April 30, 1949.

49. *Austin American,* April 29, 1949; Donald Jones to James Nabrit, Jr., January 14, 1949 (NAACP Papers).

Chapter 18

1. Newspaper clipping from the *Houston Post,* March 20, 1949 (in the "Negro History" scrapbook, HMRC); *Dallas Morning News,* September 26 and 30, 1948.

2. Barchus, "Dynamics of Black Demands," 4.

3. Quoted in the *Houston Chronicle,* July 31, 1949.

4. Heman Sweatt to Thurgood Marshall, February 19, 1949, and Thurgood Marshall to Heman Sweatt, February 23, 1949 (NAACP Papers).

5. Sweatt to Marshall, February 19, 1949.

6. Quoted in Barchus, "Dynamics of Black Demands," 58.

7. Heman Sweatt to Thurgood Marshall, March 1, 1950 (NAACP Papers).

8. Transcript of press conference with Heman Marion Sweatt, April 4, 1950 (NAACP Papers).

9. See *McLaurin v. Oklahoma State Regents,* 339 U.S. 637 (1950), and *Henderson v. United States,* 339 U.S. 816 (1950). On May 17, 1942, Elmer W. Henderson, an African American passenger and employee of the United States, was traveling on a first-class ticket on the Southern Railway from Washington, D.C., to Atlanta, Georgia. While in Virginia, Henderson went to the dining car as soon as dinner was announced. "In accordance with the practice then in effect," two end tables nearest the kitchen were reserved for Negroes. The court described the racial segregation in the dining car: "At each meal those tables were to be reserved initially for Negroes and, when occupied by Negroes, curtains were to be drawn between them and the rest of the car. If the other tables were occupied before any Negro passengers presented themselves at the diner then those two tables also were to be available for white passengers, and Negroes were not to be seated at them while in use by white passengers." When Henderson entered the diner, some of the seats had already been taken by white passengers, so the steward refused to allow Henderson to sit at the end table. The steward did, however, offer to serve Henderson at his Pullman seat. Henderson declined the offer and agreed to return to his seat to await word that an end-table seat had become available. The steward never called, and Henderson missed dinner that evening. The question *Henderson* brought before the Court was whether the rules and practices of the Southern Railway Company, which racially

divided each dining car so as to allot some tables exclusively to white passengers and others to Negro passengers, and which called for a curtain or partition between them, violated a section of the Interstate Commerce Act that made it unlawful for a railroad in interstate commerce "to subject any particular person . . . to any undue or unreasonable prejudice or disadvantage in any respect whatsoever."

10. Thurgood Marshall to Maceo Smith and Thurgood Marshall to Heman Sweatt, telegrams, November 7, 1949 (NAACP Papers).

11. Thurgood Marshall to Joe Greenhill, November 22, 1949 (NAACP Papers).

12. Thurgood Marshall to Robert Redfield, and Thurgood Marshall to Dr. and Mrs. Lewis Mitchell, both dated March 10, 1949 (NAACP Papers).

13. Thurgood Marshall to Carolyn Mitchell, June 14, 1947 (NAACP Papers).

14. Quoted in the *Austin American,* March 27, 1950.

15. *Houston Informer,* undated January 1950 issue; Price Daniel quoted in the *Austin American,* March 27, 1950; Barchus, "Dynamics of Black Demands," 64–65. The list of southern state officials signing on to the *amici* is in *Sweatt v. Painter* 339 U.S. 629 (1950).

16. Dr. Dick Cason to Theophilus Painter, August 24, 1949 (President's Office Records, DBCAH); Barchus, "Dynamics of Black Demands," 68.

17. *Austin American,* October 13, 1949; *Daily Texan,* October 13, 1949; Barchus, "Dynamics of Black Demands," 57–58.

18. L. N. D. Wells, Jr. to Thurgood Marshall, February 15, 1950 (NAACP Papers).

19. John Q. Barrett, "Teacher, Student, Ticket: John Frank, Leon Higginbotham, and One Afternoon at the Supreme Court—Not a Trifling Thing," 312; Entin, "Desegregating the American Law School"; *Austin American,* January 20, 1950. The quotations from the law teachers' brief can be found in Shabazz, *Advancing Democracy,* 100.

20. Quoted in the *Austin American,* January 20, 1950.

21. Greenhill Papers, provided to the author in November 2005, and Joe Greenhill to Bill Pugsley, November 20, 2003.

22. The states were Ohio (1870), New York (1872), Pennsylvania (1873), California (1874), and Indiana (1874); Greenhill, interviewed by Brands, February 10, 1986; Michael J. Klarman, "Why *Brown v. Board of Education* was a Hard Case"; Greenhill Papers.

23. Joe Greenhill, interviewed by Brands, February 10, 1986; Konvitz, "Legally-Enforced Segregation."

24. Klarman, "Why *Brown* Was a Hard Case," 6–14.

25. Davis and Clark, *Thurgood Marshall,* 144; Barchus, "Dynamics of Black Demands," 69.

26. Donald Jones to Thurgood Marshall, January 23, 1950; Heman Sweatt to Thurgood Marshall, March 1, 1950; Maceo Smith to Heman Sweatt, March 1, 1950 (all in NAACP Papers).

27. Maceo Smith to J. M. Tolbert, March 16, 1950 (NAACP Papers).

28. Joe Greenhill, personal files and interview by the author, September 9, 2005.

29. "Chief Counsel for Equality"; Thurgood Marshall to William Durham, March 16, 1950 (NAACP Papers).

30. Barrett, "Teacher, Student, Ticket," 316; *Dallas Morning News,* April 5, 1950.

31. *United States Law Week* 18, no. 39 (April 11, 1950): 3277; Barrett, "Teacher, Student, Ticket," 316.

32. Remarkably, there are no transcripts or recordings of the oral arguments in *Sweatt v. Painter;* for what is probably the best account of them, see the summary in *United States Law Week* 18: 3277; see also Barrett, "Teacher, Student, Ticket," 316; Barchus, "Dynamics of Black Demands," 65.

33. *United States Law Week* 18: 3277; *Dallas Morning News,* April 5, 1950; Goldman and Gallen, *Thurgood Marshall,* 89.

34. *United States Law Week* 18: 3277.

35. Ibid.

36. Joe Greenhill very kindly provided a copy of his "Brief of Argument in the U.S. Supreme Court" for *Sweatt v. Painter* (1950).

37. Barrett, "Teacher, Student, Ticket," 316.

38. Barchus, "Dynamics of Black Demands," 60–64.

39. Charles H. Thompson to Thurgood Marshall, April 5, 1950 (NAACP Papers).

40. McNeil, *Groundwork,* 209–211.

41. Tushnet, *NAACP's Legal Strategy,* 131.

42. The first full-length biography of Clark was recently published; see Mimi Clark Gronlund, *Supreme Court Justice Tom C. Clark* (Gronlund is Clark's daughter).

43. Tom Clark, Memorandum to Supreme Court Justices (Tom Clark Papers, Tarlton Law Library, University of Texas at Austin).

44. Ibid.

45. Ibid.

46. The student is quoted in Thompson, "Separate but Not Equal."

47. Clark, Memorandum to Supreme Court Justices (Tom Clark Papers).

48. Kirk, *One Life,* 112–113.

49. Ibid., 115.

50. Ibid.; R. O'Hara Lanier to W. Astor Kirk, January 5, 1950, and W. Astor Kirk to R. O'Hara Lanier, January 9, 1950 (both in NAACP Papers).

51. Kirk, *One Life,* 117.

52. Quoted in ibid., 121.

53. Quoted in the *Austin American,* February 7, 1950.

54. Shabazz, *Advancing Democracy,* 92.

55. T. S. Painter to Herman A. Barnett, August 19, 1949; Donald Jones to Roy Wilkins, August 23, 1949; Donald Jones to Regional Advisory Board Members, September 1, 1949 (all in NAACP Papers); Lanier, "Higher Education for Negroes in Texas," 220; Barchus, "Dynamics of Black Demands," 55–56.

Chapter 19

1. Climatic data on Houston, Texas, are taken from http://www.weatherbase.com.

2. Gillette, "NAACP in Texas," 80–85.

3. Ibid.; Marshall quoted in Gillette, "Heman Marion Sweatt," 177–178.

4. The opinion is *Sweatt v. Painter,* 339 U.S. 629 (1950); the quotation is at 631. Further quotations from the decision will not include the extensive citations and footnotes normally found in a Supreme Court opinion. Other sources will be noted as usual, but this chapter is largely my interpretation of the opinion itself.

5. Justice Tom Clark, interviewed by Joe Frantz, October 7, 1969, 21 (LBJ Library); available at http://www.lbjlib.utexas.edu/Johnson/archives.hom/oralhistory .hom/Clark-T/Clark-T.pdf (accessed September 20, 2009).

6. See *McLaurin v. Oklahoma,* 339 U.S. 637 (1950).

7. During the litigation of *Henderson v. United States,* 339 U.S. 816 (1950), astute court observers noted that enforced racial segregation was on its deathbed when the Truman administration refused to defend its own Interstate Commerce Commission's rules separating the races in rail transportation. Indeed, Attorney General J. Howard McGrath took the unusual step of appearing before the Court personally to support Elmer Henderson. Justice Harold Burton wrote for the unanimous Court (save for Justice Clark, who did not vote): "The question here is whether the rules and practices of the Southern Railway Company, which divide each dining car so as to allot ten tables exclusively to white passengers and one table exclusively to Negro passengers, and which call for a curtain or partition between that table and the others, violate 3 (1) of the Interstate Commerce Act. That section makes it unlawful for a railroad in interstate commerce 'to subject any particular person . . . to any undue or unreasonable prejudice or disadvantage in any respect whatsoever.'" *Henderson* was not as far-reaching as *Sweatt* and *McLaurin,* since the Court's interpretation did not extend to the Fourteenth Amendment: "Since 3 (1) of the Interstate Commerce Act invalidates the rules and practices before us, we do not reach the constitutional or other issues suggested." See Entin, "Desegregating the American Law School."

8. Entin, "Desegregating the American Law School."

9. Juan Williams, *Thurgood Marshall,* 185.

10. Carter, *Matter of Law,* 92.

11. Thurgood Marshall, "The Supreme Court as Protector of Civil Rights: Equal Protection of the Laws," in *Marshall: Speeches,* 124; NAACP press release, June 8, 1950 (NAACP Papers).

12. Roscoe Dunjee to Thurgood Marshall, June 6, 1950, and NAACP press release, June 8, 1950 (both in NAACP Papers); Shabazz, *Advancing Democracy,* 104; *Austin American,* June 6, 1950.

13. *Dallas Morning News,* June 6, 1950; "Negro History," vol. 1, 71 (HMRC).

14. Carter Wesley, *Houston Informer,* June 10, 1950.

15. Thurgood Marshall to Heman Marion Sweatt, June 8, 1950 (NAACP Papers).

16. Quoted in the *Austin American,* June 6, 1950.

17. Ibid.; *Dallas Morning News,* May 20, 1979.

18. Quoted in the *Austin American,* June 6, 1950.

19. Ibid.

20. *Alcalde,* October 1950; *Austin American,* July 18, 1950.

21. *Houston Informer,* June 24, 1950; McElroy is quoted in the *Austin American,* June 27, 1950. After making a thorough search, the Office of the Registrar at UT Austin could find no record of George McElroy ever enrolling as a student.

22. Associated Press dispatch reported by the *Amarillo Daily News,* June 8, 1950; *Austin American,* July 19 and 20, 1950.

23. Blackstock, *Higher Education for Negroes,* 12–18; *Austin American,* July 19 and 20, 1950.

24. Dr. George Cross, quoted in the *Houston Informer,* June 17, 1950. The Tennessee and Florida officials are quoted in the *Austin American,* June 6, 1950.

25. Quoted in the *Austin American,* June 6, 1950.

26. Ibid.

27. Unidentified and undated clipping in the Greenhill Papers.

28. Statement of Walter White, June 6, 1950 (NAACP Papers); Shabazz, *Advancing Democracy,* 105; *Austin American-Statesman,* June 3, 2000.

29. Donald Jones to Herman Barnett, October 17, 1950 (NAACP Papers); Blackstock, *Higher Education for Negroes,* 65; Shabazz, *Advancing Democracy,* 85.

30. W. Astor Kirk to A. Maceo Smith, October 10, 1950 (NAACP Papers).

31. William Astor Kirk, interviewed by Karen Riles, July 14, 2004 (oral-history transcript, Austin History Center).

32. See *United States v. Texas,* 339 U.S. 707 (1950); Patricia Lefforge Davis, *"Sweatt v. Painter,"* 79; *The Handbook of Texas Online,* s.v. "Tidelands Controversy," http://www.tshaonline.org/handbook/online/articles/TT/mgt2.html (accessed June 21, 2008).

33. *The Handbook of Texas Online,* s.v. "Tidelands Controversy."

34. Shabazz, *Advancing Democracy,* 105; Maceo Smith to Thurgood Marshall, telegram, June 9, 1950, and Thurgood Marshall to Maceo Smith, June 30, 1950 (NAACP Papers).

35. Carter Wesley, *Houston Informer,* June 17 and December 19, 1950.

36. Quoted in *Tyler Courier Times Telegraph,* September 30, 1956. The contract was made public during the trial of *Texas v. NAACP,* no. 56-649, 7th Judicial District of Smith County, Texas. Incredibly, much of the trial record was purged, and the Smith County clerk of court no longer has a copy of the contract, which was introduced as an exhibit; see also Texas Commission on Democracy in Education, "Advancing the Cause of Democracy in Education."

37. *Life,* October 16, 1950. The significance of six African Americans registering for UT Law and twenty-seven enrolled at TSUN Law should be considered in light of the fact that there was a total of twenty-four black attorneys in Texas at the time of the *Sweatt* trial.

38. Thurgood Marshall to Heman Sweatt, June 8, 1950 (NAACP Papers).

39. Gillette, "Heman Marion Sweatt," 181–182; Keeton was quoted in the *Dallas Morning News,* September 20, 1950.

40. Morton to A. Maceo Smith, September 22, 1950, cited in Banks, "Pursuit of Equality," 472.

41. Page Keeton, "Law, Sweatt, and UT," *Third Coast,* August 1985; *Austin American,* September 20, 1950.

42. *Austin American,* September 20, 1950.

43. Heman Sweatt's permanent record data was provided to me by the registrar of the University of Texas at Austin.

44. Blackstock, *Higher Education for Negroes,* 71; Patricia Lefforge Davis, *"Sweatt v. Painter,"* 29.

45. Blackstock, *Higher Education for Negroes,* 23–24, 68, 71, 73.

46. Pitre, *Struggle against Jim Crow,* 103.

47. The best coverage of the 1951 annual meeting of the Texas State Conference of Branches is in the *Daily Texan,* October 7, 1951.

Chapter 20

1. Quoted in Klarman, "Why *Brown* Was a Hard Case."

2. Quoted in Juan Williams, *Thurgood Marshall,* 82.

3. Ibid.; Johnson, "Vinson Court and Racial Segregation"; Carter, *Matter of Law,* 131.

4. Strasser, "*Brown*'s Decision of Invalidity," 769.

5. See A. Leon Higginbotham's foreword to McNeil, *Groundwork,* xvi–xvii.

6. Quoted in Leon Friedman and Fred L. Israel, eds., *The Justices of the United States Supreme Court: Their Lives and Major Opinions,* 3:2321–2330.

7. Ibid., 4:2453–2455.

8. Ibid., 3:2373–2380.

9. Ibid., 3:2403–2404.

10. Ibid., 4:2549–2563.

11. Ibid., 4:2617–2623.

12. Ibid., 4:2665–2667.

13. Ibid., 4:2699–2703.

14. Bunche, "Negro in Political Life."

15. Marshall, "Reminiscences," 431.

16. Fisher, *Black and White,* 94; Marshall quoted in Juan Williams, *Thurgood Marshall,* 285.

17. Greenhill, Figg, and Whipple quoted in an unidentified clipping (Greenhill Papers).

18. Quoted in ibid.

19. Quoted in Juan Williams, *Thurgood Marshall,* 215.

20. Quoted in an undated and unidentified clipping entitled "Chief Counsel for Equality" (Greenhill Papers).

21. Quoted in Carter, *Matter of Law,* 153.

22. Greenhill interview with the author; Thompson, "Separate but Not Equal"; Carter, *Matter of Law,* 153.

23. Quoted in the *Daily Texan,* March 19, 1948.

24. Carter Wesley, *Houston Informer,* June 10, 1950.

25. Barchus, "Dynamics of Black Demands," 81.

26. Heman Sweatt to Thurgood Marshall, October 28, 1950 (NAACP Papers).

27. Ibid.

28. Theophilus S. Painter to Primus C. Wade, November 3, 1950 (President's Office Records, DBCAH).

29. *Daily Texan,* October 18, 1950.

30. Heman Sweatt quoted in ibid.; Heman Sweatt to Thurgood Marshall, October 28, 1950 (NAACP Papers).

31. Examples of Sweatt's 1970s recollection are in Gillette, "NAACP in Texas,"

89–94, and Gillette, "Heman Marion Sweatt," 181–182; Griffith, "'Courage and the Refusal to Be Swayed.'"

32. J. H. Morton to A. Maceo Smith, September 22, 1950, as cited in Banks, "Pursuit of Equality," 472; Heman Sweatt is quoted in Griffith, "'Courage and the Refusal to Be Swayed,'" which shows Gillette, "Heman Marion Sweatt" as a source.

33. Quoted in Bernie Weberman and Steve Jackson, "Sweatt Paints Dim Past."

34. The location of Heman Sweatt's domicile is taken from the return address of his letters to Thurgood Marshall and others in the NAACP Papers. The locations of Dr. Lewis Mitchell's and James Morton's homes are from the *Austin City Directory,* 1950.

35. W. Page Keeton, interviewed by H. W. Brands, July 28, 1986, available online at: http://www.houseofrussell.com/legalhistory/sweatt/docs/koh.htm (accessed August 19, 2009); Page Keeton, "Law, Sweatt, and UT."

36. Thurgood Marshall to Heman Marion Sweatt, November 6, 1950 (NAACP Papers).

37. Fisher, *Black and White,* 145–147; Greenhill interview.

38. Guy B. Johnson, "Racial Integration in Public Higher Education."

39. Unidentified clipping, dated November 22, 1950 ("Heman Marion Sweatt" scrapbook, DBCAH).

40. Carter Wesley, *Houston Informer,* June 10, 1950.

41. John P. Frank, "Can the Courts Erase the Color Line?" 308.

42. Ibid., 316.

43. Marshall, "Recent Efforts to Achieve Racial Integration," 150. Other articles about the unequal academic preparation of African Americans and whites include Joseph R. Houchins, "The Negro in Professional Occupations in the United States," and Harry E. Groves, "A Re-Examination of the 'Separate-But-Equal' Doctrine in Public Education."

44. Dean Page Keeton's reminiscences are found in the following: Keeton, "Law, Sweatt, and UT"; Keeton interviewed by Brands, July 28, 1986; and *Austin American-Statesman,* October 7, 1982; see also Patricia Lefforge Davis, "*Sweatt v. Painter,*" 91.

45. Keeton interviewed by Brands, June 2, 1986. Dwonna Goldstone responded to Keeton's statement that Sweatt was "impossible" and that he "couldn't write a simple sentence": "These charges [from Keeton] are difficult to believe considering Sweatt had graduated with honors from Wiley College, had received a master's degree from the University of Michigan, and had done coursework at Columbia University." (*Integrating the Forty Acres,* 163n36.) None of Goldstone's three assertions is factually correct. Among all the documents establishing Sweatt's qualification to be admitted to UT Law, there is no memorable reference to Sweatt as an honor graduate either in the NAACP correspondence or the record of *Sweatt v. Painter.* The statements that he had a master's degree from Michigan and completed coursework at Columbia are just wrong. Goldstone (and other historians) can evaluate the veracity of Keeton's statement by reviewing Sweatt's surviving correspondence and other samples of his writing.

46. Heman Sweatt's correspondence with J. Frank Dobie is in the J. Frank Dobie Manuscript Collection, Harry Ransom Humanities Research Center, University of Texas at Austin. The Sweatt correspondence, dated February and March 1947, con-

sists of three letters, one of which includes a synopsis of Sweatt's proposed novel. Dobie did not keep a copy of the drafts he marked up, nor is there a copy of the letter Dobie wrote when he returned the drafts.

47. Information about Heman Sweatt's academic performance is taken from his official transcript.

48. Quoted in the *Dallas Morning News,* May 20, 1979.

49. Ibid.

50. James Leonard Sweatt III, MD, interviewed by the author, July 7, 2008.

51. Ibid.; *Daily Texan,* February 10, 1987.

52. Sweatt quoted in the *Daily Texan,* February 10, 1987; Keeton quoted in unidentified newspaper clipping ("Heman Sweatt" vertical file, HMRC).

53. *Dallas Morning News,* May 20, 1979.

54. Ibid.; Hemella L. Sweatt, MD, interviewed by the author on April 6, 7, and 8, 2006.

55. *Dallas Morning News,* August 2, 1951.

56. *Houston Post,* April 29, 1972.

57. Weberman and Jackson, "Sweatt Paints Dim Past."

58. Hemella L. Sweatt, MD, interviews with the author.

59. Heman Sweatt to Hemella Sweatt, September 2, 1982, provided to the author by Hemella L. Sweatt, MD.

60. Ibid.; James Leonard Sweatt III, MD, interview with the author.

61. Heman Sweatt to Hemella Sweatt, September 30, 1982.

Chapter 21

1. Gillette, "Heman Marion Sweatt," 172–173.

2. Richard B. McCaslin, "Steadfast in His Intent: John Hargis and the Integration of the University of Texas at Austin."

3. Nia Dorian Becnel, "John Chase," *Texas Architect,* November–December 1989, 47.

4. "*Hopwood*'s Long-Range Effect: An Eviction of Blacks from Political Power," *Journal of Blacks in Higher Education* 17 (Autumn 1997): 53–54; George Washington, Jr., quoted in Goldstone, *Integrating the Forty Acres,* 143.

5. Quoted in *Utmost,* Winter 1982.

6. *The Handbook of Texas Online,* s.v. "Theophilus Shickel Painter."

7. *Austin American-Statesman,* December 21, 1985.

8. See http://www.utexas.edu/welcome/rankings.html (accessed July 15, 2008).

9. Information on Texas Southern University was taken from its website, http://www.TSU.edu.

10. *Houston Post,* February 15, 1976; Greenhill interview.

11. Patricia Lefforge Davis, "*Sweatt v. Painter,*" 93.

12. *Austin American-Statesman,* January 25, 1993.

13. Greenhill interview.

14. Ibid.

15. *The Handbook of Texas Online,* s.v. "Marion Price Daniel, Sr.," http://www.tshaonline.org/handbook/online/articles/DD/fda94.html (accessed July 15, 2008).

16. In the interest of full disclosure: I was deposed during the litigation of *Fisher*

v. Texas in my capacity as director of admissions research at UT Austin. As part of my duties, I help craft freshman and transfer admission policies and conduct research validating the admissions process. Since attorneys for the plaintiffs have announced that they will appeal Judge Sparks's ruling, my involvement with this case is likely to be ongoing.

17. Pitre, *Struggle against Jim Crow*, 144; *Houston Informer*, October 22, 1960.

18. *Houston Informer*, February 20, 1954.

19. *Houston Post*, November 11, 1969.

20. *Dallas Morning News*, December 20, 1971.

21. *The Handbook of Texas Online*, s.v. "Joseph J. Rhoads."

22. *Houston Post*, March 8, 1971.

23. Kirk, *One Life*, 120.

Bibliography and Notes on Sources

Interviews

Sweatt v. Painter was adjudicated sixty years ago, and almost all of the major partic-ipants are deceased. As of June 2009, of the attorneys only Robert Carter, Thurgood Marshall's assistant, and Joe Greenhill, the assistant attorney general, are alive to-day. Robert Carter, a federal judge in New York, declined my request for an inter-view. In a letter to me, he indicated that he was not Heman Sweatt's attorney and does not remember enough of the details of the case to be of any value to my project. Joe Greenhill granted me an interview, and afterward we corresponded. His letters to me will eventually be deposited with my papers in the Dolph Briscoe Center for American History at the University of Texas at Austin.

For information on the Sweatt family, I contacted and interviewed James Leon-ard Sweatt III, MD, of Dallas, a nephew of Heman Sweatt, who is in posses-sion of materials his uncle Wendell Sweatt (Heman's brother) left him. Some of Dr. Sweatt's pictures are used in this book. I also interviewed Anna Sweatt, He-man's sister-in-law through her marriage to Wendell. For information on Heman Sweatt's later years, I interviewed his daughter, Hemella L. Sweatt, MD, of Ohio.

For information on the African American community in Austin during the 1940s and 1950s, I interviewed Ms. Ada Anderson, of Austin, and W. Astor Kirk, of Maryland.

Oral-history projects at the Tarlton Law Library and the Lyndon B. Johnson Presidential Library relate to many of the major players of this story, including Page Keeton, Joe Greenhill, and Thurgood Marshall. These interviews are posted on the websites of Thomas Russell of the University of Denver, the LBJ Presidential Li-brary, and the Tarlton Law Library. During the writing of his doctoral disserta-tion, "The NAACP in Texas, 1937–1957," Michael L. Gillette interviewed many of the major participants, including Heman Sweatt, Carter Wesley, and W. J. Durham. These interviews have not been made public, and Dr. Gillette respectfully declined to make them available to me for this book.

It should be noted that the interviews I conducted were intended to supplement my more traditional approach to writing history, that is, by relying on contemporaneous primary documents. Previous experience in true-crime writing has taught me that eyewitness testimony, reminiscences, and oral history should be used with great care.

Court Cases

Because of the nature of this work, the richest sources of information come from the many court cases bound up with the story of Heman Marion Sweatt. The cases include but are not limited to the following:

> *Berea College v. Kentucky* (1908)
>
> *California Regents v. Bakke* (1978)
>
> *Cumming v. Richmond County Board of Education* (1899)
>
> *Dred Scott v. Sandford* (1857)
>
> *Gong Lum v. Rice* (1927)
>
> *Grovey v. Townsend* (1935)
>
> *Henderson v. U.S.* (1950)
>
> *Love v. Griffith* (1924)
>
> *McCabe v. Atchinson* (1914)
>
> *McLaurin v. Oklahoma Regents* (1950)
>
> *Missouri ex rel. Gaines v. Canada* (1938)
>
> *Newberry v. U.S.* (1921)
>
> *Nixon v. Condon* (1932)
>
> *Nixon v. Herndon* (1927)
>
> *Pearson v. Murray* (Maryland, 1936)
>
> *Plessy v. Ferguson* (1896)
>
> *Sipuel v. Oklahoma Regents* (1948)
>
> *Smith v. Allwright* (1944)
>
> *Sweatt v. Painter* (1950)
>
> *Texas v. NAACP et al.* (Texas, 7th District, 1957)
>
> *U.S. v. Classic* (1941)

The texts of the rulings in many of these cases are available online at www .FindLaw.com.

Archives

Particularly helpful and convenient are the Heman Sweatt Archives posted on the Internet by Thomas Russell, professor of Law at the University of Denver (http:// www.houseofrussell.com/legalhistory/sweatt/). They include images of the Charles

T. McCormick Papers, interview transcripts, state court proceedings of *Sweatt v. Painter,* Justice Tom Clark's memo to the Supreme Court, various newspaper articles, and other digitized materials. Especially valuable are the McCormick letters documenting the establishment of the 13th Street school.

Another essential archive is the Dolph Briscoe Center for American History at the University of Texas at Austin. Among other treasures, it contains the Lee Stanley Smith Papers, which are a little-known but extremely valuable source for the history of African American higher education in Texas. Lee Smith is a friend of mine, and he provided me with important information.

The center also houses the President's Office Records, a collection of business correspondence of UT presidents; the papers of Homer Rainey and Theophilus Painter were particularly useful. The center's vertical file and scrapbook on Heman Marion Sweatt are so complete as to nearly eliminate the need for arduous searches for newspaper articles.

The Houston Metropolitan Research Center (HMRC) at the Houston Public Library has a multitude of vertical files on Houstonians like Lonnie Smith, as well as books, manuscripts, articles, theses, and dissertations collectively called the "Red Bibliography." The most valuable in that collection is a series of scrapbooks entitled "Negro History," which present an amazing diversity of materials and viewpoints.

The Perry-Castañeda Library and the Tarlton Law Library at the University of Texas at Austin both have portions of the NAACP Papers on microfilm. The frequency with which this source is used by every writer on the history of civil rights in Texas is a measure of its value.

Newspapers

In general, African American newspapers provided the most complete coverage of the Heman Sweatt saga; the story was important to their readers. Carter Wesley's *Houston Informer* and Clifton Richardson, Jr.'s *Houston Defender* should be read with the understanding that the publishers themselves were active participants in the struggles being documented. Nonetheless, the papers provide news and details not found in white-owned organs such as the *Houston Chronicle, Houston Post, Dallas Morning News,* or *Austin American.*

The student-run *Daily Texan* provided the most thorough coverage of the trial and matriculation of Heman Marion Sweatt. It is important to remember, however, that its reporters and editors were also engaged in a learning process.

Books, Journal Articles, and Unpublished Papers

Adams, Effie Kaye. *Tall Black Texans: Men of Courage.* Dubuque, Iowa: Kendall-Hunt, 1972.

Atwood, Rufus B. "The Origin and Development of the Negro Public College, with Special Reference to the Land Grant College." *Journal of Negro Education* 31, no. 3 (Summer 1962): 240–250.

Banks, Melvin James. "The Pursuit of Equality: The Movement for First Class Citizenship among Negroes in Texas, 1920–1950." PhD diss., Syracuse University, 1962.

Barchus, Gale Leslie. "The Dynamics of Black Demands and White Responses for Negro Higher Education in the State of Texas, 1945–1950." Master's thesis, University of Texas at Austin, 1970.

Barr, Alwyn, and Robert Calvert, eds. *Black Leaders: Texans for Their Times.* Austin: Texas State Historical Association, 1981.

Barrett, John Q. "Teacher, Student, Ticket: John Frank, Leon Higginbotham, and One Afternoon at the Supreme Court—Not a Trifling Thing." *Yale Law and Policy Review* 20, no. 2 (2002): 311–323.

Becnel, Nia Dorian. "John Chase." *Texas Architect,* November–December 1989.

Beeth, Howard, and Cary D. Wintz, eds. *Black Dixie: Afro-Texan History and Culture in Houston.* College Station: Texas A&M Univ. Press, 1992.

Bishop, David W. "*Plessy v. Ferguson:* A Reinterpretation." *Journal of Negro Education* 62, no. 2 (April 1977): 125–133.

Blackstock, Graham. *Staff Monograph on Higher Education for Negroes,* Texas Legislative Council, November 1950.

Blaustein, Albert P., and Clarence Clyde Ferguson, Jr. *Desegregation and the Law: The Meaning and Effect of the School Segregation Cases.* New Brunswick, N.J.: Rutgers Univ. Press, 1957.

Brewer, J. Mason. *A Pictorial and Historical Souvenir of Negro Life in Austin, Texas, 1950–51: Who's Who and What's What.* Austin, 1951.

Brophy, William Joseph. "The Black Texan, 1900–1950: A Quantitative History." PhD diss., Vanderbilt University, 1974.

Brown, Aaron. "Graduate and Professional Education in Negro Institutions." *Journal of Negro Education* 27, no. 3 (Summer 1958): 233–242.

Bryant, Ira B. *Texas Southern University: Its Antecedents, Political Origin, and Future.* Houston: Armstrong, 1975.

Bryson, Conrey. *Dr. Lawrence A. Nixon and the White Primary.* Rev. ed. El Paso: Texas Western Press, 1992.

Bullock, Henry Allen. "The Availability of Education in the Texas Negro Separate School." *Journal of Negro Education* 16, no. 3 (Summer 1947): 425–432.

Bunche, Ralph. "The Negro in the Political Life of the United States." *Journal of Negro Education* 10, no. 3 (July 1941): 567–584.

Carter, Robert L. *A Matter of Law: A Memoir of Struggle in the Cause of Equal Rights.* New York: New Press, 2005.

Clark, Felton G. "The Development and Present Status of Publicly-Supported Higher Education for Negroes." *Journal of Negro Education* 27, no. 3 (Summer 1958): 221–232.

Davis, Jackson. "The Outlook for the Professional and Higher Education of Negroes." *Journal of Negro Education* 2, no. 3 (July 1933): 403–410.

Davis, Michael D., and Hunter R. Clark. *Thurgood Marshall: Warrior at the Bar, Rebel on the Bench.* Secaucus, N.J.: Carol, 1992.

Davis, Patricia Lefforge. "*Sweatt v. Painter:* Integration in Texas Higher Education." Master's thesis, University of Texas at Austin, 1971.

Du Bois, W. E. B. *The Souls of Black Folk.* 1903. Reprint, New York: Cosimo Classics, 2007.

Eby, Frederick H. *The Development of Education in Texas*. New York: Macmillan, 1925.

Entin, Jonathan L. "Desegregating the American Law School: The Road to *Brown*," *In Brief* [Case Western Reserve University law alumni magazine], Fall 1985, 19–24. There is a copy in the "Heman Sweatt" vertical file at the DBCAH.

Farnsworth, Robert M. *Melvin B. Tolson*. Columbia: Univ. of Missouri Press, 1984.

Ficker, Douglas J. "From *Roberts* to *Plessy:* Educational Segregation and the 'Separate but Equal' Doctrine." *Journal of Negro History* 84, no. 4 (Autumn 1999): 301–314.

Fireside, Harvey. *Separate and Unequal: Homer Plessy and the Supreme Court Decision That Legalized Racism*. New York: Carroll and Graf, 2004.

Fisher, Ada Lois Sipuel. *A Matter of Black and White: The Autobiography of Ada Lois Sipuel Fisher*. With Danny Goble. Norman: Univ. of Oklahoma Press, 1996.

Flasch, Joy. *Melvin B. Tolson*. New York: Twayne, 1972.

Frank, John P. "Can the Courts Erase the Color Line?" *Journal of Negro Education* 21, no. 3 (Summer 1952): 304–316.

Friedman, Leon, and Fred L. Israel, eds. *The Justices of the United States Supreme Court: Their Lives and Major Opinions*. 4 vols. New York: Chelsea House, 1997.

Gillette, Michael Lowery. "Heman Marion Sweatt: Civil Rights Plaintiff." In Barr and Calvert, *Black Leaders*, 136–188.

———. "The NAACP in Texas, 1937–1957." PhD diss., University of Texas at Austin, 1984.

Goldman, Roger, and David Gallen. *Thurgood Marshall: Justice for All*. New York: Carroll and Graf, 1992.

Goldstone, Dwonna. *Integrating the Forty Acres: The Fifty-Year Struggle for Racial Equality at the University of Texas*. Athens: Univ. of Georgia Press, 2006.

Goldstone, Naomi. "'I Don't Believe in Segregation': *Sweatt v. Painter* and the Groundwork for *Brown v. Board of Education*." *Judges' Journal* 43, no. 2 (Spring 2004): 19–24.

Gray, William H., Jr. "Trends in the Control of Private Negro Colleges." *Journal of Negro Education* 11, no. 1 (January 1942): 18–28.

Green, George Norris. *The Establishment in State Politics: The Primitive Years, 1938–1957*. Westport, Conn.: Greenwood, 1979.

Greene, Casey Edward. "Apostles of Hate: The Ku Klux Klan in and Near Houston, Texas, 1920–82." Master's thesis, University of Houston–Clear Lake, 1995.

Greene, Lorenzo. "Sidelights on Houston Negroes as Seen by an Associate of Dr. Carter G. Woodson in 1930." In Beeth and Wintz, *Black Dixie*, 134–154.

Griffith, Vivé. "'Courage and the Refusal to Be Swayed': Heman Marion Sweatt's Legal Challenge that Integrated the University of Texas." In *TxTell: UT Stories*. http://txtell.lib.utexas.edu/stories/s0010-full.html.

Gronlund, Mimi Clark. *Supreme Court Justice Tom C. Clark: A Life of Service*. Austin: Univ. of Texas Press, 2010.

Grose, Charles William. "Black Newspapers in Texas, 1868–1970." PhD diss., University of Texas at Austin, 1972.

Groves, Harry E. "A Re-Examination of the 'Separate-But-Equal' Doctrine in Public Education." *Journal of Negro Education* 20, no. 4 (Autumn 1951): 520–534.

Haynes, Robert V. "Black Houstonians and the White Democratic Primary, 1920–45." In Beeth and Wintz, *Black Dixie,* 192–210.

Hine, Darlene Clark. "Blacks and the Destruction of the Democratic White Primary." *Journal of Negro History* 62, no. 1 (January 1977): 43–59.

———. *Black Victory: The Rise and Fall of the White Primary.* Columbia: Univ. of Missouri Press, 1979.

———. "The Elusive Ballot: The Black Struggle against the Texas White Primary, 1932–45." *Southwestern Historical Quarterly* 81 (April 1978): 371–392.

Hornsby, Alton, Jr. "The 'Colored Branch University' Issue in Texas—Prelude to *Sweatt v. Painter.*" *Journal of Negro History* 61, no. 1 (January 1976): 51–60.

Houchins, Joseph R. "The Negro in Professional Occupations in the United States." *Journal of Negro Education* 22, no. 3 (Summer 1953): 405–415.

Houston, Charles Hamilton. "The Need for Negro Lawyers," *Journal of Negro Education* 4, no. 1 (January 1935): 49–52.

Hubbell, John T. "The Desegregation of the University of Oklahoma, 1946–1950." *Journal of Negro History* 57, no. 4 (October 1972): 370–384.

Jenkins, Martin D. "The Availability of Higher Education for Negroes in the Southern States." *Journal of Negro Education* 16, no. 3 (Summer 1947): 459–473.

Johnson, Guy B. "Racial Integration in Public Higher Education in the South." *Journal of Negro Education* 23, no. 3, (Summer 1954): 317–329.

Johnson, Whittington B. "The Vinson Court and Racial Segregation, 1946–1953." *Journal of Negro History* 63, no. 3 (July 1978): 220–230.

Jones, Carolyn. *Volma: My Journey.* Austin: Eakin, 1998.

Jones, William H. "Desegregation of Public Education in Texas—One Year Afterward." *Journal of Negro Education* 24, no. 3 (Summer 1955): 348–360.

Keeton, Page. "Law, Sweatt, and UT." *Third Coast,* August 1985.

Kelleher, Daniel T. "The Case of Lloyd Lionel Gaines: The Demise of the Separate but Equal Doctrine." *Journal of Negro History* 56, no. 4 (October 1971): 262–271.

Kennedy, Hugh. *When Baghdad Ruled the Muslim World.* Cambridge, Mass: Da Capo, 2004.

Kilpatrick, James Jackson. *The Southern Case for School Segregation.* New York: Crowell-Collier, 1962.

Kirk, W. Astor. *One Life: My Civil Rights Story.* Suitland, Md.: Magic Valley, 2007.

Klarman, Michael J. "Why *Brown v. Board of Education* Was a Hard Case." *Judges' Journal* 43, no. 2 (Spring 2004): 6–14.

Kluger, Richard. *Simple Justice: The History of "Brown v. Board of Education" and Black America's Struggle for Equality.* New York: Knopf, 1975.

Konvitz, Milton R. "The Extent and Character of Legally-Enforced Segregation." *Journal of Negro Education* 20, no. 3 (Summer 1951): 425–435.

Lanier, Raphael O'Hara. "The History of Higher Education for Negroes in Texas, 1930–55, with Particular Reference to Texas Southern University." EdD diss., New York University, 1957.

Lavergne, Gary. "College Admissions as Conspiracy Theory." *Chronicle of Higher Education Review,* November 9, 2007.

Linder, Douglas O. "Before *Brown:* Charles H. Houston and the *Gaines* Case." http://papers.ssrn.com/sol3/papers.cfm?abstract_id=1109108 (accessed August 18, 2009).

Marquart, James W., Sheldon Ekland-Olson, and Jonathan R. Sorensen. *The Rope, the Chair, and the Needle: Capital Punishment in Texas, 1923–1990.* Austin: Univ. of Texas Press, 1994.

Marshall, Thurgood. "An Evaluation of Recent Efforts to Achieve Racial Integration in Education through Resort to the Courts." *Journal of Negro Education* 21 (1952): 316–327.

———. "The Reminiscences of Thurgood Marshall." In *Thurgood Marshall: His Speeches, Writings, Arguments, Opinions, and Reminiscences,* 413–514.

———. "The Rise and Collapse of the White Democratic Primary." *Journal of Negro Education* 26, no. 3 (Summer 1957): 249–254.

———. *Thurgood Marshall: His Speeches, Writings, Arguments, Opinions, and Reminiscences.* Edited by Mark V. Tushnet. Chicago: Lawrence Hill, 2001.

———. "The Supreme Court as Protector of Civil Rights: Equal Protection of the Laws." In *Thurgood Marshall: His Speeches, Writings, Arguments, Opinions, and Reminiscences,* 116–125.

———. "Tribute to Charles H. Houston." *Amherst Magazine,* Spring 1978. Reprinted in *Thurgood Marshall: His Speeches, Writings, Arguments, Opinions, and Reminiscences,* 272–276.

Martin, Robert E. "The Relative Political Status of the Negro in the United States." *Journal of Negro Education* 22, no. 3 (Summer 1953): 363–379.

McCaslin, Richard B. "Steadfast in His Intent: John Hargis and the Integration of the University of Texas at Austin." *Southwestern Historical Quarterly* 95 (July 1991): 20–41.

McNeil, Genna Rae. *Groundwork: Charles Hamilton Houston and the Struggle for Civil Rights.* Philadelphia: Univ. of Pennsylvania Press, 1993.

Montgomery, Thomas Sears. *The Senior Colleges for Negroes in Texas: A Study Made at the Direction of the Bi-Racial Conference on Education for Negroes in Texas.* Austin: n.p., 1944.

Moon, F. D. "Higher Education and Desegregation in Oklahoma." *Journal of Negro Education* 27 (Summer 1958): 300–310.

National Urban League. *A Review of the Economic and Cultural Problems of Houston, Texas: As They Relate to the Conditions in the Negro Population, April–May, 1945.* New York: National Urban League, 1945. A copy of this report is located in the HMRC.

Pitre, Merline. "Black Houstonians and the 'Separate but Equal' Doctrine: Carter W. Wesley versus Lulu B. White." *Houston Review* 12, no. 1 (1990): 23–36.

———. *In Struggle against Jim Crow: Lulu B. White and the NAACP, 1900–1957.* College Station: Texas A&M Univ. Press, 1999.

Rainey, Homer P. *The Tower and the Dome.* Boulder, Colo.: Pruell, 1971.

Ransom, Leon A. "Legal Status of Negro Education under Separate School Systems." *Journal of Negro Education* 8, no. 3 (July 1939): 395–405.

Red, George N. "Present Status of Negro Higher and Professional Education." *Journal of Negro Education* 17, no. 3 (Summer 1948): 400–409.

Richardson, Clifton F., Sr. "Houston's Colored Citizens: Activities and Conditions among the Negro Population in the 1920s." In Beeth and Wintz, *Black Dixie,* 128–133.

Shabazz, Amilcar. *Advancing Democracy: African Americans and the Struggle for Access and Equity in Higher Education in Texas.* Chapel Hill: Univ. of North Carolina Press, 2004.

Shores, Louis. "Library Service and the Negro." *Journal of Negro Education* 1, no. 3–4 (October 1932): 374–380.

Slater, Robert Bruce. "The First Black Graduates of the Nation's 50 Flagship State Universities." *Journal of Blacks in Higher Education* 13 (Autumn 1996): 72–85.

SoRelle, James M. "The Darker Side of 'Heaven': The Black Community in Houston, Texas, 1917–45." PhD diss., Kent State University, 1980.

———. "Race Relations in 'Heavenly Houston,' 1919–45." In Beeth and Wintz, *Black Dixie*, 175–191.

Stefkovich, Jacqueline A., and Terrence Leas. "A Legal History of Desegregation in Higher Education." *Journal of Negro Education* 63, no. 3 (Summer 1994): 406–420.

St. James, Warren D. *The National Association for the Advancement of Colored People: A Case Study in Pressure Groups.* New York: Exposition, 1958.

Strasser, Mark. "Was *Brown*'s Declaration of Per Se Invalidity Really out of the Blue? The Evolving 'Separate but Equal' Education Jurisprudence from *Cumming* to *Brown*." *Howard Law Journal* 47, no. 3 (Spring 2004): 769–794.

Terry, William Edward. "Origin and Development of Texas Southern University." EdD diss., University of Houston, 1968.

"Texas Southern University: The Stepchild of the Texas Higher Education System," *Journal of Blacks in Higher Education*, no. 25 (October 31, 1999): 64–66.

Thompson, Charles Henry. "Separate but Not Equal: The *Sweatt* Case." *Southwest Review* 33, no. 3 (Spring 1948): 105–112.

Tolson, Melvin B. *Caviar and Cabbage: Selected Columns by Melvin B. Tolson from the "Washington Tribune," 1937–1944.* Edited by Robert M. Farnsworth. Columbia: Univ. of Missouri Press, 1982.

Tushnet, Mark V. *The NAACP's Legal Strategy against Segregated Education, 1925–1950.* Chapel Hill: Univ. of North Carolina Press, 1987.

Valien, Preston. "Desegregation in Higher Education: A Critical Summary." *Journal of Negro Education* 27, no. 3 (Summer 1958): 373–380.

Washington, Booker T. *Up from Slavery.* 1901. Reprint, Secaucus, N.J.: Carol, 1997.

Weberman, Bernie, and Steve Jackson. "Sweatt Paints Dim Past." *Texas Law Forum* 16, no. 1 (October 3, 1974): 8.

Williams, David A. "The History of Higher Education for Black Texans, 1872–1977." PhD diss., Baylor University, 1978.

Williams, Juan. *Thurgood Marshall: American Revolutionary.* New York: Three Rivers, 1998.

Index